THE
ULTIMATE
DINOSAUR
BOOK

THE
ULTIMATE
DINOSAUR
BOOK

DAVID LAMBERT

Foreword by John H. Ostrom, PhD

DK PUBLISHING, INC

www.dk.com

in association with

THE NATURAL HISTORY MUSEUM • LONDON

A DK PUBLISHING BOOK
www.dk.com

Consultant Editors
Dr. Angela Milner (The Natural History Museum, London)
Dr. Ralph E. Molnar (Queensland Museum, Australia)
John H. Ostrom, PhD (Peabody Museum, Yale University)

Project Editor
Mary Lindsay

Project Art Editor
Jillian Haines

Editors
Edward Bunting, Fiona Courtenay-Thompson,
Mark Ronan

US Editor
Mary Ann Lynch

Designers
Johnny Pau, Anne Renel, Clare Shedden

Editorial Assistant
Jeanette Cossar

Design Assistant
Philip Ormerod

Managing Editor
Ruth Midgley

Managing Art Editors
Philip Gilderdale, Stephen Knowlden

Photographers
Andy Crawford, Lynton Gardiner (US), Steve Gorton
Colin Keates (The Natural History Museum, London),
Miguel Pereira (Argentina), Tim Ridley

Illustrators
Roby Braun, Simone End, Andrew Hutchinson,
Steve Kirk, Janos Marffy, Andrew Robinson,
Graham Rosewarne, John Sibbick, John Temperton

Model Makers
Roby Braun, David Donkin, Graham High and Jeremy Hunt
(Centaur Studios), John Holmes

Production
Sarah Fuller, Hilary Stephens

FIRST AMERICAN EDITION, 1993
6 8 10 9 7
Published in the United States by DK Publishing, Inc.
95 Madison Avenue, New York, NY 10016

PUBLISHED IN GREAT BRITAIN BY DORLING KINDERSLEY LIMITED.
DISTRIBUTED BY HOUGHTON MIFFLIN COMPANY, BOSTON.

LIBRARY OF CONGRESS CATALOGING-IN-PUBLICATION DATA

LAMBERT, DAVID, 1932-
THE ULTIMATE DINOSAUR BOOK/BY DAVID LAMBERT;
FOREWORD BY JOHN H. OSTROM. -- 1ST AMERICAN ED.
P. CM.
INCLUDES INDEX.
ISBN 1-56458-304-X
1. DINOSAURS. I. TITLE.
QE862.D5L4246 1993
567.9'1--dc20   93-21885
                                      CIP

Computer page make-up by
Cooling Brown, Hampton-on-Thames, Middlesex
Reproduced by
Colourscan, Singapore

Printed and bound by Neografia in Slovakia

CONTENTS

FOREWORD 7

THE ESSENTIAL DINOSAUR 8

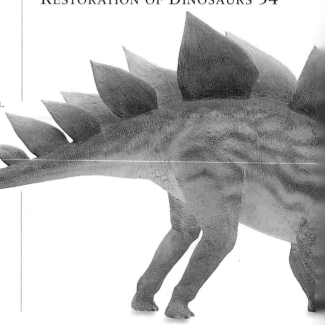

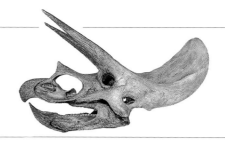

DINOSAUR PROFILES 36

A TO Z OF DINOSAURS 168

THEROPODS 38
Bipedal predatory dinosaurs with birdlike legs and feet. Most were armed with fangs as well as toe- and finger-claws.

THYREOPHORANS 110
Quadrupedal plant-eaters, including the plated stegosaurs and armored ankylosaurs, with bodies fortified by bony studs and spikes or plates.

With entries for all the currently known dinosaur genera, this dinosaur dictionary also includes cross-references for names not now in standard use.

ORNITHOPODS 130
Bipedal and bipedal/quadrupedal dinosaurs with distinctive hipbones, bony tendons that stiffened the tail, and jaws and cheek teeth remarkably designed for chewing vegetation.

SAUROPODOMORPHS 82
Chiefly quadrupedal, plant-eating dinosaurs—some of which were immense—with long necks, bulky bodies, and long tails.

MARGINOCEPHALIANS 152
Plant-eaters with a ridge or shelf at the back of the skull; within this group were the thick-headed and "parrot-beaked" dinosaurs.

FOREWORD

ALTHOUGH DINOSAURS are now extinct, the dinosaur clan was successful for a *very* long time—about 160 million years, more or less. During that time they became intricately adapted to a wide range of conditions and environments. This adaptation contributed to the success of dinosaurs, and to their incredible diversification. We probably know only a small fraction of the many kinds that actually existed and a small amount of all there is to know about these wondrous prehistoric creatures. This book should convince you of that—and also perhaps explain the "dinomania" of today and past decades.

Could there have been certain distinctly dinosaurian traits or conditions that contributed to dinosaurs' earthly dominance and longevity? Could one of these traits have been a tendency toward warm-bloodedness, as some have theorized? Could this have produced a more efficient physiology? Or did dinosaurs have a particularly high fertility rate, or did they perform some special postnatal care, or did they simply live a very long time?

How long did an average *Diplodocus* live? And not only how much did an adult *Brachiosaurus* weigh, but how much and what fodder did it consume in a normal day? How did *Apatosaurus* breathe? There is no evidence whatsoever that any dinosaur had a muscular diaphragm, so what expanded their lungs? And is it really true that there are no living dinosaur descendants?

It is questions like these that lured me into my own quest for past life. My discovery of the first fragments of *Deinonychus*, and then the entire specimen, seemed to be the ultimate discovery—and it was, at that moment. But even today, nearly 30 years after that discovery, new questions keep coming to mind about this amazing animal of 100 million years ago. And other dinosaur discoveries are made almost daily. This book should provide answers to some of *your* questions, but, more importantly, it should also trigger others. Where dinosaurs are concerned, the quest goes on.

John H. Ostrom
Curator of Vertebrate Paleontology
Peabody Museum of Natural History, Yale University

THE ESSENTIAL DINOSAUR

T HIS SECTION begins with a definition of the dinosaurs and looks at how they evolved. It describes the world the dinosaurs inhabited, examining how they lived and how they may have died out. Finally, it surveys the sequence of events from fossilization to discovery, excavation, study, and reconstruction, resulting in today's magnificently lifelike museum displays.

WHAT IS A DINOSAUR?

I N POPULAR IMAGINATION dinosaurs were just immense, slow-witted, slow-moving, prehistoric versions of living reptiles. Most scientists agree that they were reptiles, and certainly some grew as large as a great whale. Yet there were also dinosaurs no bigger than a chicken, dinosaurs as alert as an ostrich, and dinosaurs as swift as a horse. They came in two-legged, four-legged, clawed, hoofed, fanged, and toothless forms. Some even had beaks. In fact, they made up a group almost as varied as—and in their time, much more successful than—mammals. Despite variations, all dinosaurs shared a basic body plan. This was so different from that of other reptiles that some scientists grant them the status of a subclass (a major subdivision) within the class Reptilia. These pages name the characteristics that enable an anatomist to identify a fossil creature as a dinosaur.

ORNITHISCHIAN PELVIS
This Hypsilophodon *pelvis has the typically ornithischian backward-sloping pubis. The forward-pointing part of the pubic bone is the prepubis.*

Prepubis · Ilium · Ischium · Pubis

SAURISCHIAN PELVIS
This Allosaurus *pelvis has the typically saurischian forward-sloping pubis. The broad pubic "foot" is specific to certain predatory dinosaurs. Every dinosaur pelvis had a paired pubis, ilium, and ischium.*

Ilium · Pubis · Ischium

■ DINOSAUR FEATURES ■

The skull of a dinosaur had long bones known as vomers, which ran from the front of the snout to the level of the antorbital fenestrae (skull holes in front of the eyes). All but perhaps the most primitive dinosaurs had at least three sacral vertebrae anchoring the hip girdle to the spine. The shoulder girdle had a backward-facing glenoid fossa (the humerus or upper arm bone socket); the humerus had a long, low deltopectoral crest; and the fourth finger of each hand had no more than three phalanges (finger bones). There were also key features in the bones of the hips, thighs, legs, and feet. A dinosaur's hind limbs evolved to hold the body vertical, like the legs of a mammal. They stayed erect because each femur (thighbone) had a sharply inturned neck and ball-shaped head, which slotted into the fully open acetabulum (hip socket). This meant that the shaft of the femur turned down instead of sticking out sideways like a lizard's. A supra-acetabular crest helped prevent dislocation of the femur.

The shaft of the femur bore a fourth trochanter (a bump securing leg-retracting muscles), as well as a greater and a lesser trochanter. The knee joint was aligned below the hip socket, so that the whole hind limb could swing to and fro like a human's, rather than with a sprawling motion like a lizard's. The tibia (shinbone) was far larger than the fibula (calf bone) and bore a bony frontal ridge (the cnemial crest). The bottom end of the tibia was notched to take a bony projection arising from the astragalus (the main ankle bone). The high ankle joint formed a simple hinge, and the elongated foot bones indicate that dinosaurs walked on their toes. The middle toe tended to be the longest; some dinosaurs had very short outer toes, or none at all. Close relatives of dinosaurs shared some, but not all, of these features.

HIND LIMB OF TYRANNOSAURUS
The Tyrannosaurus *hind-limb bones (above and right) show key dinosaurian features, such as a reduced fibula, an ascending process of the astragalus, and a high ankle joint.*

Pelvic girdle · Acetabulum · Ball-shaped head · Femur · Ischium · Knee joint · Fibula · Tibia · Ankle joint · Foot

Cnemial crest · Fibula · Tibia · Astragalus · Ankle joint · Metatarsal · Phalanx

STANCES COMPARED
The dinosaur and the elephant, with their erect stance, walk more efficiently than the crocodilian, with its bent knees and elbows, or the lizard, with its sprawling, reptilian gait.

ORNITHOPOD DINOSAURS

This scene shows Lambeosaurus, Parasaurolophus, *and* Corythosaurus. *These three genera are all hadrosaurs (duck-billed dinosaurs) and belong to the family Lambeosauridae, the suborder Ornithopoda, and the order Ornithischia.*

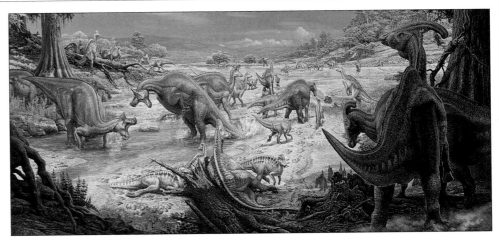

■ DINOSAUR GROUPS ■

All known dinosaurs are divided into two large groups: Saurischia ("lizard-hipped") and Ornithischia ("bird-hipped"). Most saurischians had forward-jutting pubes (pubic hip bones), while in ornithischians each pubis slanted back, parallel to the ischium (another hipbone). Some saurischians had pubes aligned like those of ornithischians, but there were other, more consistent differences between the groups. These included the saurischians' elongated neck bones and the ornithischians' predentary bone at the tip of the toothless lower jaw. There were two major saurischian subgroups: the carnivorous, bipedal theropods and the plant-eating, mostly quadrupedal sauropodomorphs. Ornithischians (all plant-eaters) were divided into three main groups: birdlike ornithopods, armored thyreophorans, and horned or thick-skulled marginocephalians. A few kinds of small, early bipedal ornithischians seem to have been more primitive than the other ornithischian groups.

DINOSAUR CLADOGRAM

The cladogram (right) shows the relationships among the key groups of dinosaurs. A clade consists of a group of animals that share uniquely evolved features and therefore a common ancestry. On the far right are shown one suborder, eight infraorders, and two families (names ending in -idae). The dotted line represents an uncertain relationship.

KEY

- ● Order
- ● Suborder
- ○ Intermediate group
- ∙∙∙ Relationship uncertain

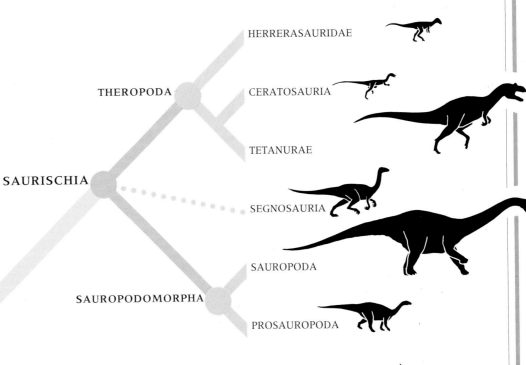

DINOSAURIA

THEROPODA
HERRERASAURIDAE
CERATOSAURIA
TETANURAE

SAURISCHIA
SEGNOSAURIA

SAUROPODOMORPHA
SAUROPODA
PROSAUROPODA

THYREOPHORA
SCELIDOSAURIDAE
STEGOSAURIA
ANKYLOSAURIA

ORNITHISCHIA

MARGINOCEPHALIA
PACHYCEPHALOSAURIA
CERATOPSIA

CERAPODA
ORNITHOPODA

ORIGINS, ANCESTORS, AND DESCENDANTS

D INOSAURS ORIGINATED from microscopic marine organisms several thousand million years ago. From these evolved true plants and animals. The processes of genetic change and natural selection led to the appearance of new forms of life. In the Paleozoic era (about 570–248 million years ago) soft-bodied creatures gave rise to fish with internal bony skeletons. Fish produced amphibians that walked on land, which in turn gave rise to reptiles. Reptiles dominated land life in later Paleozoic times. One group of reptiles evolved into archosaurs or "ruling reptiles." This group included dinosaurs, which ruled the Mesozoic era (about 248–65 million years ago). Many scientists now believe that modern birds are descendants of the dinosaurs.

THE AGES OF THE EARTH

The spiral ribbon (below) represents the Earth through time. The last 570 million years, which are rich in fossil material, are marked off in geological periods. Seven animals representing predominant groups are illustrated close to the periods in which they lived. The conodont animal (the first vertebrate), the amphibian (the first tetrapod), and the reptile (the first amniote) here represent three major evolutionary innovations inherited by the dinosaurs. Dinosaurs themselves are symbolized by a theropod, a sauropod, and a ceratopsian.

JURASSIC PERIOD
208–144 MYA: this was the heyday of the sauropods: huge, plant-eating dinosaurs. Among the largest of all was immense, giraffe-like Brachiosaurus.

TRIASSIC PERIOD
248–208 MYA: new groups of reptiles replaced the older forms. Dinosaurs evolved, diversified, and spread. Early kinds included the slim, predatory theropod Coelophysis.

CRETACEOUS PERIOD
144–65 MYA: herds of large, horned dinosaurs, such as Triceratops, multiplied, but so did little mammals. This period saw the end of the Age of Dinosaurs.

CAMBRIAN PERIOD
570–510 MYA: invertebrates and eel-like conodont animals filled the seas. These were possibly the earliest of all known vertebrates (animals with backbones).

TERTIARY PERIOD
65–2 million years ago.

PERMIAN PERIOD
290–248 million years ago.

CARBONIFEROUS PERIOD
362–290 MYA: amniotes in the form of reptiles evolved from amphibians.

SILURIAN PERIOD
438–408 million years ago.

ORDOVICIAN PERIOD
505–438 million years ago.

DEVONIAN PERIOD
408–362 MYA: in this period fish with lungs and fleshy fins gave rise to amphibians.

QUATERNARY PERIOD
2–0 MYA: Homo sapiens has evolved from Homo erectus. Mammals and birds are now the chief land vertebrates.

PRE-CAMBRIAN
4,600–570 million years ago.

12

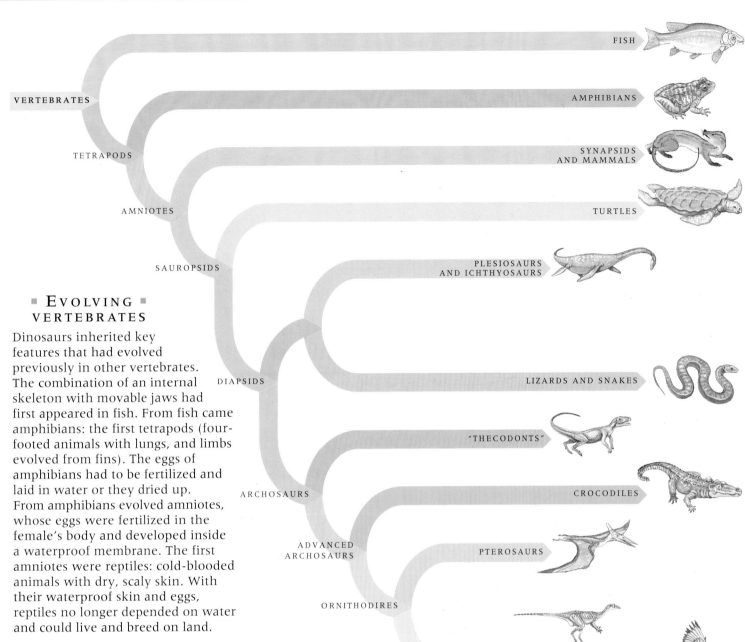

FISH

VERTEBRATES

AMPHIBIANS

TETRAPODS

SYNAPSIDS
AND MAMMALS

AMNIOTES

TURTLES

SAUROPSIDS

PLESIOSAURS
AND ICHTHYOSAURS

■ EVOLVING ■
VERTEBRATES

Dinosaurs inherited key
features that had evolved
previously in other vertebrates.
The combination of an internal
skeleton with movable jaws had
first appeared in fish. From fish came
amphibians: the first tetrapods (four-
footed animals with lungs, and limbs
evolved from fins). The eggs of
amphibians had to be fertilized and
laid in water or they dried up.
From amphibians evolved amniotes,
whose eggs were fertilized in the
female's body and developed inside
a waterproof membrane. The first
amniotes were reptiles: cold-blooded
animals with dry, scaly skin. With
their waterproof skin and eggs,
reptiles no longer depended on water
and could live and breed on land.

DIAPSIDS

LIZARDS AND SNAKES

"THECODONTS"

ARCHOSAURS

CROCODILES

ADVANCED
ARCHOSAURS

PTEROSAURS

ORNITHODIRES

DINOSAURS
AND BIRDS

■ EVOLVING AMNIOTES ■

Synapsids were mammal-like reptiles
characterized by a skull opening low
down in the cheek. They dominated
the land in Permian times, giving rise
to true mammals before becoming
extinct. Sauropsids (with two openings
in the roof of the mouth) include
turtles and tortoises. Diapsids (with
two openings in the part of the skull
behind each eye) produced plesiosaurs
and ichthyosaurs, lizards and snakes,
and the archosaurs. Archosaurs have
an extra skull opening in front of each
eye, perhaps to hold an excess salt-
removing gland. Primitive archosaurs
included a mixed group of thecodont
("socket-toothed") reptiles, some
similar to dinosaurs and crocodilians.

Certain advanced archosaurs gave rise
to two new groups: true crocodilians
and ornithodires ("bird necks"). The
latter included pterosaurs, dinosaurs,
and modern birds, all of which walk
on their toes. They have an ankle
joint forming a simple hinge, a shelf
above the hip socket, and thighbones
with an enlarged ridge (fourth
trochanter). Dinosaurs evolved
distinctive skull, spinal, shoulder,
upper arm, hand, hip-, calf, and ankle
bones. Strong similarities between the
bones of predatory dinosaurs and
modern birds suggest that birds may
be feathered dinosaurs with wings.

VERTEBRATE EVOLUTION

Starting with fish (top of diagram), this
simplified family tree shows the sequence
in which different groups of vertebrates
evolved. The lines of extinct groups are
shorter. Groups below amphibians belong
to the class Reptilia (reptiles). Birds and
mammals are each traditionally placed in a
separate class. Scientists have worked out
the relationships of dinosaurs to other
groups of animals by comparing key
characteristics in fossil bones. Identifying
sets of derived characteristics inherited from
a common ancestor has enabled scientists to
decide which of these organisms evolved
first, and which are most closely related.

TRIASSIC WORLD

T HE TRIASSIC PERIOD (about 248–208 million years ago) was the first phase of the Mesozoic era ("Age of Middle Life"), often called the Age of Dinosaurs. All lands formed one supercontinent, known as Pangaea ("all earth"), of which the northern part was called Laurasia and the southern part Gondwana. Everywhere the climate was mild, warm, or hot. No ice sheets covered polar lands, but deserts spread into inland regions. Flowering plants had not yet evolved; conifers, palmlike cycads, and ferns grew in moist areas. Life on land was dominated by prehistoric reptiles suited to dry conditions. Reptiles also took to the air and seas. In the Late Triassic, many of the older reptiles were wiped out, but new kinds took their place. The most successful of these proved to be the dinosaurs.

Dicroidium was a Triassic seedfern.

TRIASSIC SUPERCONTINENT
Black outlines show modern continents superimposed on the Triassic supercontinent Pangaea. Despite an extensive area of water, the Tethys Sea, the north (Laurasia) and south (Gondwana) remained joined.

■ LANDS ■

Laurasia comprised North America, Europe, and much of what is now Asia. Gondwana included Africa, Arabia, India, Australia, Antarctica, and South America. The South Pole was located over the ocean. The whole of Pangaea was slowly drifting north as one great landmass. This supercontinent began to show the first signs of a future breakup after the Middle Triassic, when cracks appeared in parts of eastern North America, west and central Europe, and northwest Africa.

■ PLANTS ■

The plants that flourished in Laurasia were those adapted to dry climates, such as ginkgoes, seed ferns, and somewhat palmlike cycads and cycadeoids. The biggest trees were conifers. Ginkgoes formed a fairly open canopy of medium-size trees, and cycads ranged from short, squat forms to taller, palmlike species. Tree ferns created an understory in the forests, and low ferns formed

savannas in drier open areas that would be grasslands today. Moist, open land supported dense growths of horsetails. Close to the equator and in drier regions, patchy conifer and cycad forests thrived. Stands of tall seedferns formed forests in Gondwana. Later in the Triassic period ferns were replaced by cycadeoids and conifers.

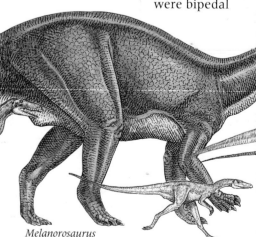

EUPARKERIA
Euparkeria was a lightly built, agile archosaur. A precursor of crocodiles and dinosaurs, it lived in Early Triassic southern Africa.

■ LIFE ON LAND ■

Reptiles ruled life on land during the Triassic period. Plant-eaters included hippopotamus-like dicynodonts, squat, piglike rhynchosaurs, and mammal-like herbivorous cynodonts. There were formidable flesh-eating cynodonts as well. Dicynodonts, rhynchosaurs, and most cynodonts died out in the first of two mysterious mass extinctions. The thecodonts that largely took their place died out in the second of these extinctions. Survivors included turtles, land crocodilians, dinosaurs, and tiny mammals. Both of the main dinosaur groups emerged during the Late Triassic. Among saurischian dinosaurs were bipedal

TRIASSIC DINOSAURS
Herrerasaurus, Staurikosaurus, *and* Coelophysis *were all carnivores.* Mussaurus, Melanorosaurus, Technosaurus, *and* Plateosaurus *typify early plant-eating dinosaurs.*

Mussaurus

Herrerasaurus

Melanorosaurus

Staurikosaurus

TRIASSIC COUNTRYSIDE
*Conifers, palmlike cycads, and ferns flourish in a
well-watered valley. An area
of desert lies beyond.*

EUDIMORPHODON
*Eudimorphodon ("true two-form tooth") from
Late Triassic north Italy was one of the earliest
known pterosaurs. It grew about 3ft 3in (1m) long.*

flesh-eating theropods and
quadrupedal prosauropods: the first
big, high-browsing herbivores. Early
ornithischians were small, bipedal
herbivores. With no sea to stop them,
dinosaurs quickly colonized the world.

■ LIFE IN THE AIR ■

Small reptiles with wings of skin or
scales took gliding flights from tree to
tree. These "wings" may have been
supported by long ribs, or they may
simply have been feathery scales
growing from arms and legs or webs
of skin between front and hind limbs.
Late Triassic animals like these may
have given rise to furry-bodied, warm-
blooded "reptiles" called pterosaurs.
These had large heads, short bodies,
and long skin wings supported by
elongated fourth finger bones. Unlike
their gliding ancestors, pterosaurs
were capable of powered flight.

■ LIFE IN WATER ■

Various reptile groups invaded the
shallow Triassic seas. Sharp-toothed,
fish-eating nothosaurs grew up to
13 feet (4m) long and had small
heads, long tails and bodies, and
paddlelike limbs. Seallike placodonts
crushed shellfish between broad, flat
back teeth. Dolphinlike
ichthyosaurs, up to
about 50 feet (15m)
long, were the reptiles
best adapted to the sea. Among their
prey were the big, swimming mollusks
called ammonoids.

Coelophysis

Technosaurus

Plateosaurus

JURASSIC WORLD

T HE JURASSIC PERIOD (about 208–144 million years ago) marked the middle of the Mesozoic era. By this time the supercontinent Pangaea was breaking up in earnest. Rifts in the continental crust produced the Atlantic Ocean. Africa began to split from South America, and India prepared to drift toward Asia. Climates were now warm worldwide, and moist winds from invading seas brought rain to inland deserts. Plants spread into once-barren lands, providing food for abundant and widespread dinosaurs (including the largest of all land animals). Above them flew the first small birds, which themselves may have evolved from small dinosaurs. The seas were shared by new, large swimming reptiles, and bony fish built on "modern" lines.

Megazostrodon, a shrewlike mammal.

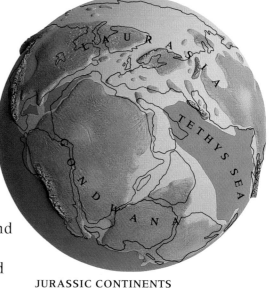

JURASSIC CONTINENTS
Black outlines show the modern landmasses, but in Jurassic times. Seas now began to cut into Pangaea and to divide Laurasia from Gondwana.

■ LANDS ■

When the Jurassic period began, old mountains had been worn away, but, as Pangaea started splitting up, new ones were formed. Floods of basalt lava oozed from geological rifts that ran all the way from southern Africa through Antarctica into Tasmania. Episodes of mountain building wracked western North America, and volcanoes pushed up in the Andes. During the Jurassic, Tibet joined Eurasia, and, as the period ended, Africa brushed against southern Europe, losing chunks of crust that formed portions of land as far apart as Arabia and Spain.

■ PLANTS ■

Jurassic lands were generally greener and more lush than they had been in Triassic times, and vegetation types were more uniform worldwide. Tall forest conifers included relatives of today's giant sequoias, pines, and Chile pine (monkey puzzle). Other plentiful trees included ginkgoes, while palmlike cycadeoids were the main small trees and shrubby plants. In conifer forests tall treeferns often made up the understory. The most common low-growing plants were ferns and horsetails. These grew prolifically and may have been important as a food source for sauropod dinosaurs. No flowering plants had appeared yet.

MARINE REPTILE
Ichthyosaurus was a sleek, swimming reptile with a long snout, paddle-shaped limbs, and a tall tail fin. It was born and lived in the sea.

■ LIFE ON LAND ■

In the Early Jurassic, the main plant-eating vertebrates were prosauropod and ornithischian dinosaurs, and small, mammal-like reptiles. But, by Late Jurassic times, huge sauropods predominated. These browsed on both high- and low-level vegetation. Sauropods relied mainly on swallowed stones rather than teeth to pulverize their food. Stegosaurs, the next most abundant plant-eating dinosaurs, had toothless beaks and weak cheek teeth. There were also early ankylosaurs and ornithopods. Large theropods killed and ate herbivores, but small coelurid and compsognathid theropods chased small game or may have scavenged.

JURASSIC DINOSAURS
Sauropods like Diplodocus *were the major Late Jurassic plant-eaters. Ornithischians included* Dryosaurus, Stegosaurus *(derived from beasts like* Scelidosaurus*), and* Camptosaurus. *The large theropod* Allosaurus *ate such herbivores.*

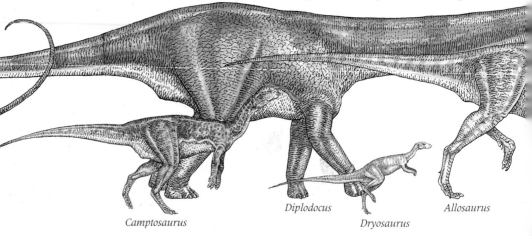

Camptosaurus

Diplodocus

Dryosaurus

Allosaurus

JURASSIC COUNTRYSIDE

Tall conifers, relatives of the Chile pine, tower above an understory of treeferns, palmlike cycadeoids, and cycads. The ground is covered with a dense undergrowth of ferns and horsetails.

ARCHAEOPTERYX

Archaeopteryx *may indicate that there is a link between birds and dinosaurs. It has been suggested that birds are winged theropods.*

▪ LIFE IN THE AIR ▪

The skin-winged pterosaurs dominated life in the air. Rhamphorhynchoid pterosaurs had a long tail that served as a stabilizer and rudder; pterodactyloid pterosaurs lacked a tail. Many of these creatures had spiky teeth, adapted for spearing fish as they swooped low over water. Early birds also appeared. The best-known, *Archaeopteryx,* had bones, teeth, and claws that resembled a small theropod's, but also had feathered wings and tail and was capable of flight.

▪ LIFE IN WATER ▪

By the Jurassic period, both nothosaurs and placodonts had died out, but ichthyosaurs persisted. They shared shallow seas with a group of marine crocodilians whose limbs had also evolved into flippers, and with teleosts (fish with a bony skeleton and a suction-feeding mechanism). Other sea creatures included barrel-bodied plesiosaurs, which traveled through the water like sea lions, and pliosaurs, which were short-necked plesiosaurs with big heads and strong, sharp teeth. By Late Jurassic times, ichthyosaurs and marine crocodilians were in declinc.

Stegosaurus

Scelidosaurus

CRETACEOUS WORLD

T HE CRETACEOUS PERIOD (about 144–65 million years ago) marked the last phase of the Mesozoic era and the climax of the Age of Dinosaurs. During this period, thick chalk beds covered the floors of shallow seas that invaded North America and Europe; Laurasia and Gondwana fragmented into the continents that we know today; and colliding slabs of continental and oceanic crust thrust up the Rockies and other mountain ranges. Near the Equator, climates stayed warm but grew drier, and forests became thinner. Elsewhere the seasons grew more marked, and flowering plants began to appear. Animals on the now-isolated continents began to evolve separately from one another, explaining why more kinds of dinosaurs appeared in Late Cretaceous times than ever before.

Magnolia: a survivor from the Cretaceous.

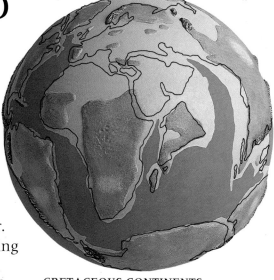

CRETACEOUS CONTINENTS
Black outlines show the shapes of modern landmasses in their Late Cretaceous positions. Shallow seas then covered immense tracts of continental crust.

▪ LANDS ▪

Early in the Cretaceous period a land bridge linked East Asia and western North America, forming one faunal region known as Asiamerica. Gradually over the Cretaceous period a shallow sea split North America in half, and western North America became an island with its own dinosaur genera. A shallow sea separated Euramerica (eastern North America, Europe, and Greenland) from Asia. Also, the southern lands of Africa, Antarctica, India, South America, and Australia gradually drifted apart. With Euramerica, these southern lands shared "old-fashioned" types of dinosaurs, so all arguably made up one great faunal region, known as the Eurogondwanan region.

▪ PLANTS ▪

Typically Mesozoic plants, such as cycadeoids, ginkgoes, conifers, and ferns, still dominated the land in Early Cretaceous times. But small, weedy, flowering plants (angiosperms) also started to appear. As these prolific plants spread from the tropics into cooler regions, some evolved into

CRETACEOUS DINOSAURS
Ornithischians, like Hypsilophodon, Iguanodon, *and* Torosaurus *were replacing sauropod herbivores like* Saltasaurus. *Formidable carnivores included* Deinonychus *and* Tyrannosaurus.

FRESHWATER CROCODILIAN
Sarcosuchus, *an Early Cretaceous crocodilian up to 49ft (15m) long, lived in Africa and South America.*

shrubs and small trees. By the Late Cretaceous, oaks, maples, walnuts, and other trees were competing with the still-abundant conifers.

▪ LIFE ON LAND ▪

By the Late Cretaceous, small mammals were diversifying fast and snakes had evolved from lizards, but dinosaurs still dominated life on land. New plant-eating ornithischian

families appeared, equipped with teeth and jaws that were engineered for chewing the new flowering plants. Low-browsing, armored ankylosaurs multiplied, too, but the less well-defended stegosaurs grew scarcer. The great, long-necked sauropods also began to diminish in northern lands, although they still predominated in the south. Cretaceous theropods ranged from birdlike ornithomimids to some of the largest of all land carnivores, the tyrannosaurids.

▪ LIFE IN THE AIR ▪

Winged creatures of Cretaceous times ranged from the world's first tiny moths and small social bees to the biggest animals that ever flew: giant pterosaurs. Among the largest pterosaurs were the

Deinonychus   *Saltasaurus*   *Hypsilophodon*   *Iguanodon*

CRETACEOUS COUNTRYSIDE
Flowering herbaceous plants and shrubby trees have started to colonize this heavily browsed river valley in western North America.

PTERANODON
This toothless pterosaur had wings up to 23ft (7m) across and soared like an albatross. It ate fish caught with its long beak.

huge *Quetzalcoatlus* and *Pteranodon*. New finds published in the early 1990s show that birds were also diversifying. By the Early Cretaceous, little *Sinornis* from China and *Concornis* from Spain had ridged breastbones, like modern flying birds. Later, diving and running birds that did not fly appeared, among them the turkey-size *Mononykus*, with a ridged breastbone and a long, bony, dinosaurian tail core.

■ LIFE IN WATER ■

Cretaceous water creatures included immense relatives of vertebrates living today. The largest freshwater species were crocodilians and the huge, crocodile-like champsosaurs, while the marine turtle *Archelon* outgrew the largest leatherback living today. Seagoing, flippered lizards, known as mosasaurs, grew to 33ft (10m) in length and swam with undulations of a deep, flattened tail. The flippered, swimming plesiosaurs included such short-necked forms (called pliosaurs) as the formidable *Kronosaurus*, with a head 10ft (3m) long, and long-necked fish-eaters, such as *Elasmosaurus*, which had no fewer than 70 cervical (neck) vertebrae. During this period the ichthyosaurs died out.

Tyrannosaurus

Torosaurus

DINOSAUR ANATOMY

S URVIVING FOSSILS reveal the bony frameworks of dinosaurs. It is possible to guess at the internal anatomy and muscles of dinosaurs by looking at those of living crocodilians, birds, and mammals. These animals also help us deduce how dinosaur bodies may have worked. Like those of living animals, dinosaur skeletons were largely designed to support muscles used for locomotion; to protect internal organs such as the brain, heart, and lungs; and to house bone marrow, which manufactured blood. Different groups of dinosaurs had specialized bones. For instance, heavy dinosaurs had thick, solid limb bones to support great weight, while lightweight dinosaurs had hollow, thin-walled limb bones. Huge "windows" in big theropod skulls and deep cavities scooped out of sauropod vertebrae removed unnecessary weight. The digestive systems, teeth, and claws of carnivores and herbivores varied according to diet and methods of attack and defense.

■ SKELETON ■

Skull and mandible formed braincase and jaws. Holes in the skull were for muscles, nostrils, and glands. Teeth were specialized according to diet; new teeth replaced old ones, which fell out. Cervical, dorsal, sacral, and caudal vertebrae formed the spine that supported the head, body, and tail. Ribs shielded the vital organs. Some dinosaurs also had belly ribs, called gastralia. Limb bones acted as levers worked by muscles. The forelimbs consisted of the scapula and coracoid bones (shoulder bones), the humerus (upper arm bone), the radius and ulna (lower arm bones), and the carpals (wrist bones). The metacarpals and

Troodon had big eyes and a wide visual field.

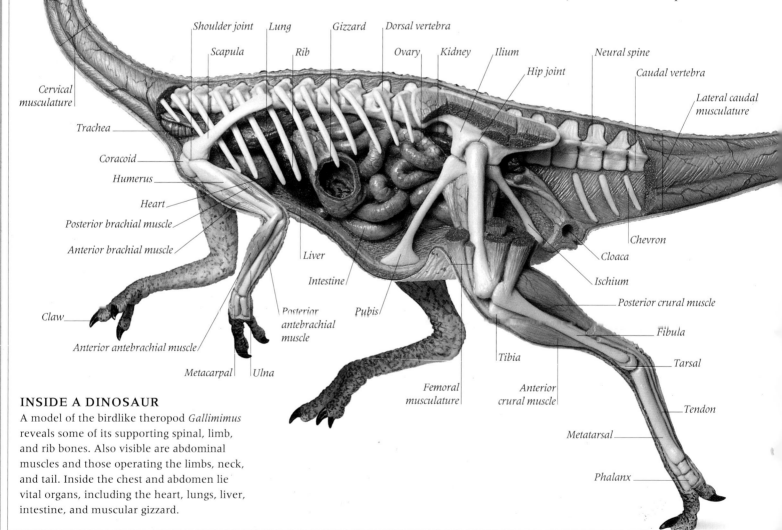

INSIDE A DINOSAUR

A model of the birdlike theropod *Gallimimus* reveals some of its supporting spinal, limb, and rib bones. Also visible are abdominal muscles and those operating the limbs, neck, and tail. Inside the chest and abdomen lie vital organs, including the heart, lungs, liver, intestine, and muscular gizzard.

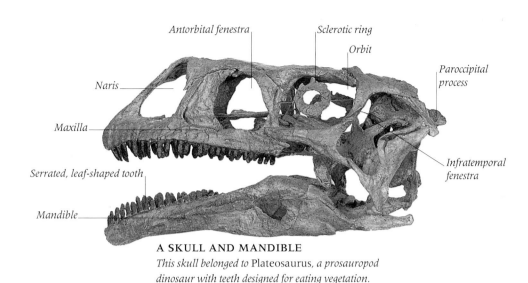

A SKULL AND MANDIBLE
This skull belonged to Plateosaurus, *a prosauropod dinosaur with teeth designed for eating vegetation.*

Either way, the mild to hot climate probably meant dinosaurs never cooled enough to become lethargic like ordinary, cold-blooded, reptiles.

▪ CONTROL SYSTEMS ▪

Interacting nervous and hormonal systems coordinated body functions. The brain sent signals to the nerves, which operated muscles. Immense sauropods had tiny brains, but some small theropods, like *Troodon*, had brains as "big" and complex as a bird's. The large theropod *Tyrannosaurus* had a brain well-designed to control limb movements and process sight and scent messages, but its cerebrum ("thinking part") was very small.

phalanges formed the palm and finger bones. The pelvic (hip) bones were fused to the sacral vertebrae. The structure of the hind limbs was as follows: femur (thigh bone), tibia (shin bone), fibula (calf bone), tarsals (ankle bones), metatarsals (upper foot bones), and phalanges (toe bones).

▪ SOFT ANATOMY ▪

Bones were bound together by ligaments, and muscles were often attached to bones by tendons. Paired, opposing muscles contracted and

relaxed to move limbs to and fro. The digestive system consisted of a convoluted gut. Flesh-eaters would have had a fairly short, simple alimentary tract, but herbivores needed a long, complex intestine to break down fibrous vegetation. Body wastes, sperm, and eggs all left the body through the cloaca.

▪ HEART-LUNG SYSTEM ▪

A dinosaur's heart-lung system may have functioned like those of warm-blooded humans or cold-blooded reptiles. Theropods probably had efficient hearts that kept their body temperatures high, as in birds or mammals. Sauropods might have been warm-blooded in another way: their vast bodies could have stored up enough heat from the sun to keep them warm all through the night.

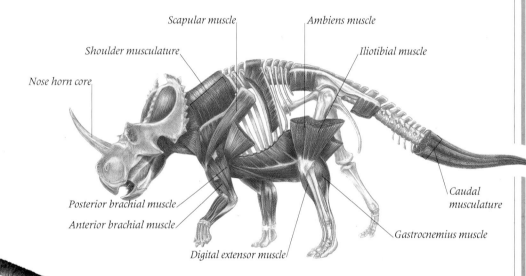

DINOSAUR MUSCULATURE
Sheets and bands of muscle appear here superimposed on the skeleton of the horned dinosaur Centrosaurus.

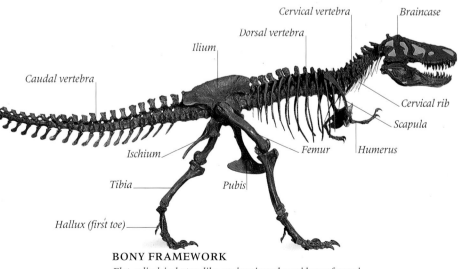

BONY FRAMEWORK
Flat, cylindrical, straplike, and various shaped bones formed the skeleton of big, bipedal, predatory Tyrannosaurus.

LIFE AND BEHAVIOR

L IKE PRESENT-DAY ANIMALS, dinosaurs lived in a variety of different ways. For example, some species lived in herds or packs, while others kept to themselves, and some were plant-eaters while others ate flesh. The three most important aspects in which dinosaur life and behavior varied were their ways of feeding, fighting (both attack and defense), and breeding.

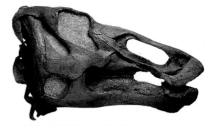
EDMONTOSAURUS SKULL

ALBERTOSAURUS SKULL

SKULLS AND TEETH
The skull of Edmontosaurus *has a toothless beak and batteries of cheek teeth for grinding tough vegetation.* Albertosaurus's *skull has strong jaws and the large, serrated fangs of a meat-eater.*

■ FEEDING ■

Most kinds of dinosaur were either herbivores (plant-eaters) or carnivores (meat-eaters). Among the herbivores, wide-mouthed browsers, such as *Maiasaura* and *Euoplocephalus*, probably snatched mouthfuls of mixed plants, while narrow-mouthed dinosaurs, such as *Edmontonia* and *Stegosaurus*, picked out specific plants. Ankylosaurs had primitive, small teeth with gaps between them. Horned dinosaurs had more advanced and efficient teeth that formed a continuous cutting edge. The vegetation that a dinosaur could eat was limited by the animal's height. Little *Lesothosaurus* and low-slung *Scelidosaurus* cropped ground-hugging plants, although some small plant-eaters may have reared on their hind limbs to browse. In contrast, the long-necked sauropods and prosauropods were tall enough to feed on leafy twigs in the upper levels of trees. Flesh-eating dinosaurs fed on plant-eating dinosaurs and other animals. Large theropods, such as *Tyrannosaurus* and *Allosaurus*, could have picked off plant-eaters that were even larger than themselves. Small predators – *Deinonychus*, for example – mainly hunted small plant-eaters, although by hunting in packs, they may have brought down ornithopods as large as *Iguanodon*. Smaller, more agile theropods, like *Compsognathus*, probably ate small lizards and large insects. A few dinosaurs had extremely specialized diets. Crocodile-jawed *Baryonyx* probably ate fishes, while the toothless *Oviraptor* may have fed on eggs or shellfish, and segnosaurs may have lived mainly on termites.

■ FIGHTING ■

Most theropods had sharp teeth and claws for piercing the tough, scaly hides of plant-eating dinosaur prey. Size and mobility largely determined how a theropod attacked. Large theropods, such as tyrannosaurids, may have stalked herds of plant-eaters, rushing in to kill a lagging individual by tearing a hole in its neck. In contrast, dromaeosaurids may have hunted in packs, swarming over their prey and using their

STRATEGY FOR ATTACK
Allosaurus, *a large theropod, attacks a much bigger sauropod. When hunting such large prey, theropods would have isolated one animal from its herd before attacking.*

second-toe claws to gash open its belly. A small, light hunter, such as *Ornitholestes*, might have sprinted after lizards and seized them in its sharp-toothed jaws or with its clawed hands. All plant-eating dinosaurs had some defense against theropod attacks. Tough hides, some with bony studs or spikes, protected titanosaurid sauropods, stegosaurs, scelidosaurids, and ankylosaurs. However, it was the sheer size of most sauropods, duck-billed ornithopods, and ceratopsid dinosaurs that deterred predators, particularly since large plant-eaters often traveled in herds. When threatened, many large plant-eating dinosaurs could have stood their ground and counter attacked. Prosauropods, sauropods, and iguanodontids could strike out with their large thumb-claws. Diplodocids and titanosaurids might have lashed out with their whiplike tails. *Shunosaurus* and ankylosaurid dinosaurs could even swing their tails to deliver crushing blows with their bony tail clubs. Less well-protected plant-eaters relied on different

survival strategies. *Scelidosaurus*, for example, might have crouched down, exposing only its armored back. Defenseless bipeds, such as the ostrich dinosaurs and the hypsilophodontids, would simply have sprinted away.

■ BREEDING ■

Like modern birds, many dinosaurs practiced courtship rituals, made nests, laid eggs, and even tended their young. Male duckbills, ceratopsid dinosaurs, and some theropods had crests or horns on their heads that were probably used in courtship rituals. *Pachycephalosaurus* males had head-butting contests to win herds of females. After mating, female dinosaurs laid hard-shelled eggs. In many cases, the eggs were laid in mud nests or hollows scooped in sand and covered with vegetation or sand. Some dinosaurs grouped their nests in breeding colonies, and certain species returned to the same nesting sites year after year. The mothers of some species stayed by the nests to protect the eggs and the small hatchlings. Most young dinosaurs apparently grew up quite quickly, although young duckbills were probably fed and tended by their mothers for up to several months after hatching. Despite parental care, most young dinosaurs probably fell prey to flesh-eating theropods before reaching adulthood.

DINOSAUR EGGS
The small, horned dinosaur Protoceratops *laid long eggs resembling large potatoes. Each clutch was laid in the form of a ring or spiral in a bowl-shaped hollow dug in the sand.*

COLONIAL NESTING
Maiasaura *mothers here tend their nests, eggs, and young. Nesting in colonies gave these duck-billed dinosaurs mutual protection and improved their offspring's chances of survival.*

AN ARMORED DINOSAUR'S DEFENSE
Sharp spines stuck out from Edmontonia's *flanks and shoulders, providing a good defense. A tyrannosaur would have hesitated before attacking such a heavily armored dinosaur.*

EXTINCTION THEORIES

H AVING SURVIVED for 150 million years, dinosaurs seemed indestructible. Groups cut off from one another on diverging continents were fast evolving in different directions, and there were now more kinds of dinosaurs alive than ever. Yet, 10 million years later, the creatures we usually think of as dinosaurs were all extinct, as were all pterosaurs, marine crocodiles, plesiosaurs, many marine invertebrates, and all land animals above the size of a large dog. Scientists dispute why and how scores of groups suddenly died out about 65 million years ago. Various theories, some bizarre and some plausible, have been advanced to explain this mass extinction.

This position was thought to be caused by poisoning but is the result of drying.

EGG-THIEF
Small, omnivorous mammals like this one could have raided dinosaur nests. But egg-stealing did not kill off the dinosaurs.

■ THE LAST DINOSAURS ■

The last dinosaurs known lived in western North America and included *Tyrannosaurus* and *Triceratops*. Fossil evidence suggests that dinosaurs did not all disappear all at once, but over an extended period. Fossil remains in one rock formation in Montana suggest that dinosaur genera there dwindled from 19 to seven in the last few hundred thousand years before the time of the final extinction. Although in geological terms the Age of Dinosaurs ended abruptly, the precise timescale is not known. The extinction might have happened in an hour, or could have taken up to 100,000 years.

■ "SELF-DESTRUCTION" ■

The least convincing explanations of dinosaur extinction are those that blame the dinosaurs themselves. One suggestion was that vicious carnivores ate all the herbivores, then starved to death. A second notion was that dinosaurs evolved into creatures too clumsy to fend for themselves. Horned, crested, and thick-skulled dinosaurs were interpreted as the incompetent products of "racial degeneration." Defective hormones that led to dangerously thin eggshells, and stupidity resulting from shrinking brains, are other unsupported notions.

■ ENEMY AGENTS ■

A second group of ideas suggests that a sort of "biological warfare" killed the dinosaurs. For instance, newly evolving flowering plants might have held poisons fatal to dinosaurs. The co-evolution of dinosaurs with plants makes this theory unlikely. A virus may have caused a fatal pandemic— but it is unlikely that any germ could kill a group as diverse as the dinosaurs. Perhaps small, prolific mammals ate all the dinosaurs' eggs—but monitor lizards eat crocodiles' eggs without making crocodiles extinct. None of these theories seems believable.

■ GLOBAL CHANGE ■

Harsh changes affecting lands, seas, and climates may possibly have wiped out many dinosaurs and other animals. By the Late Cretaceous, such changes were taking place as a result of continental drift, mountain-building, and sea-level changes. As areas of shallow sea disappeared, many marine creatures lost their habitats. Away from the Equator, climates cooled, seasons grew more marked, and hardy plant species evolved. If dinosaurs were cold-blooded, they might have grown too sluggish to survive, and even a small temperature change could have made their eggs all hatch out as one sex, ending future breeding.

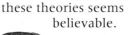

ORODROMEUS HATCHLINGS
Colonial nesting casts doubt on beliefs that stressed, overcrowded females laid fatally thin eggs.

▪ VOLCANIC ▪ ERUPTIONS

Climatic change brought about by volcanic eruptions is another possible cause of the demise of the dinosaurs. At the end of the Cretaceous, floods of lava were erupting through the Earth's crust in what is now central India—building the Deccan Plateau. For thousands of years this process sent enormous amounts of carbon dioxide and acids into the air. Spread around the world by winds, these materials could well have caused the global atmospheric temperature to rise, acid rain to fall, and the ozone in the atmosphere, which shuts out deadly radiation, to diminish.

▪ CATASTROPHES ▪ FROM SPACE

"Extraterrestrial" theories are those that suggest, for instance, that the extinction followed a burst of lethal radiation from an exploding star, or solar radiation admitted by a sudden reversal of the Earth's magnetic field. Another, likelier theory is that a large asteroid crashed into the Earth: such a collision would have formed a gigantic crater, vaporizing rock and flinging up dust and water droplets into the stratosphere. Clouds would have been carried around the world by high-level winds, shrouding the planet and causing cold, stormy weather. Plants would have died,

GUNNARITES
All such ammonites (coiled-shell sea molluscs) also died out about the same time as the dinosaurs became extinct.

along with many animals—especially land animals too large to hibernate. Evidence for such a catastrophe, cited in 1979, is a thin, worldwide deposit of the rare element iridium, which is frequently found in meteorites. Associated finds included shocked quartz (impact-fractured sand grains) and fossil proof of a sudden loss of flowering plants in North America. The recent discovery in Mexico of Chicxulub, a buried crater 186 miles (300km) across, provided further circumstantial evidence. It now seems likely that asteroids might also have caused other mass extinctions.

▪ THE SURVIVORS ▪

Most scientists believe the last true dinosaurs died out at the end of the Mesozoic era. Dinosaur fossils have been identified in rocks dating from the Cenozoic era (65 MYA to present day), but the finds are small and are probably older material dislodged from Mesozoic rocks. There is some support for the theory that birds are winged, feathered theropods. If this were so, with some 9,000 species living today, birds might claim to be the most successful "dinosaurs" of all!

METEOR CRATER, ARIZONA
A small meteorite punched out this crater (above). That of a big asteroid would have been vast.

VOLCANIC ERUPTIONS
Vast volcanoes erupting for half a million years could have caused catastrophic climatic changes.

FOSSILIZATION

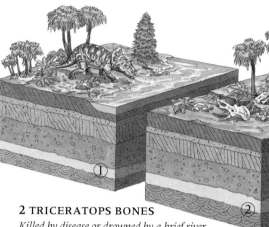

1 TRICERATOPS ALIVE
A Triceratops drinks from a river flowing through an open woodland of ferns, conifers, and other plants. This scene is set more than 65 million years ago.

WHEN LAND organisms die their bodies usually disappear, eaten by scavengers, rotted by bacteria, or degraded by the weather. Fossils are exceptions to this rule: they are the remains of long-dead organisms that escaped destruction by being covered up by sediments. The remains turned into fossils while sediments above them hardened into heavy sheets of rock. In time, some of these rock strata were uplifted and eroded to reveal the fossils. Perhaps no more than one dead dinosaur in a million was fossilized, and relatively few of these have so far been exposed. Fossil bones and teeth are our main clues to dinosaur life, but there are also fossil footprints, droppings, eggs, and the remains of prehistoric plants.

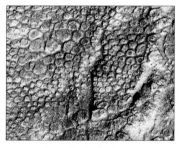

A fossilized imprint of a hadrosaur's belly skin.

2 TRICERATOPS BONES
Killed by disease or drowned by a brief river flood, the Triceratops is now reduced to scattered bones, beside and in the now dried-up riverbed.

▪ HOW FOSSILS ▪ FORMED

Fossilization often took place when death occurred in or near water, or in marshland. The soft parts of the dinosaur's body usually soon rotted away. However, the harder bones and teeth took much longer, and sometimes even the skin persisted in dinosaurs that were dried out and mummified by drought. Future fossils tended to be bones or other objects that were quickly cloaked by mud or sand dumped by moving water or wind. This process shut out the oxygen essential to bacteria that cause decay, but let mineral-saturated water percolate into the pores and bigger cavities in bones, filling these with calcite, iron sulphide, silica, or even opal. Permineralization, as this process is called, increased the weight and hardness of the bones. The pressure exerted by the mass of sediments that gradually accumulated overhead often deformed the permineralized bones.

▪ INSIDE THE EARTH ▪

Compacted under the weight of the overlying sediments, and bound by natural cement, these sediments hardened, their once-loose particles forming layers of sedimentary rocks. Over many millions of years, thousands of feet of sedimentary rock strata piled up on sagging plains and offshore seabeds. Beneath the weight of these rocks, fragile dinosaur bones collapsed, but fossil teeth and stronger bones endured. In this way, dinosaurs once living on the surface of the land were trapped deep within the Earth's crust. But not irrevocably. The giant jigsaw pieces, or tectonic plates, that form our planet's crust move slowly on convection currents in the Earth's mantle. Where two of these plates collided, or one overrode another, fossil-rich rock strata folded up and tilted into mountain ridges. Attacked by the elements, these mountains slowly crumbled, and their fossil treasures were laid bare.

▪ MOLDS, CASTS, AND ▪ PETRIFICATIONS

Not all fossilized dinosaur bones are heavy and permineralized. Freezing Alaskan rock, for example, has preserved bones that are darkened but lightweight, chemically unaltered since death. At the other extreme, acid-rich groundwater, such as that found in porous sandstones, has completely dissolved bones, leaving only bone-shaped holes, or molds. Sometimes minerals filled these cavities, creating bone-shaped casts. Bones completely "turned into stone" by mineral replacement are called petrifications.

A DINOSAUR TRACKWAY
Spiky footprints in Queensland's Late Cretaceous rocks may show where many small, bipedal dinosaurs fled from a large, predatory dinosaur. This event occurred about 100 million years ago.

COPROLITES
Experts identified these stones as the fossil droppings of a dinosaur. The shape, size, and contents (such as seeds and broken bones) of such coprolites hold clues to the bulk and feeding habits of the dinosaur they came from.

3 LIFE GOES ON

The skull of the drowned Triceratops *lies buried under silt dumped by the river. The rest of the skeleton has been destroyed by animal scavengers, bacteria, and weathering.*

4 BONE TO FOSSIL

Fifteen million years after the Triceratops *died, the same chemicals that helped to cement silt into rock have transformed its buried skull into a stony fossil. The land above is now inhabited by mammals.*

TRICERATOPS AND TAPHONOMY

The scene showing a dead *Triceratops*'s scattered bones (2) is based on taphonomy, or the study of what happens to animals after they die and before sediments cover them. Taphonomy shows that large, heavy skeletons held together by strong ligaments break up less readily than small ones. Small dinosaurs quickly decomposed and had their bones crunched up or dispersed by scavengers or river currents. Rivers could have separated the smaller bones of beasts as heavy as *Triceratops*, but only bits of skull or other bones tended to survive from fragile forms such as *Troodon*. Few dinosaurs under 110lb (50kg) survive as articulated skeletons.

5 THE ICE AGE

Woolly mammoths roam an Ice Age land 20,000 years ago. Mountain-building Earth movements have brought the skull of the Triceratops *closer to the surface.*

6 TRICERATOPS REVEALED

Frost, ice, rain, sun, and wind have eroded mountain slopes and gnawed deeply into layered rocks formed more than 65 million years ago. The Triceratops *skull is now unearthed by fossil hunters.*

JUMBLED BONES

These jumbled bones (above) belonged to several Coelophysis, *victims of a flash flood.*

PTEROSAUR FOSSILS

One rock (below left) preserves pterosaur bones. The other rock (below right) contains their mold.

■ TRACE FOSSILS ■

Trace fossils are fossils that reveal traces of ancient animal activity. Ichnites are fossil footprints made in soft mud that hardened into rock. Distinctive ichnites are often given names, known as ichnogenera. Fossil footprints can indicate the size, weight, and stance of a dinosaur, and they may identify their maker as a theropod, sauropod, ornithopod, ceratopsian, or ankylosaur. Footprints forming a trackway can show how fast a dinosaur moved (the longer its stride the greater its speed), and parallel tracks may reflect herding habits. Track sites with millions of footprints mark where sauropod herds followed a Late Jurassic shore in western North America. Fossil clues to dinosaur diet include bitten leaves and coprolites (fossilized droppings), some of which still hold traces of food. Evidence of breeding activity comes from broken fossil eggshells, whole eggs, complete clutches, nests, embryos, and young. Proof of injury lies in bones scratched by teeth or broken by a fall (and sometimes subsequently healed). Abnormally swollen or fused bones are clues to bone disease. Fossilized wood, leaves, and old lake- and river-beds provide clues to the dinosaurs' environments.

DINOSAUR FINDS

I N THE YEAR 1824 the English naturalist and clergyman William Buckland published the first scientific account of a dinosaur – *Megalosaurus*. The following year, amateur paleontologist Gideon Mantell described the teeth and bones of *Iguanodon*. The comparative anatomist Sir Richard Owen coined the term Dinosauria for the very few dinosaurs then known in 1841, and in 1887 Professor Harry Govier Seeley grouped all dinosaurs into the Saurischia and Ornithischia according to their hip design. While theoretical understanding grew, the hunt for fossil dinosaurs expanded, and in the course of the nineteenth century the search spread from England to mainland Europe and the Americas. Since 1900, paleontologists have unearthed dinosaurs from Mesozoic rocks in every continent, and each year brings fresh discoveries.

EDWARD DRINKER COPE (1840–1897)
Cope gave names to a number of different dinosaurs.

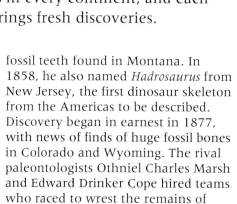

FOSSIL JAWBONE
This Megalosaurus *jawbone formed the basis of the first scientific description of a dinosaur.*

■ FINDS IN EUROPE ■

Dinosaur discovery very quickly spread from England and led to exciting fossil discoveries elsewhere in Europe. In 1837, Hermann von Meyer described *Plateosaurus*, a Triassic prosauropod found in Germany, and in 1861 he named *Archaeopteryx*, a bird closely linked to dinosaurs. In 1878, Belgian miners made the dramatic discovery of more than 30 complete *Iguanodon* skeletons in a deep coal mine. Since the 1860s, searchers in southern France have found clutches of large eggs laid by a Late Cretaceous sauropod. Numerous Late Cretaceous dinosaurs have been found across Europe, but England remains the best source of Early Cretaceous dinosaurs.

■ UNITED STATES FINDS ■

Early finds of fossil dinosaur bones and footprints in New England went unrecognized. But, in 1856, anatomist Joseph Leidy named *Troodon* from

fossil teeth found in Montana. In 1858, he also named *Hadrosaurus* from New Jersey, the first dinosaur skeleton from the Americas to be described. Discovery began in earnest in 1877, with news of finds of huge fossil bones in Colorado and Wyoming. The rival paleontologists Othniel Charles Marsh and Edward Drinker Cope hired teams who raced to wrest the remains of sauropods from the Late Jurassic rocks of Morrison and Canyon City,

Colorado, and Como Bluff, Wyoming. Over 20 dinosaur genera, including *Apatosaurus* and *Camarasaurus*, were named by these scientists. Fresh finds by Henry Fairfield Osborn, William J. Holland, and Earl Douglass came in the early 1900s. Since the middle of this century, excavations by Sankar Chatterjee, David Gillette, John Horner, James Jensen, Robert Long, John Ostrom, and many more have thrown light on dinosaurs from all

OTHNIEL CHARLES MARSH (1831–1899)
Marsh (center back row) funded Wild West fossil hunts and named dozens of dinosaurs.

three Mesozoic periods. Finds include *Seismosaurus*, *Deinonychus*, and whole colonies of nesting hadrosaurs. With about 110 genera, the United States led the world by the 1990s.

▪ FINDS IN CANADA ▪

In 1884, Joseph Tyrrell's discovery of the first *Albertosaurus* skull launched a great dinosaur hunt that continues in the badlands beside Alberta's Red Deer River. Thomas Chesmer Weston and Lawrence Lambe prospected for dinosaurs from riverboats. In 1910, Barnum Brown competed with Charles Sternberg and sons, who were collecting for the Canadian Geological Survey. Work stopped in 1917, but by this time, a wealth of Late Cretaceous horned and duck-billed dinosaurs had been found. In the 1980s, Philip Currie and other fossil-hunters renewed the search, and by the 1990s the area of Alberta now known as Dinosaur Provincial Park had yielded more dinosaur specimens than any comparable area on Earth.

▪ FINDS IN ASIA ▪

Chinese dinosaur discovery began in earnest under Young Chung Chien, whose work continued from the 1930s into the 1970s. Since then, further discoveries have been made under Dong Zhiming. With 95 named genera in 1990, China ranked second only to the United States. In the early 1920s, American teams of scientists led by Roy Chapman Andrews and Walter Granger revealed Mongolia's Gobi Desert as one of the world's richest sources of dinosaur remains. Since then, Russian, Mongolian, Polish, and American teams have worked this desert. Russian paleontologists have also opened dinosaur quarries in remote parts of Siberia.

▪ DINOSAURS FROM GONDWANA ▪

By the early 1900s dinosaur finds had been made in South America, Africa, India, and Australia – the now inhabited parts of Gondwana. Most South American finds were made in Argentina, but Brazil was the site of the major discovery of *Staurikosaurus*. Other

EAST-WEST COLLABORATION
Dong Zhiming (right) and Philip Currie take part in a Sino-Canadian excavation in Inner Mongolia.

SHUNOSAURUS (A CHINESE SAUROPOD)
This skeleton is one of scores of finds that have made China one of the top two sources of fossil dinosaurs.

important finds included the theropod *Carnotaurus*, sail-backed *Amargasaurus*, and *Eoraptor* (the most primitive of all known dinosaurs). The Argentinian paleontologist José Bonaparte named a number of South American genera. African discoveries began in the early 1900s, and by the 1990s at least 16 nations had recorded dinosaur finds. They included early forms in Morocco and South Africa, sail-backed dinosaurs in the Sahara Desert, and mixed Late

Jurassic dinosaurs in what is now Tanzania. Dinosaur detection in India dates from the 1860s. By the 1990s it had produced a primitive sauropod, the last known stegosaur, and a giant theropod. Organized Australian discovery dates only from about 1980. By the 1990s Ralph Molnar, Thomas Rich, and others had raised Australia's tally to nearly a dozen genera, including armored *Minmi*.

▪ NEW LOCATIONS ▪

Since 1980, dinosaur fossils have emerged in some unexpected places. In 1980, Ralph Molnar described a theropod vertebra discovered in the North Island of New Zealand. By 1990, Yoshikazu Hasegawa had studied scraps of perhaps nine dinosaur genera unearthed on the Japanese islands of Honshū and Kyūshū, and in 1992, *Wakinosaurus*, a large Kyūshū theropod, was named by Yoshihiko Okazaki. During the 1980s, both Polar regions yielded dinosaur fossils. In 1985, teams from the universities of California and Alaska found many Late Cretaceous bones in the North Slope of Alaska. In 1986, Argentinian paleontologists noted a dinosaur from Antarctica, and by 1993 Antarctic finds included a sauropod and a horned theropod.

JOSE BONAPARTE
Since the 1960s, the work of this paleontologist from Argentina has revealed valuable information on South American dinosaurs. Among the dinosaurs named by Bonaparte are Carnotaurus, Riojasaurus, *and* Patagosaurus.

MUSSAURUS
Found in Argentina and named in 1979, this "mouse lizard" was a tiny young prosauropod.

EXCAVATING DINOSAURS

D IGGING UP DINOSAURS means first finding where their remains are likely to be. Dinosaur hunters must concentrate on rocks formed from sediments laid down in Mesozoic times. Only certain regions of the world with special kinds of countryside provide rich hunting grounds. Sometimes amateurs discover dinosaurs by chance, but most finds result from paleontologists' systematic fossil hunts. Once located, a small, isolated dinosaur fossil may be collected single-handedly in a few minutes, but prying a big fossil from hard rock can take a large team weeks or months of wielding an arsenal of machines and tools. Excavation is only part of the work; measuring and recording full details of the find are equally important. Once they are excavated, the fragile bones need careful cushioning and labeling before being transported to an often distant museum.

EXCAVATING AN ANKYLOSAUR
A Polish paleontologist's delicate work with knife and brush lays bare the forepart of Saichania. *This ankylosaur may have been suffocated by a sandstorm in the Gobi Desert nearly 80 million years ago.*

❋ WHERE TO EXCAVATE ❋

The best places for hunting dinosaurs are exposed Mesozoic rocks derived from sediments that accumulated on land or close inshore. This can mean roadside cuttings, quarries, sea cliffs, riverbanks, and even coal mines. But the most extensive, dinosaur-rich outcrops occur among badlands and remote deserts, such as parts of western North America, the Gobi Desert, Patagonia, and some sandy tracts of the Sahara. Here erosion lays bare great tracts of fossil-bearing Mesozoic rock. Unfortunately, much dinosaur-bearing rock can never be explored. It lies deeply buried under other rocks, soil, water, or ice; has been deformed by heat and pressure; or has been removed completely by erosion.

❋ DINOSAUR DISCOVERY ❋

This can be accidental or planned. For example, the discovery of *Iguanodon* is said to have begun when a doctor's wife noticed a fossil tooth in a heap of roadside stones. Farmers and road and railroad workers have also made important finds. And amateur and weekend fossil-hunters, often armed with no more than a geological hammer, have also been known to strike fossil "gold,"

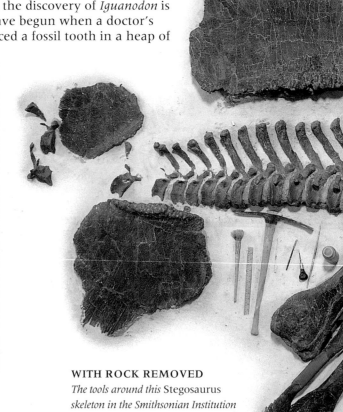

UNEARTHING OPISTHOCOELICAUDIA
Six workers here use hammers and picks to remove sandy rock from this headless fossil sauropod in southern Mongolia.

WITH ROCK REMOVED
The tools around this Stegosaurus *skeleton in the Smithsonian Institution were used to free it from its rocky matrix.*

as when Joan Wiffen discovered New Zealand's first known dinosaur, an unnamed theropod; William Walker discovered *Baryonyx*; and Eddie and Vivian Jones located new dinosaurs in Colorado. But a large number of major discoveries have occurred on long-term expeditions to remote regions, usually organized by universities or museums. Teams of paleontologists set off in trucks loaded with gear for excavating, surveying, and packing fossil finds.

⁂ EXCAVATION METHODS ⁂

Fossil-hunters usually walk along dry streambeds and adjacent to slopes, scouring the ground for dark, shiny, or otherwise unusual "stones." Such scraps may well be fossil fragments washed down from bones embedded in the rocks above. A single dinosaur bone projecting from a hill may prove an isolated find, or it may lead to an entire skeleton hidden underground. Picks and shovels are used to clear soil and soft rock from around a large fossil skeleton. In some deserts, bones can be exposed by

merely brushing away the uppermost layer of the sand. Large skeletons entombed in hard rock present much greater problems. To get at a hidden skeleton a team may have to raze half a hillside with explosives, bulldozers, and power drills. Careful work can then be carried out with a variety of tools, including toothbrushes, to free the fossil from its surrounding matrix. Fragile bones are often removed while still embedded in large chunks of rock.

⁂ RECOVERING AND REMOVING ⁂

Once the bones lie exposed, scientists can number and photograph them, and plot their position on a plan. Later, this detailed survey may help anatomists reconstruct the skeleton and may also help scientists understand what happened to the dinosaur after its death. Bones are prepared for removal by painting resin on crumbly fossils to stop them from disintegrating. Big bones can be protected with burlap soaked in plaster or with plastic foam.

EXCAVATING COELOPHYSIS
After tunneling under rock rich in Coelophysis *fossils, members of a Carnegie Museum team protect the fragile rock surface with burlap and plaster.*

TRANSPORTING COELOPHYSIS
Members of the Carnegie Museum team (above) prepare to slide a block of plastered rock containing Coelophysis *fossils down a timber slope. This quarry is at Ghost Ranch, Abiquiu, New Mexico.*

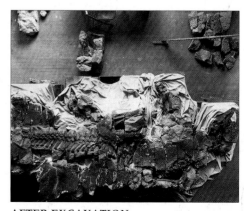

AFTER EXCAVATION
The blocks of solid rock and plaster enclosing a Stegosaurus *skeleton (above) were removed before it was displayed at the Smithsonian Institution (left).*

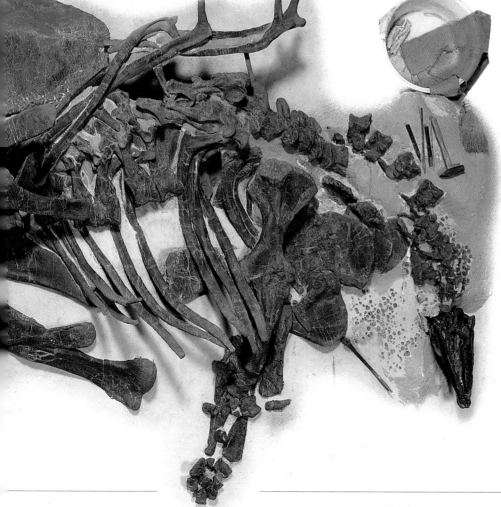

DINOSAURS IN MUSEUMS

R ECOVERING A DINOSAUR fossil is the first step on a journey of discovery. When a museum laboratory has prepared the specimen, a paleontologist compares it with known dinosaurs. Differences may indicate a brand-new genus. A description of the specimen is then published in a scientific journal. When studies are complete, experts may reconstruct the creature's skeleton and put it on display. These pages show the creation of a major sauropod exhibit for one American museum. Thanks to international collaboration, hundreds of such dinosaur displays have been developed around the world. At least three dozen institutions hold about 500 original specimens from Alberta's Dinosaur Provincial Park alone, area for area perhaps the world's richest "gold mine" of articulated fossil dinosaurs.

RECONSTRUCTED BAROSAURUS SKELETON

Among the most ambitious of any reconstructed dinosaurs, this rearing *Barosaurus* skeleton towers over 49ft (15m) above the floor of the American Museum of Natural History. Steel rods concealed inside its bones support their weight, which is substantial, even though the bones are in fact lightweight plastic and fiberglass replicas of the originals. This method of reconstructing dinosaur skeletons is far more effective than earlier methods, where the original, heavy fossil bones were supported by obtrusive scaffolding on the outside of the skeleton.

✳ IN THE LABORATORY ✳

Work in the museum laboratory begins with freeing a fossil from its rock matrix. The protective jacket is cut away by a preparator, who then strengthens the exposed, fragile bone with chemical solutions. A saw or hammer and chisel can then be used to remove the outer rock. If that is softer than the fossil it surrounds, shot-blasting (where tiny high-speed plastic pellets bombard the specimen inside a steel and glass cabinet) can be used. If the rock is a limestone, the preparator can use dilute acetic acid to dissolve the rock, leaving the fossil unharmed. Final treatment, though, is often slow, painstaking work with a magnifying glass or microscope and dental drill, dental pick, and needle. Removing a great dinosaur like *Seismosaurus* from rock that is as hard as concrete could take anything up to ten years. Extracting the rock inside a fossil skull or eggshell may be impossible, but X-rays or CAT scans may detect an internal embryo or brain cavity.

WELDING STEEL SUPPORTS
Sparks fly as a welder, wearing a protective mask, fuses metal rods together (above). The rods provide internal support for the tail vertebrae of the mounted Barosaurus *skeleton.*

MOUNTING AN ALLOSAURUS
A team positions an Allosaurus *skeleton in the American Museum of Natural History, New York.*

❊ SCIENTIFIC STUDY ❊

A paleontologist first compares the prepared, newly discovered bones with equivalent bones from known dinosaurs. Bones with unusual features may reveal a new dinosaur genus. The paleontologist draws or photographs these to illustrate a scientific paper in which the bones are described. Details of skull, teeth, limb bones, and vertebrae may help the writer draw conclusions about the size, appearance, and behavior of the dinosaur. Finally, the article gives the animal a scientific name unique to that species. Independent experts must approve the description of the new dinosaur before a scientific journal can accept it for publication.

POSITIONING THE LEGS AND TAIL

A museum worker on a cherry picker positions Barosaurus's tail vertebrae. Another lowers the hip girdle and hind limb bones onto a supporting metal framework.

❊ RECONSTRUCTION ❊

Once scientists have worked out how the dinosaur bones fit together, a museum may want to reconstruct the skeleton for display in a lifelike pose. Skeletons seldom survive intact, but museum staff can make fiberglass models of the missing bones. Heavy, mineralized bones need thick rods and bars to hold them up. Nowadays, most big mounted skeletons are light fiberglass replicas, made as shown on page 35, and supported by slim, metal rods invisibly threaded inside.

❊ HIDDEN TREASURE TROVES ❊

The dinosaurs the public sees are often a fraction of the fossils kept in storage. For instance, the Earth Sciences Museum, Brigham Young University, Provo, Utah, has a stockpile of 100 tons of big fossilized bones, still encased in plaster. Many a museum basement is similarly crammed with labeled bones, laid on racks or placed in drawers. For years most of these lie there unexamined, waiting for a scientist to study them. Sometimes a paleontologist identifies a "brand-new" dinosaur from one or two bones found a century ago and left in storage, undescribed or misidentified.

BONES IN STORAGE

Shelves in the basement of the American Museum of Natural History hold the bones of Barosaurus *and of many other dinosaurs.*

❊ BACKROOM WORK ❊

Much of what we know of dinosaurs springs from backroom work in museum and university laboratories. Once, the only guide to when these creatures lived was the relative ages of fossil-bearing rock layers laid down on top of one another, the youngest layer usually uppermost. Now, radiometric dating can be used in order to pinpoint the age of dinosaurs within a million years or so. In radiometric dating, special instruments are used to measure the radioactive elements in certain rocks. These elements decay into others at known rates, so their relative proportions allow scientists to work out the age of the rock, and thus also the age of the fossils within it.

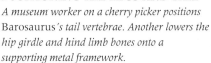

AN EARLY RECONSTRUCTION

Wooden trestles featured in this early effort to mount a Diplodocus *skeleton in Pittsburgh's Carnegie Museum.*

RESTORATION OF DINOSAURS

W HILE RECONSTRUCTION is the task of piecing together fossil bones to rebuild a skeleton, restoration is fleshing out the bones to show the creature as it looked in life. Clues to the shape of muscles and intestines can be found by examining the rare fossils of soft tissues that are known, by looking at muscle attachment points on fossilized bones, and by making comparisons with living animals. Modeling a dinosaur is a skill that requires good knowledge of the creature's size, shape, and stance, and of such questions as whether it had fleshy cheeks, or whether it dragged its tail or carried it aloft. By keeping up-to-date with new theories and discoveries, artists and sculptors have transformed the popular images of many dinosaurs.

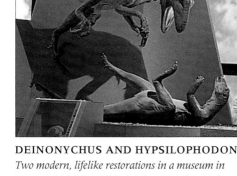

DEINONYCHUS AND HYPSILOPHODON
Two modern, lifelike restorations in a museum in Taiwan depict the stiff-tailed, ferocious theropod Deinonychus, *with its sickle claws poised to strike its prey, a terrified, fallen* Hypsilophodon.

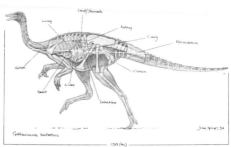

"OLD STYLE" HYPSILOPHODON MODEL
Old models show Hypsilophodon *perched in trees. New models depict it as a ground-based sprinter.*

RESTORING GALLIMIMUS
Below are some of the stages in the creation of one of the lifelike model dinosaurs shown in this book. This birdlike theropod was restored with one side of its body dissected to expose bones and internal organs. The other side shows skin color and texture.

✳ RESTORATION ✳

A reconstructed skeleton gives artists and model-makers the basis for lifelike restorations of the animal. The anatomy of modern reptiles, birds, and mammals serves as a guide to the sizes, shapes, and positions of the internal organs and the muscles that give the body bulk. Skin texture of a model is based partly on fossil skin impressions showing non-overlapping scales covering the body, and partly on the scaly skins of the legs of crocodiles and birds. Color must remain intelligent guesswork based on what we know of living animals. Big dinosaurs might have been drab, like elephants. Smaller

ones could have been striped or spotted as a form of camouflage. Like some modern birds and reptiles, though, breeding males could have had brightly colored heads and areas of skin. All of these features can be incorporated into models built to any scale. Robotics specialists can even construct life-size, lifelike dinosaurs that move their heads and bellow horribly. Inside the models, pneumatic machinery powers metal skeletons supporting polyurethane bodies. The bodies of these dinosaurs are sheathed in silicone rubber skin painted in convincing colors, shades, and patterns. Weatherproof models are posed realistically in the open air, for instance in a park or a small wood.

THE SKETCH
A pencil sketch delineates the details of the internal anatomy of Gallimimus. *The muscles and internal organs are based on those of living animals. Next, an articulated cardboard "skeleton" is made.*

THE ARMATURE
The armature for the model is made from wire and wood, and based on the reconstructed skeleton. This then forms the framework on which the sculptor will add other substances to build up solid body structures.

BULKING OUT
Modeling clay is used to build the exposed bones on the dissected side of the model. The neck, body, and tail are bulked out with scrim (fabric) and plaster and sealed with shellac. The claws are cast in resin.

❋ DINOSAURS TODAY ❋ AND YESTERDAY

Modern restorations incorporate scientific theories of the appearance and behavior of dinosaurs. Straight thigh bones with sharply turned-in heads indicate that dinosaurs stood with their hind limbs upright, like our own. The ossified (bony) tendons encasing their caudal vertebrae show that most ornithischians had stiffened tails, while teeth set in from the jaw rims indicate that ornithischians had fleshy cheeks. The lack of a tail imprint between their fossil footprints suggests that sauropods did not drag their tails. The restudying of even well-studied dinosaurs has led to revelations. We now know that *Tyrannosaurus* walked with its back horizontal and its tail held off the ground, *Iguanodon*'s stiff tail prevented it from standing like a kangaroo, and *Hypsilophodon* ran fast but may not have climbed trees, as was once supposed. Scientific studies even support theories of jousting pachycephalosaurs and head-wrestling ceratopsids.

RESTORING BARYONYX'S SKULL

The biological sculptor John Holmes checks a measurement in this reconstruction of the skull and mandible of *Baryonyx*. Only parts of the actual bones have been discovered. Missing areas are filled in with clay. Careful anatomical drawings of the skull's likely proportions have already been made with reference to other theropod skulls.

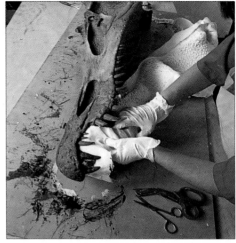

MAKING A RUBBER MOLD
The clay and bone reconstruction of Baryonyx's *skull is now used to produce a rubber mold. The skull is first painted with coats of liquid silicone rubber that solidify after adding a catalyst. The resulting rubber mold is then gently peeled away from the skull (above). The next stage is to make a fiberglass cast.*

MAKING A FIBERGLASS CAST
The rubber mold of the Baryonyx *skull now becomes the basis for making casts. The pale rubber mold is painted with a coat of dark liquid resin (above). Fiberglass mat is embedded in later coats of resin. The complete structure forms a rigid, lightweight facsimile of the original clay skull.*

THE CLAY SCULPTURE
To produce a finished clay restoration, the basic shape is built up with small amounts of clay. Skin textures and other details are worked into the surface. A rubber mold is then made from the clay sculpture.

THE RESIN CAST
Using the rubber mold, a cast is made from a special mix of mineral and polyester resin reinforced with glass, metal rods, and carbon fiber. The cast is then cleaned to prepare it for the final stage.

COLORING THE CAST
The final stage in making a model of Gallimimus *involves hand-painting and air-brushing the internal and external features of the model with oil paint. The glass eyes give the final realistic touch.*

DINOSAUR PROFILES

THIS SECTION presents illustrated profiles of 55 different genera selected so as to represent all the major dinosaur groups. Included throughout the section are specially commissioned photographs showing skulls, skeletons, and other items from museums around the world. These are supplemented with dramatic photographs of models plus color illustrations and archival materials.

THEROPODS

THE BIPEDAL THEROPODS ("beast feet") include all known predatory dinosaurs. Typical examples had birdlike features, such as hollow bones; an S-shaped neck; long, muscular hind limbs; and clawed, four-toed feet, the first toe short and high-positioned. Many theropods may have been warm-blooded, and scientists believe a few may have had feathers. Small, early forms gave rise to heavy big-game hunters, and to ostrichlike omnivores (and possibly herbivores) with toothless beaks. One group of small, feathered, warm-blooded theropods may have given rise to true birds. Theropods spread worldwide and spanned the Age of Dinosaurs, but many left scanty remains. A number of relationships shown here are open to dispute.

The small, but ferocious theropod Gasosaurus, *found in China.*

DROMAEOSAURUS SKULL

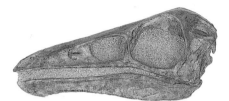

DROMICEIOMIMUS SKULL

ALBERTOSAURUS SKULL

THREE THEROPOD SKULLS
These photographs contrast the skulls of small, sharp-toothed Dromaeosaurus, *fanged* Albertosaurus, *and birdlike, toothless* Dromiceiomimus.

■ PRIMITIVE THEROPODS ■

These lacked the distinctive features of the Ceratosauria or Tetanurae. *EORAPTOR*, from early Late Triassic Argentina, was a primitive theropod no bigger than a large dog. STAURIKOSAURIDAE was a family named after the genus *Staurikosaurus*. It lived in early Late Triassic Brazil. HERRERASAURIDAE, a worldwide Late Triassic/Early Jurassic group, had "old-fashioned" hind limb bones.

■ CERATOSAURIA ■

Ceratosaurs were small to large theropods with a kinked upper jaw, a crested snout, unusual vertebrae, possibly four fingers per hand, birdlike hip bones with rod-shaped pubes, and a stiffened rear half of the tail. NOASAURIDAE contained the Late Cretaceous *Noasaurus*. This small dinosaur had a swiveling toe-claw. ALVAREZSAURIDAE contained the Late

Cretaceous Argentinian genus *Alvarezsaurus*, which resembled the (unrelated) ornithomimids. ABELISAURIDAE included nine or so genera with fused ankle bones and unusual skulls. These big beasts lived in Early to Late Cretaceous times. VELOCISAURIDAE included *Velocisaurus*, a small, Late Cretaceous beast with unusual upper foot bones. CERATOSAURIDAE were big theropods named after *Ceratosaurus* of Late Jurassic North America. COELOPHYSIDAE were lightly built theropods occurring widely from Late Triassic to Early Jurassic times. HALTICOSAURIDAE were primitive, early theropod dinosaurs that may have belonged to the infraorder Tetanurae. MEGALOSAURIDAE were a family of big, robust beasts that may have lived from Early

Jurassic to Late Cretaceous times. *EUSTREPTOSPONDYLUS* was a big, Middle Jurassic predator from England.

■ TETANURAE ■

Tetanurae had tails that were stiffened for most of their length. There were two main subgroups.

SUBGROUP CARNOSAURIA

ALLOSAURIDAE were large to huge, mainly Late Jurassic theropods with a worldwide distribution. ITEMIRIDAE were a family containing the small, Late Cretaceous *Itemirus*. DRYPTOSAURIDAE included the large, slender-legged *Dryptosaurus* from Late Cretaceous North America. TYRANNOSAURIDAE comprised about nine genera from Late Cretaceous Asia and North America, including some of the largest-ever land-based carnivores. AUBLYSODONTIDAE were small, Late Cretaceous hunters of big game. SPINOSAURIDAE were huge, with a tall dorsal "sail." The genus *Spinosaurus*

THREE THEROPODS
Models shown to scale contrast the enormous Allosaurus *with the large* Gallimimus *and the tiny* Compsognathus.

lived in Late Cretaceous Africa.
BARYONYCHIDAE, from North Africa
and Early Cretaceous Europe, had
long heads and hooked thumb-claws.

SUBGROUP COELUROSAURIA

ORNITHOMIMIDAE were widely
distributed, ostrichlike, Late Jurassic
to Late Cretaceous theropods.
DEINOCHEIRIDAE came from Late
Cretaceous Asia and might have been
huge relatives of the Ornithomimidae.
OVIRAPTORIDAE were Late Cretaceous,
Asian, birdlike beasts with short, deep
heads and strong beaks.
CAENAGNATHIDAE were small, Late
Cretaceous, Asian and North
American relatives of the oviraptorids.
ELMISAURIDAE were small, Late
Cretaceous, Asian and North
American beasts with birdlike feet.
THERIZINOSAURIDAE were Asian, Late
Cretaceous theropods with scythelike
finger-claws.
TROODONTIDAE were small, alert,
Late Cretaceous, northern theropods
with a swiveling toe-claw.
DROMAEOSAURIDAE were fairly
small, Cretaceous, northern
theropods with
a "ramrod"   THEROPODA
tail and a savage,
swiveling second-toe claw.
ARCHAEOPTERYGIDAE included the
genus *Archaeopteryx*, a primitive, Late
Jurassic, European bird. (Some
scientists—though far from all—
believe that all birds *are* dinosaurs.)
AVIMIMIDAE contained one genus,
Avimimus, which was a toothless,
long-legged, birdlike, running
dinosaur from Late Cretaceous Asia.
COELURIDAE were small, Late Jurassic
to Late Cretaceous theropods with a
worldwide distribution.
COMPSOGNATHIDAE had one genus,
Compsognathus, a tiny, two-fingered
dinosaur that lived in Europe in Late
Jurassic times.

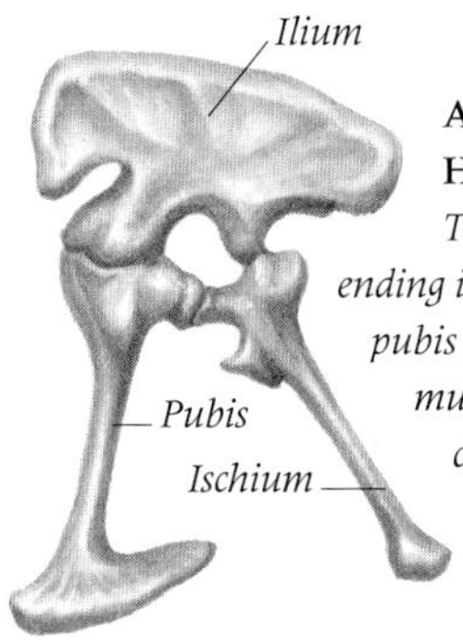

ALLOSAURUS HIP BONES

Ilium

Pubis

Ischium

*These show a long pubis
ending in a broad "foot". The
pubis and foot secured the
muscles that kept hind limbs
close to the body. When
Allosaurus lay down, the
"foot" might have helped
to support its weight.*

THEROPOD FAMILY TREE

This diagram shows possible relationships
among theropod families (the names ending
in -idae), each containing one genus or
several genera. Names of individual genera
not allocated to a family appear in italics.
The infraorders Ceratosauria and Tetanurae
are briefly described in the main text. Key
subgroups below this level included the
Maniraptora, dinosaurs that many
scientists now think gave rise
to birds. If so, strictly speaking,
birds are tetanuran theropods.

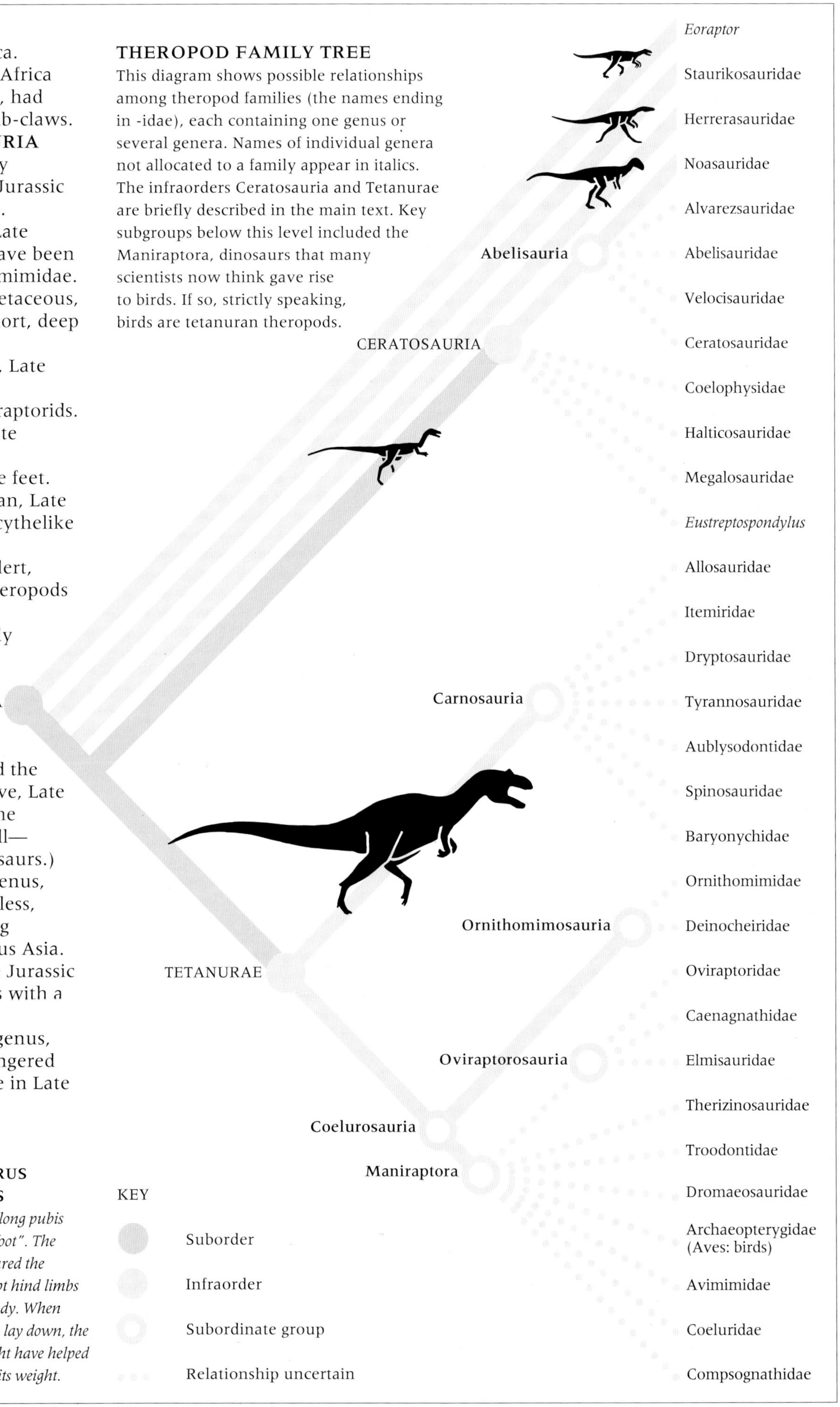

Abelisauria

CERATOSAURIA

Carnosauria

Ornithomimosauria

TETANURAE

Oviraptorosauria

Coelurosauria

Maniraptora

Eoraptor

Staurikosauridae

Herrerasauridae

Noasauridae

Alvarezsauridae

Abelisauridae

Velocisauridae

Ceratosauridae

Coelophysidae

Halticosauridae

Megalosauridae

Eustreptospondylus

Allosauridae

Itemiridae

Dryptosauridae

Tyrannosauridae

Aublysodontidae

Spinosauridae

Baryonychidae

Ornithomimidae

Deinocheiridae

Oviraptoridae

Caenagnathidae

Elmisauridae

Therizinosauridae

Troodontidae

Dromaeosauridae

Archaeopterygidae
(Aves: birds)

Avimimidae

Coeluridae

Compsognathidae

KEY

Suborder

Infraorder

Subordinate group

Relationship uncertain

HERRERASAURUS

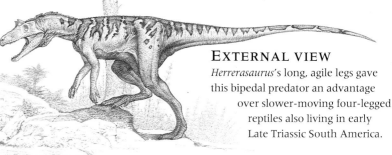

H ERRERASAURUS ("Herrera's lizard") is named after Victorino Herrera, the Andean goat farmer who first stumbled on its skeleton. One of the earliest known dinosaurs, this medium-size, bipedal carnivore had sharp teeth, short arms, and formidable, curved claws on its three-fingered hands. "Old-fashioned" features of the leg and foot bones seemed to hint at a dinosaur more primitive than any in the two main dinosaur groups. The later discovery of a complete skull, however, revealed that *Herrerasaurus* had a sliding lower jaw joint in common with some other theropods. This extra hinge gave killers like *Herrerasaurus* a fearsome grasping bite.

EXTERNAL VIEW
Herrerasaurus's long, agile legs gave this bipedal predator an advantage over slower-moving four-legged reptiles also living in early Late Triassic South America.

SKULL
Herrerasaurus's skull was long and narrow, with small nostril holes. A flexible joint in the mandible (lower jaw) let the front half move against the rear half, to give a grasping bite. Similar jaws help some lizards overcome their prey.

Infratemporal fenestra

Braincase

Orbit

Naris

Mandible

Curved, pointed tooth

Scaly skin

※ LIFE AND BEHAVIOR ※

Herrerasaurus inhabited an upland region where plants grew thickly in the rainy season but then died back during long months of drought. Striding on long, birdlike legs through the dense clumps of vegetation that fringed the rivers, this dinosaur hunted and perhaps ambushed its prey. Tracks left in sand or trampled through the undergrowth probably betrayed potential victims, such as the small, bipedal plant-eating dinosaur *Pisanosaurus*. But a far more plentiful prey would have been certain squat, four-legged reptile herbivores, such as the tusked, piglike rhynchosaurs, and the armored quadrupeds named aetosaurs. Darting in to surprise a browsing rhynchosaur, an adult *Herrerasaurus* could have clawed and bitten fatal gashes in its hide. Sometimes a young *Herrerasaurus* might have scavenged from the carcass of a rhynchosaur. There were relatively few species of predatory dinosaurs in the Late Triassic; the main predators at this time were the large, crocodile-like rauisuchids. Arguably, the upright stance, long hind limbs, and clawed, grasping hands made *Herrerasaurus* and its relatives relatively faster and potentially more dangerous than most competitors. Rauisuchids eventually died out, and the theropods dominated predatory life on land for over 150 million years.

Long tail acts as a counterbalance

SOUTH AMERICAN SCENE
Two young Herrerasaurus *(left) here vie with a big rauisuchid* Saurosuchus *for the remains of a dead rhynchosaur, watched by the small, primitive theropod* Eoraptor *(center) and by two mammal-like reptiles (right).*

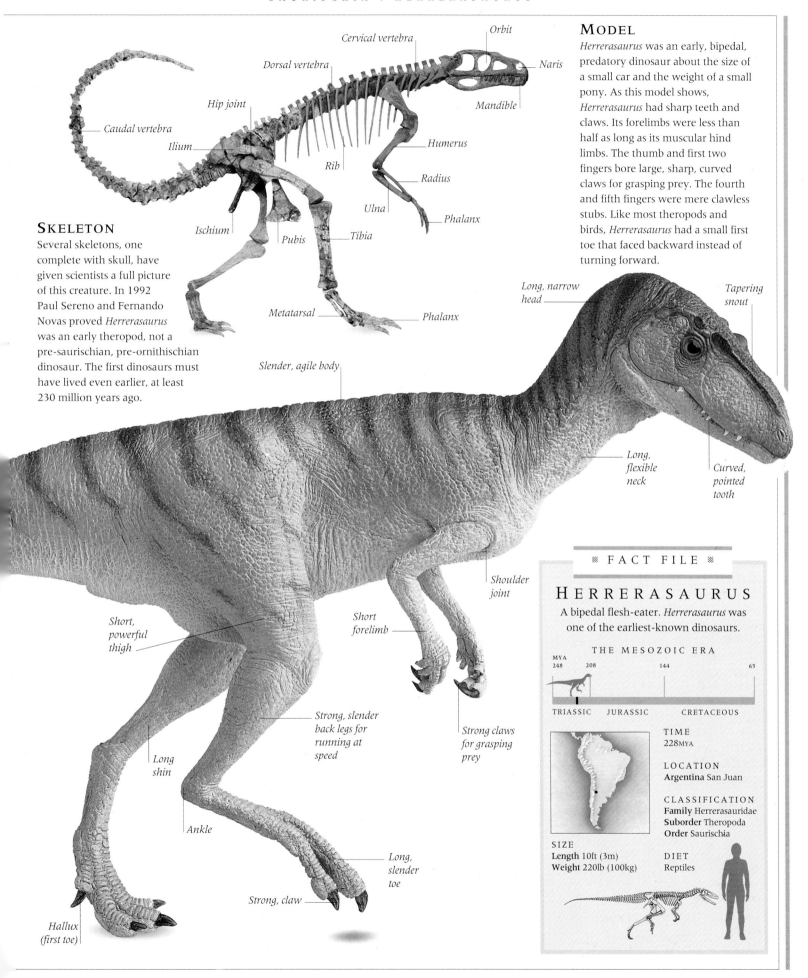

Orbit

Cervical vertebra

Dorsal vertebra

Naris

Hip joint

Mandible

Caudal vertebra

Ilium

Humerus

Rib

Radius

Ulna

Ischium

Phalanx

Pubis

Tibia

Metatarsal

Phalanx

SKELETON

Several skeletons, one complete with skull, have given scientists a full picture of this creature. In 1992 Paul Sereno and Fernando Novas proved *Herrerasaurus* was an early theropod, not a pre-saurischian, pre-ornithischian dinosaur. The first dinosaurs must have lived even earlier, at least 230 million years ago.

Slender, agile body

MODEL

Herrerasaurus was an early, bipedal, predatory dinosaur about the size of a small car and the weight of a small pony. As this model shows, *Herrerasaurus* had sharp teeth and claws. Its forelimbs were less than half as long as its muscular hind limbs. The thumb and first two fingers bore large, sharp, curved claws for grasping prey. The fourth and fifth fingers were mere clawless stubs. Like most theropods and birds, *Herrerasaurus* had a small first toe that faced backward instead of turning forward.

Long, narrow head

Tapering snout

Long, flexible neck

Curved, pointed tooth

Shoulder joint

Short, powerful thigh

Short forelimb

Strong, slender back legs for running at speed

Strong claws for grasping prey

Long shin

Ankle

Long, slender toe

Strong, claw

Hallux (first toe)

※ FACT FILE ※

HERRERASAURUS

A bipedal flesh-eater. *Herrerasaurus* was one of the earliest-known dinosaurs.

THE MESOZOIC ERA

MYA			
248	208	144	65

TRIASSIC   JURASSIC   CRETACEOUS

TIME
228MYA

LOCATION
Argentina San Juan

CLASSIFICATION
Family Herrerasauridae
Suborder Theropoda
Order Saurischia

SIZE
Length 10ft (3m)
Weight 220lb (100kg)

DIET
Reptiles

CERATOSAURUS

T HE LARGEST and in some ways the most primitive of the ceratosaurs, *Ceratosaurus* ("horned lizard") somewhat resembled its more advanced rival *Allosaurus*. Both were powerful, sizable predators; each had a huge, deep head, vast jaws with curved fangs, a short, thick neck, short arms, and long, muscular legs. But *Ceratosaurus* was probably less heavily built. Its name derives from the bony horn on its snout. Other distinctive features were its unusual hip- and hind-limb bones, the small bony plates along its back, and a heavy tail stiffened in a way that let only the end half waggle.

LIFE AND BEHAVIOR

Limb design reveals that *Ceratosaurus* could put on a burst of speed to chase fast-running dryosaurid herbivores. Grappling with its teeth and claws, it could have tackled even larger dinosaurs, such as *Camptosaurus* and *Stegosaurus*, and it probably also killed and ate young or sick sauropods. Even a healthy, full-grown *Diplodocus* might have fallen prey if *Ceratosaurus* roamed in packs. However, the few, solitary *Ceratosaurus* fossil finds suggest this was unlikely. Some of the finds were in a quarry, together with more plentiful fossils of *Allosaurus*; but whether this implies that *Ceratosaurus* was a rarer beast is uncertain. Both lived on the fern savannas and wooded flood plains of Late Jurassic western North America. *Ceratosaurus* might also have roamed similar countryside in East Africa. Two *Ceratosaurus* species have been named from fossils found in Tanzania. One bone certainly resembles the femur of a *Ceratosaurus*. The tibia seems to be very distinctive, and several recognizable examples have been found at Tanzanian sites, making identification reasonably certain. The fossil evidence also suggests that *Ceratosaurus* males were larger and stronger than the females.

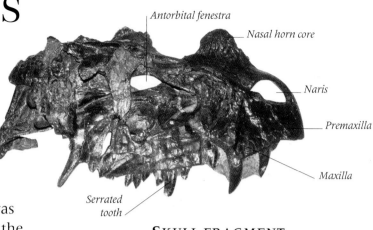

SKULL FRAGMENT

The lightly built skull was made up of bony struts and sheets. A bladelike horn protruded from the snout and a pair of smaller horns jutted

Antorbital fenestra
Nasal horn core
Naris
Premaxilla
Maxilla
Serrated tooth

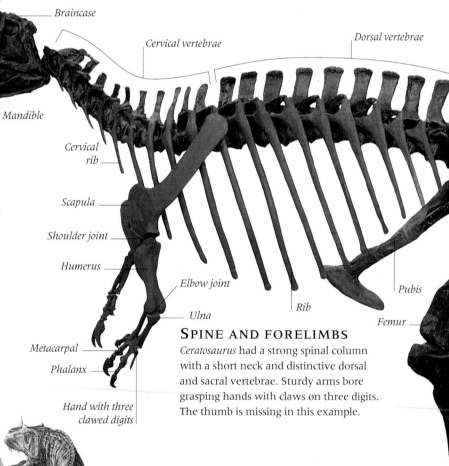

Nasal horn core
Naris
Antorbital fenestra
Braincase
Cervical vertebrae
Dorsal vertebrae
Mandible
Cervical rib
Scapula
Shoulder joint
Humerus
Elbow joint
Ulna
Rib
Pubis
Femur
Metacarpal
Phalanx
Hand with three clawed digits
Fibula
Metatarsal
Phalanx

SPINE AND FORELIMBS

Ceratosaurus had a strong spinal column with a short neck and distinctive dorsal and sacral vertebrae. Sturdy arms bore grasping hands with claws on three digits. The thumb is missing in this example.

CONFRONTATION
In this illustration, startled pterosaurs are shown flying away as a snarling Ceratosaurus *confronts a sauropod far larger than itself. However, it seems unlikely that a lone* Ceratosaurus *would have dared to attack a dinosaur as large as this.*

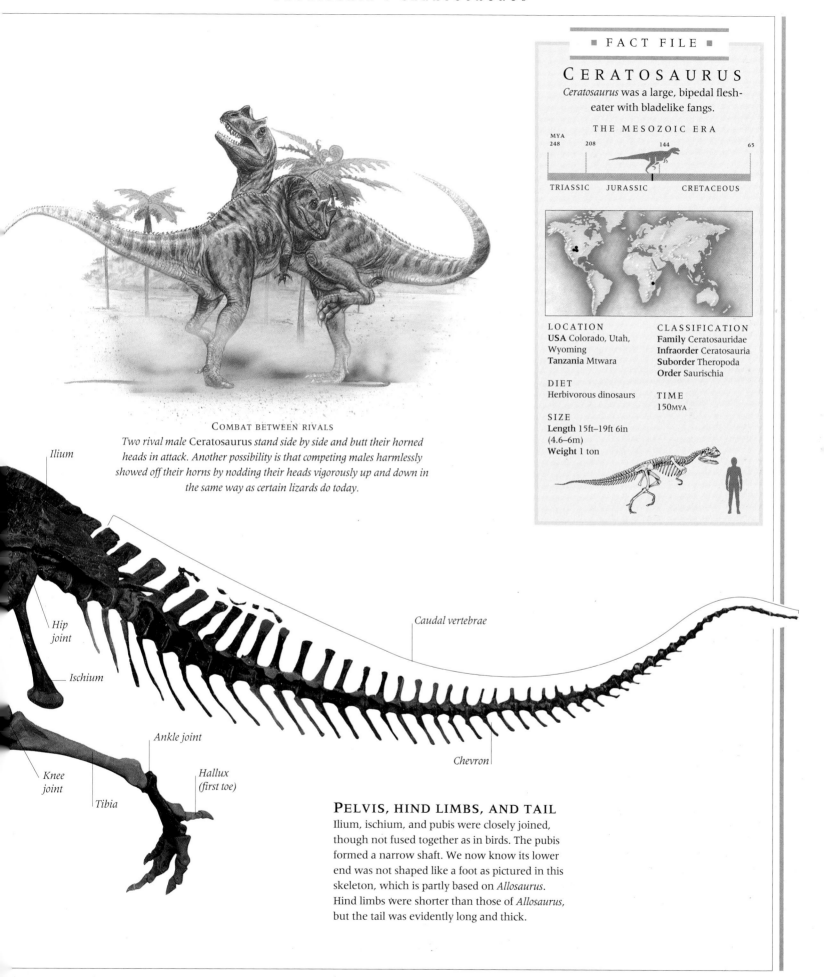

■ FACT FILE ■

CERATOSAURUS

Ceratosaurus was a large, bipedal flesh-eater with bladelike fangs.

THE MESOZOIC ERA

MYA 248	208	144	65
TRIASSIC	JURASSIC	CRETACEOUS	

LOCATION
USA Colorado, Utah, Wyoming
Tanzania Mtwara

DIET
Herbivorous dinosaurs

SIZE
Length 15ft–19ft 6in (4.6–6m)
Weight 1 ton

CLASSIFICATION
Family Ceratosauridae
Infraorder Ceratosauria
Suborder Theropoda
Order Saurischia

TIME
150MYA

COMBAT BETWEEN RIVALS

Two rival male Ceratosaurus *stand side by side and butt their horned heads in attack. Another possibility is that competing males harmlessly showed off their horns by nodding their heads vigorously up and down in the same way as certain lizards do today.*

Ilium

Hip joint

Ischium

Knee joint

Tibia

Ankle joint

Hallux (first toe)

Caudal vertebrae

Chevron

PELVIS, HIND LIMBS, AND TAIL

Ilium, ischium, and pubis were closely joined, though not fused together as in birds. The pubis formed a narrow shaft. We now know its lower end was not shaped like a foot as pictured in this skeleton, which is partly based on *Allosaurus*. Hind limbs were shorter than those of *Allosaurus*, but the tail was evidently long and thick.

DILOPHOSAURUS

N ICKNAMED "the terror of the Early Jurassic," *Dilophosaurus* ("two-ridge lizard") is the earliest big theropod that is well known from adequate remains. About a half-dozen partial skeletons of young and adult specimens have been found in Arizona, and the late 1980s brought news of a discovery in China. *Dilophosaurus* was a long, lithe hunter, lighter than its relative *Ceratosaurus*. The build and enormously long tail are reminiscent of *Dilophosaurus*'s smaller cousin *Coelophysis*. Both shared the kinked upper jaw typical of the ceratosaurs. Uniquely, *Dilophosaurus* bore a tall, fragile head crest of two parallel bony ridges that jutted out in semicircles from its head.

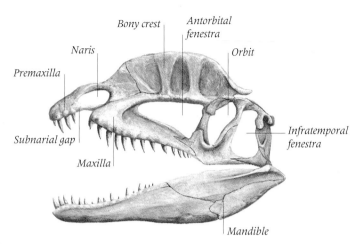

CRESTED SKULL

The light skull was distinguished by its tall, double crest, and by an unusually deep gap between the premaxilla and the maxilla (top jaw). This is known as the subnarial gap, and a large one is typical of the ceratosaurs, but most notable in *Dilophosaurus*.

■ LIFE AND BEHAVIOR ■

Long, agile legs and clawed feet equipped this predator for chasing Arizona's early plant-eating dinosaurs. *Dilophosaurus* probably outsprinted the small, lightly armored ornithischian *Scutellosaurus* and the bigger, bulkier prosauropod *Massospondylus*. Dashing in upon such prey, *Dilophosaurus* could have savaged them to death with a three-pronged attack: biting with its long teeth as it struck out with the sharp claws on its toes and fingers. *Dilophosaurus* must have aimed at making short, clean kills. Long struggles could have put its slender double crest at risk. So fragile was the crest that some scientists think *Dilophosaurus* fed

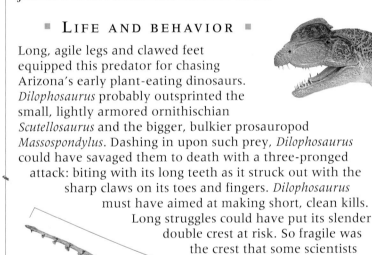

THREAT DISPLAY

A male *Dilophosaurus* might have threatened rivals by making an open-jawed threat display like this one, or he might have bobbed his head up and down to show off his skull crest. Outright fighting seems unlikely.

only on carrion. These sceptics also argue that the jaws were too weak to deliver a lethal bite. (Most scientists disagree.) If the creature killed at all, the sceptics claim, it would have disemboweled its victims by raking their bellies open with its sharp claws. Although a liability in battle, the fragile head crests could have helped prevent fighting between rival males if, as fossil finds suggest, *Dilophosaurus* lived in packs. When males confronted one another, individuals with the smallest crests probably gave way without a struggle. The large-crested winner would then stay to rule a territory and mate with females in his herd. If this was so, the crests may have been covered with brightly colored skin for display, like the comb of a farmyard rooster. It is likely that only the males were equipped with this attractive headgear.

SKELETON

The tail was as long as the whole of the rest of the animal, and helped *Dilophosaurus* maintain balance as it raced around after agile prey. The neck was strong but flexible. Each short and sturdy forelimb bore a four-fingered, grasping hand, with sharp claws on the first three fingers. The hind limbs were long and powerful, and ended in three forward-facing, elongated, sharp-clawed toes. As in other ceratosaurian theropods, the pubic hipbones did not end in an expanded "foot."

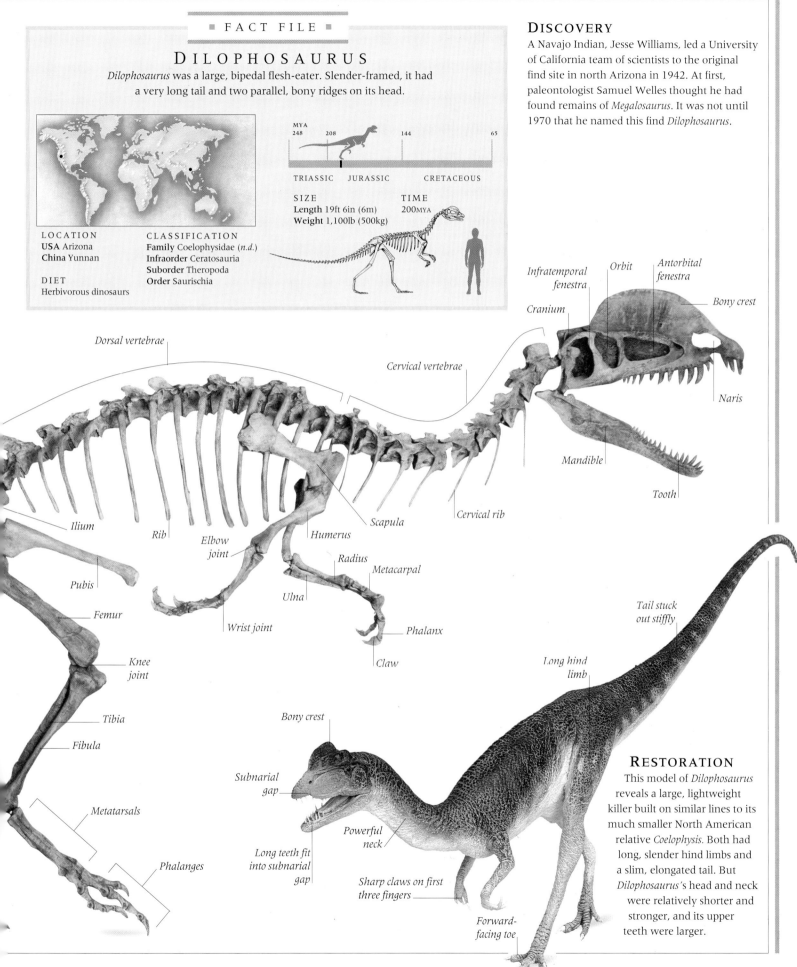

■ FACT FILE ■

DILOPHOSAURUS

Dilophosaurus was a large, bipedal flesh-eater. Slender-framed, it had a very long tail and two parallel, bony ridges on its head.

MYA
248   208   144   65

TRIASSIC   JURASSIC   CRETACEOUS

SIZE
Length 19ft 6in (6m)
Weight 1,100lb (500kg)

TIME
200MYA

LOCATION
USA Arizona
China Yunnan

DIET
Herbivorous dinosaurs

CLASSIFICATION
Family Coelophysidae (*n.d.*)
Infraorder Ceratosauria
Suborder Theropoda
Order Saurischia

DISCOVERY
A Navajo Indian, Jesse Williams, led a University of California team of scientists to the original find site in north Arizona in 1942. At first, paleontologist Samuel Welles thought he had found remains of *Megalosaurus*. It was not until 1970 that he named this find *Dilophosaurus*.

Infratemporal fenestra
Orbit
Antorbital fenestra
Cranium
Bony crest
Naris
Cervical vertebrae
Mandible
Tooth

Dorsal vertebrae

Cervical rib

Ilium
Rib
Scapula
Humerus
Elbow joint
Radius
Metacarpal
Pubis
Ulna
Femur
Phalanx
Wrist joint
Claw
Knee joint
Tail stuck out stiffly
Tibia
Long hind limb
Fibula

Metatarsals

Bony crest

Subnarial gap

Powerful neck

Long teeth fit into subnarial gap

Phalanges

Sharp claws on first three fingers

RESTORATION
This model of *Dilophosaurus* reveals a large, lightweight killer built on similar lines to its much smaller North American relative *Coelophysis*. Both had long, slender hind limbs and a slim, elongated tail. But *Dilophosaurus*'s head and neck were relatively shorter and stronger, and its upper teeth were larger.

Forward-facing toe

COELOPHYSIS

O NE OF THE EARLIEST well-known dinosaurs, *Coelophysis* ("hollow form") was a flesh-eater, built like a large, slender bird, with a narrow, almost storklike head, an S-shaped neck, a slim body, and long, birdlike legs. Some internal features were also birdlike, including hollow, thin-walled bones, and the fusion of bones at the hips and spine, as well as those of the ankles and upper feet. Other features were unlike those of a bird: the skin was probably scaly, the long jaws bristled with teeth, and the forelimbs were arms with three-fingered hands. A long, reptilian tail balanced the forepart of the body.

RESTORATION

In this restoration, a lightly built, slim *Coelophysis* is propelled forward by its long, powerful legs. With neck and tail extended, the flesh-eater pursues prey across its open, semidesert habitat.

■ LIFE AND BEHAVIOR ■

Troops of hunting *Coelophysis* trekked across a red, sandy, semidesert plain with a distant view of a green fringe of trees and ferns that lined a riverbank. Among the animals in each troop, some were noticeably more robust in build, with longer arms and stronger shoulders than others. These may possibly have been the males, while the females could have been the slighter forms. If a lizard broke cover and scuttled away, one of the sharp-eyed hunters would race after it, neck and tail stretched out. With a sudden, snakelike, jabbing movement of the head, the dinosaur would impale the lizard between sharp, saw-edged teeth. *Coelophysis* could maneuver a large lizard between its jaws before swallowing it headfirst, as herons handle fish today. If its prey were a larger creature, it might have held the carcass in its clawed hands to tear it apart with its jaws. Jumbled bones discovered in one fossil adult's stomach cavity suggest that *Coelophysis* sometimes turned cannibal and ate its own young, but this probably happened only if food grew scarce. In normal times, the principal prey of a hunting pack of *Coelophysis* could have included *Revueltosaurus* and *Technosaurus*, which were small, but meaty, early plant-eating dinosaurs. Living in a crowd also gave *Coelophysis* some protection from attack by the large, aggressive reptiles known today as rauisuchids, and from starikosaurid dinosaurs. But perhaps the most pressing danger of all to *Coelophysis* came from the terrible jaws of parasuchians, otherwise known as phytosaurs. These were crocodile-like carnivores that lurked in rivers and seized reptiles coming down to the water to drink.

Labels on skeleton diagram: Naris, Orbit, Cervical vertebra, Mandible, Dorsal vertebra, Ischium, Sacral vertebra, Caudal vertebra, Humerus, Phalanx, Pubis, Ilium, Chevron, Radius, Femur, Tibia, Neural spine, Ulna, Fibula, Tarsal, Metacarpal, Hallux (first toe), Phalanx, Metatarsal

SKELETON

Several features of the *Coelophysis* skeleton echo the anatomy of birds: some of the limb bones were hollow with thin walls, and four sets of bones were fused together—the sacral vertebrae, pelvic bones, tarsals (ankle bones), and metatarsals (foot bones).

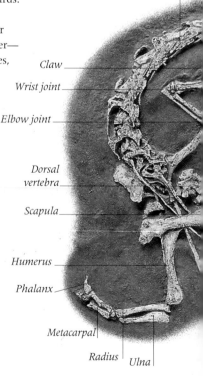

Labels on fossil: Cervical vertebra, Claw, Wrist joint, Elbow joint, Dorsal vertebra, Scapula, Humerus, Phalanx, Metacarpal, Radius, Ulna

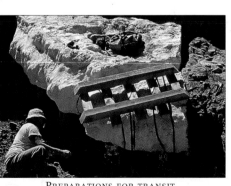

PREPARATIONS FOR TRANSIT

At a quarry in New Mexico, a rock containing Coelophysis *fossils is protected with plaster and made ready to be moved out on wooden skids.*

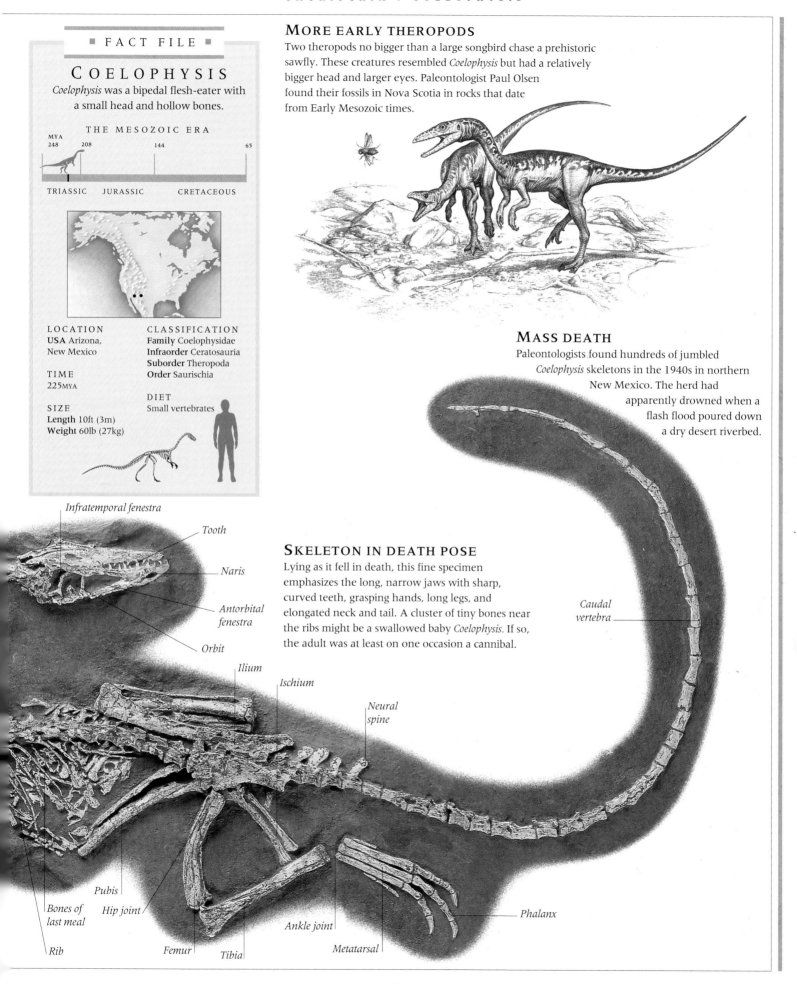

COELOPHYSIS

Coelophysis was a bipedal flesh-eater with a small head and hollow bones.

THE MESOZOIC ERA

MYA			
248	208	144	65

TRIASSIC   JURASSIC   CRETACEOUS

LOCATION
USA Arizona,
New Mexico

TIME
225MYA

SIZE
Length 10ft (3m)
Weight 60lb (27kg)

CLASSIFICATION
Family Coelophysidae
Infraorder Ceratosauria
Suborder Theropoda
Order Saurischia

DIET
Small vertebrates

MORE EARLY THEROPODS

Two theropods no bigger than a large songbird chase a prehistoric sawfly. These creatures resembled *Coelophysis* but had a relatively bigger head and larger eyes. Paleontologist Paul Olsen found their fossils in Nova Scotia in rocks that date from Early Mesozoic times.

MASS DEATH

Paleontologists found hundreds of jumbled *Coelophysis* skeletons in the 1940s in northern New Mexico. The herd had apparently drowned when a flash flood poured down a dry desert riverbed.

SKELETON IN DEATH POSE

Lying as it fell in death, this fine specimen emphasizes the long, narrow jaws with sharp, curved teeth, grasping hands, long legs, and elongated neck and tail. A cluster of tiny bones near the ribs might be a swallowed baby *Coelophysis*. If so, the adult was at least on one occasion a cannibal.

Infratemporal fenestra

Tooth

Naris

Antorbital fenestra

Orbit

Ilium

Ischium

Neural spine

Caudal vertebra

Pubis

Hip joint

Bones of last meal

Rib

Femur

Tibia

Ankle joint

Metatarsal

Phalanx

CARNOTAURUS

I N 1985, Argentinian paleontologist José Bonaparte announced news of a big, bizarre dinosaur unlike anything described before. *Carnotaurus* ("carnivorous bull") had a deeper, shorter, more bull-like head than other theropods. Most extraordinary were the pointed, winglike horns above its eyes—perhaps butting weapons used by combating rivals. Other remarkable features included small, forward-facing eyes, spinal bones with winglike projections, very short arms, and prominent rows of scales along the back and sides.

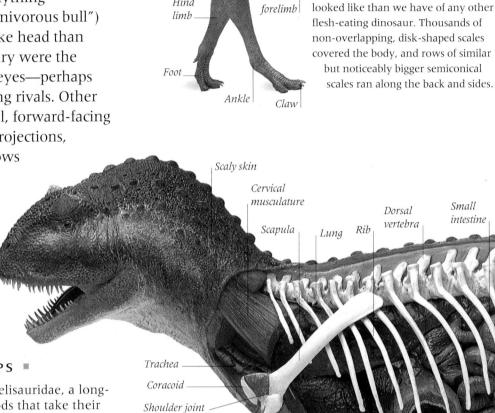

Tail
Semiconical, bony scales
Thick neck
Winglike horn
Hind limb
Short forelimb
Foot
Ankle
Claw

EXTERNAL VIEW

Thanks to some good fossilized skin impressions preserved in rock, we have a better idea of what *Carnotaurus* looked like than we have of any other flesh-eating dinosaur. Thousands of non-overlapping, disk-shaped scales covered the body, and rows of similar but noticeably bigger semiconical scales ran along the back and sides.

■ LIFE AND BEHAVIOR ■

Carnotaurus lived alongside *Chubutisaurus*, a sauropod three times its length. Perhaps it killed and ate *Chubutisaurus* young and hunted moderately sized adult ornithopods. Short-armed *Carnotaurus* evidently assaulted prey or tackled carrion headfirst.

■ RELATIONSHIPS ■

Carnotaurus proved to belong to the Abelisauridae, a long-lived family of "old-fashioned" theropods that take their group name from *Abelisaurus*, a dinosaur named in 1985. Details of *Abelisaurus* bones prove it was related to *Carnotaurus*, although *Abelisaurus* had no horns, a longer head, and a hooked nose. A third abelisaurid, named *Xenotarsosaurus* ("strange ankle lizard") was described in 1986. A further look at *Genyodectes*, named in 1901, showed it was another South American abelisaurid. Scientists next noted abelisaurid features in skull fragments from South America, India, and France. A pattern appeared to be emerging. The apparent distribution of abelisaurids would suggest that they spread across the southern supercontinent Gondwana (which included South America and India) after it separated from the northern supercontinent Laurasia (North America, Europe, and Asia). The French abelisaurid could be explained by a land bridge where Gondwana briefly touched Laurasia.

JOSE BONAPARTE
This Argentinian paleontologist has dug up or described dinosaurs that lived in what is now Argentina in all three periods of the Mesozoic.

Scaly skin
Cervical musculature
Scapula
Lung
Rib
Dorsal vertebra
Small intestine
Trachea
Coracoid
Shoulder joint
Humerus
Heart
Liver
Gizzard
Large intestine
Pubis
Hind limb
Retroarticular process
Tooth
Hallux (first toe)
Toe

LOWER JAW

For a beast with a formidably deep, powerful-looking skull that incorporated strong jaw-closing muscles, the lower jaw seems slim and was perhaps even weakly built. It has also been suggested that the teeth are unusually slender for a big theropod. The combination of deep skull and shallow mandible (lower jaw) makes it difficult to visualize *Carnotaurus*'s likely prey.

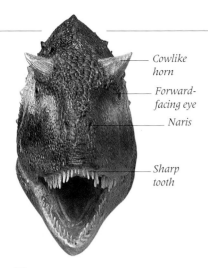

Cowlike horn

Forward-facing eye

Naris

Sharp tooth

HEAD FROM FRONT

This front view of a model head of *Carnotaurus* emphasizes the short, broad, cowlike horns that poked out sideways from above the eyes. The deep snout might imply large nasal organs and a keen sense of smell.

MOUNTED SKELETON

Posed as if frozen in mid-stride, a skeletal *Carnotaurus* forms one of the most striking dinosaur exhibits in a Buenos Aires museum. The discovery of a fossilized individual that lacked only half of the tail and parts of the feet made this reconstruction possible.

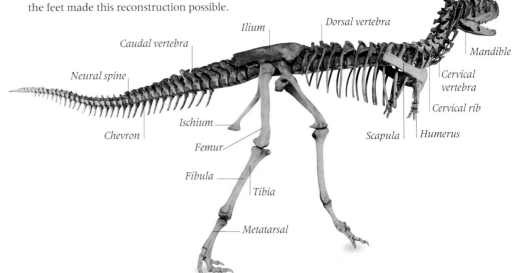

Naris

Braincase

Ilium

Dorsal vertebra

Caudal vertebra

Neural spine

Mandible

Cervical vertebra

Cervical rib

Ischium

Chevron

Scapula

Humerus

Femur

Fibula

Tibia

Metatarsal

MODEL OF A CARNIVORE

This model, built up on a replica *Carnotaurus* skeleton, shows the external appearance and internal anatomy of one of the most bizarre of all meat-eating dinosaurs. External peculiarities included the deep, horned, bull-like head, and dwarfed, useless-looking forelimbs. Unusual internal features included small "wings" projecting from some vertebrae.

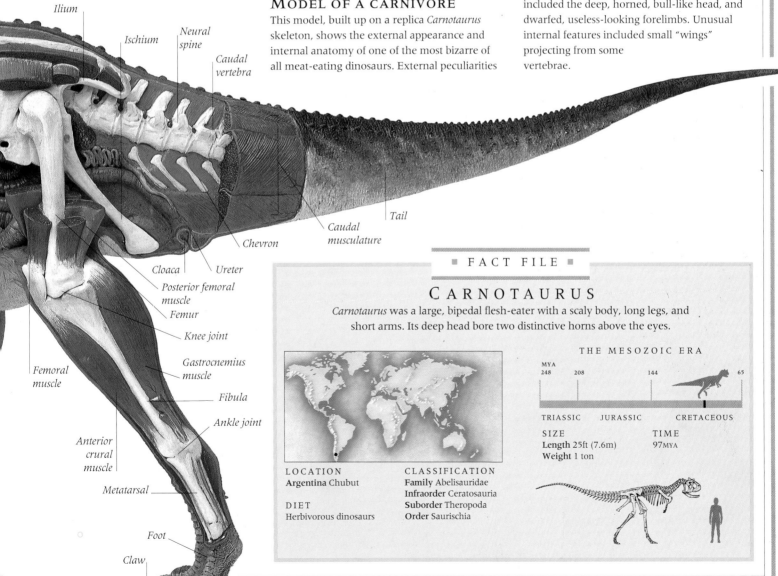

Ilium

Ischium

Neural spine

Caudal vertebra

Femoral muscle

Chevron

Caudal musculature

Tail

Cloaca

Ureter

Posterior femoral muscle

Femur

Knee joint

Gastrocnemius muscle

Fibula

Ankle joint

Anterior crural muscle

Metatarsal

Foot

Claw

■ FACT FILE ■

CARNOTAURUS

Carnotaurus was a large, bipedal flesh-eater with a scaly body, long legs, and short arms. Its deep head bore two distinctive horns above the eyes.

THE MESOZOIC ERA

MYA
248   208   144   65

TRIASSIC   JURASSIC   CRETACEOUS

SIZE
Length 25ft (7.6m)
Weight 1 ton

TIME
97MYA

LOCATION
Argentina Chubut

DIET
Herbivorous dinosaurs

CLASSIFICATION
Family Abelisauridae
Infraorder Ceratosauria
Suborder Theropoda
Order Saurischia

EUSTREPTOSPONDYLUS

T HANKS TO THE DISCOVERY OF a fine skeleton in Oxfordshire, England, *Eustreptospondylus* ("well-curved vertebra") was Europe's best-known large, carnivorous dinosaur for many years. This predator had short arms, thick-walled leg bones, and large, weight-saving "windows" in the skull. A short spine rising from the neck bone nearest the skull, and a winglike ridge on each thighbone, seem typical of carnosaur theropods. Skull, neck, and ankle bones share certain features with North America's *Allosaurus*.

■ LIFE AND BEHAVIOR ■

Eustreptospondylus shared what is now England with various plant-eaters. It was a big carnivore, longer than such early, plated ornithischians as *Lexovisaurus* and such early, armored ornithischians as *Sarcolestes*. Even a half-grown *Eustreptospondylus*, such as the fossilized specimen found in Oxfordshire that would have been about the size of a lion, could have tackled these inoffensive, plodding herbivores. Such sauropods as *Cetiosaurus* and *Cetiosauriscus* were evidently longer and certainly much heavier than a full-grown *Eustreptospondylus*, but they, too, formed potential meals for this large, rapacious theropod.

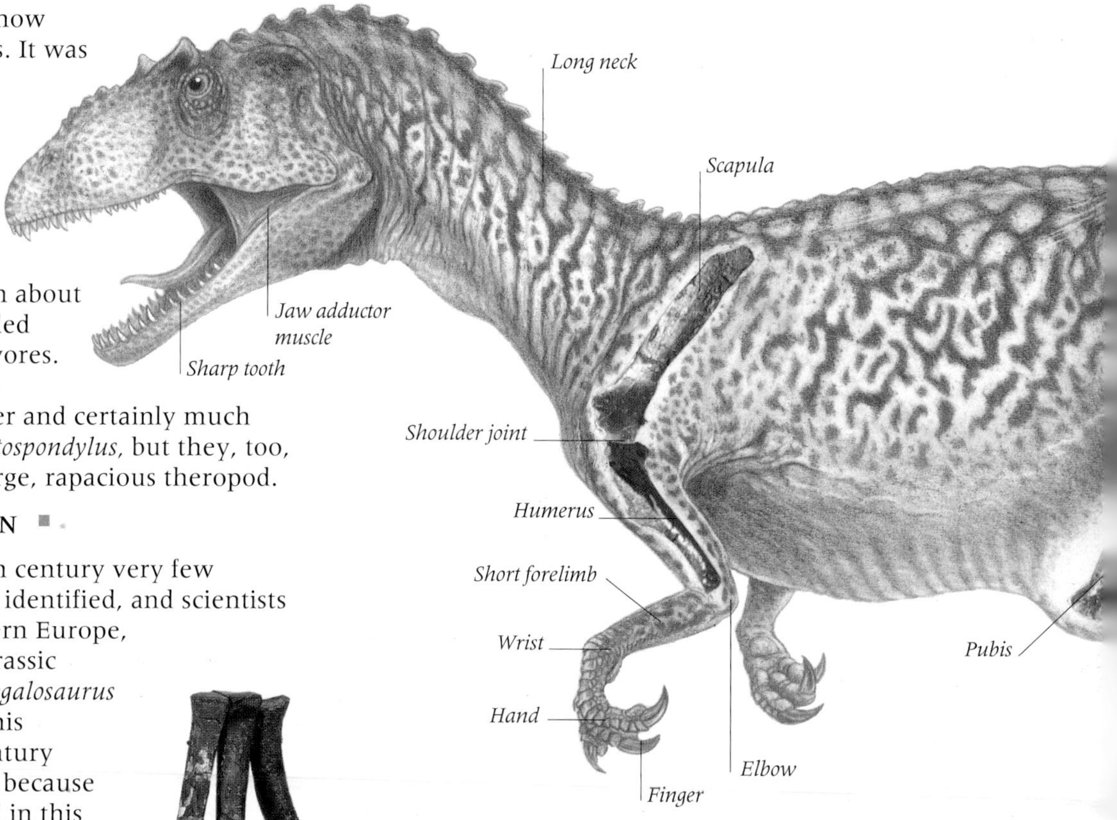

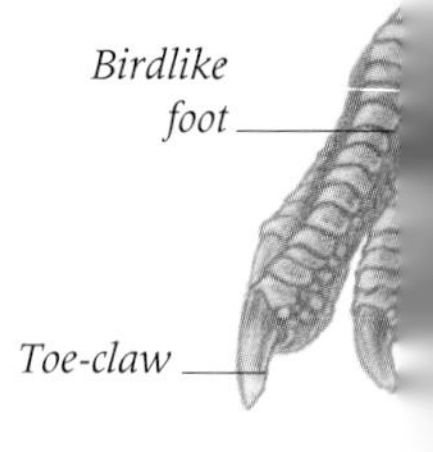

■ CLASSIFICATION ■

In the early part of the nineteenth century very few dinosaurs had been discovered or identified, and scientists had the impression that, in Western Europe, there had been only one large Jurassic predatory dinosaur. The name *Megalosaurus* (see box opposite) was given to this conceptual animal. For over a century there was considerable confusion because widely differing finds were placed in this genus. In 1964 the British paleontologist Alick Walker proved that the animal shown on this page could not have been a *Megalosaurus*, and considered the name *Streptospondylus*, which various earlier scientists had proposed. This name turned out to be inadmissible because it had, even earlier, been given to a genus of crocodile. Walker added the prefix Eu- ("well"), producing the name *Eustreptospondylus* for the genus, and created the name *oxoniensis* ("from Oxford") for this species.

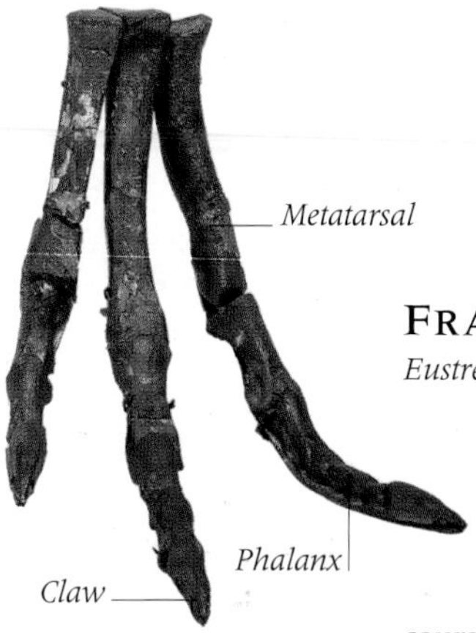

RUNNING PREDATOR

This illustration shows bipedal *Eustreptospondylus* running swiftly as though chasing prey. Its victims might have included *Cetiosaurus*, hypsilophodontids, and stegosaurs, all of which lived in Middle Jurassic England.

Long neck

Scapula

Jaw adductor muscle

Sharp tooth

Shoulder joint

Humerus

Short forelimb

Wrist

Hand

Pubis

Elbow

Finger

Metatarsal

Birdlike foot

Toe-claw

Claw

Phalanx

FRAGMENT OF FOOT

Eustreptospondylus had a theropod's three-toed foot. The metatarsals (upper foot bones) are only partly visible here. At the top end (not seen here) the middle metatarsal is tapered, reflecting a change that took place in the course of the evolution of the theropods—by the time *Tyrannosaurus* evolved, the top of this central metatarsal was reduced to a sharp point.

■ FACT FILE ■

EUSTREPTOSPONDYLUS

Eustreptospondylus was a bipedal flesh-eater. The large head was armed with sharp teeth.

THE MESOZOIC ERA

MYA
248   208   144   65

TRIASSIC   JURASSIC   CRETACEOUS

CLASSIFICATION
Family Unknown
Infraorder Ceratosauria
Suborder Theropoda
Order Saurischia

TIME
165MYA

DIET
Herbivorous
dinosaurs

LOCATION
England
Buckinghamshire,
Oxfordshire

SIZE
Length 23ft (7m)
Weight 485lb (220kg)

Hip joint

Ilium

FLESHING OUT THE BONES

The articulated hip- and major limb bones featured in this restoration of *Eustreptospondylus* were taken from the skeletal remains of an immature individual on display in the University Museum, Oxford, England.

Tail

Ischium

Femur

Thigh

Knee
joint

Tibia

Fibula

Hind limb

Ankle

Hallux
(first toe)

MEGALOSAURUS

Megalosaurus ("great lizard") was a 30ft (about 9m) Middle Jurassic theropod, discovered in England, and named in 1824 from half a lower jaw that bristled with large, curved teeth. Scientists went on to apply the name *Megalosaurus* to many different large theropod finds, though most of these were of uncertain identity. Some taxonomic errors persisted more than 100 years.

Old tooth

New tooth pushing
out old tooth

Interdental plate

Dentary
bone

JAW AND TEETH

The jaw features replacement teeth and separate interdental plates.

RESTORATION

As shown (right), Europe's *Megalosaurus* was a big, robust predator. It belonged to the Megalosauridae, a family that also included North America's *Torvosaurus*.

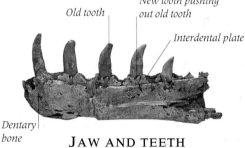

ALLOSAURUS

A LLOSAURUS ("OTHER LIZARD") was one of the biggest carnivorous dinosaurs before the tyrannosaurids appeared some 50 million years later. *Allosaurus*'s long, muscular hind limbs supported a body nearly as heavy as an elephant's. The huge but lightweight skull consisted largely of bony struts, with bony ridges above the eyes. The immense, expandable jaws had long, curved, saw-edged teeth. A thick, S-curved neck supported the head, and a long, deep tail counterbalanced the heavy front end of this terrifying theropod. Curved, tapering claws armed the three fingers of each short, strong arm. Each foot had three claw-bearing toes; the short first toe turned slightly backward.

▪ LIFE AND BEHAVIOR ▪

Allosaurus must have been a formidable enemy of medium-to-large plant-eating dinosaurs. A lone *Allosaurus* could have hunted and attacked beasts the size of *Camptosaurus*. The predator probably lurked in dense undergrowth. When an unsuspecting *Camptosaurus*—or any meaty prey—meandered past, the *Allosaurus* might have lunged suddenly forward onto its victim, grappling with its sharp finger-claws while simultaneously plunging its fanglike teeth deep into its victim's vulnerable neck flesh. Sauropods much larger than the largest *Allosaurus* would have proved more difficult to overcome. Perhaps packs of *Allosaurus* dogged herds of sauropods, singling out and slaughtering any young or sickly individuals that lagged behind the rest. Sauropods like *Apatosaurus* and *Diplodocus* probably went around in herds for mutual protection from gangs of theropods.

Other hints that *Allosaurus* patrolled the land in troops include more than 10,000 disarticulated bones discovered in one quarry in Utah. Usually, the fossil bones of herbivore victims far outnumber the bones of the theropods that preyed upon them. Here, however, it seems that *Allosaurus* far outnumbered its prey. Even more intriguingly, the *Allosaurus* bones came from animals of every age and size, including the very young. Some scientists suspect that the theropods had flocked in from far and wide to feast on a few big herbivores trapped in marshy ground; it is possible that the theropods might also have become stuck and died.

Supraoccipital crest
Orbit
Antorbital fenestra
Maxillary fenestra
Postorbital bone
Braincase
Naris
Serrated tooth
Infratemporal fenestra
Mandible
Mandibular fenestra

Small, triangular horn

Elastic tissue at corner of mouth

Curved, serrated tooth

SKULL AND HEAD

Allosaurus's great head (above) was less heavy than it appeared. Many skull bones (top) were load-bearing bars that separated "windows" for nostrils, eyes, and muscles. The sturdiest bones supported the teeth and jaw muscles.

Caudal vertebrae

Neural spine

Chevron

HIGH-ANKLED FOOT

Allosaurus's high-ankled, scaly foot resembled the foot of a gigantic flightless bird, far heavier than any now alive. Three big toes bore the body's weight. The high, tiny first toe faced back. The toe-claws were bony cores sheathed in horn.

JAW MOVEMENTS

Allosaurus could open its jaws far apart (left), and then expand them (below) to engulf a huge chunk of meat. It bit flesh from its victims by pulling its skull back over its lower jaw so that its narrow-bladed teeth cut through tough, living tissue. Movable joints between the skull bones made all this possible.

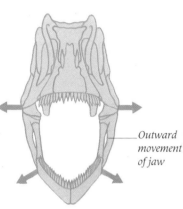

Outward movement of jaw

■ FACT FILE ■

ALLOSAURUS

Allosaurus was a large, bipedal predator. It had huge jaws armed with bladelike teeth, a bulky body, muscular hind limbs, and sharp claws.

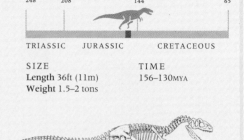

MYA			
248	208	144	65

TRIASSIC   JURASSIC   CRETACEOUS

SIZE
Length 36ft (11m)
Weight 1.5–2 tons

TIME
156–130MYA

LOCATION
USA Colorado, Montana, New Mexico, Oklahoma, South Dakota, Utah, Wyoming
Tanzania Mtwara
Australia Victoria

CLASSIFICATION
Family Allosauridae
Infraorder Tetanurae
Suborder Theropoda
Order Saurischia

DIET
Herbivorous dinosaurs

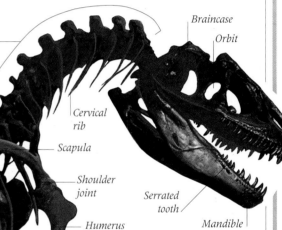

Cervical vertebrae

Braincase

Orbit

Dorsal vertebrae

Cervical rib

Scapula

Ilium

Hip socket

Shoulder joint

Serrated tooth

Mandible

Humerus

Femur

Metacarpal

Ischium

Ulna

ALLOSAURUS SKELETON

The skull was long, deep, and narrow. As in other carnosaurs, big neural spines anchored strong neck, back, and tail muscles; there was also a bladelike ilium, a pubis ending in a "foot," and a femur (thighbone) longer than the tibia (shinbone).

Wrist joint

Phalanx

Tibia

Pubis

Knee joint

THE FOSSIL RECORD

Allosaurus was named in 1877 from a Colorado discovery. Later finds of over 60 individuals came mostly from Utah's spectacular Cleveland-Lloyd Dinosaur Quarry. A tibia from East Africa has been attributed (perhaps mistakenly) to *Allosaurus*.

Naris

Thick neck

Long tail

Short Forelimb

Scaly skin

Clawed hand

Thigh

Hind limb

Metacarpal

Fibula

Hallux (first toe)

Phalanx

RESTORATION

This model of *Allosaurus* emphasizes the large head, gaping jaws, thick "bulldog" neck, short back, narrow belly, and long, deep tail. Short arms, with long, three-fingered, claw-tipped hands, contrast with vast, weight-bearing legs, which supported this creature weighing up to two tons.

TYRANNOSAURUS

T YRANNOSAURUS ("TYRANT LIZARD") was one of the last, largest, and most powerful of all predatory dinosaurs. Arguably the biggest flesh-eating land animal of any age, this two-legged theropod grew as heavy as an elephant, as long as a tennis court is wide, and tall enough to peer into an upstairs room. Saw-edged teeth armed the mighty jaws of its immense head, 4ft (1.2m) long, and strong claws tipped the main toes of each gigantic, birdlike foot. Compared to its massive legs, the small, two-fingered "hands" and arms no longer than our own, appear absurdly puny. Despite its size, *Tyrannosaurus* was lightly constructed, with hollow bones and great windows in the skull.

■ LIFE AND BEHAVIOR ■

Alone, in pairs, or possibly in packs, *Tyrannosaurus* probably trailed migrating herds of horned and duck-billed dinosaurs, picking off the weak, young, and sick. Another tactic might have been to wait in ambush and then charge, jaws wide

open, bringing down its victim with its teeth after a short chase at speeds of 20mph (32km/h) or more. Some experts disagree with this theory. They believe that *Tyrannosaurus* moved more slowly, eating only corpses found already dead; yet no large, land-based carnivore living today survives on carrion alone. *Tyrannosaurus* could have pierced big herbivores' thick hides with its serrated teeth, then twisted its head to and fro to saw off the flesh. Or perhaps the teeth were used to stab smaller dinosaurs that could be eaten whole. The contrast between *Tyrannosaurus*'s huge body and tiny, two-fingered hands long puzzled paleontologists. Although the forelimbs bore sharp claws, they seemed too puny for use in an attack and too short to bring food to the mouth. We know that the arms were muscular. Perhaps they propped up the front of the animal as it rose from lying to standing, or perhaps the fingers became grappling hooks when *Tyrannosaurus* savaged its victims.

HEAD IN FRONT VIEW

Forward-facing eyes helped *Tyrannosaurus* judge distance well as it moved in to attack, with jaws agape to bare its rows of fangs. The tips of its upper teeth formed a curve as sharp as a scalpel. When *Tyrannosaurus* bit into a victim, it probably pulled one side of its jaws backward, so that each sharp-edged tooth cut backward too. Teeth plowed through flesh like butchers' knives.

Heavy tail balancing the body

Muscular thigh

DISCOVERY

The first fairly complete *Tyrannosaurus* was found in 1902. In 1905, American paleontologist Henry Fairfield Osborn described and named the dinosaur. For many years, scientists knew of only three partial skeletons. Then, in the 1960s, fresh discoveries shed new light on the animal's anatomy.

HEAD MOVEMENTS
Strobe photography shows the wide range of side-to-side head movements that could have helped Tyrannosaurus *detect prey and also tear flesh from its victims.*

Toe

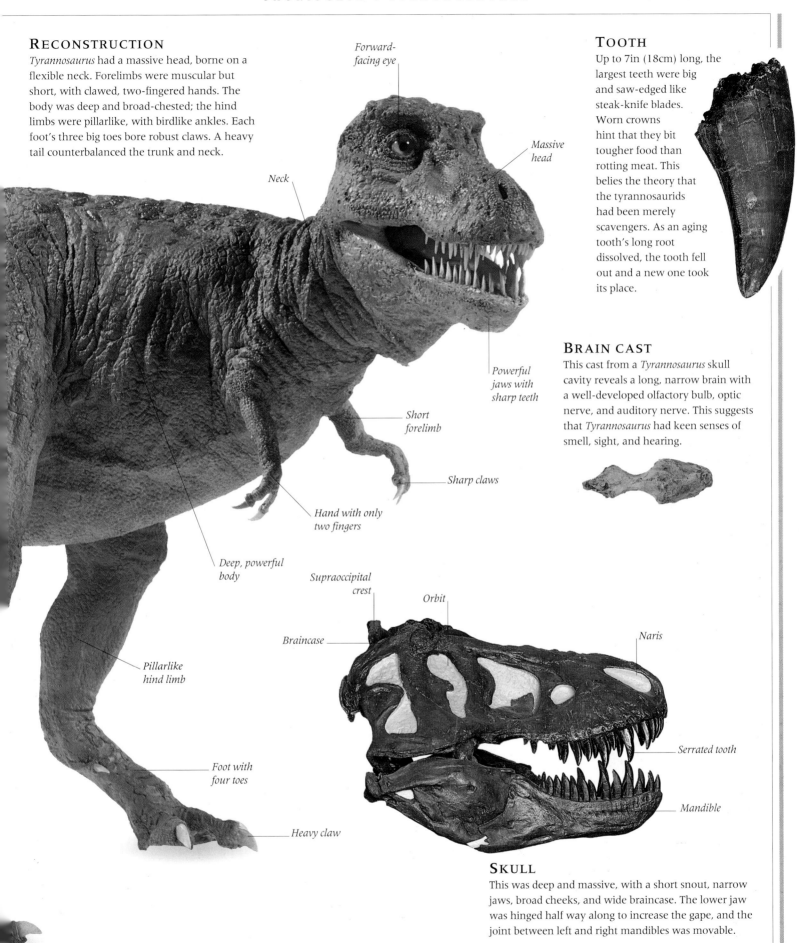

RECONSTRUCTION

Tyrannosaurus had a massive head, borne on a flexible neck. Forelimbs were muscular but short, with clawed, two-fingered hands. The body was deep and broad-chested; the hind limbs were pillarlike, with birdlike ankles. Each foot's three big toes bore robust claws. A heavy tail counterbalanced the trunk and neck.

Forward-facing eye

Massive head

Neck

Powerful jaws with sharp teeth

Short forelimb

Sharp claws

Hand with only two fingers

Deep, powerful body

Pillarlike hind limb

Foot with four toes

Heavy claw

TOOTH

Up to 7in (18cm) long, the largest teeth were big and saw-edged like steak-knife blades. Worn crowns hint that they bit tougher food than rotting meat. This belies the theory that the tyrannosaurids had been merely scavengers. As an aging tooth's long root dissolved, the tooth fell out and a new one took its place.

BRAIN CAST

This cast from a *Tyrannosaurus* skull cavity reveals a long, narrow brain with a well-developed olfactory bulb, optic nerve, and auditory nerve. This suggests that *Tyrannosaurus* had keen senses of smell, sight, and hearing.

Supraoccipital crest

Orbit

Braincase

Naris

Serrated tooth

Mandible

SKULL

This was deep and massive, with a short snout, narrow jaws, broad cheeks, and wide braincase. The lower jaw was hinged half way along to increase the gape, and the joint between left and right mandibles was movable.

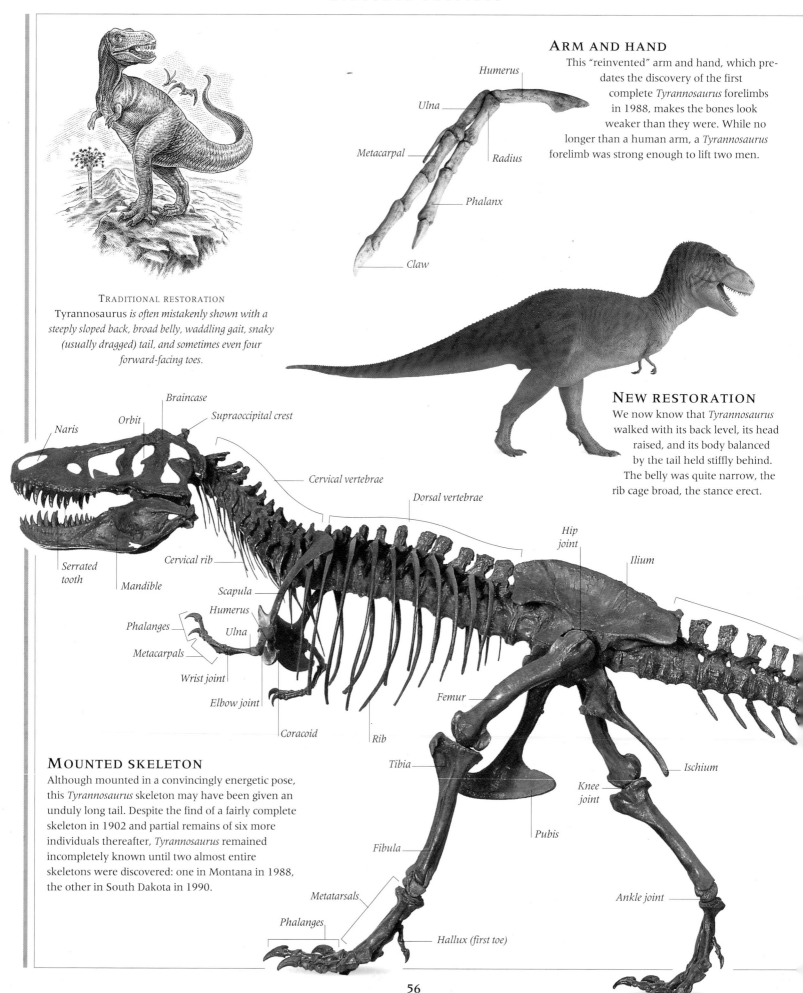

ARM AND HAND

This "reinvented" arm and hand, which pre-dates the discovery of the first complete *Tyrannosaurus* forelimbs in 1988, makes the bones look weaker than they were. While no longer than a human arm, a *Tyrannosaurus* forelimb was strong enough to lift two men.

Humerus

Ulna

Metacarpal

Radius

Phalanx

Claw

TRADITIONAL RESTORATION

Tyrannosaurus is often mistakenly shown with a steeply sloped back, broad belly, waddling gait, snaky (usually dragged) tail, and sometimes even four forward-facing toes.

NEW RESTORATION

We now know that *Tyrannosaurus* walked with its back level, its head raised, and its body balanced by the tail held stiffly behind. The belly was quite narrow, the rib cage broad, the stance erect.

Naris

Orbit

Braincase

Supraoccipital crest

Cervical vertebrae

Dorsal vertebrae

Hip joint

Ilium

Serrated tooth

Mandible

Cervical rib

Scapula

Humerus

Phalanges

Ulna

Metacarpals

Wrist joint

Elbow joint

Coracoid

Rib

Femur

Tibia

Ischium

Knee joint

Pubis

Fibula

MOUNTED SKELETON

Although mounted in a convincingly energetic pose, this *Tyrannosaurus* skeleton may have been given an unduly long tail. Despite the find of a fairly complete skeleton in 1902 and partial remains of six more individuals thereafter, *Tyrannosaurus* remained incompletely known until two almost entire skeletons were discovered: one in Montana in 1988, the other in South Dakota in 1990.

Metatarsals

Ankle joint

Phalanges

Hallux (first toe)

ANATOMY OF THE LEG

Makers of this model of the leg of *Albertosaurus*—a relative of *Tyrannosaurus*—visualized the position of the leg muscles from grooves and ridges on the bones.

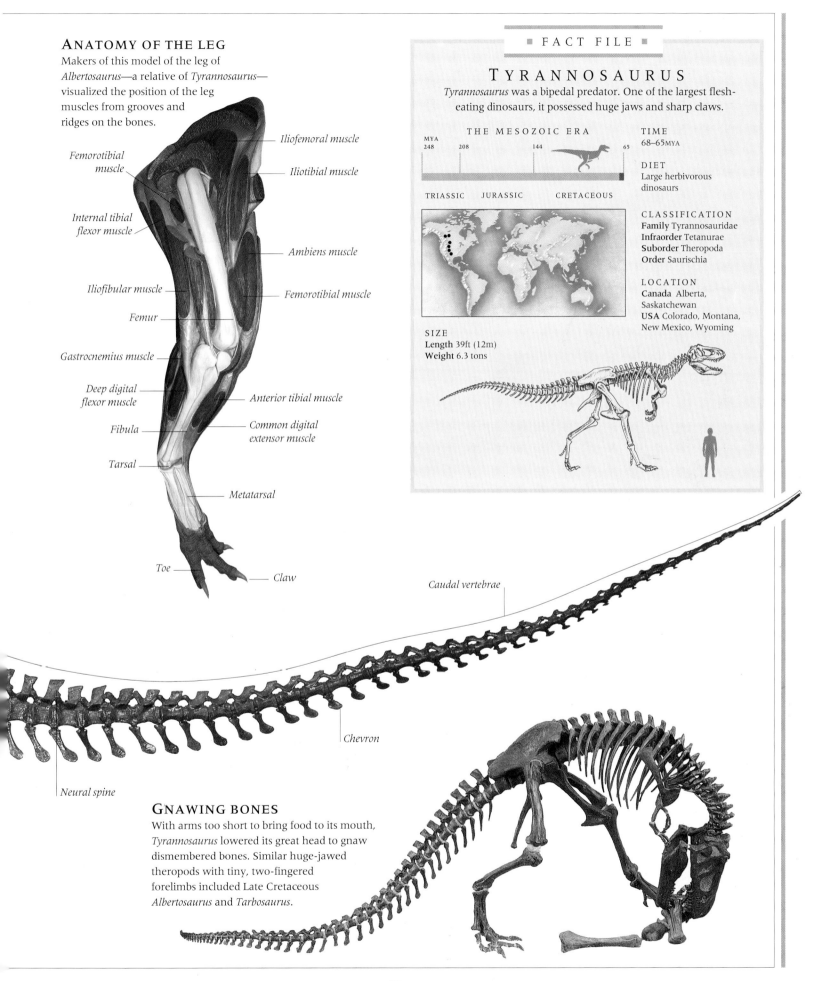

Femorotibial muscle

Internal tibial flexor muscle

Iliofibular muscle

Femur

Gastrocnemius muscle

Deep digital flexor muscle

Fibula

Tarsal

Toe

Iliofemoral muscle

Iliotibial muscle

Ambiens muscle

Femorotibial muscle

Anterior tibial muscle

Common digital extensor muscle

Metatarsal

Claw

■ FACT FILE ■

TYRANNOSAURUS

Tyrannosaurus was a bipedal predator. One of the largest flesh-eating dinosaurs, it possessed huge jaws and sharp claws.

THE MESOZOIC ERA

MYA 248	208	144	65
TRIASSIC	JURASSIC	CRETACEOUS	

TIME
68–65MYA

DIET
Large herbivorous dinosaurs

CLASSIFICATION
Family Tyrannosauridae
Infraorder Tetanurae
Suborder Theropoda
Order Saurischia

LOCATION
Canada Alberta, Saskatchewan
USA Colorado, Montana, New Mexico, Wyoming

SIZE
Length 39ft (12m)
Weight 6.3 tons

Caudal vertebrae

Chevron

Neural spine

GNAWING BONES

With arms too short to bring food to its mouth, *Tyrannosaurus* lowered its great head to gnaw dismembered bones. Similar huge-jawed theropods with tiny, two-fingered forelimbs included Late Cretaceous *Albertosaurus* and *Tarbosaurus*.

BARYONYX

BARYONYX ("HEAVY CLAW") takes its name from its murderously large and hooklike thumb-claws. In 1983, the chance find of one of these thumb-claws in southern England led to the discovery of the only known skeleton of this strange, big, predatory dinosaur—the best preserved of any dating from its time (around 120 million years ago). The most unusual features of *Baryonyx* were its long, narrow, crocodile-like jaws filled with sharp teeth. It also had a longer, straighter neck than most big theropods and strong arms and hind limbs; its body was balanced by a stiffened tail.

CROCODILE SKULL

WILLIAM WALKER
Amateur fossil-hunter William Walker with the Baryonyx *thumb-claw he found in a clay pit in Surrey, England, in 1983.*

TWO SKULLS COMPARED

Long, low jaws and sharp, somewhat rounded teeth made *Baryonyx*'s 3ft 7in (1.1m) head less like that of a flesh-eating dinosaur than that of a present-day crocodile, a reptile whose jaws were specifically designed to seize and grasp slippery prey. Other notable aspects of *Baryonyx*'s skull are the kinked upper jaw and position of the nostrils, features that are similar in *Dilophosaurus*.

◾ LIFE AND BEHAVIOR ◾

Baryonyx's homeland was the warm flood plain that stretched from where London now stands, south into France and Belgium. The carnivorous predator prowled through conifer and cycad forests, ferny glades, and horsetail meadows fringing rivers, lakes, and swamps. It probably waded into water and caught big fish with its great thumb-claws, much as grizzly bears snatch salmon from Alaskan rivers. Or it might have crouched on all fours on the shore, its long neck craned out just above the water, seizing passing fish in its jaws. The long mouth armed with narrow, pointed teeth would have been ideal for gripping slippery prey. Half-digested fish scales found in *Baryonyx*'s rib cage prove that fish of roughly 3ft (about 1m) in length formed at least part of this creature's diet. However, it has been pointed out that no present-day, large land animal eats only fish, and one scientist has therefore surmised that *Baryonyx* also hunted terrestrial prey. Another possibility is that *Baryonyx* scavenged meat from the corpses of dinosaurs it found already dead, probing deep inside the carcasses with its long, narrow, sharp-toothed jaws.

Stiffened tail acts as a counterbalance

FOSSILIZED SKELETON

Reconstructing a *Baryonyx* skeleton involved making model bones to take the place of bones that were missing. Parts of the skull, ribs, tail, arms, and legs had to be based on other theropods or modeled from bones on the left side of the body, then fitted together.

Cervical vertebra

Orbit

Naris

Ulna

Mandible

Radius

Humerus

Femur

Pubis

Ischium

Tibia

Fibula

Chevron

Neural spine

Caudal vertebra

Ankle

Foot

Toe

Toe-claw

Phalanx

THUMB-CLAW

Baryonyx's sharp, curved thumb-claw resembled the strong hook on a fisherman's gaff (a tool used to lift heavy fish out of water). This fossil (right) was reconstructed from fragments that fell out of a large, hard siltstone nodule struck by fossil hunter William Walker's geological hammer. With its (long-lost) horny sheath, the claw must have measured 14in (about 35cm).

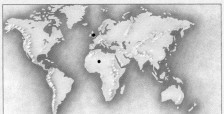

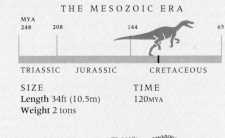

■ FACT FILE ■

BARYONYX

Baryonyx was a large, bipedal predator. Its body was long and it had jaws like those of a crocodile, sharp teeth, and big thumb-claws.

THE MESOZOIC ERA
MYA
248
208
144
65
TRIASSIC
JURASSIC
CRETACEOUS

SIZE
Length 34ft (10.5m)
Weight 2 tons

TIME
120MYA

LOCATION
England Surrey
Niger

DIET
Fish, carrion

CLASSIFICATION
Family Baryonychidae
Infraorder Tetanurae
Suborder Theropoda
Order Saurischia

Narrow, pointed tooth
Scaly skin
Long, straight neck
Long, narrow jaw
Wrist
Elbow
Forelimb
Powerful hind limb
Hand
Hooked thumb-claw
Finger
Finger-claw

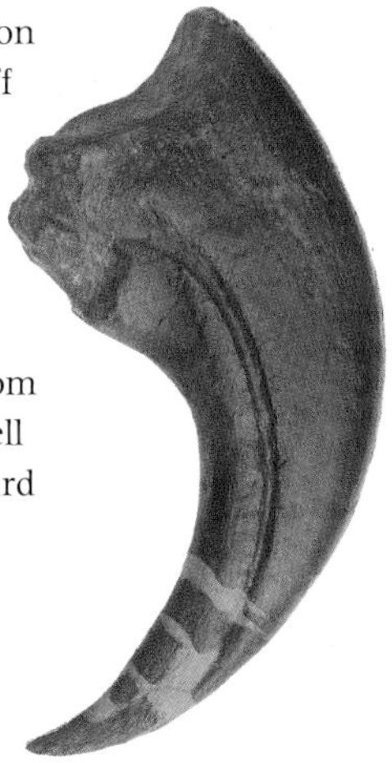

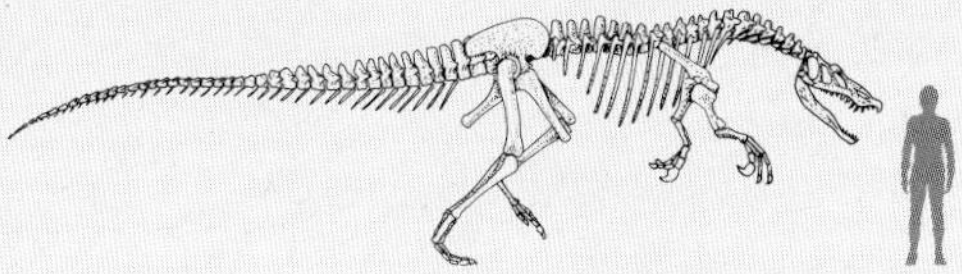

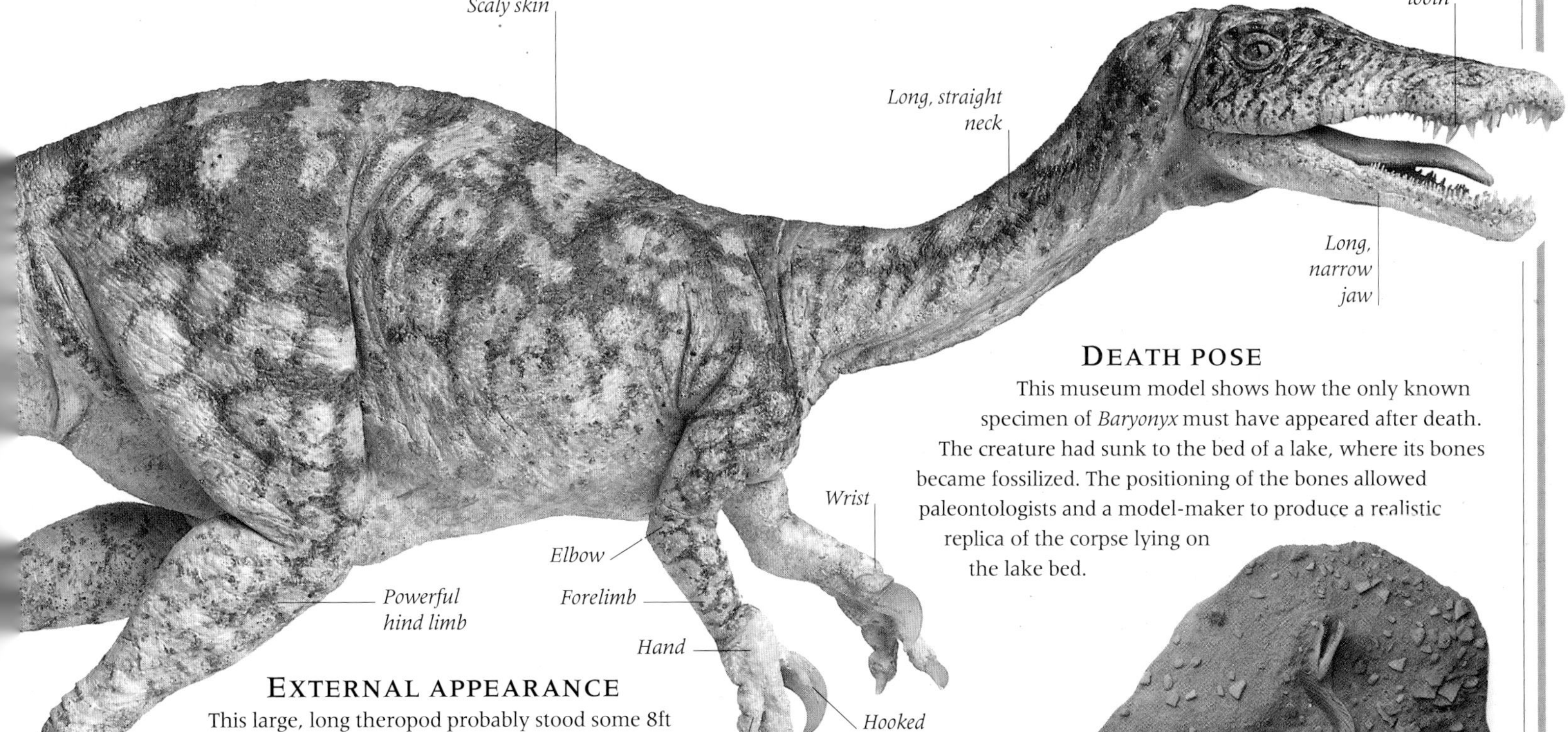

EXTERNAL APPEARANCE

This large, long theropod probably stood some 8ft (about 2.5m) high at the hips. *Baryonyx* probably prowled around on its hind limbs, with the long, stiffened tail balancing the chest, and the neck and head held low and jutting forward. (Most other big theropods usually held their necks shaped like a letter S.) The arms were very powerfully built for ambushing fish and lifting them out of the water, or for tackling carrion. *Baryonyx* probably did not go down on all fours.

DEATH POSE

This museum model shows how the only known specimen of *Baryonyx* must have appeared after death. The creature had sunk to the bed of a lake, where its bones became fossilized. The positioning of the bones allowed paleontologists and a model-maker to produce a realistic replica of the corpse lying on the lake bed.

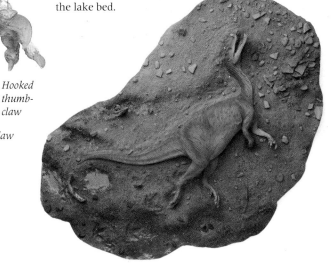

SPINOSAURUS

A WORLD WAR II bombing raid destroyed the few bones then known of one of the longest and strangest of all carnivorous dinosaurs. *Spinosaurus* ("thorn lizard") was as long as *Tyrannosaurus*, but less heavily built. Its most unusual feature was a tall skin "sail" that was held aloft by bony "swords" rising up to 5ft 5in (1.6m) from its backbone. Skull and jaw fragments seem to suggest that *Spinosaurus* had a long, low skull and a kinked snout. Similar traits are found in crocodiles and in the skull of the theropod *Baryonx*.

WARMING UP
Two Spinosaurus *align themselves so that the sun's rays warm up the blood coursing through their tall skin sails.*

■ LIFE AND BEHAVIOR ■

There has been considerable discussion about the shape of *Spinosaurus*'s head. One theory suggests that it had a long, low head and crocodile-like teeth designed for eating fish rather than killing other dinosaurs. This large theropod may have preyed mainly on big species of freshwater fish, skewering its victims between its piercing, narrow teeth. Like a heron, *Spinosaurus* may have stood on the banks of lakes and rivers and grabbed prey in its jaws. Or perhaps it stood in shallow water, hooking out fish by means of long, sharp thumb-claws like *Baryonyx*'s. This is purely guesswork, however, for no *Spinosaurus* claw bones have survived. Scientists disagree as to whether *Baryonyx* and *Spinosaurus* belonged to a single group of predatory dinosaurs. While they show similarities, there are also differences. For instance, *Spinosaurus* seems to have had far fewer teeth. suggesting that it may have scavenged flesh from the decaying corpses of big dinosaurs.

CATCHING FISH
A Spinosaurus *seizes a slippery catch between jaws armed with piercing teeth like a crocodile's.*

Tail

Lateral caudal musculature

Chevron

■ SKIN SAIL ■

A large skin "sail" makes it unlikely that *Spinosaurus* overpowered and ate large dinosaurs, since a struggling victim could have fractured the sail's bony props. The sail's function is open to debate. If *Spinosaurus* were cold-blooded, the sail might have acted as a solar-heating panel, making *Spinosaurus* warm and active in the early morning, when other cold-blooded dinosaurs were still relatively cold and sluggish. *Spinosaurus* could have attacked them when they were incapable of escaping or fighting back. Alternatively, rival males might have used their sails to try to dominate each other, possibly slightly raising and lowering them for threat displays.

SAIL-BACKED DINOSAURS

Spinosaurus was the largest but not the only theropod to sport a sail on its back. Other sail-backed theropods included *Acrocanthosaurus* and *Becklespinax,* with their much lower sails. Unrelated sail-backed dinosaurs living in North Africa at the same time as *Spinosaurus* were the ornithopod *Ouranosaurus* and the sauropod *Rebbachisaurus.*

■ FACT FILE ■

SPINOSAURUS

Spinosaurus was a huge, bipedal predator, with a skin "sail", a bulky body, and crocodile-like jaws.

THE MESOZOIC ERA

MYA				
248	208	144		65

TRIASSIC   JURASSIC   CRETACEOUS

CLASSIFICATION
Family Spinosauridae
Infraorder Tetanurae
Suborder Theropoda
Order Saurischia

TIME
100–95MYA

DIET
Fish, dinosaurs

LOCATION
Egypt Marsa Matrûh
Morocco Taouz
Tunisia

SIZE
Length 49ft (15m)
Weight 3.9 tons

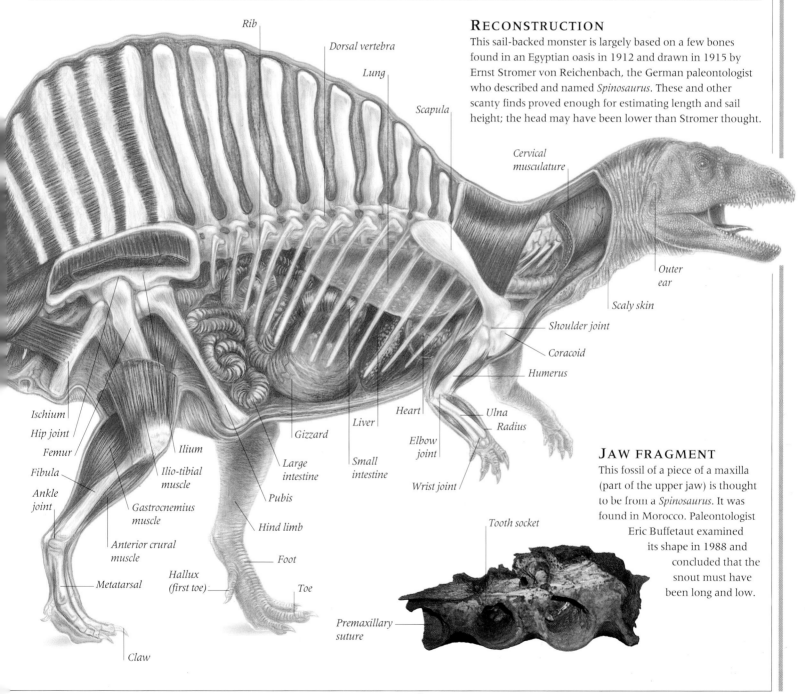

Rib

Dorsal vertebra

Lung

Scapula

Cervical musculature

Outer ear

Scaly skin

Shoulder joint

Coracoid

Humerus

Heart

Ulna

Radius

Liver

Elbow joint

Wrist joint

Gizzard

Small intestine

Large intestine

Pubis

Hind limb

Foot

Ischium

Hip joint

Femur

Fibula

Ankle joint

Ilium

Ilio-tibial muscle

Gastrocnemius muscle

Anterior crural muscle

Metatarsal

Hallux (first toe)

Toe

Claw

Premaxillary suture

Tooth socket

RECONSTRUCTION

This sail-backed monster is largely based on a few bones found in an Egyptian oasis in 1912 and drawn in 1915 by Ernst Stromer von Reichenbach, the German paleontologist who described and named *Spinosaurus*. These and other scanty finds proved enough for estimating length and sail height; the head may have been lower than Stromer thought.

JAW FRAGMENT

This fossil of a piece of a maxilla (part of the upper jaw) is thought to be from a *Spinosaurus*. It was found in Morocco. Paleontologist Eric Buffetaut examined its shape in 1988 and concluded that the snout must have been long and low.

GALLIMIMUS

T HREE NEARLY COMPLETE skeletons from Mongolia's Gobi Desert make "chicken mimic" the best-known ornithomimid, or ostrich dinosaur. Over twice the length of a modern-day ostrich, *Gallimimus* was the largest of a group of lightly built, birdlike theropods from Africa, East Asia, and western North America. It had a long, toothless beak, a slim neck, a short body, a stiffened

EXCAVATION
Excavation exposes a Gallimimus pelvis at Altan Ula, in Mongolia. This dinosaur was one of several found in that country in the late 1960s and early 1970s by a joint Polish-Mongolian team of paleontologists, among whom were Zofia Kielan-Jaworowska and Halszka Osmólska from Poland, and Mongolia's Rinchen Barsbold.

tail, three-fingered hands, and slender legs. It also had a bird's intelligence and big, outward-facing eyes.

■ LIFE AND BEHAVIOR ■

Although *Gallimimus* has in the past been thought of as a plant-eating dinosaur, recent work has led to the conclusion that its diet was more carnivorous than herbivorous, and its grasping hand was probably used for catching small animals. *Gallimimus* would have snapped up large insects and their larvae, perhaps small vertebrates, and anything else it could swallow whole. *Gallimimus* lived deeper inland than its North American cousins, in a climate that was drier overall but in which droughts and rainy seasons alternated. The ornithomimid walked along the banks of rivers, perhaps in company with plant-eating duckbills, armored dinosaurs, and sauropods. With its head carried high above its narrow shoulders, *Gallimimus* scanned the land, alert to the threat of ambush by such carnosaurs as *Tarbosaurus*. Other enemies might have included *Deinocheirus* and *Therizinosaurus*, mysterious theropods known only from huge, gangling forelimbs armed with formidable claws. *Gallimimus*'s only defense against such large, hungry predators was to run away, increasing stride as it gained speed—possibly running as fast as a modern-day ostrich.

DYNAMIC RESTORATION
A restored *Gallimimus* is shown here scanning the land for danger, ready to break into a sprint.

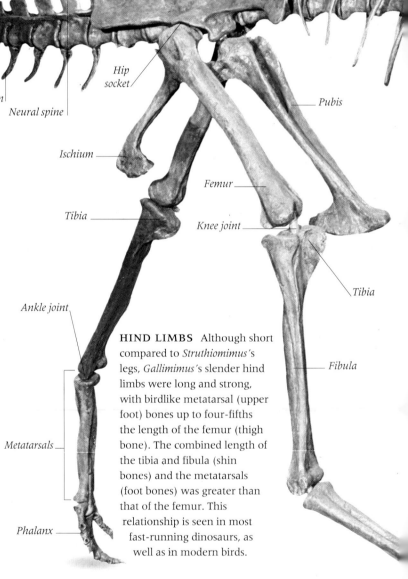

Caudal vertebrae

Ilium

Chevron

Neural spine

Hip socket

Pubis

Ischium

Femur

Tibia

Knee joint

Tibia

Ankle joint

Fibula

Metatarsals

HIND LIMBS Although short compared to *Struthiomimus*'s legs, *Gallimimus*'s slender hind limbs were long and strong, with birdlike metatarsal (upper foot) bones up to four-fifths the length of the femur (thigh bone). The combined length of the tibia and fibula (shin bones) and the metatarsals (foot bones) was greater than that of the femur. This relationship is seen in most fast-running dinosaurs, as well as in modern birds.

Phalanx

DEATH POSE

Ornithomimids have been found with the head and tail pulled back: they may have died of thirst in deserts or temporary droughts. Dry air would have helped shrink the ligaments that tugged their necks and tails upward. Lack of drinking water nearby might also have been the reason why these corpses were preserved in such complete form—fewer carrion-eaters, who would otherwise have dismembered the corpses and scattered the bones, would have survived.

Skull

Orbit

Naris

Mandible

Cervical vertebrae

Dorsal vertebrae

Rib

Scapula

Humerus

Radius

Ulna

Wrist joint

Metacarpal

Phalanx

SKELETON

This convincing reconstruction of a *Gallimimus* skeleton benefited from the discovery of the remains of several specimens in southern Mongolia. These include two almost complete skeletons, one skeleton complete except for the skull, a skull with other pieces of a skeleton, and bits and pieces from various specimens. Compared to *Struthiomimus*, *Gallimimus's* small, light skull was longer, its hands were shorter, and its claws were more curved.

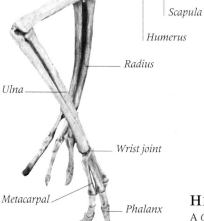

HEAD AND NECK

A *Gallimimus* head and neck in close-up show how the eyes were held: they were high above the ground and their fields of vision did not overlap. This would make it hard to judge distance well, but with one eye on each side of the head and a neck it could twist around, *Gallimimus* would have been able to get an all-around view.

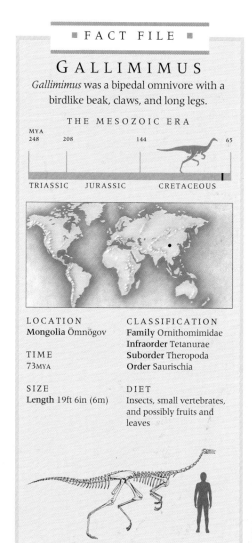

■ FACT FILE ■

GALLIMIMUS

Gallimimus was a bipedal omnivore with a birdlike beak, claws, and long legs.

THE MESOZOIC ERA

MYA 248	208	144	65
TRIASSIC	JURASSIC	CRETACEOUS	

LOCATION
Mongolia Ömnögov

TIME
73MYA

SIZE
Length 19ft 6in (6m)

CLASSIFICATION
Family Ornithomimidae
Infraorder Tetanurae
Suborder Theropoda
Order Saurischia

DIET
Insects, small vertebrates, and possibly fruits and leaves

STRUTHIOMIMUS

S TRUTHIOMIMUS ("ostrich mimic") is the best-known of North America's large, bird-like, running dinosaurs. An almost complete skeleton found in Alberta shows striking similarities to the skeleton of a modern ostrich (*Struthio*). Both have a small head, large eye sockets, a toothless beak, a long neck, a short back, long legs with longer shins than thighs, elongated upper foot bones, and three large, forward-facing toes with claws. Unlike the ostrich, *Struthiomimus* had gangling arms with clawed, three-fingered hands, and a long tail with a stiffened end; and it was probably covered in bare, scaly skin.

LIFELIKE MODEL
From the Royal Tyrrell Museum, Alberta.

■ LIFE AND BEHAVIOR ■

This dinosaur probably ranged over low, open countryside west of North America's great inland sea. Its large eyes and peripheral vision gave it early warning of attack. Confronted by a small, hostile theropod, *Struthiomimus* could have delivered powerful kicks to drive it away. However, this would not have deterred larger predators, such as a tyrannosaur or a dromaeosaur pack, and *Struthiomimus* would have had to rely instead on speed, outrunning its enemies to escape. As it fled, it would probably have had the knack of sharply and suddenly changing direction every now and then, in order to throw off its pursuers, its tail swinging from side to side to maintain its balance. Some scientists think *Struthiomimus* might have been able to sprint away almost as fast as a modern horse can gallop. But emergencies demanding this sort of reaction should not have occurred often, for the dinosaur was constantly on the alert for danger. Most scientists are convinced that *Struthiomimus* was an unfussy feeder. Its long claws—like those of a present-day sloth—were suited to hooking leafy twigs or picking fruits from bushes and low trees; these could then be snipped off by its sharp-edged, horny beak. Extra joints within the skull probably helped this dinosaur to work both halves of the beak, enabling it to manipulate foods held in the mouth, much as parrots dehusk nuts. *Struthiomimus* probably also fed on insects and small animals. By lowering its neck and making sudden lunging movements of its head, it could have snapped up large insects, lizards, and small, shrewlike mammals in the undergrowth.

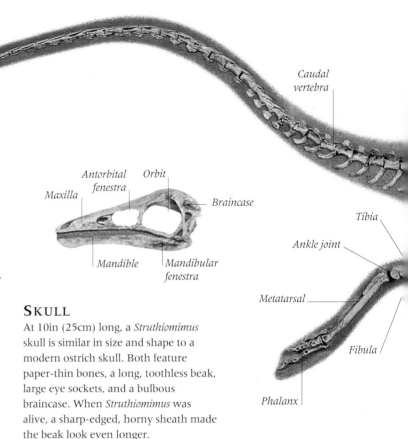

Caudal vertebra

Tibia

Ankle joint

Metatarsal

Fibula

Phalanx

Antorbital fenestra *Orbit*

Maxilla

Braincase

Mandible *Mandibular fenestra*

SKULL

At 10in (25cm) long, a *Struthiomimus* skull is similar in size and shape to a modern ostrich skull. Both feature paper-thin bones, a long, toothless beak, large eye sockets, and a bulbous braincase. When *Struthiomimus* was alive, a sharp-edged, horny sheath made the beak look even longer.

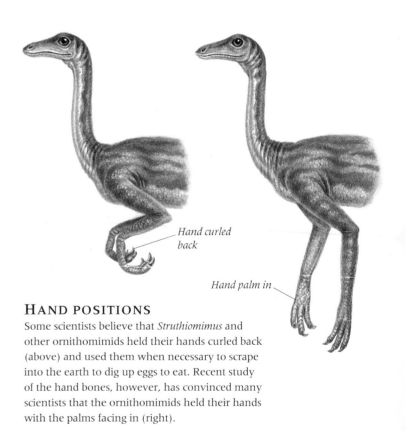

Hand curled back

Hand palm in

HAND POSITIONS

Some scientists believe that *Struthiomimus* and other ornithomimids held their hands curled back (above) and used them when necessary to scrape into the earth to dig up eggs to eat. Recent study of the hand bones, however, has convinced many scientists that the ornithomimids held their hands with the palms facing in (right).

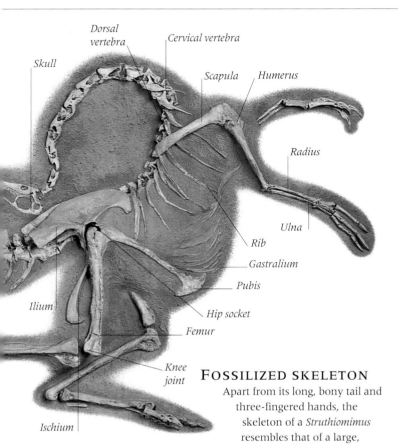

Skull

Dorsal
vertebra

Cervical vertebra

Scapula   Humerus

Radius

Ulna

Rib

Gastralium

Pubis

Ilium

Hip socket

Femur

Knee
joint

Ischium

FOSSILIZED SKELETON

Apart from its long, bony tail and
three-fingered hands, the
skeleton of a *Struthiomimus*
resembles that of a large,
running bird. After death this
individual dried out. As its ligaments shrank,
they pulled the cervical vertebrae (neck bones)
back into an agonized, unnatural-looking pose.

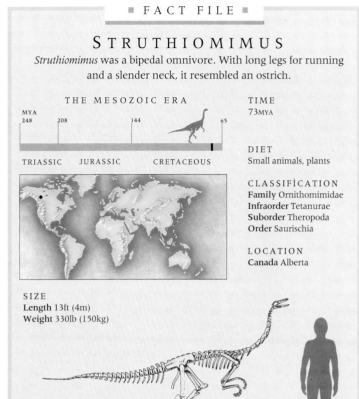

■ FACT FILE ■

STRUTHIOMIMUS

Struthiomimus was a bipedal omnivore. With long legs for running
and a slender neck, it resembled an ostrich.

THE MESOZOIC ERA

MYA
248   208   144   65

TRIASSIC   JURASSIC   CRETACEOUS

TIME
73MYA

DIET
Small animals, plants

CLASSIFICATION
Family Ornithomimidae
Infraorder Tetanurae
Suborder Theropoda
Order Saurischia

LOCATION
Canada Alberta

SIZE
Length 13ft (4m)
Weight 330lb (150kg)

RUNNING ABILITY

Convergent evolution made *Struthiomimus* (far right) a
sprinter very like a modern ostrich (right). Studies of its limb
bones convinced American paleontologist Dale Russell that
a scared *Struthiomimus* could run very fast indeed. Some
experts believe it could reach an ostrich's top speed of
50mph (80km/h). Even at half that speed a *Struthiomimus*
would have matched an Olympic
100m sprinter.

OVIRAPTOR

O VIRAPTOR ("EGG-THIEF") was a birdlike theropod with a bizarrely shaped head. The strong, toothless jaws ended in a horny beak; two sharp, bony prongs jutted down from the roof of the mouth, and the head was surmounted by a crest. The rest of *Oviraptor*'s body was more like that of a typical theropod, with muscular arms, clawed, three-fingered hands, long legs with three-toed feet, and a long, muscular tail.

■ LIFE AND BEHAVIOR ■

This toothless theropod gets its name from the notion that it stole and ate horned dinosaurs' eggs: the first *Oviraptor philoceratops* to be discovered had a smashed skull and was found lying on a nest of *Protoceratops* eggs. *Oviraptor* had strong jaws, and inside its mouth there were bony prongs with which it could easily have crushed the hard eggshells of other dinosaurs. A very similar method is used by egg-eating snakes, which use the sharp bones in their necks to smash eggs. Had an *Oviraptor* been surprised at the nest, running away would have been the best strategy in the face of its strong but slow enemies. Evidence also suggests that one *Protoceratops* stamped an *Oviraptor* to death before it could escape or put up a fight.

■ TWO SPECIES ■

There were two *Oviraptor* species, both of which lived in late Cretaceous Mongolia. The animal shown in the main picture on these pages is *Oviraptor philoceratops*, which lived in semi-desert. In this habitat, eggs would have been important as a source of liquid as well as nourishment. A second species,

DISCOVERY
An expedition from the American Museum of Natural History found Oviraptor *in the Gobi Desert in 1923.*

Oviraptor mongoliensis had a tall, domed crest, much larger than that of *Oviraptor philoceratops*. This animal lived near lakes and rivers rich in shellfish. One scientist concluded that it swam in search of food, sculling along with its deep tail, scooping up such shellfish as snails and mussels with its hands and crunching them between its jaws.

OVIRAPTORID SKULL

An oviraptorid's toothless skull was deep but lightweight. Many of the skull bones were mere struts, which enclosed huge holes for eyes, nostrils, and jaw muscles. Some crestless skulls first attributed to *Oviraptor* young came from adults of a different type of oviraptorid: *Conchoraptor* or *Ingenia*.

Nasal bump

Orbit

Braincase

Space for jaw muscles

Toothless beak

Powerful lower jaw

Cervical musculature

Dorsal vertebra

Cervical vertebra

Ambiens muscle

Wrist joint

Posterior brachial muscle

Anterior brachial muscle

Scapular muscle

Pubis with "foot-shaped" end

Elongated "sprinter's" shins

Radius

Phalanx

Ankle joint

Ulna

Strongly curved claw

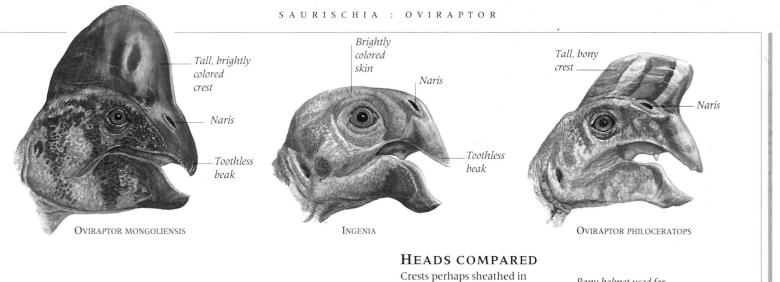

Tall, brightly colored crest

Naris

Toothless beak

OVIRAPTOR MONGOLIENSIS

Brightly colored skin

Naris

Toothless beak

INGENIA

Tall, bony crest

Naris

OVIRAPTOR PHILOCERATOPS

HIPS, HIND LIMBS, AND TAIL

As in most theropods, *Oviraptor* had slim hips, and its pubis ended in a "foot." It had elongated shins and three weight-bearing toes per foot. The long tail's core was formed of 40 caudal vertebrae.

HEADS COMPARED

Crests perhaps sheathed in colored horn crowned the males' heads in *Oviraptor mongoliensis* and *Oviraptor philoceratops*. They resemble the bony helmet of a cassowary, a bird that butts its way through forest undergrowth headfirst. Oviraptorids like *Ingenia* probably had brightly colored skin but no crest.

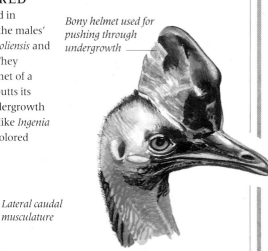

Bony helmet used for pushing through undergrowth

CASSOWARY

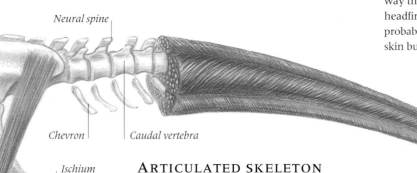

Neural spine

Chevron

Caudal vertebra

Ischium

Ilio tibial muscle

Gastrocnemius muscle

Lateral caudal musculature

ARTICULATED SKELETON

Areas of muscle have been added to the neck, limbs, and tail on this illustration of an *Oviraptor philoceratops* skeleton. The fossil skeleton's upper jaw bones protruded beyond the lower jaw, but the latter was probably extended by a horny beak. Hands with "thumbs" shorter than the fingers, and the strongly curved claws, helped convince scientists that *Oviraptor* did not belong in the same group of toothless theropods as the ostrich dinosaurs such as *Struthiomimus*.

Fibula

Digital exterior muscle

Tibia

Ankle joint

Hallux (first toe)

Phalanx

OVIRAPTOR

Oviraptor was a bipedal, birdlike predator. It had a deep beak containing two toothlike bones, strong forelimbs with curved claws, and a long tail.

THE MESOZOIC ERA

MYA
248   208   144   65

TRIASSIC   JURASSIC   CRETACEOUS

SIZE   TIME
Length 6ft 6in (2m)   83–73MYA
Weight 73lb (33kg)

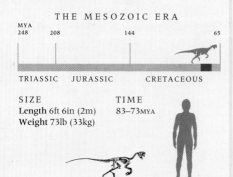

LOCATION
Mongolia Ömnögov

DIET
Molluscs, eggs

CLASSIFICATION
Family Oviraptoridae
Infraorder Tetanurae
Suborder Theropoda
Order Saurischia

TROODON

N AMED IN 1856 from a small, sharp tooth, athletic *Troodon* ("wounding tooth") was at first believed to be a lizard, and then a bone-headed dinosaur. *Troodon's* tooth was not matched with bones until the 1980s. The bones showed that this dinosaur had been a sharp-eyed, birdlike theropod with a bigger brain for its body size than almost any other dinosaur. Its hands could grasp, and had large, sharp, hooklike claws. Its extremely long, slim legs ended in elongated feet with three weight-bearing toes, each second toe bearing a deep, curved claw a bit like that of *Deinonychus*. Despite this similarity, some scientists believe that *Troodon* and *Deinonychus* were not closely related.

Partly forward-facing eye

Naris

Wide mouth

Long, flexible neck

HEAD IN FRONT VIEW

This model stresses *Troodon's* alert, birdlike head and large, partly forward-facing eyes. The overlapping visual fields of the two eyes may have allowed accurate judgment of distance, helping *Troodon* to pounce upon fast-moving, ratlike mammals and young, agile, hypsilophodontids. Since we cannot observe *Troodon's* behavior, we cannot tell for certain if it hunted at night.

Partly forward-facing eye

Sharp finger-claw

Long, slim leg

Large, swiveling second-toe claw

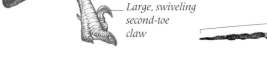

■ LIFE AND BEHAVIOR ■

Scientists suspect that *Troodon's* anatomy made this theropod a deadly hunter of small mammals that ventured out to feed at dusk. Most dinosaurs had eyes on the sides of their heads, but *Troodon's* large eyes faced partly forward, more like ours. This would have probably given it binocular vision, making this predator particularly good at focusing upon small, swiftly moving animals no bigger than a rat. If the retinas of its eyes were well endowed with low-light sensitive rods, *Troodon* could see the creatures even if they scampered around at night, safe from day-active predatory dinosaurs. *Troodon* could have stalked through forest glades, watching for the slightest movement.

■ RANGE OF PREY ■

There is much discussion among experts about the prey that this agile theropod might have hunted. If *Troodon* glimpsed a mammal running for cover, it might have darted after it to grasp it between rows of coarsely serrated teeth. *Troodon* also seems to have been fierce enough to have attacked larger animals, which it could have seized with the sharp claws on its hands and feet. But its second-toe claws were not designed to deal such powerful blows as those of *Deinonychus*. Unlike that dinosaur, *Troodon* could not kick a big, plant-eating dinosaur to death while clinging to its back. Although *Troodon* might not have hunted big game, its prey probably included lizards, snakes, mammals, and young dinosaurs. Another difference between *Troodon* and *Deinonychus* was that while *Deinonychus* had a system of bony tendons that stiffened the tail for use as a balancing rod in fast running or in combat, *Troodon* lacked this feature.

EXTERNAL FEATURES

Elongated legs allowed *Troodon* to take enormous strides and thus to run extremely fast, probably with its big second-toe claw held well above the ground. Such theropods probably ran faster than any others living at the time, except perhaps for the fleet-footed avimimid dinosaurs of Asia.

Serrated cutting edge

SAW-EDGED TOOTH

Troodon's small, triangular, saw-edged teeth were flattened from side to side like a knife blade, and curved along their length. Along their cutting edges they were armed with big, hooked denticles. There were up to 25 teeth on each side of the upper jaw, with precisely 25 on each side of the lower jaw.

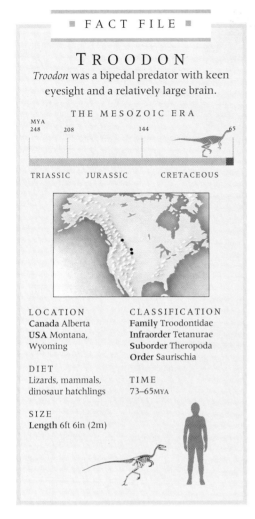

TROODON

Troodon was a bipedal predator with keen eyesight and a relatively large brain.

THE MESOZOIC ERA

MYA 248	208	144	65
TRIASSIC	JURASSIC	CRETACEOUS	

LOCATION
Canada Alberta
USA Montana, Wyoming

CLASSIFICATION
Family Troodontidae
Infraorder Tetanurae
Suborder Theropoda
Order Saurischia

DIET
Lizards, mammals, dinosaur hatchlings

TIME
73–65MYA

SIZE
Length 6ft 6in (2m)

TROODON AND DINOSAUROID

In the early 1980s, the American paleontologist Dale Russell suggested that, had dinosaurs survived, the big-brained, bipedal, birdlike *Troodon,* with grasping hands (left), might have given rise to an intelligent and human-looking descendant like the "dinosauroid" (right).

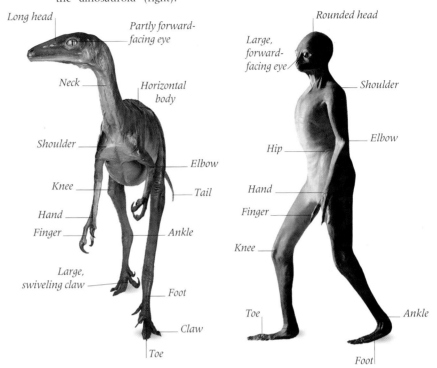

Long head
Partly forward-facing eye
Neck
Horizontal body
Shoulder
Elbow
Knee
Tail
Hand
Finger
Ankle
Large, swiveling claw
Foot
Claw
Toe

Rounded head
Large, forward-facing eye
Shoulder
Elbow
Hip
Hand
Finger
Knee
Toe
Ankle
Foot

SKELETON

Bones in *Troodon*'s skull, wrists, and hands, and the hinged claws on the second toes of its feet, show some similarity to the formidable dromaeosaurid *Deinonychus*. But *Troodon* had no bony tendons to stiffen the tail.

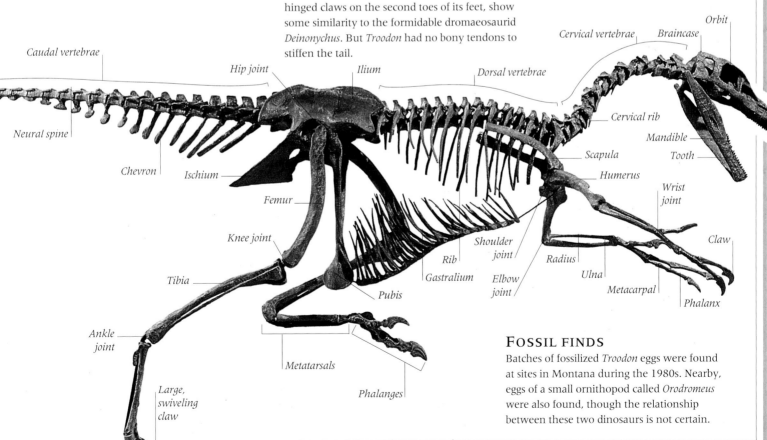

Caudal vertebrae
Hip joint
Ilium
Dorsal vertebrae
Cervical vertebrae
Braincase
Orbit
Neural spine
Cervical rib
Mandible
Tooth
Chevron
Ischium
Scapula
Femur
Humerus
Wrist joint
Knee joint
Shoulder joint
Radius
Claw
Tibia
Rib
Gastralium
Elbow joint
Ulna
Metacarpal
Ankle joint
Pubis
Phalanx
Large, swiveling claw
Metatarsals
Phalanges

FOSSIL FINDS

Batches of fossilized *Troodon* eggs were found at sites in Montana during the 1980s. Nearby, eggs of a small ornithopod called *Orodromeus* were also found, though the relationship between these two dinosaurs is not certain.

DEINONYCHUS

T HE DISCOVERY IN the 1960s of new, more complete fossils of this agile killer undermined old notions that dinosaurs were small-brained, sluggish reptiles. *Deinonychus*—"terrible claw"—was no longer than a small car and no heavier than a human, yet for its size it was more formidably armed than almost any other theropod. Large fangs rimmed the powerful jaws. Long, strong arms bore three-fingered, grasping hands with sharp claws. Most fearsome was the scythelike claw on the second toe of each of its muscular legs.

Bladelike tooth

Stiffened tail

Grasping hand

Strong arm

"Terrible claw"

RESTORATION
This museum model depicts *Deinonychus* striped somewhat like a tiger. We know that the tiger's stripes break up its outline as it hides in long grass or prowls through the dappled sunlight of a forest floor. *Deinonychus* had no grass to hide in, but it would have benefited from camouflage when it lurked among tall ferns or under trees. Its true coloration, though, remains a matter of guesswork.

Bony tendon

Caudal vertebra

Chevron extensions

■ LIFE AND BEHAVIOR ■

Scientists suspect that *Deinonychus* scoured the countryside in packs. Each individual would have snapped up any lizards or small mammals in its path, but gang members joined forces to attack large animals. Working together, they could bring down dinosaurs much bigger than themselves, as wolves combine for killing caribou and Cape hunting dogs subdue a zebra. One clue to such behavior is a fossil site containing the remains of four *Deinonychus* and a much larger *Tenontosaurus*. What took place here can only be guessed at, but one interpretation is that a hunting pack of *Deinonychus*, including many more than four animals, had raced in upon the horse-size ornithopod, stiffened tails swinging to balance violent body movements as they leapt to the attack. The deaths of at least four *Deinonychus* suggest that heavy losses may have occurred during incidents of this kind. Scientists think that for large prey, *Deinonychus* probably jumped into the attack, then balanced on one foot and kicked with the other, tearing deep gashes in the victim's belly. Alternatively it could have performed a two-footed, hopping pounce to land on the victim. Threatened by such a gang, a *Tenontosaurus* might have rolled over onto its attackers or turned suddenly to swing at them with its heavy tail. Such tactics may have killed several of the assailants. But meanwhile, the rest would have swarmed all over the ornithischian, inflicting other wounds. Weakened from loss of blood, the victim would have soon collapsed and died.

STIFFENED TAIL
Deinonychus's long tail stuck out like a ramrod thanks to unique stiffening devices that locked together all caudal vertebrae (tailbones) except those closest to the body. From above each vertebra, a forked, rodlike, bony tendon overlapped as many as the next eight vertebrae. Below each vertebra, a forward-pointing extension of the chevron interlocked with neighboring chevrons, further stiffening the tail.

A TENONTOSAURUS IS ATTACKED
Three Deinonychus *(shown here with blue-green backs) attack a big ornithopod called* Tenontosaurus. *With their combined assault, they killed creatures several times their size.*

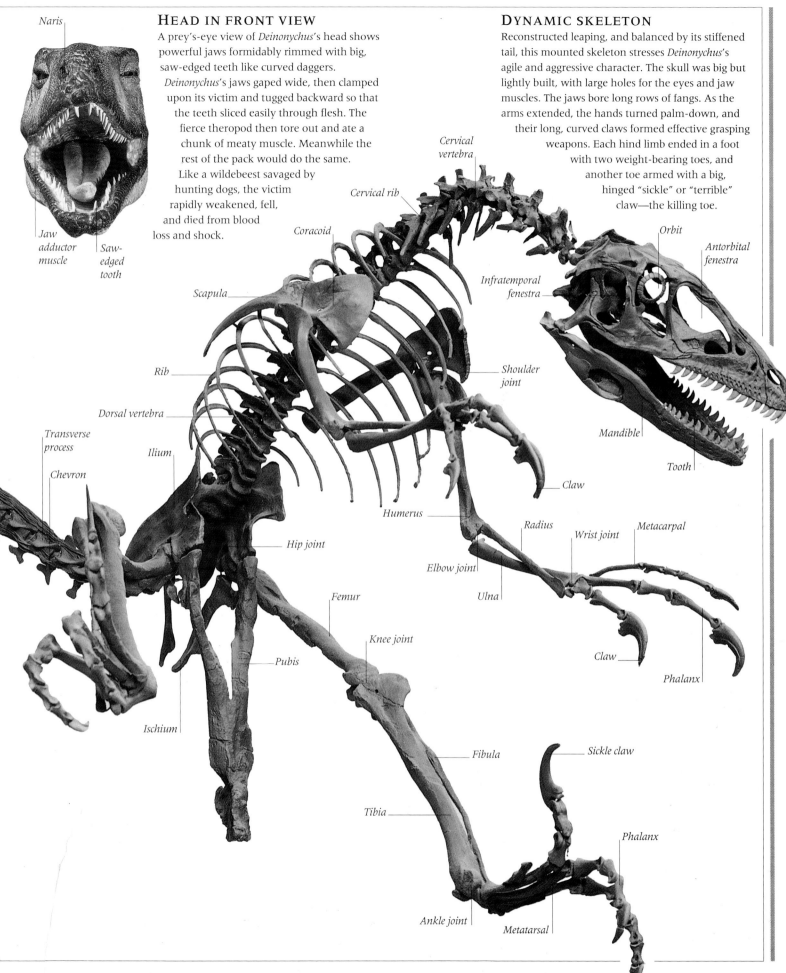

HEAD IN FRONT VIEW

A prey's-eye view of *Deinonychus*'s head shows powerful jaws formidably rimmed with big, saw-edged teeth like curved daggers.
Deinonychus's jaws gaped wide, then clamped upon its victim and tugged backward so that the teeth sliced easily through flesh. The fierce theropod then tore out and ate a chunk of meaty muscle. Meanwhile the rest of the pack would do the same. Like a wildebeest savaged by hunting dogs, the victim rapidly weakened, fell, and died from blood loss and shock.

DYNAMIC SKELETON

Reconstructed leaping, and balanced by its stiffened tail, this mounted skeleton stresses *Deinonychus*'s agile and aggressive character. The skull was big but lightly built, with large holes for the eyes and jaw muscles. The jaws bore long rows of fangs. As the arms extended, the hands turned palm-down, and their long, curved claws formed effective grasping weapons. Each hind limb ended in a foot with two weight-bearing toes, and another toe armed with a big, hinged "sickle" or "terrible" claw—the killing toe.

Naris

Jaw adductor muscle

Saw-edged tooth

Cervical vertebra

Cervical rib

Coracoid

Scapula

Rib

Dorsal vertebra

Transverse process

Chevron

Ilium

Hip joint

Femur

Knee joint

Pubis

Ischium

Tibia

Ankle joint

Metatarsal

Infratemporal fenestra

Shoulder joint

Humerus

Claw

Radius

Elbow joint

Ulna

Fibula

Orbit

Antorbital fenestra

Mandible

Tooth

Wrist joint

Metacarpal

Claw

Phalanx

Sickle claw

Phalanx

FOOT BONES

Deinonychus's foot had a long, swiveling second toe-claw, known as the "terrible claw," and typical of dromaeosaurids, the theropod family to which *Deinonychus* belonged. *Deinonychus* could menacingly raise each foot's second toe while supporting itself on the long third and fourth toes.

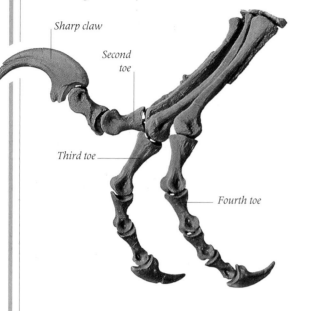

Sharp claw

Second toe

Third toe

Fourth toe

Eye faced chiefly sideways

Powerful, sturdy neck

Shoulder

Scaly skin

Powerful jaws capable of opening wide

Hand turned palm-down

Elbow

Hand with claws capable of grasping

"Terrible claw"

Toe

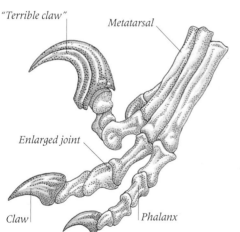

"Terrible claw"

Metatarsal

Enlarged joint

Claw

Phalanx

LIKE A BIRD

Deinonychus could run, swerve, and keep its balance as skillfully as a big, flightless bird. In fact, this fierce predator was built much like a bird, even having a somewhat backward-angled pubis. But unlike such birdlike theropods as *Troodon*, *Deinonychus* differed from birds in having a full-length third metatarsus (upper foot bone).

SWIVELING TOE-CLAW

Deinonychus probably retracted its long second toe (above) mainly to avoid blunting the sharp claw tip by scraping it on the ground when walking or running; big heels on the phalanges (toe bones) improved the leverage exerted by toe-retracting muscles. An attacking *Deinonychus* swung the toe down and forward in a slashing arc (right), delivering stabbing blows. For its body size, its swiveling claws were unusually large, like the immense canines of an extinct saber-toothed cat.

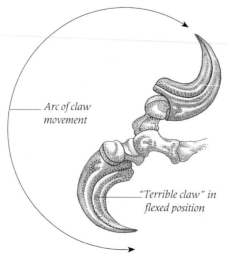

Arc of claw movement

"Terrible claw" in flexed position

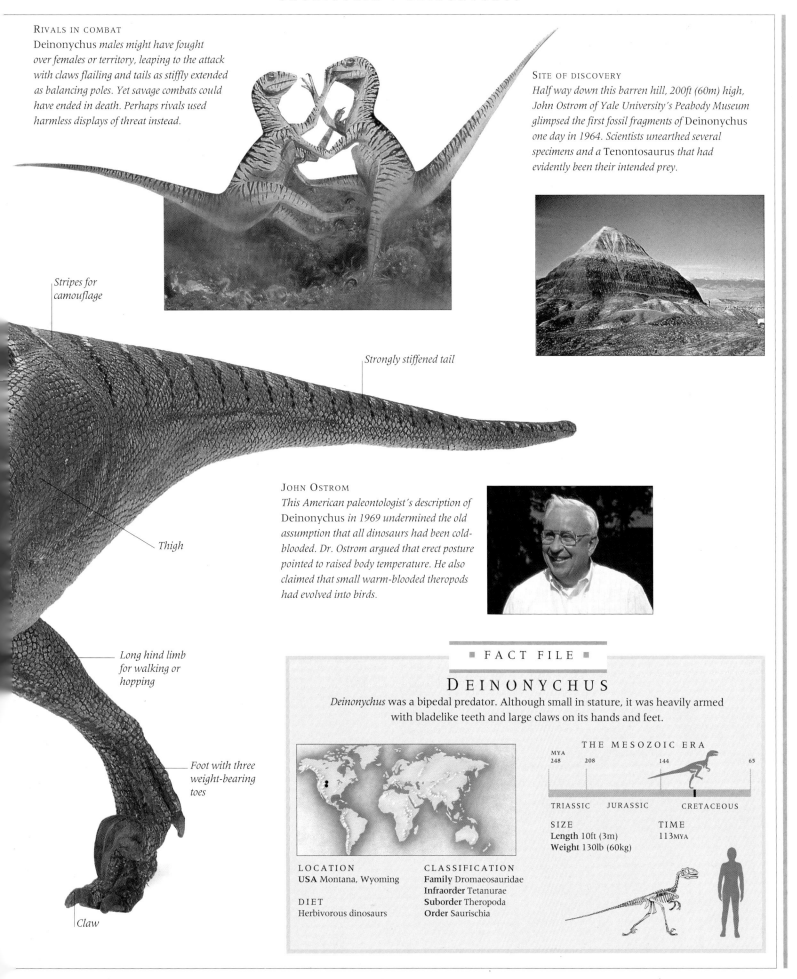

RIVALS IN COMBAT

Deinonychus *males might have fought over females or territory, leaping to the attack with claws flailing and tails as stiffly extended as balancing poles. Yet savage combats could have ended in death. Perhaps rivals used harmless displays of threat instead.*

SITE OF DISCOVERY

Half way down this barren hill, 200ft (60m) high, John Ostrom of Yale University's Peabody Museum glimpsed the first fossil fragments of Deinonychus *one day in 1964. Scientists unearthed several specimens and a* Tenontosaurus *that had evidently been their intended prey.*

Stripes for camouflage

Strongly stiffened tail

Thigh

JOHN OSTROM

This American paleontologist's description of Deinonychus *in 1969 undermined the old assumption that all dinosaurs had been cold-blooded. Dr. Ostrom argued that erect posture pointed to raised body temperature. He also claimed that small warm-blooded theropods had evolved into birds.*

Long hind limb for walking or hopping

Foot with three weight-bearing toes

Claw

■ FACT FILE ■

DEINONYCHUS

Deinonychus was a bipedal predator. Although small in stature, it was heavily armed with bladelike teeth and large claws on its hands and feet.

THE MESOZOIC ERA

MYA 248	208	144	65
TRIASSIC	JURASSIC		CRETACEOUS

SIZE
Length 10ft (3m)
Weight 130lb (60kg)

TIME
113 MYA

LOCATION
USA Montana, Wyoming

DIET
Herbivorous dinosaurs

CLASSIFICATION
Family Dromaeosauridae
Infraorder Tetanurae
Suborder Theropoda
Order Saurischia

ARCHAEOPTERYX

L ONG FAMOUS as the first known bird, the 150 million-year-old *Archaeopteryx* ("ancient wing") is also sometimes called a feathered dinosaur because its hands, hips, legs, and skull were very like those of small theropods. *Archaeopteryx* had long, slim jaws that bristled with sharp teeth; clawed, grasping fingers that sprouted from its wings; and a long tail with a bony core. Like both birds and theropods, *Archaeopteryx* had three long, forward-pointing toes and a backward-angled hallux (first toe). Scientific research suggests that *Archaeopteryx* evolved from a small predatory dinosaur and possibly gave rise to modern birds.

▪ LIFE AND BEHAVIOR ▪

A comparison between the bones of *Archaeopteryx* and those of modern flying birds suggests that it was less capable of powerful, flapping flight than, for example, the pigeon. Scientists once thought that *Archaeopteryx* took off by running and then leaping off the ground, vigorously flapping its wings. This theory has been weakened to some extent by the observation that *Archaeopteryx* lacked the well-developed supracoracoideus muscles of birds that take off from level ground. It is more probable that *Archaeopteryx* hauled itself up treetrunks by its finger claws and then launched itself out on short, brief, fluttering flights. Low, scrubby conifers were the tallest trees in *Archaeopteryx*'s habitat, on the semidesert islands in what is now Germany. It has been suggested that *Archaeopteryx* might have swum and fished in the islands' offshore lagoons. However, it is more likely that it patrolled the muddy beaches, scavenging the flesh of stranded fish, king crabs, ammonites, and worms, or snapping up the moths, flies, and dragonflies blown down to the coast by winds heading out to sea. Some early birds were very likely blown into the sea, where they drowned.

ARBOREAL MODEL
Archaeopteryx *appears perched in a tree.*

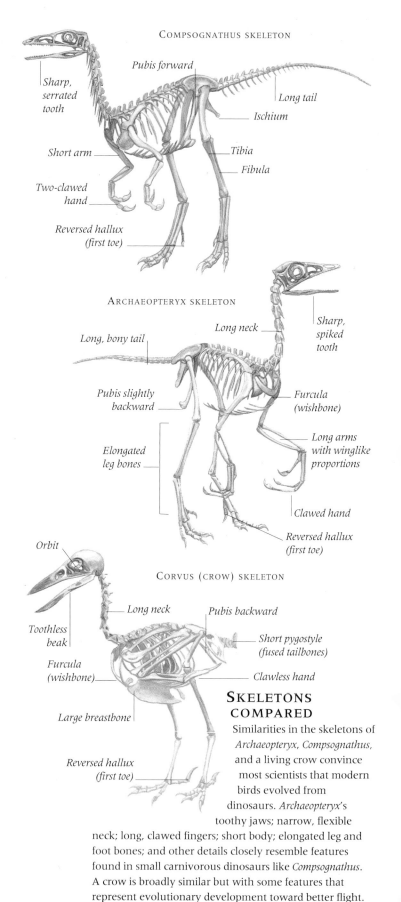

COMPSOGNATHUS SKELETON

Sharp, serrated tooth

Pubis forward

Long tail

Ischium

Short arm

Tibia

Fibula

Two-clawed hand

Reversed hallux (first toe)

ARCHAEOPTERYX SKELETON

Long, bony tail

Long neck

Sharp, spiked tooth

Pubis slightly backward

Furcula (wishbone)

Elongated leg bones

Long arms with winglike proportions

Clawed hand

Reversed hallux (first toe)

Orbit

CORVUS (CROW) SKELETON

Long neck

Pubis backward

Toothless beak

Short pygostyle (fused tailbones)

Furcula (wishbone)

Clawless hand

Large breastbone

SKELETONS COMPARED

Similarities in the skeletons of *Archaeopteryx*, *Compsognathus*, and a living crow convince most scientists that modern birds evolved from dinosaurs. *Archaeopteryx*'s toothy jaws; narrow, flexible neck; long, clawed fingers; short body; elongated leg and foot bones; and other details closely resemble features found in small carnivorous dinosaurs like *Compsognathus*. A crow is broadly similar but with some features that represent evolutionary development toward better flight.

Reversed hallux (first toe)

FEATHER IMPRESSIONS

Feather impressions plainly show up in a slab of limestone containing a fossil *Archaeopteryx*. Only very fine-grained rock preserves traces of such fragile things as feathers. This rock comes from a Bavarian quarry.

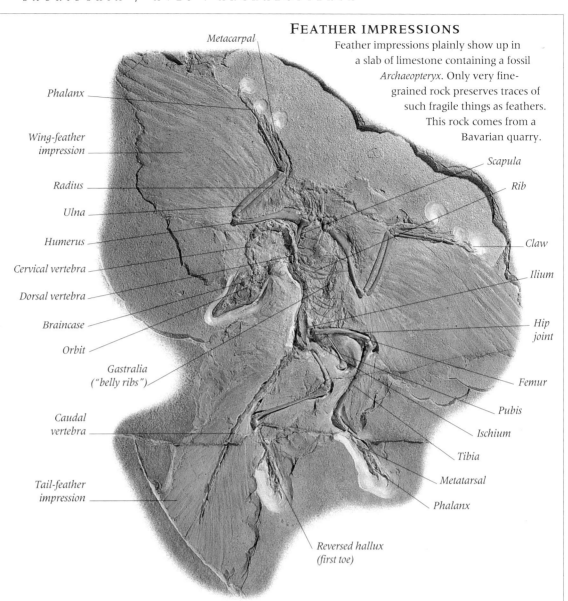

Metacarpal

Phalanx

Wing-feather impression

Radius

Ulna

Humerus

Cervical vertebra

Dorsal vertebra

Braincase

Orbit

Gastralia ("belly ribs")

Caudal vertebra

Tail-feather impression

Scapula

Rib

Claw

Ilium

Hip joint

Femur

Pubis

Ischium

Tibia

Metatarsal

Phalanx

Reversed hallux (first toe)

MOUNTED SKELETON

A mounted museum skeleton depicts an *Archaeopteryx* on the ground. Like a young Hoatzin (a living bird), it might have used its clawed fingers to climb low trees.

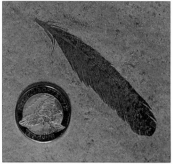

FOSSILIZED FEATHER

This fossil feather belonged to *Archaeopteryx*. Its asymmetric primary wing feathers match those of pigeons and prove that *Archaeopteryx* could fly or glide.

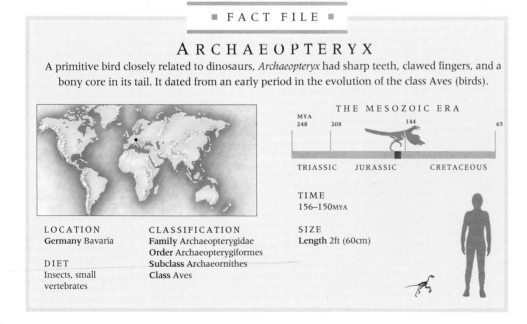

■ FACT FILE ■

ARCHAEOPTERYX

A primitive bird closely related to dinosaurs, *Archaeopteryx* had sharp teeth, clawed fingers, and a bony core in its tail. It dated from an early period in the evolution of the class Aves (birds).

THE MESOZOIC ERA

MYA
248   208   144   65

TRIASSIC   JURASSIC   CRETACEOUS

TIME
156–150MYA

SIZE
Length 2ft (60cm)

LOCATION
Germany Bavaria

DIET
Insects, small vertebrates

CLASSIFICATION
Family Archaeopterygidae
Order Archaeopterygiformes
Subclass Archaeornithes
Class Aves

TAKING OFF

Archaeopteryx spreads its wings in preparation for flight.

AVIMIMUS

T HE ONLY KNOWN member of its family, "bird mimic" seems to have been a birdlike, running dinosaur—a lightweight, long-legged creature, with a short, deep head, toothless beak, long, curved neck, well-developed tail, and short forelimbs. No fossil feathers have been found, but the rough ridge on one forearm bone resembles a modern bird's attachment for flight feathers, and the fused bases of the upper hand bones suggest a forelimb ending in a birdlike carpometacarpus. The Russian scientist who described *Avimimus* thought it could even fold its "wings" like a bird.

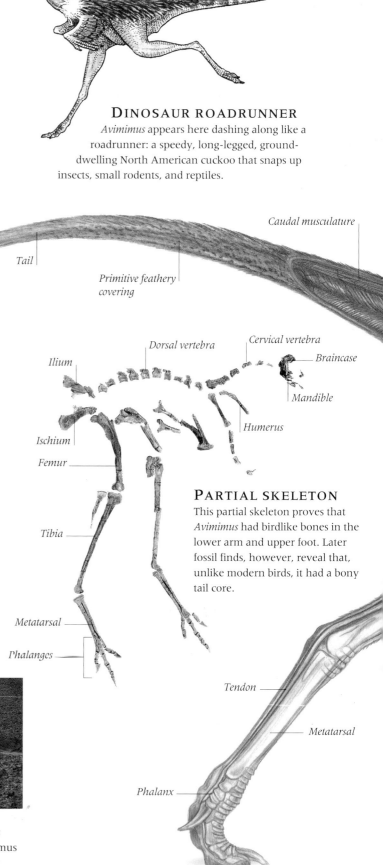

DINOSAUR ROADRUNNER

Avimimus appears here dashing along like a roadrunner: a speedy, long-legged, ground-dwelling North American cuckoo that snaps up insects, small rodents, and reptiles.

Tail | *Caudal musculature*

Primitive feathery covering

Dorsal vertebra | *Cervical vertebra*

Ilium | *Braincase*

Mandible

Ischium | *Humerus*

Femur

PARTIAL SKELETON

This partial skeleton proves that *Avimimus* had birdlike bones in the lower arm and upper foot. Later fossil finds, however, reveal that, unlike modern birds, it had a bony tail core.

Tibia

Metatarsal

Phalanges

Tendon

Metatarsal

Phalanx

※ LIFE AND BEHAVIOR ※

Scientists believe that *Avimimus* shared open plains with harmless dinosaurs, such as the ornithomimid *Gallimimus* and the sauropod *Quaesitosaurus*, as well as with dangerous enemies related to *Deinonychus*. It is likely that *Avimimus* sprinted on its long legs after small animals, darting its head down to seize them in its beak. The beak's partly ridged rim would have gripped wriggling prey too firmly for it to escape. An alternative idea is that *Avimimus* was a herbivore that used its beak for biting off and eating plants. The creature's forelimbs were probably too short to serve as a wing. If feathered, they may have served simply to keep the body warm, although another theory suggests that *Avimimus* might have used them for trapping flying insects. One scientist, however, believes that details of its skull and arm bones imply that *Avimimus* could take off and fly short distances. If so, "bird mimic" represents a line of flying dinosaurs quite separate from birds. However, most scientists discount this possibility. Some, though, do suspect that many small theropods had a covering of feathers that have left no fossil traces. (Feather impressions survive only in extremely fine-grained rocks, like the limestone that bears the imprints of *Archaeopteryx*'s wings and tail.)

SERGEI KURZANOV
Russian paleontologist Sergei Kurzanov named Avimimus *and the Avimimidae in 1981.*

WHERE AVIMIMUS LIVED
Workers rest on a dinosaur hunt in Mongolia's Gobi Desert, where Avimimus *fossils were discovered.*

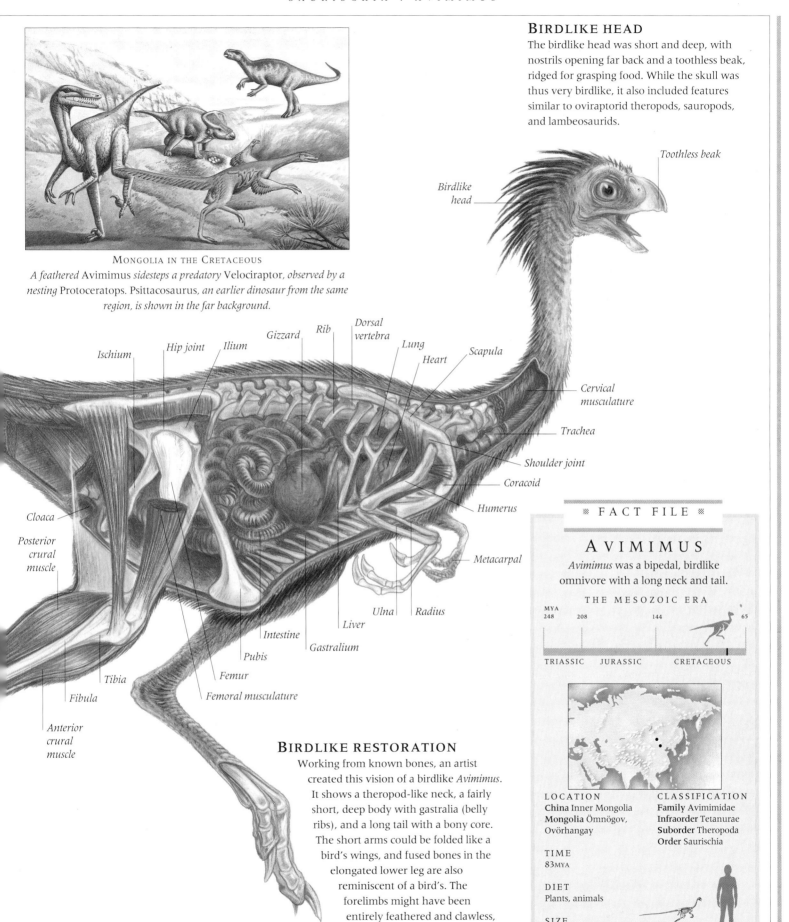

BIRDLIKE HEAD

The birdlike head was short and deep, with nostrils opening far back and a toothless beak, ridged for grasping food. While the skull was thus very birdlike, it also included features similar to oviraptorid theropods, sauropods, and lambeosaurids.

Toothless beak

Birdlike head

MONGOLIA IN THE CRETACEOUS

A feathered Avimimus *sidesteps a predatory* Velociraptor, *observed by a nesting* Protoceratops. Psittacosaurus, *an earlier dinosaur from the same region, is shown in the far background.*

Ischium

Hip joint

Ilium

Gizzard

Rib

Dorsal vertebra

Lung

Heart

Scapula

Cervical musculature

Trachea

Shoulder joint

Coracoid

Humerus

Metacarpal

Cloaca

Posterior crural muscle

Ulna

Radius

Liver

Intestine

Gastralium

Pubis

Tibia

Femur

Femoral musculature

Fibula

Anterior crural muscle

BIRDLIKE RESTORATION

Working from known bones, an artist created this vision of a birdlike *Avimimus*. It shows a theropod-like neck, a fairly short, deep body with gastralia (belly ribs), and a long tail with a bony core. The short arms could be folded like a bird's wings, and fused bones in the elongated lower leg are also reminiscent of a bird's. The forelimbs might have been entirely feathered and clawless, but the evidence for feathered wings and body is only indirect.

❋ FACT FILE ❋

AVIMIMUS

Avimimus was a bipedal, birdlike omnivore with a long neck and tail.

THE MESOZOIC ERA

MYA 248	208	144	65
TRIASSIC	JURASSIC	CRETACEOUS	

LOCATION
China Inner Mongolia
Mongolia Ömnögov, Ovörhangay

TIME
83MYA

DIET
Plants, animals

SIZE
Length 5ft (1.5m)

CLASSIFICATION
Family Avimimidae
Infraorder Tetanurae
Suborder Theropoda
Order Saurischia

ORNITHOLESTES

A WHIPLIKE TAIL comprised more than half of *Ornitholestes*'s length. Large individuals probably grew as long as a tall human, yet weighed no more than a medium-size dog. *Ornitholestes* had a stronger, deeper skull than two other well-known small theropods, *Compsognathus* and *Coelophysis*. Each hand appears to have borne a short, sharp-clawed thumb, and two, long, clawed fingers. Sharp teeth rimmed only the front half of the jaws. Some scientists believe *Ornitholestes* had a nasal crest. Possibly 16 other small theropods might belong with *Ornitholestes* in the family Coeluridae.

▪ LIFE AND BEHAVIOR ▪

The scientist who named *Ornitholestes* ("bird robber") imagined the speedy theropod killing and eating the crow-size early bird *Archaeopteryx*. Both these creatures lived at about the same time, but it is not known whether or not they lived in the same area. *Ornitholestes* might well have attacked other early birds, birdlike dinosaurs, and pterosaurs. More often, it probably ate lizards and other small creatures, such as lizardlike sphenodontians, large insects, dinosaur hatchlings, and small mammals. It searched them out as it sprinted through the fern meadows and riverside forests of Late Jurassic Wyoming. Grasping captured prey firmly between its sharp thumb- and finger-claws, *Ornitholestes* brought its victims to its jaws, where it either bit them to death or swallowed them alive. Although apparently quick and agile, *Ornitholestes* had relatively short legs, with thighs longer than the shins—a feature not usually found in fast-running dinosaurs. *Ornitholestes* seems to have been a more strongly built hunter than *Coelophysis*, its much earlier North American equivalent. If *Ornitholestes* hunted in predatory packs, it might have dared take on ornithopods as big as a half-grown *Camptosaurus*. Like jackals at a lion's kill, nimble *Ornitholestes* also might have stolen mouthfuls of flesh from the carcass of a dead sauropod. One after another, agile *Ornitholestes* could have nipped quickly in and out of the huge corpse's body cavity under the noses of its killers, a troop of *Allosaurus*, or other large flesh-eaters. These big, heavy dinosaurs, sated with flesh, would have been too slow to stop such small, maneuverable scavengers.

Whiplike tail

FOSSIL-HUNTERS
American Museum of Natural History Director Henry Fairfield Osborn and other fossil hunters posed for this photograph in 1899. At Bone Cabin Quarry, Wyoming in 1900, they found what are still the only known Ornitholestes *skull and jaws. Osborn formally named and described* Ornitholestes *in 1903.*

OLD RESTORATION

NEW RESTORATION

OLD AND NEW RESTORATIONS

Most old restorations of *Ornitholestes* show it in a somewhat sluggish pose, dragging its tail on the ground like a lizard, as in the top view above. The lower view shows today's concept of this dinosaur as a dynamic predator, with an S-shaped neck and its long tail held off the ground to balance its level-backed body. This restoration is shown with the much-disputed nasal crest.

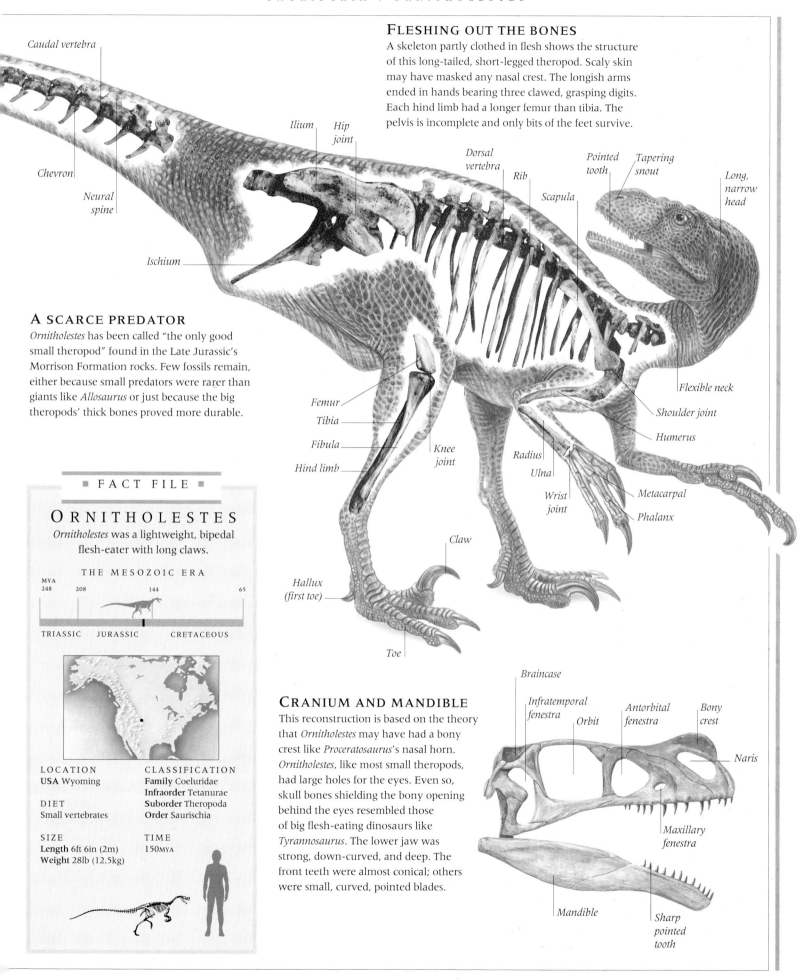

Caudal vertebra

Chevron

Neural
spine

Ilium

Hip
joint

Ischium

FLESHING OUT THE BONES

A skeleton partly clothed in flesh shows the structure
of this long-tailed, short-legged theropod. Scaly skin
may have masked any nasal crest. The longish arms
ended in hands bearing three clawed, grasping digits.
Each hind limb had a longer femur than tibia. The
pelvis is incomplete and only bits of the feet survive.

Dorsal
vertebra

Rib

Scapula

Pointed
tooth

Tapering
snout

Long,
narrow
head

Flexible neck

Shoulder joint

Humerus

A SCARCE PREDATOR

Ornitholestes has been called "the only good
small theropod" found in the Late Jurassic's
Morrison Formation rocks. Few fossils remain,
either because small predators were rarer than
giants like *Allosaurus* or just because the big
theropods' thick bones proved more durable.

Femur

Tibia

Fibula

Hind limb

Knee
joint

Radius

Ulna

Wrist
joint

Metacarpal

Phalanx

Claw

Hallux
(first toe)

Toe

■ FACT FILE ■

ORNITHOLESTES

Ornitholestes was a lightweight, bipedal
flesh-eater with long claws.

THE MESOZOIC ERA

MYA 248	208	144	65

TRIASSIC   JURASSIC   CRETACEOUS

LOCATION
USA Wyoming

DIET
Small vertebrates

SIZE
Length 6ft 6in (2m)
Weight 28lb (12.5kg)

CLASSIFICATION
Family Coeluridae
Infraorder Tetanurae
Suborder Theropoda
Order Saurischia

TIME
150MYA

CRANIUM AND MANDIBLE

This reconstruction is based on the theory
that *Ornitholestes* may have had a bony
crest like *Proceratosaurus*'s nasal horn.
Ornitholestes, like most small theropods,
had large holes for the eyes. Even so,
skull bones shielding the bony opening
behind the eyes resembled those
of big flesh-eating dinosaurs like
Tyrannosaurus. The lower jaw was
strong, down-curved, and deep. The
front teeth were almost conical; others
were small, curved, pointed blades.

Braincase

Infratemporal
fenestra

Orbit

Antorbital
fenestra

Bony
crest

Naris

Maxillary
fenestra

Mandible

Sharp
pointed
tooth

COMPSOGNATHUS

T HE AGILE little predator *Compsognathus* ("elegant jaw") was one of the smallest known dinosaurs. *Compsognathus* was delicately built and birdlike, with a narrow, pointed head, jaws armed with small, sharp teeth, a flexible neck, a compact body, and a relatively long tail. The legs were long and birdlike. Surprisingly, the short arms evidently bore two-fingered hands, like those of the huge tyrannosaurids of much later times. The sharp-toothed jaws and clawed phalanges are typical theropod features, but the short, two-fingered forelimbs and other details place *Compsognathus* in a family of its own.

■ LIFE AND BEHAVIOR ■

Compsognathus lived on the same semidesert islands (an archipelago now forming part of Europe) as the first known bird, *Archaeopteryx*. The skeletons of the two creatures are so similar that scientists mistook several *Archaeopteryx* fossils for those of *Compsognathus* before they noticed faint feather impressions in the rock that held the fossil bones of *Archaeopteryx*. Only two fossil specimens of *Compsognathus* are known: one from southern Germany is roughly the size of a chicken, and is seemingly half-grown, and the other, about the size of a turkey, from southeast France, has the fully formed bones of an adult. Despite its small size, *Compsognathus* might have been the largest carnivorous land animal on its archipelago. These semidesert islands would not have had sufficient vegetation to nourish the number of big plant-eaters that larger carnivores would have needed as a meat supply. We can imagine *Compsognathus* stalking through the undergrowth, its keen eyes quick to catch the slightest movement of large insects, lizards, or mouselike mammals. It could have outrun lizards and might have chased a young *Archaeopteryx* if it surprised one on the ground. In the morning, basking lizards still sluggish after cooling down at night would have been easy prey. *Compsognathus* probably bit large victims while gripping them with its hands; the claws were not sickle-shaped weapons for inflicting wounds. Smaller creatures would have been swallowed whole.

AGILE HUNTER
One of the tiniest of all predatory dinosaurs, Compsognathus *used its speed to catch small vertebrates.*

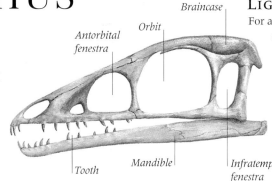

LIGHTWEIGHT SKULL
For a small theropod, the skull of *Compsognathus* was large but low. It tapered to the snout and was lightly built, with huge openings, especially the orbits (eye sockets). The mandible (lower jaw) was slender, and the teeth were sharp, curved, and far apart.

Braincase
Orbit
Antorbital fenestra
Tooth
Mandible
Infratemporal fenestra

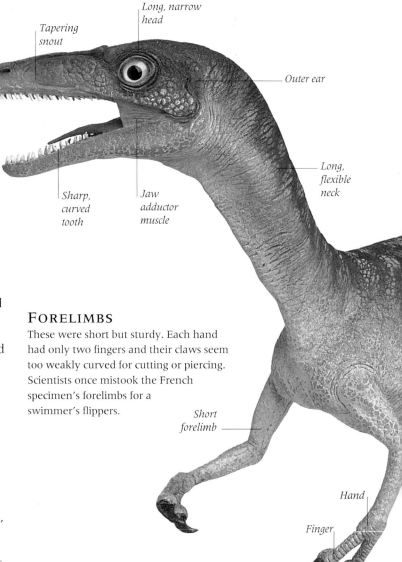

Long, narrow head
Tapering snout
Outer ear
Sharp, curved tooth
Jaw adductor muscle
Long, flexible neck

FORELIMBS
These were short but sturdy. Each hand had only two fingers and their claws seem too weakly curved for cutting or piercing. Scientists once mistook the French specimen's forelimbs for a swimmer's flippers.

Short forelimb
Hand
Finger
Claw

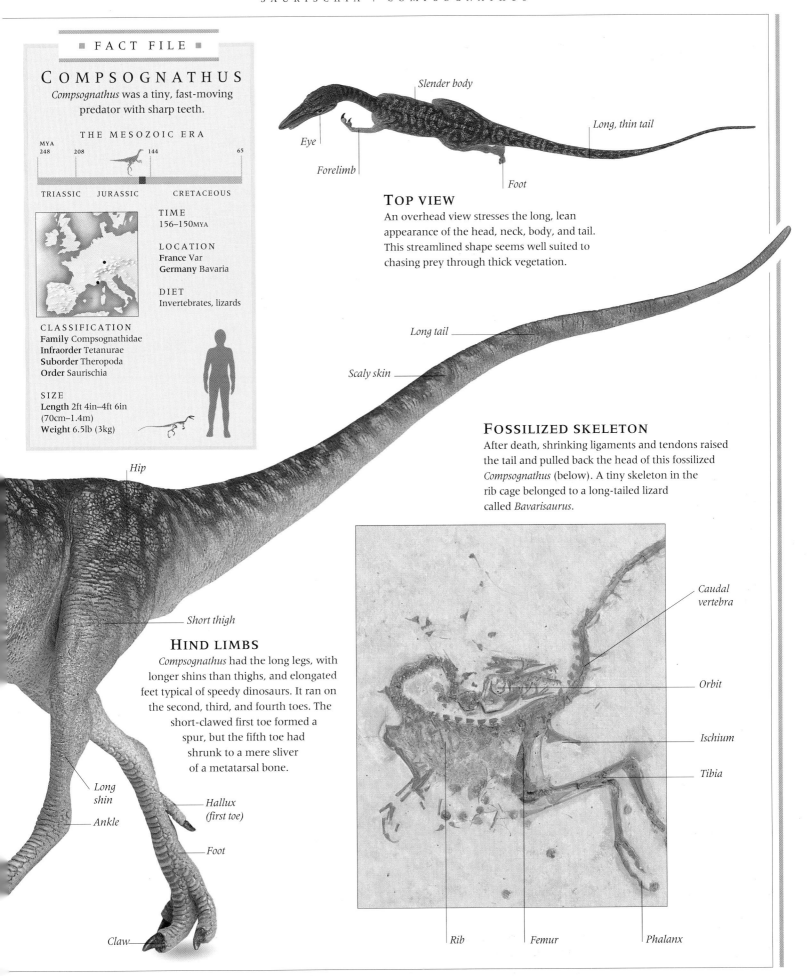

COMPSOGNATHUS

Compsognathus was a tiny, fast-moving predator with sharp teeth.

THE MESOZOIC ERA

MYA 248	208	144	65
TRIASSIC	JURASSIC	CRETACEOUS	

TIME
156–150MYA

LOCATION
France Var
Germany Bavaria

DIET
Invertebrates, lizards

CLASSIFICATION
Family Compsognathidae
Infraorder Tetanurae
Suborder Theropoda
Order Saurischia

SIZE
Length 2ft 4in–4ft 6in
(70cm–1.4m)
Weight 6.5lb (3kg)

Slender body

Eye

Forelimb

Foot

Long, thin tail

TOP VIEW

An overhead view stresses the long, lean appearance of the head, neck, body, and tail. This streamlined shape seems well suited to chasing prey through thick vegetation.

Long tail

Scaly skin

FOSSILIZED SKELETON

After death, shrinking ligaments and tendons raised the tail and pulled back the head of this fossilized *Compsognathus* (below). A tiny skeleton in the rib cage belonged to a long-tailed lizard called *Bavarisaurus*.

Hip

Short thigh

HIND LIMBS

Compsognathus had the long legs, with longer shins than thighs, and elongated feet typical of speedy dinosaurs. It ran on the second, third, and fourth toes. The short-clawed first toe formed a spur, but the fifth toe had shrunk to a mere sliver of a metatarsal bone.

Long shin

Ankle

Hallux (first toe)

Foot

Caudal vertebra

Orbit

Ischium

Tibia

Claw

Rib

Femur

Phalanx

81

SAUROPODOMORPHS

T HE SAURISCHIAN suborder Sauropodomorpha ("lizard-feet forms") comprised small to immense, bipedal to quadrupedal herbivores with small heads, long necks, bulky bodies, and long tails. There were two infraorders. Prosauropods evolved from beasts no larger than a human and gave way to sauropods, which included the heaviest and longest land animals ever. Long necks allowed sauropodomorphs to browse both high up and low down on tree leaves and ferns. These dinosaurs often moved in herds. They were the most abundant large, plant-eating dinosaurs from Late Triassic to Late Jurassic times, and to long afterward in southern continents. *Segnosaurus*, also included in this section, was a member of a puzzling group from Late Cretaceous Asia. Despite some prosauropod-like features, the segnosaurs might have been therizinosaurid theropods.

PLATEOSAURUS
This sauropodomorph had a typical prosauropod's relatively small head, bulky body, long neck and tail, and extremely large, sharp, curved thumb-claws.

HOLLOWED VERTEBRAE
Cavities in Diplodocus's cervical (neck) vertebrae reduced weight without sacrificing strength. Various advanced dinosaurs evolved this engineering stratagem.

❈ PROSAUROPODA ❈

This early infraorder included seven families of small to large, bipedal and quadrupedal dinosaurs with big, curved thumb-claws. Some were the first large, high-browsing land animals. The last died out in Early Jurassic times.
THECODONTOSAURIDAE were small, primitive, and bipedal. They lived in Late Triassic Europe and perhaps Africa.
ANCHISAURIDAE contained *Anchisaurus*, a bipedal/quadrupedal beast, 8ft (2.4m) long, from Early Jurassic North America and maybe Africa and China.
MASSOSPONDYLIDAE included a 16ft 6in (5m) dinosaur, *Massospondylus*, whose lower jaw may have ended in a beak. It lived in Early Jurassic southern Africa and North America.
YUNNANOSAURIDAE held one genus, *Yunnanosaurus*, from Early Jurassic China. It was 23ft (7m) long, with spoon-shaped teeth.

PLATEOSAURIDAE included more than half a dozen genera up to 26ft (8m) long. They lived worldwide during the Late Triassic and the Early Jurassic.
MELANOROSAURIDAE contained the first very large dinosaurs, up to 39ft (12m) long. They lived during the Late Triassic and the Early Jurassic in South America, Africa, Europe, and Asia.
BLIKANASAURIDAE held *Blikanasaurus*. This had stocky hind limbs, grew 16ft 6in (5m) long, and lived in Late Triassic southern Africa.

❈ SAUROPODA ❈

This infraorder contained about eight families of very large to immense, plant-eating quadrupeds weighing up to 49 tons or more. Many had hollowed vertebrae to reduce weight. By the Middle Jurassic, sauropods had replaced prosauropods and spread worldwide. They persisted into Late Cretaceous times. Various family relationships remain unclear.
VULCANODONTIDAE, the most primitive sauropod family, included Early Jurassic genera up to 29ft 6in (9m) long, from Africa, Europe, and Asia.
BARAPASAURIDAE were the family of *Barapasaurus*, which had distinctive vertebrae, reached 60ft (18m), and lived in Early Jurassic India.
CETIOSAURIDAE included about 15 "old-fashioned" genera up to 59ft (18m) long, with blunt heads and relatively short necks. They lived worldwide from Early Jurassic to Middle Cretaceous times.

THREE GIANT SAUROPODS
These sauropods (left) were among the largest-ever land animals. The brachiosaurid Brachiosaurus (center) attained 82ft (25m). The diplodocids Supersaurus (far left) and Seismosaurus respectively grew to 98ft (30m) and 130ft (40m).

DIPLODOCUS SKULL

CAMARASAURUS SKULL

TWO SAUROPOD SKULLS

Diplodocus's low skull and peg-like teeth contrast with Camarasaurus's deep skull and strong, spoon-shaped teeth. Variations in sauropod skull and tooth design may reflect different kinds of diet.

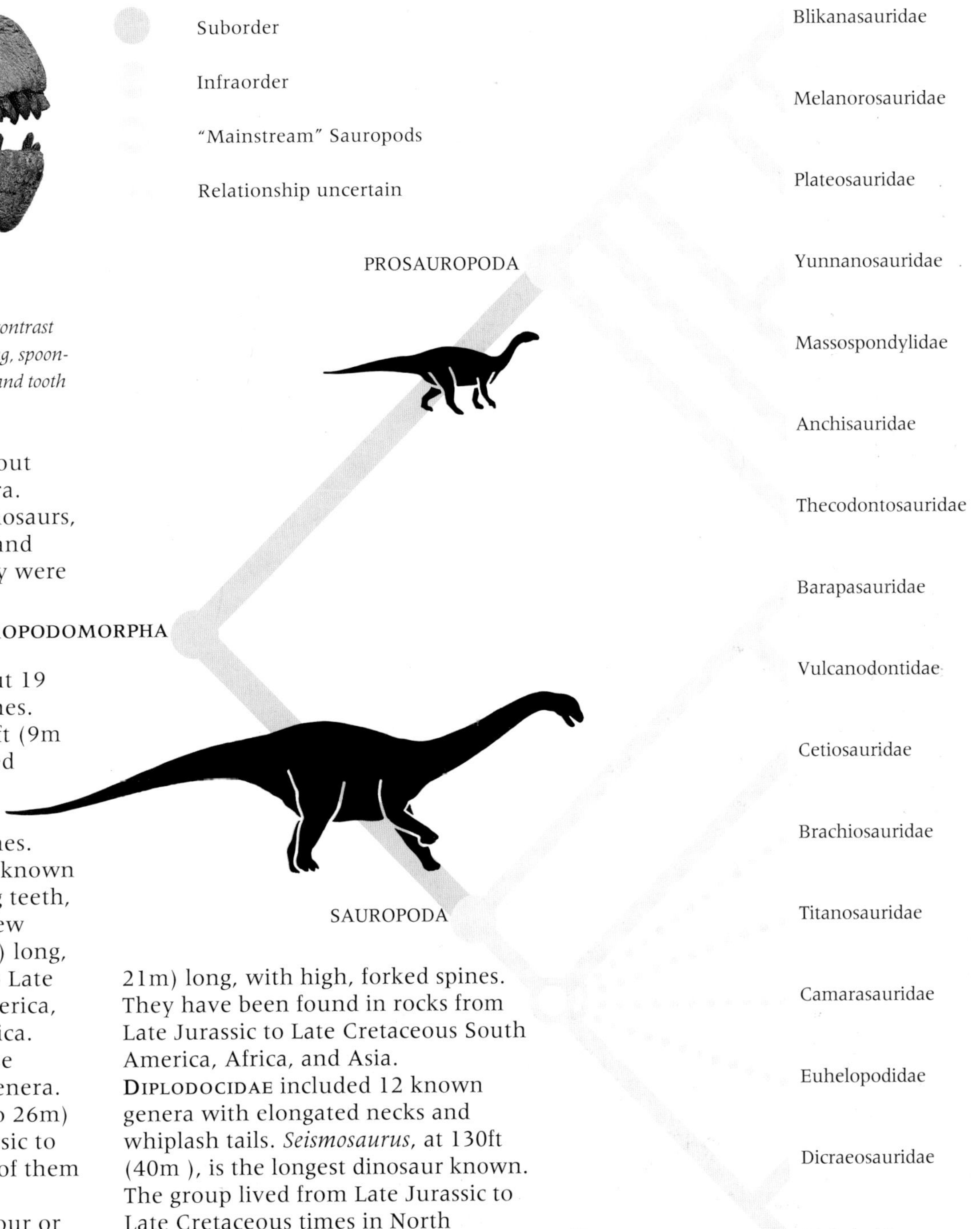

BRACHIOSAURIDAE included about 12 immense, giraffe-like genera. Among the largest, heaviest dinosaurs, they grew to 82ft (25m) long and weighed 49 tons or more. They were widespread from Middle/Late Jurassic to Early Cretaceous times.

TITANOSAURIDAE included about 19 genera with distinctive tail bones. They grew from 29ft 6in to 69ft (9m to 21m) long or more, and lived mostly in the southern continents from Late Jurassic to Late Cretaceous times.

CAMARASAURIDAE included six known genera with deep skulls, strong teeth, and hollow vertebrae. They grew from 39ft to 59ft (12m to 18m) long, and lived from Late Jurassic to Late Cretaceous times in North America, Europe, Asia, and perhaps Africa.

EUHELOPODIDAE were a Chinese family of about half a dozen genera. They were 33ft to 85ft (10m to 26m) long and lived from Late Jurassic to Early Cretaceous times. Some of them had extremely long necks.

DICRAEOSAURIDAE contained four or five genera 29ft 6in to 69ft (9m to

FAMILY TREE

This diagram shows possible relationships among sauropodomorph families (the names ending in -idae), each containing one genus or several genera. Connections between some families are unclear, and some scientists even suspect that sauropods and prosauropods did not share the same ancestor. If this is so, the Sauropodomorpha is an artificial grouping.

KEY

Suborder

Infraorder

"Mainstream" Sauropods

Relationship uncertain

PROSAUROPODA

SAUROPODOMORPHA

SAUROPODA

21m) long, with high, forked spines. They have been found in rocks from Late Jurassic to Late Cretaceous South America, Africa, and Asia.

DIPLODOCIDAE included 12 known genera with elongated necks and whiplash tails. *Seismosaurus*, at 130ft (40m), is the longest dinosaur known. The group lived from Late Jurassic to Late Cretaceous times in North America, Africa, Europe, and Asia.

DIPLODOCUS HIP BONES

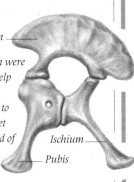

The ilium, pubis, and ischium were extremely strong in order to help support Diplodocus. Ilium, pubis, and ischium combined to frame the acetabulum, a socket that held the ball-shaped head of the femur, transmitting its load to one hind limb.

Ilium

Ischium

Pubis

Blikanasauridae

Melanorosauridae

Plateosauridae

Yunnanosauridae

Massospondylidae

Anchisauridae

Thecodontosauridae

Barapasauridae

Vulcanodontidae

Cetiosauridae

Brachiosauridae

Titanosauridae

Camarasauridae

Euhelopodidae

Dicraeosauridae

Diplodocidae

ANCHISAURUS

P ERHAPS THE FIRST dinosaur to be discovered in North America, *Anchisaurus* was somewhat longer than a human's height. It was among the smallest and most primitive of all prosauropods—plant-eating cousins of the mighty sauropods. The head was slight in comparison with the lengthy neck, back, and tail, and the capacious belly. "Near lizard" bore its weight on all fours, although its legs were far longer and more powerful than its arms. Like the bipedal *Thecodontosaurus,* it had slender, four-toed feet and five-fingered hands, armed with sickle-shaped thumb-claws.

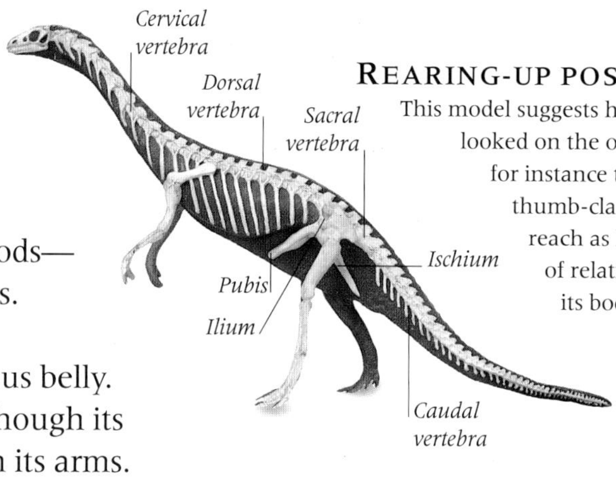

Cervical vertebra

Dorsal vertebra

Sacral vertebra

Pubis

Ilium

Ischium

Caudal vertebra

REARING-UP POSE

This model suggests how *Anchisaurus* may have looked on the occasions when it reared up, for instance to feed, possibly using its large thumb-claw to grasp branches. It could reach as high as the twigs and foliage of relatively small trees, supporting its body on the hind limbs and tail.

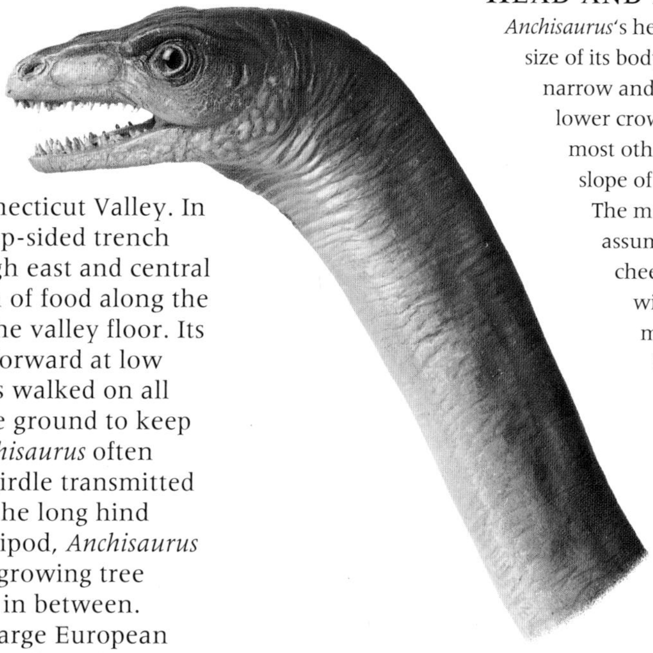

▪ LIFE AND BEHAVIOR ▪

Anchisaurus lived in what is now the Connecticut Valley. In Early Jurassic times this was a warm, steep-sided trench like the Great Rift Valley that runs through east and central Africa today. *Anchisaurus* moved in search of food along the shores of lakes that filled depressions in the valley floor. Its front-heavy body made it tend to topple forward at low speeds, so perhaps it stood and sometimes walked on all fours, holding its two thumb-claws off the ground to keep them from getting injured. However, *Anchisaurus* often reared up to feed. Then its powerful hip girdle transmitted the weight of the forepart of the body to the long hind limbs and tail. Supported by this sturdy tripod, *Anchisaurus* craned its neck to reach and snip off low-growing tree leaves with its saw-edged teeth with gaps in between. Although *Anchisaurus* lived later than its large European relative *Plateosaurus*, its teeth and jaws were less effective than that animal's, so *Anchisaurus* probably ate relatively softer plants. In dry weather, *Anchisaurus* and other creatures walked across the wet mud left behind by shrinking lakes. As the mud dried and began to harden into rock, the tracks of all these animals were preserved as fossils. From these and other fossil evidence, we know that *Anchisaurus* shared eastern North America with harmless early ornithischians and predatory theropods. If a plodding *Anchisaurus* saw a large theropod approaching, it could have risen and hurried off on its hind limbs. If taken by surprise, the best the otherwise comparatively defenseless creature could have done was to stand at bay and strike out with its sickle claws.

HEAD AND NECK

Anchisaurus's head was surprisingly small for the size of its body. The head was long and narrow and the skull relatively flat, with a lower crown than that of *Plateosaurus* and most other prosauropods. In addition, the slope of the forehead was more gradual. The model shown here is based on the assumption that *Anchisaurus* had no cheeks. This might be consistent with a mode of feeding based mainly on snatching and gulping, but anatomical evidence suggests prosauropods had cheeks.

CHEEKS

This artist's restoration (left) shows how prosauropods would have looked if they had possessed cheeks, which would have helped to retain food for chewing.

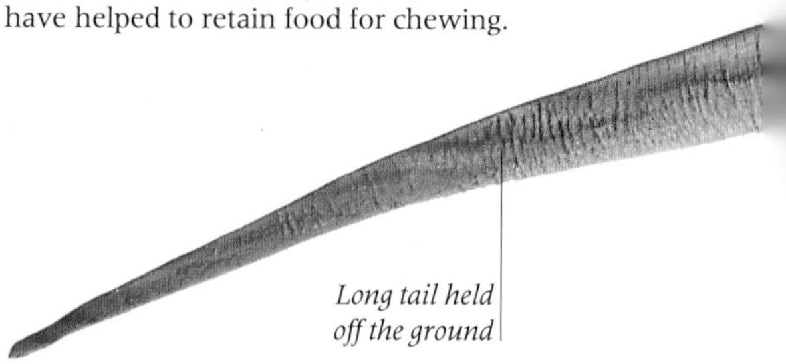

Long tail held off the ground

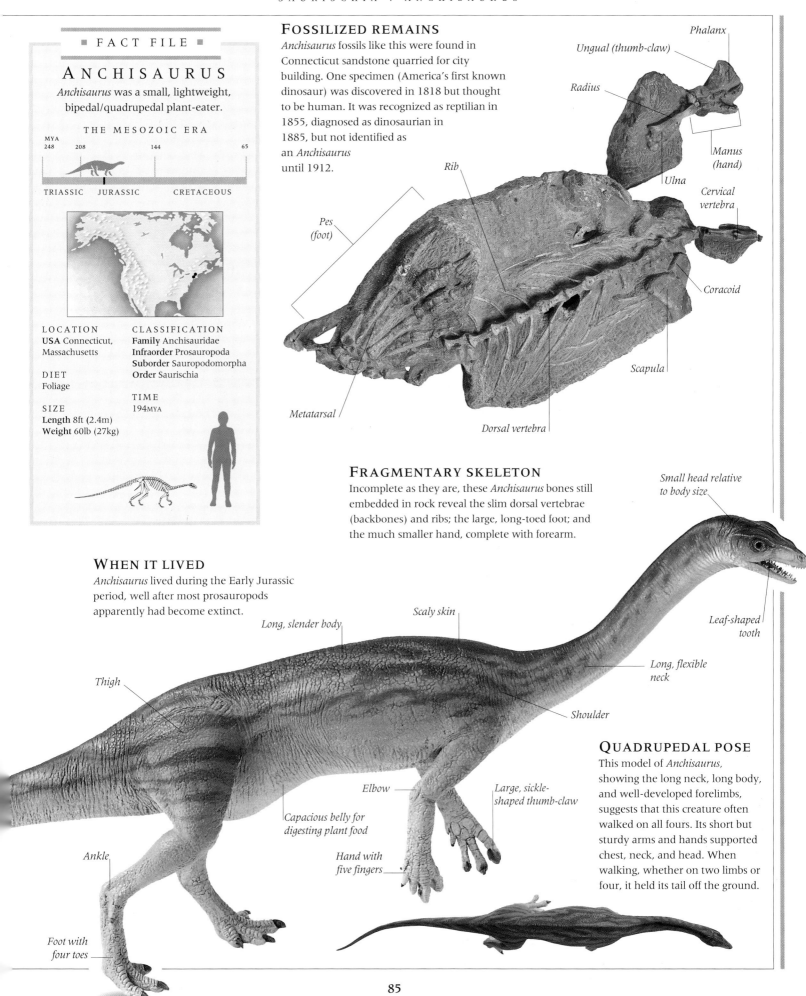

ANCHISAURUS

Anchisaurus was a small, lightweight, bipedal/quadrupedal plant-eater.

THE MESOZOIC ERA

MYA 248	208		144	65
TRIASSIC	JURASSIC		CRETACEOUS	

LOCATION
USA Connecticut, Massachusetts

DIET
Foliage

SIZE
Length 8ft (2.4m)
Weight 60lb (27kg)

CLASSIFICATION
Family Anchisauridae
Infraorder Prosauropoda
Suborder Sauropodomorpha
Order Saurischia

TIME
194MYA

FOSSILIZED REMAINS

Anchisaurus fossils like this were found in Connecticut sandstone quarried for city building. One specimen (America's first known dinosaur) was discovered in 1818 but thought to be human. It was recognized as reptilian in 1855, diagnosed as dinosaurian in 1885, but not identified as an *Anchisaurus* until 1912.

Phalanx

Ungual (thumb-claw)

Radius

Manus (hand)

Ulna

Cervical vertebra

Rib

Coracoid

Scapula

Pes (foot)

Metatarsal

Dorsal vertebra

FRAGMENTARY SKELETON

Incomplete as they are, these *Anchisaurus* bones still embedded in rock reveal the slim dorsal vertebrae (backbones) and ribs; the large, long-toed foot; and the much smaller hand, complete with forearm.

Small head relative to body size

WHEN IT LIVED

Anchisaurus lived during the Early Jurassic period, well after most prosauropods apparently had become extinct.

Scaly skin

Long, slender body

Leaf-shaped tooth

Long, flexible neck

Thigh

Shoulder

QUADRUPEDAL POSE

This model of *Anchisaurus*, showing the long neck, long body, and well-developed forelimbs, suggests that this creature often walked on all fours. Its short but sturdy arms and hands supported chest, neck, and head. When walking, whether on two limbs or four, it held its tail off the ground.

Elbow

Large, sickle-shaped thumb-claw

Capacious belly for digesting plant food

Ankle

Hand with five fingers

Foot with four toes

PLATEOSAURUS

S CORES OF SKELETONS dug up amid central Europe's Late Triassic rocks make this the best-known of the larger early dinosaurs. "Flat lizard" was one of the prosauropods, which were perhaps the ancestors of the sauropods, the largest dinosaurs ever to walk the Earth. It had a small head, long neck, bulky body, huge thumb-claws, and large, powerful hind legs. Its tail, however, was thick, and the narrow skull larger, stronger, and taller than that of *Anchisaurus*, with a deeper snout and more teeth. A ridge on the lower jaw, below the level of the tooth row, anchored the powerful muscles that worked the lower jaw. This arrangement produced a highly effective bite.

◼ LIFE AND BEHAVIOR ◼

Plateosaurus would normally have walked on all fours. Sometimes, however, it could have reared and, with its curved thumb-claws, hooked down twigs and fronds to its mouth. Small cheek pouches would hold the bitten-off leaves as the jaws worked up and down, causing the top and bottom rows of flat-sided, leaf-shaped teeth to mesh together, chopping up the mouthful. The shredded mass was then ground up inside its stomach by pebbles that rubbed against each other. Finding enough to eat could have kept each *Plateosaurus* on the move, particularly if it lived in a herd, as seems quite probable. When the herd had stripped an area of tasty, young tree-fern fronds, it would have moved on in search of more. But living together would have had advantages. If a big predator confronted them, the prosauropods could have closed ranks, reared, and struck out with their thumb-claws, inflicting wounds and driving off the enemy. At the same time, a great disadvantage would have been that in the event of a natural catastrophe—a sudden flood, for example—the whole herd might be swept away. (This seems actually to have happened in the vicinity of the present-day German town of Trossingen, where numbers of skeletons were found buried close together).

BIPEDAL FEEDING

A *Plateosaurus* rears and cranes its neck to eat leaves that grow beyond the reach of other reptiles. Prosauropods were the first large land animals to feed high above the ground. *Plateosaurus* might also have used its arms to pull branches to its mouth.

ELEVATED TAIL A museum in Tübingen, Germany shows a *Plateosaurus* skeleton as if briskly striding on two legs, with its tail off the ground. That is how experts now believe it walked when not on all fours; they reject an old notion that it dragged its tail on the ground.

Ilium

Caudal vertebrae

Ischium

Femur

Chevron

Neural spine

Tibia

Fibula

QUADRUPEDAL FEEDING

Preparators in a German museum set up this *Plateosaurus* skeleton as if about to go down on all fours to drink water or eat low-growing vegetation, as it must often have done.

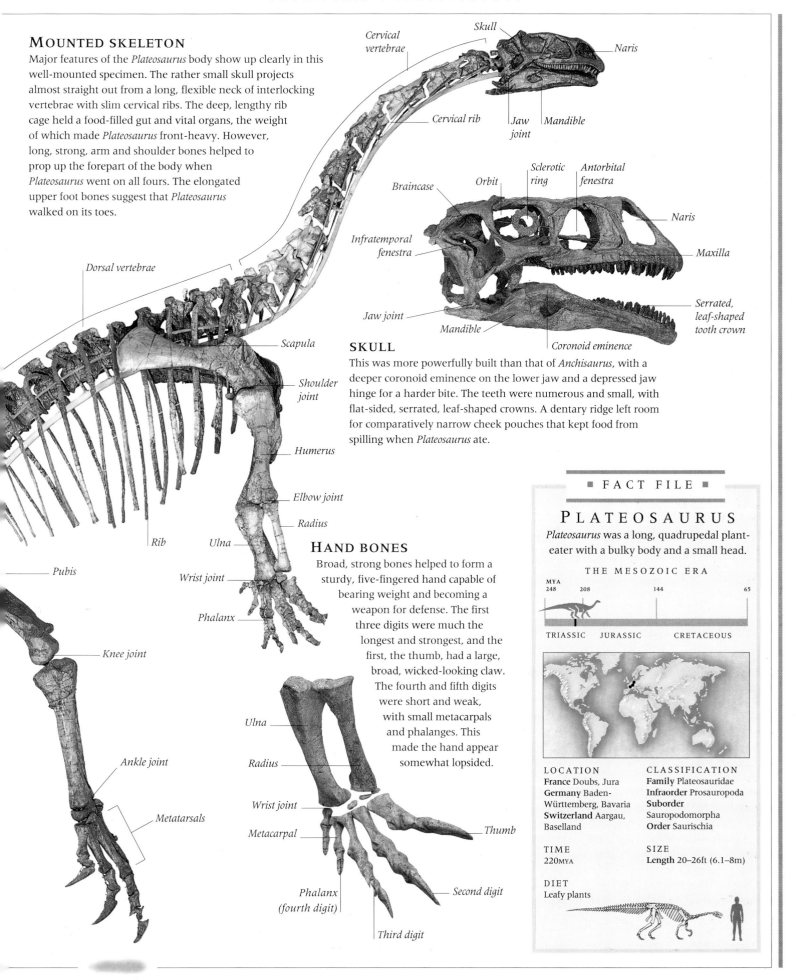

MOUNTED SKELETON

Major features of the *Plateosaurus* body show up clearly in this well-mounted specimen. The rather small skull projects almost straight out from a long, flexible neck of interlocking vertebrae with slim cervical ribs. The deep, lengthy rib cage held a food-filled gut and vital organs, the weight of which made *Plateosaurus* front-heavy. However, long, strong, arm and shoulder bones helped to prop up the forepart of the body when *Plateosaurus* went on all fours. The elongated upper foot bones suggest that *Plateosaurus* walked on its toes.

Cervical vertebrae

Skull

Naris

Cervical rib

Jaw joint

Mandible

Dorsal vertebrae

Scapula

Shoulder joint

Humerus

Elbow joint

Radius

Rib

Ulna

Wrist joint

Phalanx

Pubis

Knee joint

Ankle joint

Metatarsals

Braincase

Orbit

Sclerotic ring

Antorbital fenestra

Infratemporal fenestra

Naris

Maxilla

Jaw joint

Mandible

Coronoid eminence

Serrated, leaf-shaped tooth crown

SKULL

This was more powerfully built than that of *Anchisaurus*, with a deeper coronoid eminence on the lower jaw and a depressed jaw hinge for a harder bite. The teeth were numerous and small, with flat-sided, serrated, leaf-shaped crowns. A dentary ridge left room for comparatively narrow cheek pouches that kept food from spilling when *Plateosaurus* ate.

HAND BONES

Broad, strong bones helped to form a sturdy, five-fingered hand capable of bearing weight and becoming a weapon for defense. The first three digits were much the longest and strongest, and the first, the thumb, had a large, broad, wicked-looking claw. The fourth and fifth digits were short and weak, with small metacarpals and phalanges. This made the hand appear somewhat lopsided.

Ulna

Radius

Wrist joint

Metacarpal

Phalanx (fourth digit)

Third digit

Second digit

Thumb

■ FACT FILE ■

PLATEOSAURUS

Plateosaurus was a long, quadrupedal plant-eater with a bulky body and a small head.

THE MESOZOIC ERA

MYA
248   208   144   65

TRIASSIC   JURASSIC   CRETACEOUS

LOCATION
France Doubs, Jura
Germany Baden-Württemberg, Bavaria
Switzerland Aargau, Baselland

TIME
220MYA

DIET
Leafy plants

CLASSIFICATION
Family Plateosauridae
Infraorder Prosauropoda
Suborder Sauropodomorpha
Order Saurischia

SIZE
Length 20–26ft (6.1–8m)

MASSOSPONDYLUS

M ASSOSPONDYLUS was a medium-size prosauropod with a shorter, lower head than *Plateosaurus*, more varied teeth, and an unusual, projecting upper jaw. The overshot jaw has given rise to suggestions that the lower jaw ended in a beak, but the anatomy of the rest of the jaw does not support this theory. Some 80 partial skeletons make "massive vertebra" the world's best-known Early Jurassic prosauropod. *Massospondylus* was also remarkably widespread. Most of its fossils come from southern Africa, but in 1985 a *Massospondylus* skull was reported in North America, proving that the genus inhabited both continents when all the world's great landmasses were joined.

■ LIFE AND BEHAVIOR ■

In Arizona, *Massospondylus* shared a wooded floodplain with turtles, pterosaurs, and other creatures. It roamed southern Africa with early theropods and ornithischians, furry, mammal-like reptiles, and tiny, shrewlike mammals. Pin-headed *Massospondylus*, with its narrow head

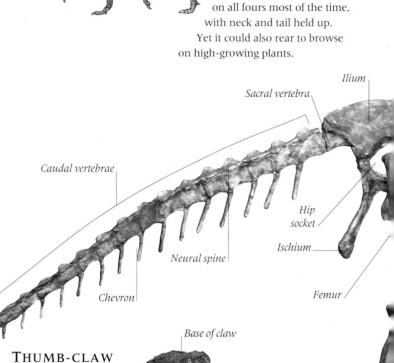

EXTERNAL VIEW
Massospondylus probably walked on all fours most of the time, with neck and tail held up. Yet it could also rear to browse on high-growing plants.

Ilium

Sacral vertebra

Caudal vertebrae

Hip socket

Ischium

Neural spine

Chevron

Femur

and bulky body, seems ideally designed for a placid, plant-eating life. In 1981, however, one scientist suggested that this prosauropod and others like it were carnivores.

■ CLUES TO THE DIET ■

Supposed clues to *Massospondylus*'s meat-eating diet included unusually tall, strong, front teeth, ridged a bit like steak-knife blades. Then, too, lack of wear on the teeth seemed to indicate that the top and bottom teeth met less effectively for crushing plants than the teeth of *Lesothosaurus*, an early plant-eating dinosaur. Furthermore, *Massospondylus*'s skull was thought too flimsy and its jaw muscles too weak for munching fibrous stems and leaves. An alternative suggestion was that *Massospondylus* tore meat with its strong, serrated front teeth, and chewed plants with the weaker, flatter teeth farther back in its jaws. In 1985, there was a counterclaim from another group of scientists: that *Massospondylus* cropped and chewed up leaves as effectively as any modern iguana. Finds of polished pebbles mixed with fossil bones hint that "millstones" in the creature's gizzard helped to mash the swallowed leaves to a pulp, allowing digestion to proceed as enzymes broke down the nutrients locked up inside the plant-cell walls.

THUMB-CLAW
Massospondylus's thumb-claws looked as vicious as those of a theropod, but were more likely to have been used defensively or as tools.

Base of claw

Curved body of claw

Top part of claw (sharp point missing)

Tibia

Fibula

Ankle joint

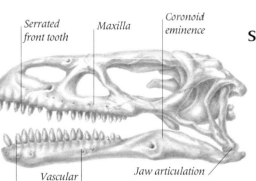

Serrated front tooth

Maxilla

Coronoid eminence

Vascular foramen

Jaw articulation

Teeth extend to the front of lower jaw

SKULL AND JAWS
The mandible (lower jaw) of *Massospondylus* had a low coronoid eminence, and the jaws were hinged just below the level of the maxillary tooth row. Vascular foramina (holes for blood vessels) hint at cheeks. An overshot upper jaw might suggest that the mandible ended in a horny beak, but this theory would not be consistent with the presence of teeth at the front of the lower jaw.

SKELETAL RECONSTRUCTION

This reconstruction presents *Massospondylus* as an elongated creature with a relatively smaller head, shallower rib cage, less deep tail, and more slender limbs than bigger, more burly prosauropods like *Lufengosaurus*, also pictured on this page, or the more robustly built European dinosaur *Plateosaurus*. The only known member of its family, *Massospondylus* may represent an evolutionary level between plateosaurids like *Lufengosaurus* and more primitive prosauropods such as *Anchisaurus*.

LUFENGOSAURUS

The worldwide distribution of prosauropods was underlined by the discovery in 1941 of this medium-size prosauropod in Early Jurassic rocks of the Lufeng Basin, Yunnan, a province of southwest China. *Lufengosaurus* had distinctive skull bones but broadly resembled its European counterpart *Plateosaurus*.

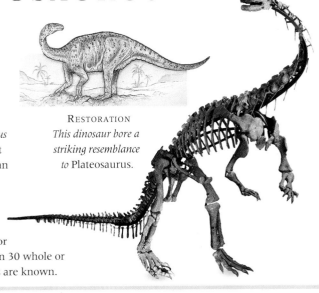

RESTORATION
This dinosaur bore a striking resemblance to Plateosaurus.

SKELETON

This mounted *Lufengosaurus* skeleton rears as if to browse or fend off a theropod. More than 30 whole or partial *Lufengosaurus* skeletons are known.

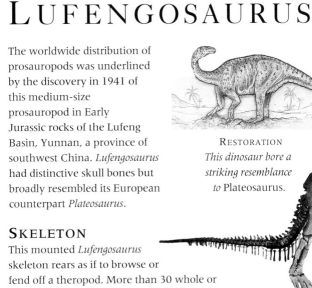

Dorsal vertebrae

Pubis

Knee joint

Rib

Cervical vertebrae

Humerus

Scapula

Elbow joint

Shoulder joint

Metatarsals

Wrist joint

Ulna

DIMINUTIVE HEAD Seen with the rest of the skeleton, the head appears incongruously minute. Yet *Massospondylus*'s small mouth must have consumed enough probably low-grade plant food to sustain and energize its relatively bulky body.

Braincase

Orbit

Mandible

Radius

Metacarpal

Phalanges

Phalanx

■ FACT FILE ■

MASSOSPONDYLUS

Massospondylus was a quadrupedal/bipedal plant-eater with a long neck and tail.

THE MESOZOIC ERA

MYA
248   208   144   65

TRIASSIC   JURASSIC   CRETACEOUS

CLASSIFICATION
Family Massospondylidae
Infraorder Prosauropoda
Suborder Sauropodomorpha
Order Saurischia

TIME
205–194 MYA

DIET
Foliage

LOCATION
USA Arizona
Lesotho Quthing
South Africa Cape Province, Orange Free State, Transvaal
Zimbabwe Matabeleland

SIZE
Length 16ft 6in (5m)

RIOJASAURUS

R IOJASAURUS ("La Rioja lizard") had a small head, long neck and tail, massive body, and four elephant-like limbs. This bus-length melanorosaurid prosauropod may have been the largest and heaviest of all land animals before the evolution of the sauropods. In fact, it matched the smaller sauropods in size and weight, and resembled them in build. The vertebrae of this huge dinosaur were made lighter by deep hollows, but its limb bones were massive and solid in order to support the vast body. *Riojasaurus* had relatively longer hands and feet than a sauropod, and more of its digits were tipped with claws.

■ LIFE AND BEHAVIOR ■

It was once believed that enormous melanorosaurid prosauropods like *Riojasaurus* were carnivores and not herbivores. This misconception largely arose because sharp, pointed teeth were found mixed up with headless melanorosaurid remains. Scientists now think that the old, worn teeth had fallen from the mouths of carnivorous dinosaurs feeding on the prosauropods' corpses. *Riojasaurus* really had leaf-shaped teeth that were designed for shredding plant fibers, not for slicing through flesh. *Riojasaurus*, with its elevated back and long neck, was one of the first land animals capable of browsing on vegetation growing high above the ground. Some scientists believe that large, long-necked plant-eating dinosaurs like this evolved in response to a drying Late Triassic climate. It is thought that lengthening dry seasons would have wiped out lush, low-growing vegetation, but that river valleys would have still held tall, deep-rooted trees: well-stocked larders for creatures tall enough to reach the leaves. This theory of a changing climate might help explain why South America's long-necked prosauropods flourished while those once abundant, low-slung, piglike reptiles, the rhynchosaurs, quickly became extinct. Another benefit of *Riojasaurus*'s enormous size was the protection afforded by sheer bulk against unexpected attack from large flesh-eating dinosaurs or from predatory, carnivorous rauisuchian reptiles.

GASTROLITHS

Like all prosauropods and sauropods, *Riojasaurus* would have swallowed stones to aid digestion. Violent, wave-like contractions of its huge gizzard rubbed down and smoothed the edges of the stones while they ground plant material to pulp for biochemical digestion.

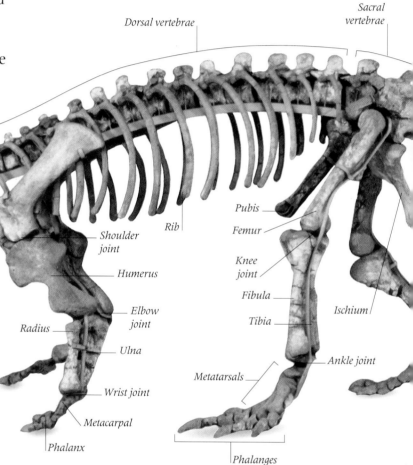

Braincase
Orbit
Cervical vertebrae
Cervical rib
Dorsal vertebrae
Sacral vertebrae
Shoulder joint
Rib
Pubis
Femur
Humerus
Knee joint
Elbow joint
Fibula
Ischium
Radius
Tibia
Ulna
Ankle joint
Wrist joint
Metatarsals
Metacarpal
Phalanx
Phalanges

RESTORATION

Riojasaurus from Argentina was one of a family of heavy, quadrupedal prosauropods: the Melanorosauridae, which included *Melanorosaurus* from South Africa and *Camelotia* from England.

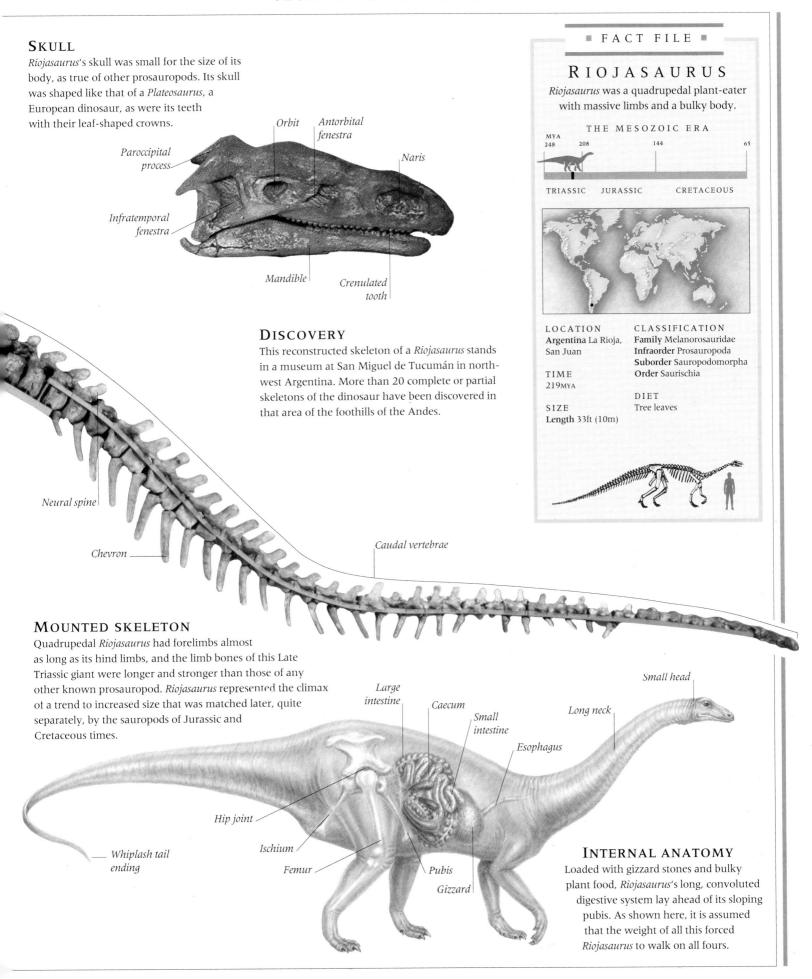

SKULL

Riojasaurus's skull was small for the size of its body, as true of other prosauropods. Its skull was shaped like that of a *Plateosaurus*, a European dinosaur, as were its teeth with their leaf-shaped crowns.

Orbit

Antorbital fenestra

Paroccipital process

Naris

Infratemporal fenestra

Mandible

Crenulated tooth

FACT FILE

RIOJASAURUS

Riojasaurus was a quadrupedal plant-eater with massive limbs and a bulky body.

THE MESOZOIC ERA

MYA 248	208	144	65

TRIASSIC   JURASSIC   CRETACEOUS

LOCATION
Argentina La Rioja, San Juan

TIME
219MYA

SIZE
Length 33ft (10m)

CLASSIFICATION
Family Melanorosauridae
Infraorder Prosauropoda
Suborder Sauropodomorpha
Order Saurischia

DIET
Tree leaves

DISCOVERY

This reconstructed skeleton of a *Riojasaurus* stands in a museum at San Miguel de Tucumán in north-west Argentina. More than 20 complete or partial skeletons of the dinosaur have been discovered in that area of the foothills of the Andes.

Neural spine

Chevron

Caudal vertebrae

MOUNTED SKELETON

Quadrupedal *Riojasaurus* had forelimbs almost as long as its hind limbs, and the limb bones of this Late Triassic giant were longer and stronger than those of any other known prosauropod. *Riojasaurus* represented the climax of a trend to increased size that was matched later, quite separately, by the sauropods of Jurassic and Cretaceous times.

Large intestine

Caecum

Small intestine

Esophagus

Small head

Long neck

Hip joint

Ischium

Whiplash tail ending

Femur

Pubis

Gizzard

INTERNAL ANATOMY

Loaded with gizzard stones and bulky plant food, *Riojasaurus*'s long, convoluted digestive system lay ahead of its sloping pubis. As shown here, it is assumed that the weight of all this forced *Riojasaurus* to walk on all fours.

CETIOSAURUS

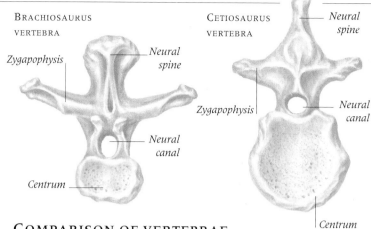

C ETIOSAURUS was the first sauropod to be discovered. This huge plant-eating dinosaur was as long as a great whale, and, when named in 1841, the largest known land animal. "Whale lizard" belonged to a primitive family called the Cetiosauridae. Its old-fashioned features included a heavy, solid backbone unlike the lighter, hollower backbones of most later sauropods. Its head was apparently blunt, with spoon-shaped teeth. The neck was moderately long, the body was capacious, and the tail was relatively short. *Cetiosaurus* supported this heavy superstructure on elephantine limbs and feet; thick pads cushioned the toes.

■ DISCOVERY ■

The first hint that colossal dinosaurs had walked the Earth was a probable *Cetiosaurus* tailbone found in Oxfordshire in 1809. In the 1830s Oxford University geologist Dean William Buckland received several huge fossil bones dug up in Oxfordshire. The great French comparative anatomist Baron Georges Cuvier identified them as whale bones—although fossils of whales were unknown in Mesozoic rocks. Cuvier's British counterpart, Richard Owen, later questioned whether the vertebrae were truly whalelike, and decided their mighty owner had the streamlined body of a water animal that swam by waggling a crocodilian tail. He named it accordingly. Subsequent fossil finds cast doubt on the idea. In 1848, Professor John Phillips discovered a thigh-bone

as tall as a human. This strongly suggested that its owner had been designed to walk on land. Then, in 1869, from Oxfordshire's same Middle Jurassic rocks, a near- complete skeleton emerged. Thomas Henry Huxley (champion of Charles Darwin and the theory of evolution through natural selection) finally arrived at the correct solution to the mystery of the giant's identity. He discerned that *Cetiosaurus* had simply been a very large, four-legged dinosaur, perhaps as heavy as five modern elephants.

COMPARISON OF VERTEBRAE

A *Cetiosaurus*'s dorsal vertebra (above right) was a massive, heavy structure, compared to the weight-saving, scooped-out dorsal vertebra of a more advanced sauropod, such as *Brachiosaurus* (above left). *Brachiosaurus* had a relatively smaller centrum but a more pronounced neural spine and zygapophyses.

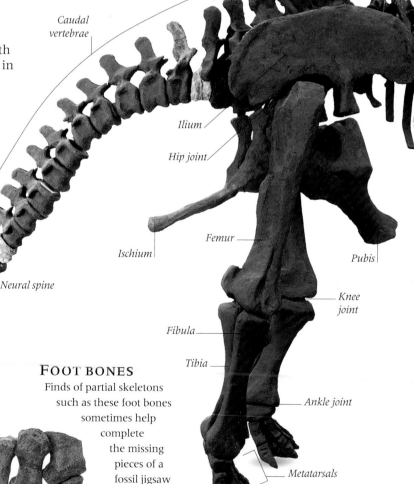

FOOT BONES

Finds of partial skeletons such as these foot bones sometimes help complete the missing pieces of a fossil jigsaw puzzle, but it is not always possible to match fossil finds with the dinosaur from which they originated.

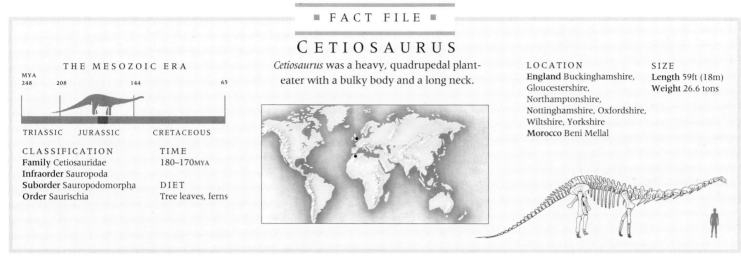

CETIOSAURUS

Cetiosaurus was a heavy, quadrupedal plant-eater with a bulky body and a long neck.

THE MESOZOIC ERA

MYA
248   208   144   65

TRIASSIC   JURASSIC   CRETACEOUS

CLASSIFICATION
Family Cetiosauridae
Infraorder Sauropoda
Suborder Sauropodomorpha
Order Saurischia

TIME
180–170MYA

DIET
Tree leaves, ferns

LOCATION
England Buckinghamshire, Gloucestershire, Northamptonshire, Nottinghamshire, Oxfordshire, Wiltshire, Yorkshire
Morocco Beni Mellal

SIZE
Length 59ft (18m)
Weight 26.6 tons

RECONSTRUCTED SKELETON

In this reconstruction, the pale bones are real fossils, and the dark bones are modern replicas created to replace missing parts, their shape deduced from isolated bones of other specimens.

RESTORATION

Cetiosaurus had pillarlike hind limbs and sturdier forelimbs than those of *Barapasaurus* or *Shunosaurus*, two other early sauropods. The larger forearm bone may have been as long as the shinbone, not shorter as in most sauropods (and as in the reconstructed skeleton on this page).

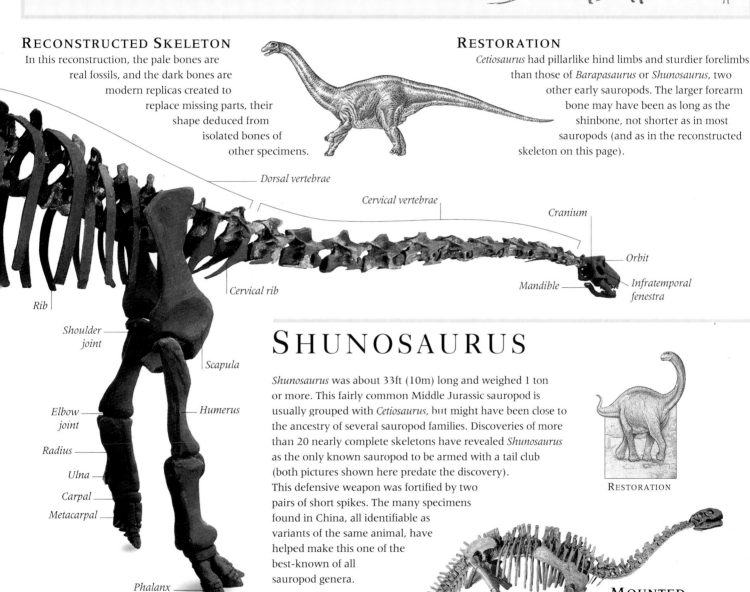

Dorsal vertebrae

Cervical vertebrae

Cranium

Orbit

Mandible

Infratemporal fenestra

Cervical rib

Rib

Shoulder joint

Scapula

Elbow joint

Humerus

Radius

Ulna

Carpal

Metacarpal

Phalanx

FOSSIL FINDS

Cetiosaurus occurs in England in rocks laid down where sea met land in Middle Jurassic times. Later uplift raised the rocks to form the Mendip Hills, the Cotswolds, and other hills that run from Dorset to North Yorkshire.

SHUNOSAURUS

Shunosaurus was about 33ft (10m) long and weighed 1 ton or more. This fairly common Middle Jurassic sauropod is usually grouped with *Cetiosaurus*, but might have been close to the ancestry of several sauropod families. Discoveries of more than 20 nearly complete skeletons have revealed *Shunosaurus* as the only known sauropod to be armed with a tail club (both pictures shown here predate the discovery). This defensive weapon was fortified by two pairs of short spikes. The many specimens found in China, all identifiable as variants of the same animal, have helped make this one of the best-known of all sauropod genera.

RESTORATION

MOUNTED SKELETON

Versions of a *Shunosaurus* skeleton without its tail club have appeared in exhibitions worldwide.

BRACHIOSAURUS

O NE OF THE LARGEST, heaviest, and longest dinosaurs, *Brachiosaurus* ("arm lizard") resembled a massive giraffe. By some estimates its weight was equivalent to ten modern-day elephants, though a recent recalculation has brought this number down to six. *Brachiosaurus'* forelimbs were much longer than its hind limbs and raised its shoulders far above hip level. The shoulders formed a high base for the neck, which swung the head from side to side and moved it up and down, from higher than a four-story building down to the ground. Compared to most sauropods, its tail was short.

MOUNTED SKELETON
A Brachiosaurus *skeleton on display in the Humboldt Museum, Berlin.*

LIFE AND BEHAVIOR

Brachiosaurus seems to have been designed for cropping leaves at high and low levels. Some scientists think it lacked muscles for raising its neck as steeply as a giraffe's and doubt that its heart could have pumped blood to the head if the neck were held high for more than a moment or two. Perhaps this sauropod stood at the edge of the woods, swinging its head up, down, and sideways, as its chisel-shaped teeth cut a swath through all vegetation in reach, even the low-growing ferns that then carpeted the ground. In its gut, gastroliths ("gizzard stones") probably ground leaves to pulp. Digestion might have depended on bacteria in a specialized hind gut, such as those in modern large plant-eating mammals. If *Brachiosaurus* were warm-blooded, it would have required more than 440lb (200kg) of low-grade conifer and cycad plant food each day, and feeding would have taken up much of its time. If it were cold-blooded, its food needs would have been less. Small herds of these immense sauropods probably spent their lives moving slowly through low-lying riverside forests. Sheer size and weight, together with their sharp claws, probably protected adults against even the largest theropod predators. However, the young would have been more at risk. If *Brachiosaurus* were warm-blooded, the young probably took at least ten years to grow to full size; if cold-blooded, they may have taken more than 100 years to reach adult size.

EXTERNAL APPEARANCE

Long forelimbs and high shoulders raised the base of the long neck high above the ground. Unlike most other sauropods, *Brachiosaurus* sloped down steeply from shoulder to hip and had a relatively short tail.

DORSAL VERTEBRAE

The dorsal vertebrae of *Brachiosaurus* were very large. To reduce their weight without significantly reducing their strength, the dorsal vertebrae had huge cavities in their sides.

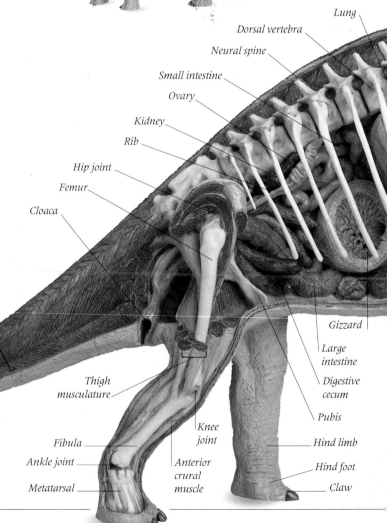

Lung

Dorsal vertebra

Neural spine

Small intestine

Ovary

Kidney

Rib

Hip joint

Femur

Cloaca

Thigh musculature

Caudal musculature

Fibula

Ankle joint

Metatarsal

Anterior crural muscle

Knee joint

Gizzard

Large intestine

Digestive cecum

Pubis

Hind limb

Hind foot

Claw

Orbit

Nasal opening

Bony strut

Cervical musculature

Mouth

Outer ear

Braincase

SKULL

The skull of *Brachiosaurus* had a low muzzle and strong jaws with chisel-shaped teeth. Light, narrow, bony struts framed the orbits (eye sockets) and the large nostril openings above. Behind the eyes, a tiny braincase held a brain that was no more than one hundred-thousandth the weight of the whole body.

MUSCULATURE

This front view of *Brachiosaurus* (right) shows how it would have appeared with the skin stripped away to reveal the muscles beneath. This reconstruction of the musculature showing how the muscles, ligaments, and tendons might have joined the bones is based on the mounted skeleton on display in the Humboldt Museum, Berlin.

Cervical musculature

Cervical vertebra

Intercostal muscle

Trachea (wind pipe)

Esophagus (food pipe)

INTERNAL ANATOMY

This cutaway model (left) shows some of the internal structures of *Brachiosaurus*. The girderlike spine supported the neck, back, and tail, and transmitted their weight to the massive limb bones. Ribs protected the heart, lungs, and other internal organs. The long gut included a gizzard and sausage-shaped ceca for digesting plant food.

Sheetlike muscles across the abdomen

Humboldt Museum skeleton is mounted with the front limbs in a bowlegged posture

Scapula

Scapular muscle

Shoulder joint

Humerus

Heart

Posterior brachial musculature

Elbow joint

Radius

Ulna

Posterior antebrachial musculature

Wrist joint

Metacarpal

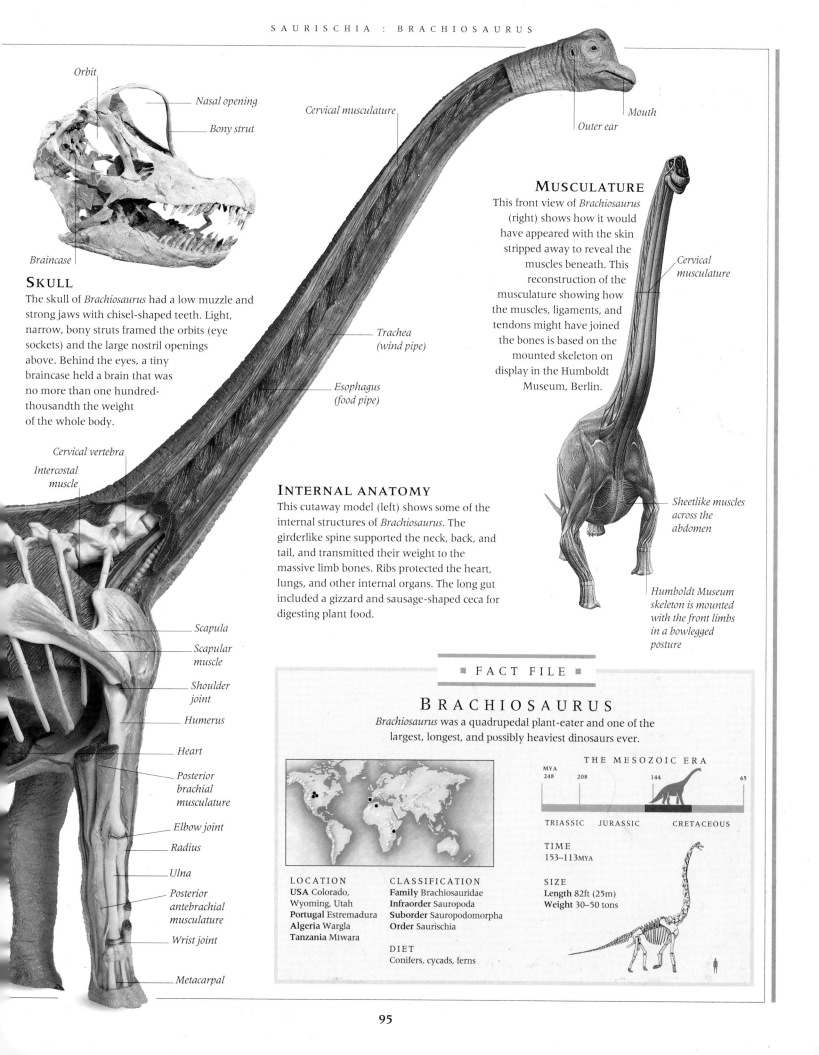

■ FACT FILE ■

BRACHIOSAURUS

Brachiosaurus was a quadrupedal plant-eater and one of the largest, longest, and possibly heaviest dinosaurs ever.

THE MESOZOIC ERA

MYA 248	208	144	65

TRIASSIC   JURASSIC   CRETACEOUS

TIME
153–113MYA

SIZE
Length 82ft (25m)
Weight 30–50 tons

LOCATION
USA Colorado, Wyoming, Utah
Portugal Estremadura
Algeria Wargla
Tanzania Mtwara

CLASSIFICATION
Family Brachiosauridae
Infraorder Sauropoda
Suborder Sauropodomorpha
Order Saurischia

DIET
Conifers, cycads, ferns

CAMARASAURUS

RESTORATION
Camarasaurus's relatively short, high snout, short neck, high shoulders, compact body, and short tail seem closer to giraffelike *Brachiosaurus* than to the long-necked, long-tailed *Diplodocus*.

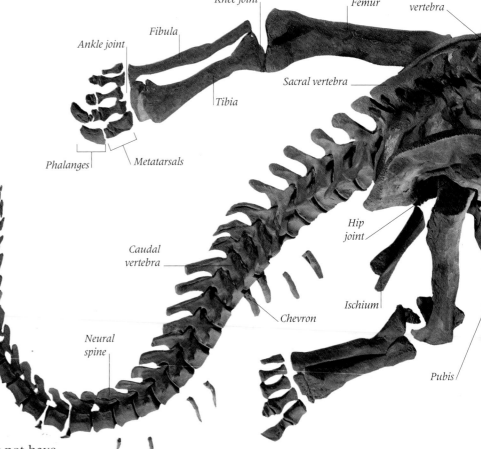

Phalanges

HUGE, WEIGHT-SAVING hollows in its vertebrae gave this sauropod its name, "chambered lizard." No other North American sauropod is known so completely from fossil bones. *Camarasaurus* was more massive than the better-known *Diplodocus* but had a shorter neck and tail, relatively long forelimbs and high shoulders, and stood with its back almost horizontal rather than rising to the hips. Whereas *Diplodocus* had a small, low, horselike head, *Camarasaurus*'s head was large and deep, with a muzzle like a bulldog's. Big eyeholes, nostrils, and other cavities reduced some skull bones to lightweight struts. The teeth all around its powerful jaws were strong and spoon-shaped.

E. D. COPE
In 1877 he named Camarasaurus.

■ LIFE AND BEHAVIOR ■

Camarasaurus's teeth seemed designed for cropping vegetation tougher than peg-toothed sauropods could tackle. One authority suggests the animal ate not only leaves but also rough-barked twigs and stiff branches, and the cycadeoid trees' harsh, fibrous, palmlike fronds. Being an unfussy feeder would possibly have compensated short-necked *Camarasaurus* and its nearest kin for being unable to reach plants in range of the longer-necked sauropods. Big skull cavities for the eyes and nostrils suggest that this sauropod had keen senses of sight and smell that would have helped it find new feeding grounds and detect where dangerous theropods lurked. *Camarasaurus* probably moved around in mixed-age herds. There is no proof for this, but without adults to protect it, a young *Camarasaurus* would have been extremely vulnerable to any hungry *Allosaurus* or *Ceratosaurus*. Even the great size, tough hide, and sharp thumb-claws of a lone adult might not have saved it from a hunting pack of big flesh-eating dinosaurs. *Camarasaurus* bones have been discovered deeply scored with the characteristic teeth-marks of *Allosaurus* and *Ceratosaurus*. It may be, however, that these predators were eating not beasts they had slain, but those they found dead.

SKELETON PRESERVED AS FOUND
Preserved as it lay after death, a fossilized *Camarasaurus* reveals key anatomical features. These include a short, deep skull; a dozen short cervical vertebrae (neck bones) with long, slim ribs; a dozen deeply hollowed-out dorsal vertebrae (back bones); about 50 short caudal vertebrae (tailbones); robust limb bones (each humerus was almost as long as a femur); and short, weight-bearing digits.

Knee joint

Fibula

Ankle joint

Femur

Dorsal vertebra

Sacral vertebra

Tibia

Phalanges

Metatarsals

Caudal vertebra

Hip joint

Ischium

Chevron

Neural spine

Pubis

FOSSIL CONDITION
Few fossil sauropods are found in so complete a condition as this *Camarasaurus*. It must have been enclosed within sand or silt almost immediately after death, or it would have been dismembered.

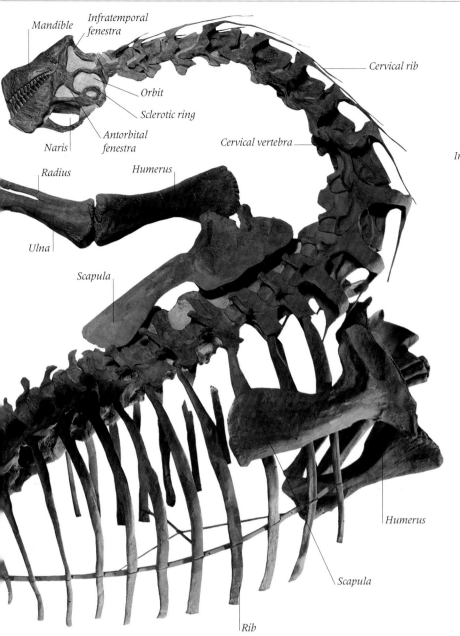

Mandible
Infratemporal fenestra
Orbit
Sclerotic ring
Antorbital fenestra
Naris
Radius
Humerus
Ulna
Cervical rib
Cervical vertebra
Scapula
Humerus
Scapula
Rib

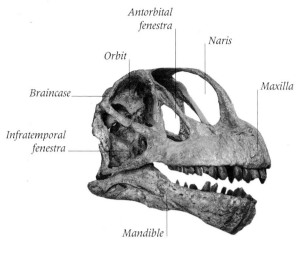

Antorbital fenestra
Naris
Orbit
Braincase
Maxilla
Infratemporal fenestra
Mandible

SKULL

A *Camarasaurus* skull was short and deep, with bony bars and windowlike openings. Each naris (nostril hole) opened in front of a cavernous hole for the eye, and behind that was another large hole, the infratemporal fenestra, for jaw muscles. Thick jawbones held deep-rooted teeth.

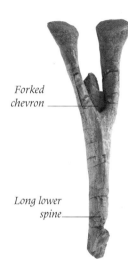

CHEVRON

Caudal vertebrae (tailbones) featured forked bones like this. These chevrons guarded a blood vessel that ran under the centra (vertebral "cores"). Each chevron's long lower spine provided a site of attachment for muscles.

Forked chevron

Long lower spine

■ FACT FILE ■

CAMARASAURUS

Camarasaurus was a quadrupedal plant-eater with long forelimbs.

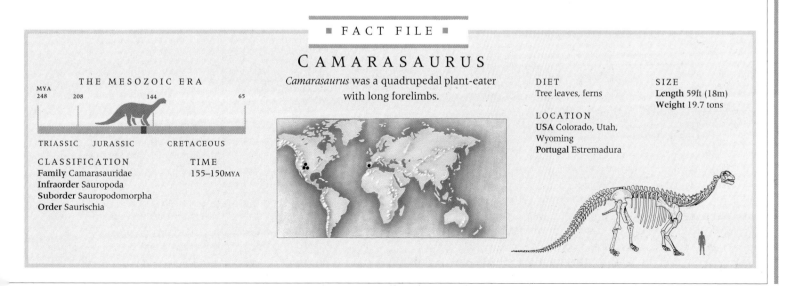

THE MESOZOIC ERA

MYA 248   208   144   65

TRIASSIC   JURASSIC   CRETACEOUS

CLASSIFICATION
Family Camarasauridae
Infraorder Sauropoda
Suborder Sauropodomorpha
Order Saurischia

TIME
155–150MYA

DIET
Tree leaves, ferns

LOCATION
USA Colorado, Utah, Wyoming
Portugal Estremadura

SIZE
Length 59ft (18m)
Weight 19.7 tons

BAROSAURUS

A N IMMENSELY LONG SAUROPOD, "heavy lizard" resembled its near relative *Diplodocus*. Both had a bulky body that stood highest at the hips. Their hind-limb bones appear identical, and other bones suggest that *Barosaurus*'s skull (which has not yet been discovered) was long and sloping like that of *Diplodocus*; but their neck and tail proportions were different. *Barosaurus*'s tail was relatively short but balanced by an extremely elongated neck that projected 30ft (about 9m) beyond its shoulders, making *Barosaurus* taller than almost any other North American dinosaur.

EARL DOUGLASS
In 1912 he excavated a Barosaurus *at the Carnegie Quarry, Utah.*

■ LIFE AND BEHAVIOR ■

Barosaurus's long neck seems designed for feeding at high elevations, like a giraffe's. Some researchers have calculated that pumping blood up to the brain demanded an amazingly large 1.6-ton heart. But the bigger a heart, the slower it beats. In 1992, scientists at Columbia University argued that a 1.6-ton heart would pump so slowly that blood forced up the neck by one heartbeat would pour back down before the next. They suggested instead that *Barosaurus* had eight hearts—two major hearts in the chest and three pairs of lesser hearts spaced out along the neck; each heart was only big enough to pump blood to the next, but all worked as a relay team to drive blood to the brain. The Columbia scientists also theorized that the resultant high blood pressure made this dinosaur prone to arterial disease and early death from heart attack or stroke. Others believe that *Barosaurus* managed with one moderately large heart aided by arterial valves in the neck to stop backflow, and waves of muscular contractions to push blood to the brain.

REARING FOR DEFENSE

Rising on her hind limbs, a *Barosaurus* towers 49ft (15m) high as she guards her vulnerable young against attack from a hungry allosaurid theropod. This lively tableau in New York's American Museum of Natural History suggests that sauropods were more active and caring than scientists once thought. However, we can only speculate on *Barosaurus*'s actual behavior. It is possible, for example, that despite the creature's apparent height, it spent much of its time horizontally, partly submerged in swamp water.

Barosaurus *mother rearing up in defense*

Attacking allosaur

Young Barosaurus *sheltering behind the tail*

TAIL The rear end of Barosaurus's tail remains undiscovered, but other tailbones lead scientists to think the tail ended in a flexible whiplash, like that of *Diplodocus*. Flexible or not, it must have carried considerable weight in order to counterbalance the long neck.

Whiplike tail

Hind limb

AFRICAN SPECIES

Fragments of the skulls, jaws, limb bones, and other bones of a dinosaur relative of *Diplodocus* that were discovered in Tanzania have been attributed by some paleontologists to *Barosaurus*. Other experts, however, do not believe that these bone fragments come from *Barosaurus*.

Claw

■ FACT FILE ■

BAROSAURUS

Barosaurus was a huge, quadrupedal plant-eater with an extremely long neck, a low head, and a bulky body. It was among the longest of the dinosaurs.

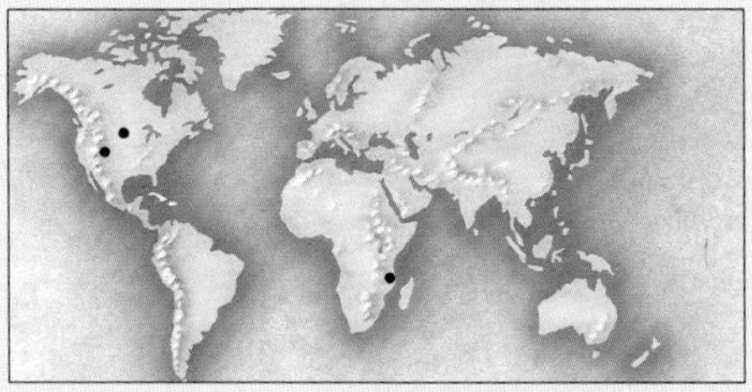

THE MESOZOIC ERA

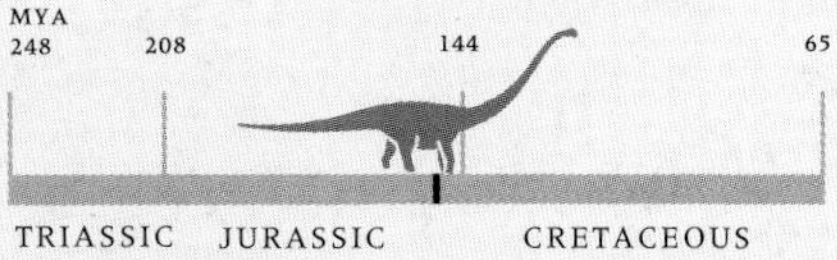

MYA 248	208	144	65
TRIASSIC	JURASSIC		CRETACEOUS

SIZE
Length 75–89ft (23–27m)

TIME
150MYA

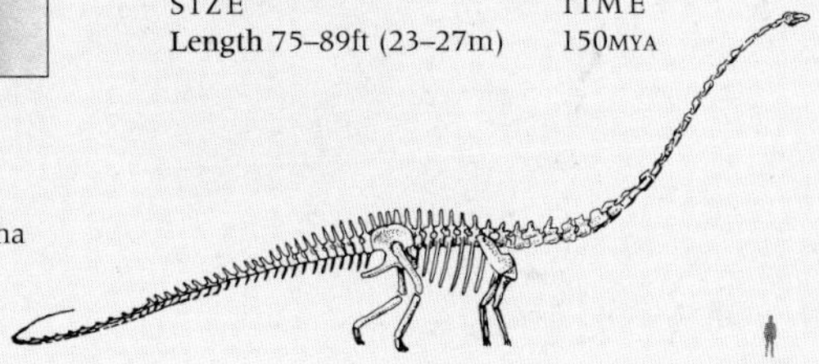

LOCATION
Tanzania Mtwara
USA South Dakota,
Utah

DIET
Tree leaves, ferns

CLASSIFICATION
Family Diplodocidae
Infraorder Sauropoda
Suborder Sauropodomorpha
Order Saurischia

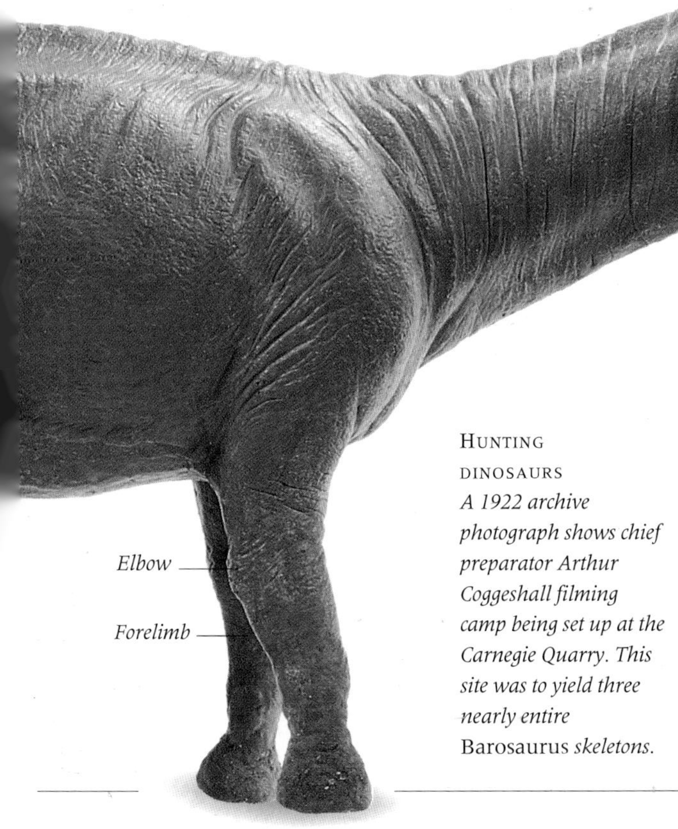

HEAD The model restores *Barosaurus*'s head as long, low and sloping, with nostrils opening above the eyes. This is guesswork based on matching parts of the skeleton with bones from similar sauropods. More than a century after Othniel Marsh named it in 1890, no *Barosaurus* skull has been found in North America.

Elongated, heavy neck supported by large, ribbed vertebrae

RESTORATION

A lifelike model restores *Barosaurus* with an immensely long neck. Supporting this were 16 or more vertebrae. Although some of these vertebrae were 3ft 3in (1m) long, bearing long, strutlike cervical ribs, they were deeply hollowed out, reducing their weight. Without this weight reduction the enormously long neck would have been too heavy to raise. In modern-day terms, if *Barosaurus* reared and craned its neck it could have nibbled leaves from treetops as high as a five-story building.

HAZARDOUS WORK
Earl Douglass and intrepid colleagues explore a fossil-rich cliff face at the Carnegie Quarry.

Elbow

Forelimb

HUNTING
DINOSAURS
A 1922 archive photograph shows chief preparator Arthur Coggeshall filming camp being set up at the Carnegie Quarry. This site was to yield three nearly entire Barosaurus *skeletons.*

99

DIPLODOCUS

T HE LONGEST COMPLETE dinosaur skeleton found so far is that of *Diplodocus* ("double beam"). This massive diplodocid sauropod resembled a walking suspension bridge and was longer than a tennis court. Four trunklike limbs, the hind limbs longer than the forelimbs, supported the body. Cantilevered from the forward end of this structure was a long, snaky neck and a small, horselike head. At the rear end, great muscles linking pelvic bones and vertebrae helped hold aloft an even longer tail that tapered to a flexible, whiplash tip. Despite this animal's tremendous length, deep huge cavities within its vertebrae suggest that *Diplodocus* possibly weighed no more than two or three present-day elephants.

ANDREW CARNEGIE
(1835–1919)
This American industrialist-philanthropist gave various museums Diplodocus *casts.*

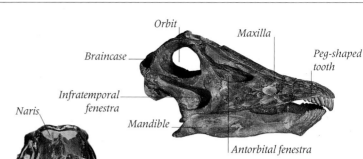

SKULL

Diplodocus's skull, seen here from in front (left) and one side (above) was small and sloping, with a tiny brain. Nostrils opened far back, above the eyes, which makes some people think that *Diplodocus* had a trunk. The peglike teeth grew only at the front of the mouth.

Labels: Orbit, Braincase, Infratemporal fenestra, Naris, Mandible, Maxilla, Peg-shaped tooth, Antorbital fenestra

■ LIFE AND BEHAVIOR ■

Diplodocus could have browsed on tall tree ferns, cycadeoids, ginkgo trees, conifers, and on the ferns and vegetation that formed the meadows of their age. Some scientists believe this dinosaur reached treetops by rearing, propped up on the tripod formed by its hind limbs and its tail. Long, skid-like bones inside the tail (the double beams that gave *Diplodocus* its name) perhaps prevented blood vessels from being crushed when the tail was pressed against the ground. Peg-shaped teeth in the front of its mouth could have combed tree leaves and fern fronds from their tough stalks. However, this dinosaur possessed no back teeth for chewing. Instead, inside a muscular stomach like a bird's crop, gastroliths (swallowed stones) mashed up the leaves. The leafy mush then passed on through the gut, probably to sausage-shaped "fermenting vats" where bacteria completed the process of digestion. Fossil footprints show that nomadic dinosaurs like *Diplodocus* migrated in herds to new feeding grounds once they had exhausted the food supply in one area. Traveling in herds was also essential from the point of view of defense against predators. Massive as *Diplodocus* was, it had evolved to do little more than eat vast quantities of plant material and had nothing but its whiplash tail with which to defend itself. Although older models and mounted skeletons depict *Diplodocus* dragging its tail, this is not supported by the fossil evidence. The absence of drag marks in fossil tracks suggests that it held its tail well off the ground.

"DOUBLE BEAM" CHEVRONS

In the middle section of the tail's length, "double beams" are seen on the chevrons (downward projections of the vertebrae). The "beams" are front and rear extensions of the chevron and may have protected the tail when pressed against the ground.

Labels: Underside of chevron, Concave surface

WHIPLASH TAIL

At least 70 and possibly more than 80 caudal vertebrae formed the bony core of *Diplodocus*'s elongated tail. Cavities lightened the first 19 vertebrae. Farther back, bones that were mere rods produced the whiplash ending to the tail.

Labels: Simple, rodlike vertebra, Caudal vertebrae, Chevron with "double beams", Unextended chevron

SUSPENSION BRIDGE STRUCTURE
Diplodocus*'s limbs were like supporting piers; the body below its spine was like a roadway held up by cables.*

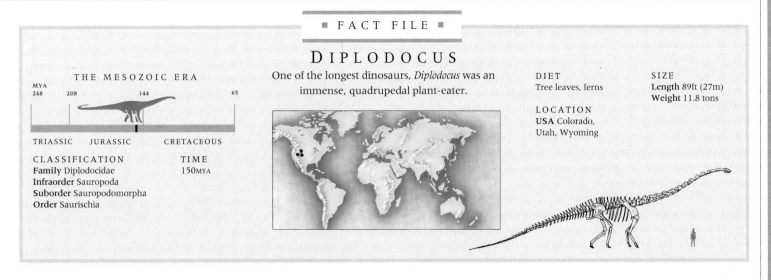

■ FACT FILE ■

DIPLODOCUS

One of the longest dinosaurs, *Diplodocus* was an immense, quadrupedal plant-eater.

THE MESOZOIC ERA

| MYA 248 | 208 | 144 | 65 |

| TRIASSIC | JURASSIC | CRETACEOUS |

CLASSIFICATION
Family Diplodocidae
Infraorder Sauropoda
Suborder Sauropodomorpha
Order Saurischia

TIME
150MYA

DIET
Tree leaves, ferns

LOCATION
USA Colorado,
Utah, Wyoming

SIZE
Length 89ft (27m)
Weight 11.8 tons

SKELETONS OLD AND NEW

Diplodocus used to be shown with a dragging tail in the Natural History Museum in London (below) before it was remounted in 1993 with a raised tail. The other skeleton (bottom) is on exhibit at the Senckenberg Museum in Frankfurt.

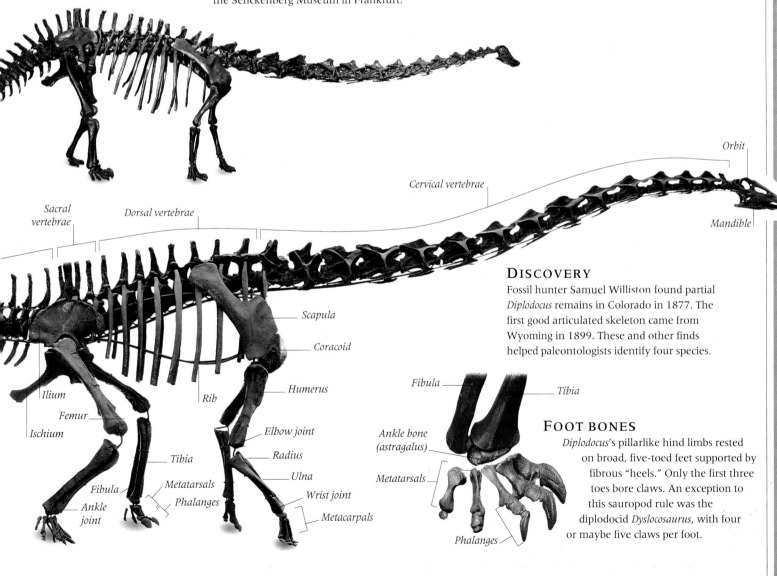

Sacral vertebrae

Dorsal vertebrae

Cervical vertebrae

Orbit

Mandible

Scapula

Coracoid

Ilium

Rib

Humerus

Femur

Ischium

Elbow joint

Tibia

Radius

Fibula

Metatarsals

Phalanges

Ulna

Ankle joint

Wrist joint

Metacarpals

Fibula

Tibia

Ankle bone (astragalus)

Metatarsals

Phalanges

DISCOVERY

Fossil hunter Samuel Williston found partial *Diplodocus* remains in Colorado in 1877. The first good articulated skeleton came from Wyoming in 1899. These and other finds helped paleontologists identify four species.

FOOT BONES

Diplodocus's pillarlike hind limbs rested on broad, five-toed feet supported by fibrous "heels." Only the first three toes bore claws. An exception to this sauropod rule was the diplodocid *Dyslocosaurus*, with four or maybe five claws per foot.

APATOSAURUS

A BOUT TWELVE skeletons, representing three species, make this one of the best-known sauropods. *Apatosaurus* constituted a sturdier, heavier, but somewhat shorter version of its close relative *Diplodocus*. The creature had a small, low, horselike head with peg-shaped teeth; a long, muscular neck; a deep, heavy body; pillarlike limbs with short, elephantine toes; and a whiplash tail containing 82 bones—even more than *Diplodocus*. *Apatosaurus* grew nearly as long as a tennis court, stood higher at the hips than an elephant, and weighed as much as four or even five elephants.

RESTORATION

Restored in line with current thinking, an *Apatosaurus* strides along with its muscular tail held clear of the ground. This stopped other sauropods from treading on its tail and may also have prevented small creatures from biting it.

THE CARNEGIE SKELETON

The *Apatosaurus* skeleton pictured on these pages stands in Pittsburgh's Carnegie Museum, which was founded by the Scottish-born, philanthropic steel magnate Andrew Carnegie (1835–1919).

▪ LIFE AND BEHAVIOR ▪

Apatosaurus herds ambled across the glades and forested riverbanks of Late Jurassic western North America, adults browsing on high treetops. It is a puzzle how *Apatosaurus*'s small jaws could have consumed enough nourishment to power its immense body. The creature probably had to eat almost all the time, stopping only to wallow in water to cool off and to kill skin parasites. At night, *Apatosaurus* might have taken brief, standing catnaps. In the case of carnosaur attack, big, tough-skinned bulls could lash out with their immense, whiplike tails, knocking over and badly damaging a predator. Or they might have reared up on their powerful hind legs, to bring their clawed forefeet crashing thunderously down on the enemy. Solidly heavy as the creature was, many of its bones—especially those of the spine— were honeycombed in structure for lightness. But even so, the creature was too massive to outrun predators. Defense was a matter of staying in herds and, probably, of a system of alarm calls that alerted the big males to come to the fore and confront the danger. Females and the younger dinosaurs would have congregated in a circle behind a wall of males.

▪ NAME CHANGE ▪

Many people know *Apatosaurus* ("deceptive lizard") better by its old name *Brontosaurus* ("thunder lizard," from the supposed sound of its heavy tread). The name was changed when "*Brontosaurus*" fossils proved identical with those of a dinosaur that had been named previously—*Apatosaurus*.

MISTAKEN IDENTITY

In 1883 this "*Apatosaurus*" tail became part of the first reconstructed sauropod skeleton. It is in fact the shorter tail of a *Camarasaurus*.

Caudal vertebra

Short tip

Chevrons extend almost to the tail-tip

HIGH-LEVEL BROWSING

Apatosaurus was capable of lifting its head high enough to browse on treetops, but probably more often ate fronds of low-growing ferns.

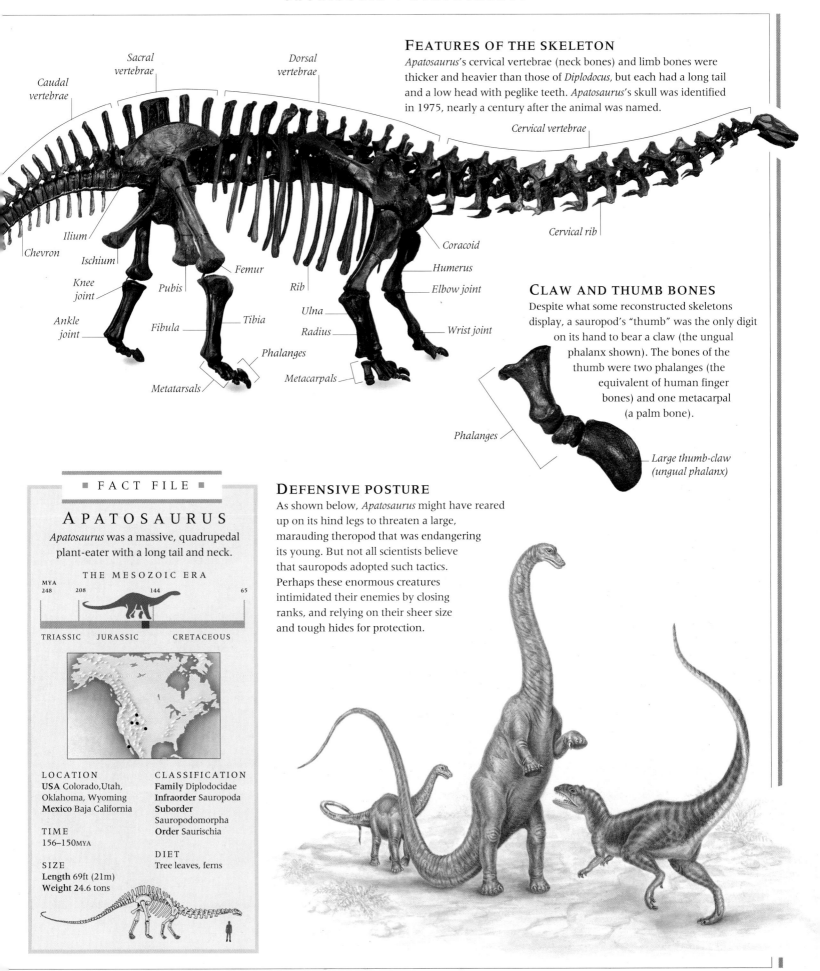

Caudal
vertebrae

Sacral
vertebrae

Dorsal
vertebrae

Chevron

Ilium

Ischium

Knee
joint

Ankle
joint

Pubis

Fibula

Tibia

Femur

Metatarsals

Phalanges

Metacarpals

Rib

Ulna

Radius

Coracoid

Humerus

Elbow joint

Wrist joint

Cervical vertebrae

Cervical rib

FEATURES OF THE SKELETON

Apatosaurus's cervical vertebrae (neck bones) and limb bones were thicker and heavier than those of *Diplodocus*, but each had a long tail and a low head with peglike teeth. *Apatosaurus*'s skull was identified in 1975, nearly a century after the animal was named.

CLAW AND THUMB BONES

Despite what some reconstructed skeletons display, a sauropod's "thumb" was the only digit on its hand to bear a claw (the ungual phalanx shown). The bones of the thumb were two phalanges (the equivalent of human finger bones) and one metacarpal (a palm bone).

Phalanges

Large thumb-claw
(ungual phalanx)

DEFENSIVE POSTURE

As shown below, *Apatosaurus* might have reared up on its hind legs to threaten a large, marauding theropod that was endangering its young. But not all scientists believe that sauropods adopted such tactics. Perhaps these enormous creatures intimidated their enemies by closing ranks, and relying on their sheer size and tough hides for protection.

■ FACT FILE ■

APATOSAURUS

Apatosaurus was a massive, quadrupedal plant-eater with a long tail and neck.

THE MESOZOIC ERA

MYA 248	208	144	65

TRIASSIC   JURASSIC   CRETACEOUS

LOCATION
USA Colorado,Utah,
Oklahoma, Wyoming
Mexico Baja California

TIME
156–150MYA

SIZE
Length 69ft (21m)
Weight 24.6 tons

CLASSIFICATION
Family Diplodocidae
Infraorder Sauropoda
Suborder
Sauropodomorpha
Order Saurischia

DIET
Tree leaves, ferns

MAMENCHISAURUS

A LARGE DINOSAUR from China, "Mamen Brook lizard" had more cervical vertebrae than any other sauropod, and the longest neck of any animal ever. Some individuals may have had necks 49ft (15m) long. Yet the neck was comparatively light: some areas of bone were eggshell-thin. Each cervical vertebra (neck bone) had two rodlike ribs to stiffen the neck, as in other sauropods. Some features of the spine are reminiscent of *Diplodocus*. Skull fragments found in the 1980s suggest *Mamenchisaurus* had a taller, blunter snout than *Diplodocus*, and teeth that were sturdier and more spoon-shaped.

■ LIFE AND BEHAVIOR ■

Scientists disagree about how this dinosaur used its ultra-long neck. Some artists have illustrated *Mamenchisaurus* with its neck jutting out almost parallel with the top of its back. This fits in with a theory that the sauropod stood in lakes, its neck floating on the water and swinging from side to side as its mouth cut a swath through the soft-leaved water plants. Most experts now reject this theory and claim that *Mamenchisaurus* lived on land and raised its neck to browse on branches high above. This appears more probable for four main reasons. First, if the dinosaur did have strong, spoon-shaped teeth, it seems unlikely that they would have been needed for cropping soft-leaved water plants. Second, the neck was lighter than it looked and should not have been difficult to lift. Third, two dorsal vertebrae near the neck apparently met at an angle that would tend to make the neck curve up from the shoulders. Elephantine limbs provide a fourth indication that *Mamenchisaurus* lived on land. This dinosaur would have lived in herds, the adults guarding the young from such hungry carnosaurs as *Szechuanosaurus* and *Yangchuanosaurus*, which occur in the same Chinese rock formation. Scientists conjecture that *Mamenchisaurus* might have belonged to a uniquely Asian family of dinosaurs, together with the two other long-necked sauropods known from Late Jurassic China: *Omeisaurus* and *Euhelopus*.

SKELETON EXPOSED

Our restoration is based on a skeleton that lacked a skull. (The head and teeth are depicted as if they resembled those of *Diplodocus*.) As many as 19 cervical vertebrae—more than any other sauropod's—supported the enormously long neck. The forelimbs were relatively longer and sturdier than those of *Diplodocus*, and the bones of the hind limbs were robust. The tail's chevron bones bore fore-and-aft extensions similar to the tail skids of *Diplodocus*; the long tail may have ended in a whiplash.

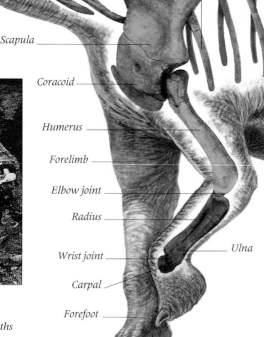

Dorsal vertebra

Cervical vertebra

Rib

Cervical rib

Scapula

Coracoid

Humerus

Forelimb

Elbow joint

Radius

Ulna

Wrist joint

Carpal

Forefoot

EXCAVATING A SKELETON
This photograph was taken during an excavation in 1957. Scientists from Beijing and Chonquing, Sichuan took three months to remove this colossus from the site.

Long, flexible neck

Naris (nostril opening) situated high up on the head

Mandible

Tooth (based on Diplodocus)

MAMENCHISAURUS

Mamenchisaurus was an immensely long, quadrupedal plant-eater. It had the longest known neck of all dinosaurs, and probably a blunt snout and strong teeth.

THE MESOZOIC ERA

MYA 248	208	144	65
TRIASSIC	JURASSIC		CRETACEOUS

SIZE
Length 82ft (25m)
Weight 26.6 tons

TIME
160MYA

LOCATION
China Sichuan, Gansu, Xinjiang

DIET
Tree leaves

CLASSIFICATION
Family Euhelopodidae
Infraorder Sauropoda
Suborder Sauropodomorpha
Order Saurischia

DEEP-SNOUTED SKULL

Mamenchisaurus's missing skull might have looked more like *Euhelopus*'s short, steep-snouted skull than *Diplodocus*'s long, low one. *Euhelopus* had larger teeth than *Diplodocus*, and these grew from the sides of the jaws as well as from the front.

Orbit

Antorbital fenestra

Naris

Maxilla

Tooth

Infratemporal fenestra

Mandible

AQUATIC RESTORATION
An old picture shows two Euhelopus *snorkeling and browsing underwater. Experts no longer believe that sauropods needed water to support their heavy bodies.*

Femur

Knee joint

Fibula

Tibia

Ankle joint

Hind limb

Tarsal

Claw

Whiplash tail

CARING PARENTS

Adults are thought to have cared well for their young, guarding them against attack by the dangerous theropod dinosaurs *Szechuanosaurus* and *Yangchuanosaurus*.

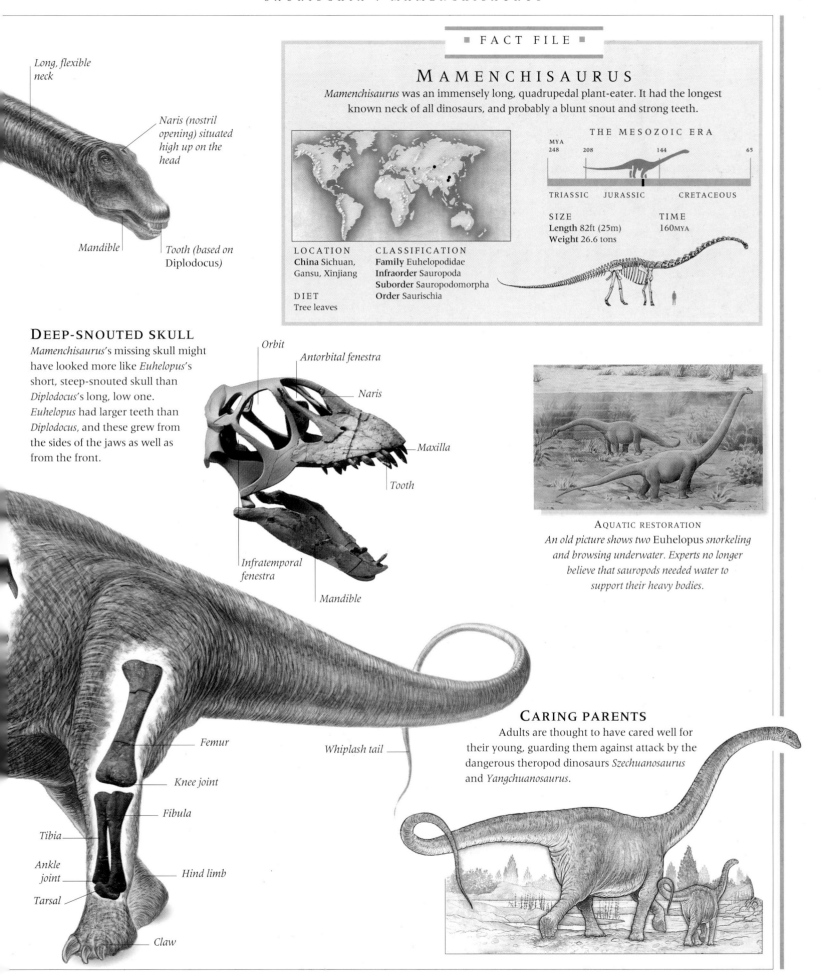

SALTASAURUS

BEFORE PALEONTOLOGISTS in
Argentina identified *Saltasaurus* ("Salta
lizard") in 1980, they had assumed that
its bony armor, long known from fossil finds in their
country, had belonged to ankylosaurs, for these were
thought to be the only dinosaurs with armor. The
discovery of *Saltasaurus* proved that some sauropods
grew armor too. Close-packed bony nodules and
ridged, bony plates as big as a human palm fortified
its back and sides. A fairly small sauropod, *Saltasaurus*
had stocky limbs, a sturdy tail tapering to a slender,
diplodocid-like whiplash, and the distinctively shaped
vertebrae characteristic of the titanosaurids.

■ LIFE AND BEHAVIOR ■

Like other sauropods, *Saltasaurus* would have walked
on land and could have raised its long neck to feed
on vegetation out of
reach of smaller
herbivores. This
titanosaurid also may have been able
to rear up on its hind limbs, supporting
its body with its tail, in order to reach even
less accessible sources of food. *Saltasaurus*'s
relatively small size made it more vulnerable than
larger sauropods to attack by big carnivorous dinosaurs. But
any animal that tried to leap upon *Saltasaurus*'s back
would have stubbed its claws and snapped off
teeth when it tried to sink them into the rock-
hard armor in *Saltasaurus*'s tough hide.

■ LOCATION ■

The same Late Cretaceous rock formations in
which *Saltasaurus* bones were discovered also
contain the skeletons of other titanosaurids like
Antarctosaurus, *Argyrosaurus*, and *Laplatasaurus*.
Very likely, most or all of these had armor plating
too. Superior defense may be only part of the
explanation why big saurischian herbivores
continued to exist in South America long after all
sauropods had died out in North America.
According to one theory, the North American
sauropods suffered from competition with duck-
billed and horned dinosaurs, which may have
been largely confined to the Northern continents
by a sea barrier. Another possibility is that the
new flowering plants, appearing in the north at
that time, were not suitable for sauropods to eat.
Whatever the cause, one titanosaurid
(*Alamosaurus*) did succeed in crossing from South
to North America, and survived there.

SALTASAURUS SPECIES
Three species of this fairly small, armored sauropod
are known: *Saltasaurus loricatus* (about six imperfect
skeletons), *Saltasaurus australis* (at least ten
individuals) and *Saltasaurus robustus* (vertebrae and
limbs possibly from three specimens).

ARMORED SKIN
The 1980 description of fossil
scraps of *Saltasaurus*'s skin, with its
bony, pea-size lumps,
supported what one
scientist had suspected
as long ago as 1896: that
titanosaurids had been
armored sauropods.

TAIL Used as a support when
the animal reared, *Saltasaurus*'s
long tail had interlocking bones
with ball-and-socket joints.

*Thick,
muscular
tail*

LATE CRETACEOUS SCENE
Three Saltasaurus, *four duck-billed dinosaurs, and a small
theropod,* Noasaurus, *visit a river in what is now Salta province in
northwestern Argentina.*

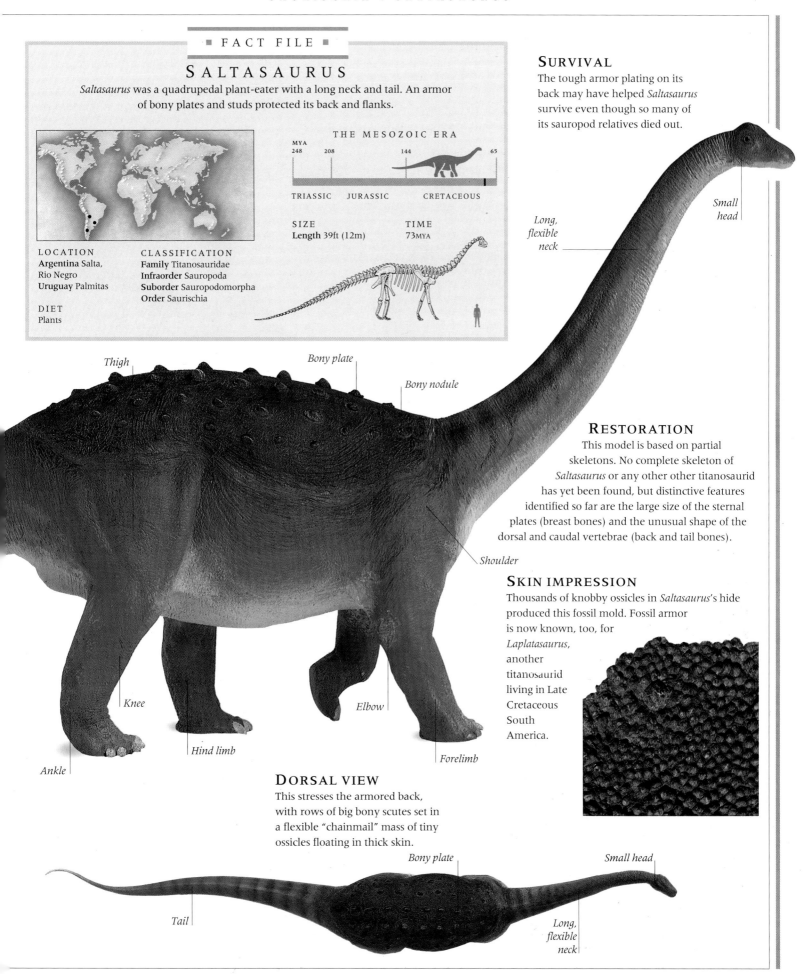

SALTASAURUS

Saltasaurus was a quadrupedal plant-eater with a long neck and tail. An armor of bony plates and studs protected its back and flanks.

THE MESOZOIC ERA

MYA
248   208   144   65

TRIASSIC   JURASSIC   CRETACEOUS

SIZE   TIME
Length 39ft (12m)   73MYA

LOCATION
Argentina Salta,
Rio Negro
Uruguay Palmitas

CLASSIFICATION
Family Titanosauridae
Infraorder Sauropoda
Suborder Sauropodomorpha
Order Saurischia

DIET
Plants

SURVIVAL

The tough armor plating on its back may have helped *Saltasaurus* survive even though so many of its sauropod relatives died out.

Small head

Long, flexible neck

Thigh

Bony plate

Bony nodule

RESTORATION

This model is based on partial skeletons. No complete skeleton of *Saltasaurus* or any other other titanosaurid has yet been found, but distinctive features identified so far are the large size of the sternal plates (breast bones) and the unusual shape of the dorsal and caudal vertebrae (back and tail bones).

Shoulder

SKIN IMPRESSION

Thousands of knobby ossicles in *Saltasaurus*'s hide produced this fossil mold. Fossil armor is now known, too, for *Laplatasaurus*, another titanosaurid living in Late Cretaceous South America.

Knee

Elbow

Hind limb

Ankle

Forelimb

DORSAL VIEW

This stresses the armored back, with rows of big bony scutes set in a flexible "chainmail" mass of tiny ossicles floating in thick skin.

Bony plate

Small head

Tail

Long, flexible neck

SEGNOSAURUS

A HEAVY-BODIED BIPED as long as the largest modern crocodile, "slow lizard" is often thought of as having a small, narrow skull with a shallow lower jaw, toothless beak, somewhat sharp yet prosauropod-like cheek teeth, and fleshy cheek pouches. *Segnosaurus* had muscular arms, and its three-fingered hands probably bore huge, curved claws. Between its broad back and bulky belly, the pubic hipbones slanted backward. Other peculiarities included short, possibly webbed, feet with four clawed toes.

❋ LIFE AND BEHAVIOR ❋

Segnosaurus belongs to the segnosaurs, an unusual group of saurischians with features that are reminiscent of theropods, prosauropods, and ornithischians. Few other dinosaurs have posed greater puzzles to scientists in their attempt to build up a picture of a particular creature's way of life. One possibility is that *Segnosaurus* might have used its strong arms and hands, probably equipped with long, sharp claws, to rake open termites' nests to feed on the insects. The great anteater, which lives in South America today, wields its claws in this way. Powerful arms and talons could also have served as defensive weapons. Some people believe that *Segnosaurus* swam in lakes or rivers, catching fish to eat—a notion that derives from the discovery, near a find of *Segnosaurus* bones, of fossil tracks preserving a series of four-toed, web-footed imprints. Yet *Segnosaurus*'s mouth seems ill-designed for gripping slippery water animals. Instead, it may have been an animal with a toothless beak, ridged teeth, and roomy cheeks, well equipped for nipping off leaves and biting them into smaller pieces. *Segnosaurus*'s hip structure also suggests a plant diet, since the back-turned pubis would have made room for the great gut needed to digest large quantities of low-grade plant material.

❋ UNUSUAL THEROPOD ❋

If the third possibility is true, it would make *Segnosaurus* into a dinosaur oddity, a plant-eating theropod. Its jaw and hip structure would be similar to those of many plant-eating dinosaurs, but no other theropod had these features. The limb bones indicate that *Segnosaurus* might have managed only a brisk walk or a slow run. Certainly, with longer thighs than shins, and short, broad feet, *Segnosaurus* would have moved around too slowly to pursue and catch active prey in the manner of most ordinary theropods.

AS A TERMITE-EATER

Segnosaurus is shown using its immensely strong arms and long, clawed hands to rake open a nest mound teeming with blind, white, antlike termites. (Like *Segnosaurus*, termites appeared during the Late Cretaceous.) *Segnosaurus* might have lapped them up by the mouthful with a long, sticky tongue.

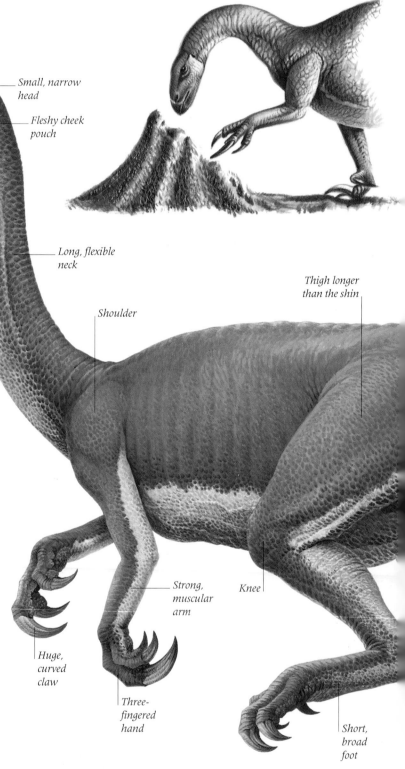

Small, narrow head

Fleshy cheek pouch

Long, flexible neck

Shoulder

Thigh longer than the shin

Strong, muscular arm

Knee

Huge, curved claw

Three-fingered hand

Short, broad foot

AS A FISH-EATER

A second scenario portrays *Segnosaurus* as a fish-eater. Mongolian scientist Altangerel Perle, who named *Segnosaurus* in 1979, thought this dinosaur capable of swimming in lakes or rivers and seizing fish in its beak. But a toothless beak might have been a clumsy fish-catching device compared to the long, narrow, pointed teeth of fish-eating crocodiles.

AS A PLANT-EATER

American paleontologist Gregory Paul made the third suggestion: that *Segnosaurus* had evolved for eating plants. Segnosaurs are now seen by some scientists as bizarre plant-eating theropods.

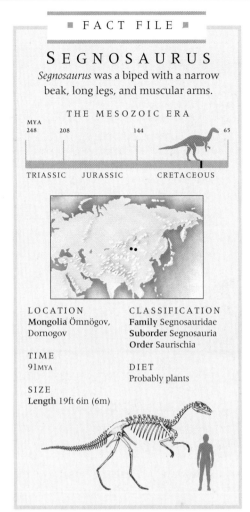

EXTERNAL APPEARANCE

Segnosaurus is here depicted as a heavy-bodied, bipedal theropod. However, other artists sometimes show segnosaurs as having walked on all fours. By the early 1990s, *Segnosaurus* was known only from three partial specimens. The various remains included the lower jaw with teeth, some limb bones, and hipbones, but no skull. The limited scope of the finds means that the exact appearance of *Segnosaurus* and other segnosaurs remains a matter for speculation.

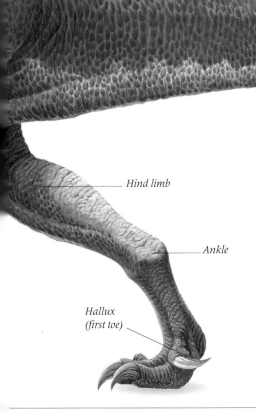

Scaly skin

Hind limb

Ankle

Hallux (first toe)

SEGNOSAURUS

Ilium

Hip socket

Ischium

Pubis

ADASAURUS

Ilium

Hip socket

Ischium

Pubis

HYPSILOPHODON

Ilium

Hip socket

Ischium

Pubis

HIPBONES COMPARED

The scientists who found segnosaurs thought their mixture of features represented a third dinosaur group, between the saurischians and ornithischians. In *Segnosaurus* the pubis sloped back against the ischium, in the same way as in the ornithischian *Hypsilophodon*. Most saurischians' pubes sloped forward or down, but there were exceptions, such as *Adasaurus*.

THYREOPHORANS

T HYREOPHORANS ("SHIELD BEARERS") were a diverse group of mainly quadrupedal, armored ornithischians, with small cheek teeth, distinctive cheek bones, heavy limbs, and rows of protective bony studs, plates, or spikes down the back. They probably browsed on low-level vegetation. These dinosaurs were primitive ornithischians with simpler teeth and jaws than ornithopods or marginocephalians. The most primitive of all thyreophorans were relatively small, Early Jurassic forms, namely *Scelidosaurus* and *Scutellosaurus*, and possibly the poorly known genera *Tatisaurus* and *Echinodon*. The rest are grouped together in the infraorders Stegosauria (chiefly Jurassic beasts) and Ankylosauria (which replaced stegosaurs). Both contained beasts that grew up to 33ft (10m) long.

An ankylosaurid tail club could have broken a tyrannosaurid's ankle.

SCELIDOSAURUS AND MINMI
Scelidosaurus *(top) was an early thyreophoran close in ancestry to such ankylosaurs as* Minmi *(above).* Minmi *was so well protected that bony armor guarded even its belly.*

NODOSAURID SPINE
This broad-based, sharply pointed, bony spine stuck up from a nodosaurid's shoulder. In life, a horny sheath made the spine more formidable.

■ SCELIDOSAURIDAE ■

This family contained *Scelidosaurus*, a 13ft (4m) long quadruped, with a small head and rows of small, bony studs shielding its body. This early thyreophoran is known from Early Jurassic English rocks, and also lived in Arizona and Tibet. *Scutellosaurus*, *Tatisaurus*, and *Echinodon* shared some features with *Scelidosaurus*. All four may be close to stegosaur and ankylosaur ancestors.

■ STEGOSAURIA ■

These dinosaurs were medium to large quadrupedal herbivores. Most had long, thick, strong hind limbs, giving them an arched back highest at the hips. Some paleontologists believe stegosaurs could have reared to browse higher up. The low head was small, with a beak and cheek teeth. The most distinctive features were two rows of tall, bony plates and/or spikes jutting up from head to tail, and at least two pairs of long tail spines. Some stegosaurs had shoulder spines too. Despite their size, the largest stegosaurs had a brain no bigger than a dog's. A large center in the hip region (often misnamed a "second brain") helped to control hind limbs and tail. Both known families of stegosaurs probably arose

in China in Early Jurassic times. One family later spread to Africa, Europe, India, and North America. Stegosaurs were an important group of dinosaurs in the Late Jurassic. Several genera survived into the Early Cretaceous, but only India's stegosaurs seem to have persisted into the Late Cretaceous. HUAYANGOSAURIDAE formed the more primitive family of stegosaurs, with a deep, short snout, a beak with upper teeth, fairly long forelimbs, and distinctive bones in the skull and hips. The family is known only from *Huayangosaurus*, a Middle Jurassic genus 15ft (4.5m) long from China. STEGOSAURIDAE basically resembled *Huayangosaurus*, but they had entirely toothless beaks. Some kinds had two rows of paired plates and/or spines jutting up from the neck, back, and tail. In *Stegosaurus* the plates alternated instead of growing side by side. Reputedly the largest stegosaur, *Stegosaurus* grew up to 29ft 6in (about 9m) long. Altogether, there were about 15 stegosaurid

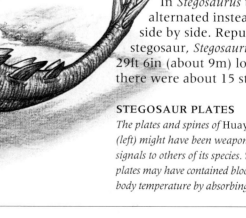

STEGOSAUR PLATES
The plates and spines of Huayangosaurus taibaii *(left) might have been weapons or used as mating signals to others of its species.* Stegosaurus's *big plates may have contained blood vessels that adjusted body temperature by absorbing and releasing heat.*

genera. This family lived from the Middle Jurassic to the Late Cretaceous. Its members occurred in Africa, Asia, Europe, India, and North America.

✳ ANKYLOSAURIA ✳

Ankylosaurs were relatively low-slung dinosaurs with broad heads; somewhat short necks; heavy, barrel-shaped bodies supported by four sturdy, erect limbs; and fairly long, muscular tails. Instead of tall plates or spines, these armored ornithischians depended upon bands of bony studs or plates, some sheathed in horn, to protect the body. These covered the neck, back, and flanks (and, in at least some specimens, the belly). Bony plates reinforced the broad, low skull, closing four "windows" left open in most other dinosaurs. A tail club or shoulder spines served as counter-offensive weapons. Ankylosaurs were replacing stegosaurs by the Early Cretaceous and became the most abundant, low-browsing, quadrupedal dinosaurs. They are chiefly known from fossils found in North America and Asia, but Australian discoveries prove that they also spread to southern continents. There were two ankylosaur families: the Nodosauridae and the Ankylosauridae.

NODOSAURIDAE were the more primitive ankylosaurs. Their skulls had an unusual palate in the shape of an hourglass. Nodosauridae lacked a tail club, but some bore dangerously long, sharp, shoulder spines. There are more than 20 named genera, ranging from about 5ft to 25ft (1.6m to 7.6m) long. Nodosaurids lived from Middle Jurassic to Late Cretaceous times and occurred in Asia, Australia, Europe, North America, and probably Antarctica.

ANKYLOSAURIDAE had skulls at least as broad as they were long, with pointed "corners" at the back, and intricate breathing passages. These dinosaurs lacked long shoulder spines but had a tail ending in a heavy, bony club. This tail club could be swung as a powerful weapon against attack by predatory dinosaurs such as the tyrannosaurids. Ankylosaurids ranged from about 18ft to 33ft (5.5m to 10m) long. They include more than a dozen named genera. This dinosaur family flourished from Early to Late Cretaceous times, in Asia and North America.

THYREOPHORAN FAMILY TREE

This diagram shows relationships among thyreophoran families (the names ending in -idae), each containing one genus or several genera. All thyreophorans had distinctive cheek bones and rows of bony studs, spikes, or plates running down the back. They were among the most primitive ornithischians, with teeth and jaws less well-evolved for slicing up or pulping vegetation than almost all the rest. Small, early, rather lightly armored forms, here represented by the Scelidosauridae, gave rise to two families of stegosaurs and two families of ankylosaurs. Stegosaurs had rows of tall plates or spikes on the neck, back, and tail. The heavily armored ankylosaurs were built like walking armored cars.

KEY

● Suborder

● Infraorder

THYREOPHORA

Stegosauria

Ankylosauria

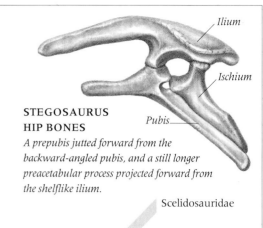

STEGOSAURUS HIP BONES
A prepubis jutted forward from the backward-angled pubis, and a still longer preacetabular process projected forward from the shelflike ilium.

Scelidosauridae

Stegosauridae

Huayangosauridae

Nodosauridae

Ankylosauridae

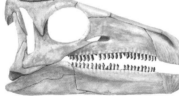

SCELIDOSAURUS SKULL

STEGOSAURUS SKULL

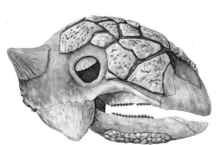

EUOPLOCEPHALUS SKULL

THREE THYREOPHORAN SKULLS

These illustrations contrast skulls taken from three thyreophorans: the scelidosaurid Scelidosaurus (top), the stegosaurid Stegosaurus (middle), and the ankylosaurid Euoplocephalus (bottom). All three have toothless beaks, although primitive, early Scelidosaurus probably had at least premaxillary (front upper) teeth. The skull of Stegosaurus was long and narrow, while that of Euoplocephalus was as wide as it was long. Narrow-beaked Stegosaurus could have selected juicy fruits or other delicacies, while broad-beaked Euoplocephalus probably cropped any low-growing plants. Bony slabs and eyelids protected Euoplocephalus's head against the formidable jaws of tyrannosaurids.

SCELIDOSAURUS

L IGHTLY ARMORED "limb lizard" was a herbivore no longer than a car. It had a small head, on a neck that was relatively long for an armored dinosaur, and a long, heavy body that was highest at the hips and underpinned by four sturdy limbs. Bony tendons probably strengthened and stiffened the tail. The hipbones and armored skin recall those of the primitive North American ornithischian *Scutellosaurus*. The teeth resemble those of the stegosaurs. Above all, the rows of ridged, bony plates and studs running down the neck, back, and tail seem prototypes for the more formidable defenses of the ankylosaurs. *Scelidosaurus* might have been ancestral to these fellow thyreophorans.

■ LIFE AND BEHAVIOR ■

Scelidosaurus ambled slowly on all fours through a leafy landscape, stopping frequently to shear off low-growing soft-leaved plants or juicy fruits with its narrow beak. With less complex teeth and jaws than later ornithischians, it would have chewed with simple up-and-down jaw movements. Young individuals perhaps added extra protein to their diet by eating insects. Some *Scelidosaurus* fossil bones are preserved in marine sediments, prompting one authority to think that *Scelidosaurus* was amphibious. More probably, these creatures lived on riverbanks, and sometimes drowned, perhaps when the river overflowed. The corpses might then have been carried out to sea, to be buried and preserved.

■ STANCE AND GAIT ■

Scelidosaurus may sometimes have reared to browse on the leafy twigs of trees, but it would seem that its normal mode of locomotion was on all fours. Certainly the body shape strongly suggests this: the hips are the highest point, but not so high as to make the hind limbs a sort of fulcrum on top of which the stiffened tail and the short neck and head might pivot. Moreover, the hands on the forelimbs appear designed for weight-bearing and were as broad as the feet on the hind limbs. Cornered, *Scelidosaurus* would have crouched, exposing only its tough, armored, upper hide to a theropod's fangs and claws. Even its head and neck bore bony reinforcements that were thick and hard enough to break off the teeth of most attackers.

SKULL

This fragmented skull of a young dinosaur was found by amateur fossil hunters in 1985 near Charmouth on England's southern coast. Identified as belonging to a *Scelidosaurus*, it has teeth in its front upper jaw, a characteristic feature in the skulls of primitive ornithischians.

Braincase
Orbit
Beak
Conical tooth
Fragment of mandible

SKIN

Scelidosaurus skin impressions show that between rows of bony studs, the skin bore a mosaic of little, rounded scales like those of *Heloderma*, the North American venomous lizard commonly known as the Gila monster.

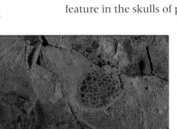

BONY PLATES

Scelidosaurus was protected by individual bony plates, known as scutes. Their shape and size depended on their location on the neck, body, or tail.

Stiffened tail for balance

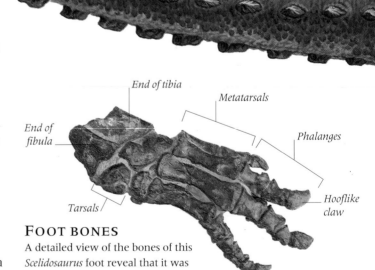

End of tibia
Metatarsals
End of fibula
Phalanges
Tarsals
Hooflike claw

FOOT BONES

A detailed view of the bones of this *Scelidosaurus* foot reveal that it was long and quite broad. There were four toes: three long and one short. The long toes helped to spread the body's weight. Fleshy pads possibly cushioned the toes.

SCUTELLOSAURUS

Like *Scelidosaurus*, *Scutellosaurus* was a primitive ornithischian close to the ancestry of ankylosaurs and stegosaurs. A lightly armored herbivore, this Early Jurassic dinosaur from Arizona was evidently descended from small, bipedal ancestors. *Scutellosaurus* could walk or run on its long hind limbs, balanced by its elongated tail. However, the weight of a lengthy body bearing rows of bony scutes made the animal front-heavy. *Scutellosaurus* often tended to go down on all fours, supporting the forepart of its body on its relatively long forelimbs and large hands.

SCUTES

Hundreds of scutes shielded *Scutellosaurus* from attack by theropods. The largest scutes ran down the back, possibly in one, but probably in two rows.

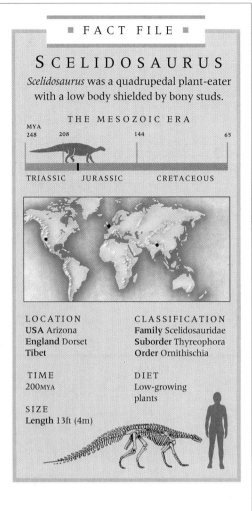

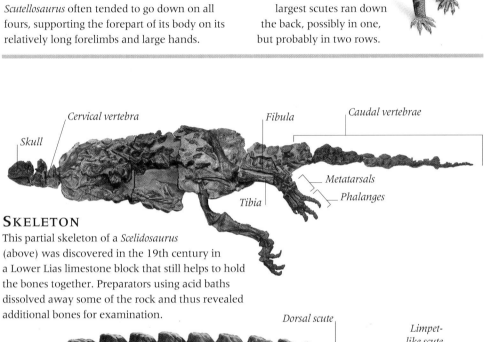

Skull

Cervical vertebra

Fibula

Caudal vertebrae

Metatarsals

Phalanges

Tibia

SKELETON

This partial skeleton of a *Scelidosaurus* (above) was discovered in the 19th century in a Lower Lias limestone block that still helps to hold the bones together. Preparators using acid baths dissolved away some of the rock and thus revealed additional bones for examination.

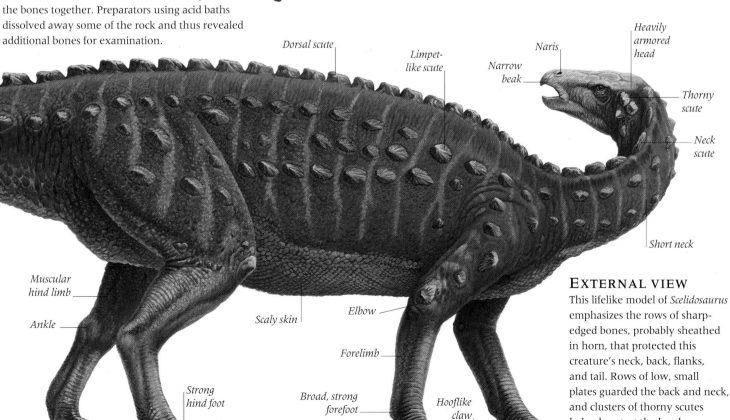

Dorsal scute

Limpet-like scute

Narrow beak

Naris

Heavily armored head

Thorny scute

Neck scute

Short neck

Muscular hind limb

Ankle

Scaly skin

Elbow

Forelimb

Strong hind foot

Broad, strong forefoot

Hooflike claw

EXTERNAL VIEW

This lifelike model of *Scelidosaurus* emphasizes the rows of sharp-edged bones, probably sheathed in horn, that protected this creature's neck, back, flanks, and tail. Rows of low, small plates guarded the back and neck, and clusters of thorny scutes helped protect the head.

STEGOSAURUS

S TEGOSAURUS ("ROOF LIZARD") gets its name from big bony plates that jutted upward from the neck, back, and upper tail. A bony plate probably protected each hip, and two pairs of spikes stuck out sideways from the end of the tail. As heavy as a big rhinoceros and about the length of a bus, *Stegosaurus* was the largest known plated dinosaur. It stood more than room-high at the hips and walked on elephantine limbs. Its small head was held low and ended in a toothless, horn-covered beak. Behind the beak were numerous teeth. It is not known if the tail drooped or was held aloft.

SEARCHING FOR FOOD
A strolling Stegosaurus *(above) had to be prepared to wield its spiky tail against aggressive carnivores. The greatest dangers probably came from* Allosaurus *and* Ceratosaurus, *but packs of smaller theropods may also have preyed on the great beast.*

■ LIFE AND BEHAVIOR ■

Fossil evidence suggests that *Stegosaurus* roamed wooded plains, browsing on low vegetation. An alternative theory holds that it was a high-level feeder, browsing at heights up to 12ft (about 3.5m) and that it was actually built to rear up. Some evidence lies in the fact that the hind limbs were longer than the forelimbs. *Stegosaurus*'s tall vertebral spines could have provided enough leverage for the back muscles to be able to lift the weight of the fore part of the body. The supple tail was better-suited to being pressed against the ground than the rigid tails of most ornithischians. In this way, tail and hind limbs could have formed a tripod when a *Stegosaurus* reared up. Most dinosaurologists are, however, unconvinced by this theory. Ideas about *Stegosaurus*'s diet, too, have changed over the years. At first, it was thought that the animal had weak teeth and that it used to feed only on soft foods; today, however, this assumption is in some doubt. On the other hand, the narrow snout may indicate that *Stegosaurus* was a selective feeder; and it may have picked out such choice items as seed-fern "fruits" and the fleshy "flowers" of cycadeoids. *Stegosaurus*'s spectacular back plates probably helped soak up and shed heat, and rival males may also have used them in harmless threat displays. There were no plates covering the flanks, but a *Stegosaurus* would have been able to fend off enemies by swishing its spiked tail, or backing into them like a porcupine. A discovery in 1992 revealed disk-shaped plates protecting the hips, and a pattern of disk-shaped bony studs that shielded the vulnerable throat.

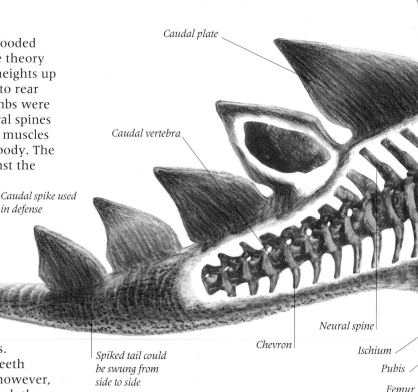

Caudal plate

Caudal vertebra

Caudal spike used in defense

Spiked tail could be swung from side to side

Chevron

Neural spine

Ischium

Pubis

Femur

Knee joint

Broad foot providing a stable base

RECONSTRUCTED SKELETON

A reconstructed skeleton, with added body outline, here reveals the robust bony framework of this large, heavy-bodied, plated dinosaur. Until 1992 scientists were unsure how its plates had been arranged upon the neck, back, and tail. Some believed they had been paired. Others thought they alternated. A third group put them in one row, with big plates overlapping. In 1992 a newly discovered skeleton, found in Colorado, proved the plates had formed two staggered rows.

ELONGATED SKULL

The skull of *Stegosaurus* (right) was narrow, elongated, and very low. Unlike a typical dinosaur skull, it lacked an antorbital fenestra (hole between the orbit and naris). A different *Stegosaurus* species might have had a shorter, blunter skull, although some experts have assigned that species to the genus *Diracodon*.

CHEEK TOOTH

The asymmetrical fossil cheek tooth (below) has been attributed to *Stegosaurus*. Denticles corrugate the front and back of the crown. Such ridges would have helped the ornithischian chew up plant foods. Most stegosaurs' teeth would have had fewer ridges.

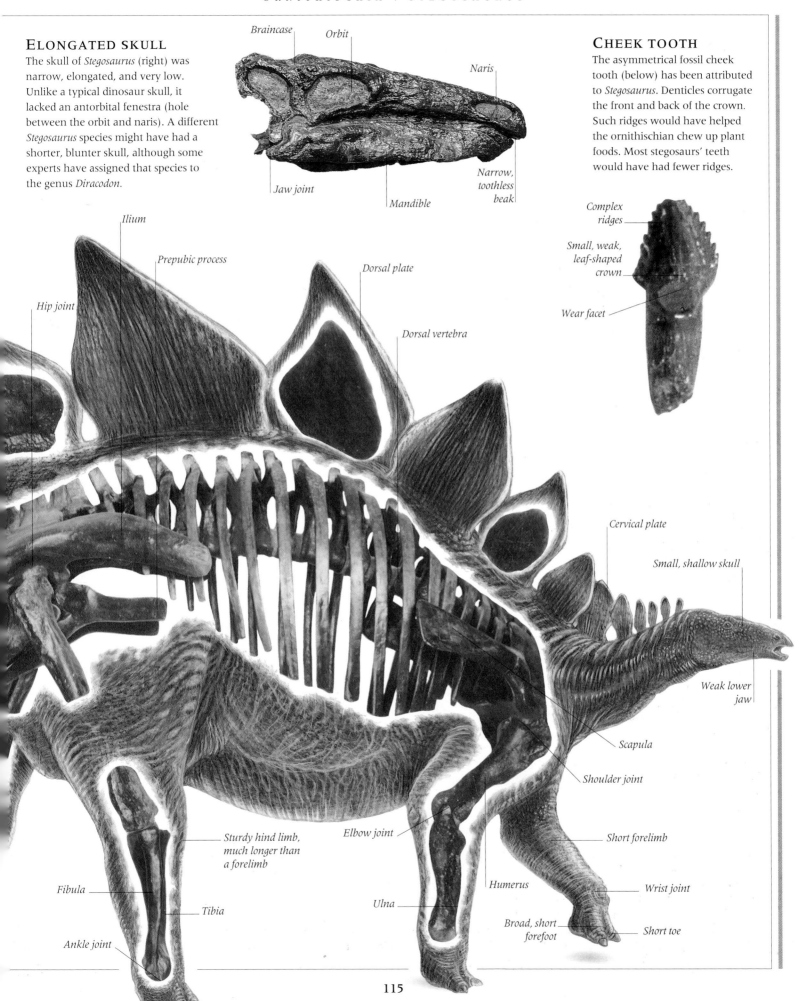

Braincase

Orbit

Naris

Jaw joint

Mandible

Narrow, toothless beak

Complex ridges

Small, weak, leaf-shaped crown

Wear facet

Ilium

Prepubic process

Dorsal plate

Hip joint

Dorsal vertebra

Cervical plate

Small, shallow skull

Weak lower jaw

Scapula

Shoulder joint

Sturdy hind limb, much longer than a forelimb

Elbow joint

Short forelimb

Fibula

Humerus

Wrist joint

Tibia

Ulna

Ankle joint

Broad, short forefoot

Short toe

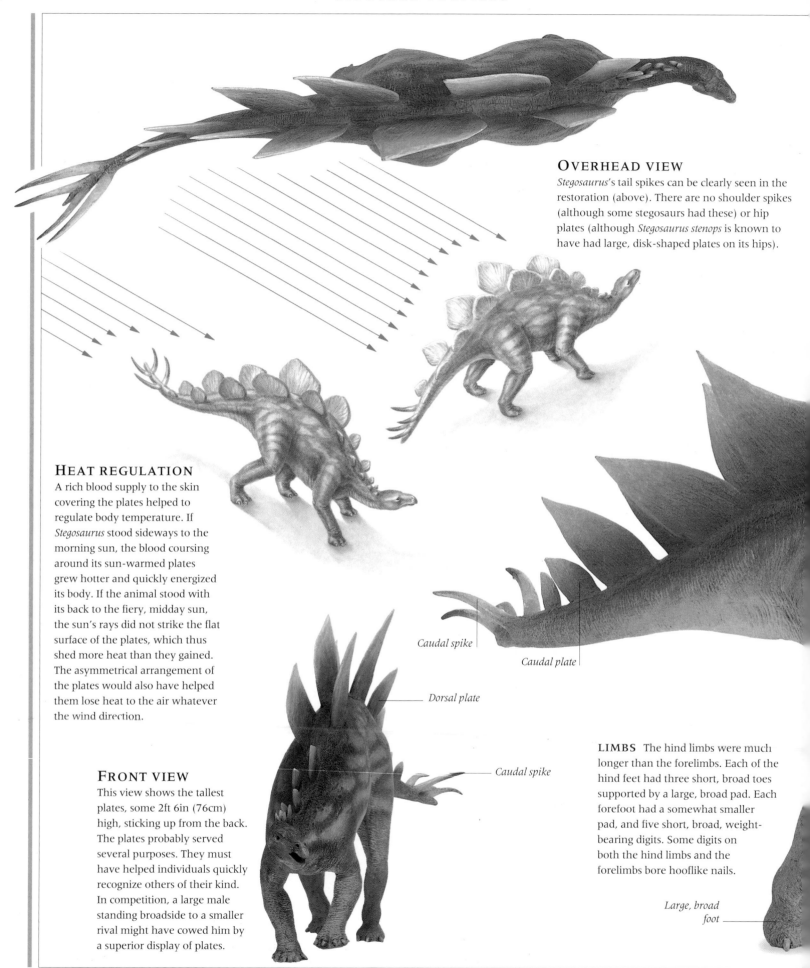

OVERHEAD VIEW

Stegosaurus's tail spikes can be clearly seen in the restoration (above). There are no shoulder spikes (although some stegosaurs had these) or hip plates (although *Stegosaurus stenops* is known to have had large, disk-shaped plates on its hips).

HEAT REGULATION

A rich blood supply to the skin covering the plates helped to regulate body temperature. If *Stegosaurus* stood sideways to the morning sun, the blood coursing around its sun-warmed plates grew hotter and quickly energized its body. If the animal stood with its back to the fiery, midday sun, the sun's rays did not strike the flat surface of the plates, which thus shed more heat than they gained. The asymmetrical arrangement of the plates would also have helped them lose heat to the air whatever the wind direction.

Caudal spike

Caudal plate

Dorsal plate

Caudal spike

FRONT VIEW

This view shows the tallest plates, some 2ft 6in (76cm) high, sticking up from the back. The plates probably served several purposes. They must have helped individuals quickly recognize others of their kind. In competition, a large male standing broadside to a smaller rival might have cowed him by a superior display of plates.

LIMBS The hind limbs were much longer than the forelimbs. Each of the hind feet had three short, broad toes supported by a large, broad pad. Each forefoot had a somewhat smaller pad, and five short, broad, weight-bearing digits. Some digits on both the hind limbs and the forelimbs bore hooflike nails.

Large, broad foot

PLATES

The thin, erect, bony plates on the neck, back, and tail were graduated in size: the biggest above the back, the smallest over the neck and tail. The largest of all plates come from *Stegosaurus stenops*, which some scientists believe is a separate genus called *Diracodon*.

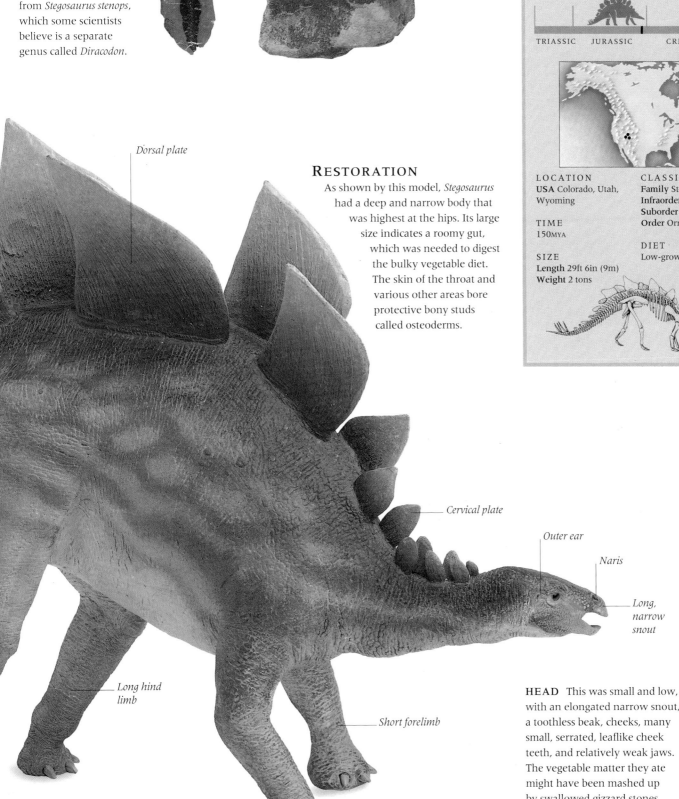

Dorsal plate

RESTORATION

As shown by this model, *Stegosaurus* had a deep and narrow body that was highest at the hips. Its large size indicates a roomy gut, which was needed to digest the bulky vegetable diet. The skin of the throat and various other areas bore protective bony studs called osteoderms.

Cervical plate

Outer ear

Naris

Long, narrow snout

Long hind limb

Short forelimb

HEAD This was small and low, with an elongated narrow snout, a toothless beak, cheeks, many small, serrated, leaflike cheek teeth, and relatively weak jaws. The vegetable matter they ate might have been mashed up by swallowed gizzard stones.

FACT FILE

STEGOSAURUS

A large quadruped, *Stegosaurus* had two rows of bony plates from neck to tail.

THE MESOZOIC ERA

MYA				
248	208		144	65

TRIASSIC   JURASSIC   CRETACEOUS

LOCATION
USA Colorado, Utah, Wyoming

TIME
150MYA

SIZE
Length 29ft 6in (9m)
Weight 2 tons

CLASSIFICATION
Family Stegosauridae
Infraorder Stegosauria
Suborder Thyreophora
Order Ornithischia

DIET
Low-growing plants

KENTROSAURUS

I N THE EARLY 1900s, scores of bones unearthed in what is now Tanzania made *Kentrosaurus* ("spiky lizard") Africa's best-known plated dinosaur. *Kentrosaurus* resembled a smaller, narrower-spined version of the Chinese stegosaur *Tuojiangosaurus*. Six pairs of small, bony plates stuck up from its neck and shoulders. Behind these, three pairs of flat spines sprouted from its back; and five pairs of very long, sharp, narrow spines guarded its tail. *Kentrosaurus* might also have had a pair of long platelike shoulder spines. As in other stegosaurs, there were no bony tendons to stiffen the tail or back.

RESTORATION
This illustration shows paired plates and spikes on the back and a spiny plate on a shoulder. *Kentrosaurus*'s tail might have been held high, as here, or simply allowed to droop.

IN EAST AFRICA
Expedition leader Werner Janensch and his assistant Salim Tombali examine dinosaur bones unearthed between 1909 and 1911 in what is now Tanzania.

◾ LIFE AND BEHAVIOR ◾

Scientists found fossils of *Kentrosaurus* where a prehistoric river had wound its way almost to the ocean. The air was always warm there, and rainy periods alternated with droughts. Even when dry weather killed shallow-rooted plants, *Kentrosaurus* could always find vegetation growing in the moist soil near the river. This dinosaur moved around on all fours and had short forelimbs and a short neck, so it is likely that it ate low-growing ferns and shrubby vegetation. However, it might also have reared up on its long, strong hind limbs and—partly propped up by its tail—reached leafy twigs. Even so, *Kentrosaurus* scarcely competed for food with the immense and much taller long-necked sauropods, such as *Dicraeosaurus*.

◾ SELF-DEFENSE ◾

Such placid animals as the sauropods posed no threat to *Kentrosaurus*. Its chief living enemies were big, predatory theropods resembling *Allosaurus* and *Ceratosaurus*. On occasions, *Kentrosaurus* might have had to defend itself by backing into an enemy approaching craftily from behind or to ward off a flank attack by lashing its spiky tail from side to side.

TRANSPORTING THE BONES
Porters carried thousands of loads of Kentrosaurus *and other dinosaur bones from Tendaguru Hill, Mtwara, to the Indian Ocean for shipment to Germany.*

TAILBONES
In most stegosaurs, the caudal neural spines (high, narrow "tops" of tail vertebrae) slope back. *Kentrosaurus* was unusual, for beyond tailbone 18, the neural spines lean forward. Other skeletal peculiarities were the protective chevrons shaped like plowshares.

Caudal spike

Backward-leaning neural spine

Forward-leaning neural spine

Caudal vertebra

Plowshare-shaped chevron

BRAIN CASTS

The small cast (right) filled the cavity occupied by *Kentrosaurus*'s brain. The much larger cast (above) filled a big hollow in two sacral vertebrae. This led to a belief that stegosaurs had two brains: one in the head and a larger one in the hips. In fact, the "second brain" was simply a nerve relay station serving the hind limbs and tail.

■ FACT FILE ■

KENTROSAURUS

Kentrosaurus was a quadrupedal plant-eater with a low head, rows of protective plates along its neck and shoulders, and spikes along its back and tail.

THE MESOZOIC ERA

MYA 248	208	144	65
TRIASSIC	JURASSIC		CRETACEOUS

LOCATION
Tanzania Mtwara

DIET
Low-growing plants

CLASSIFICATION
Family Stegosauridae
Infraorder Stegosauria
Suborder Thyreophora
Order Ornithischia

SIZE
Length 16ft (4.9m)
Weight 1 ton

TIME
156–150MYA

COMPOSITE SKELETON

This is one of two composite skeletons reconstructed in German museums from bones found in East Africa and brought to Europe in the early 1900s. The collection included hundreds of scattered parts of dismembered *Kentrosaurus* skeletons. There were more than 70 thighbones alone. Much of the material—once kept in Berlin's Humboldt Museum—was destroyed, unfortunately, in World War II. This reconstruction suggests that *Kentrosaurus* was more akin to *Tuojiangosaurus* than to *Stegosaurus*.

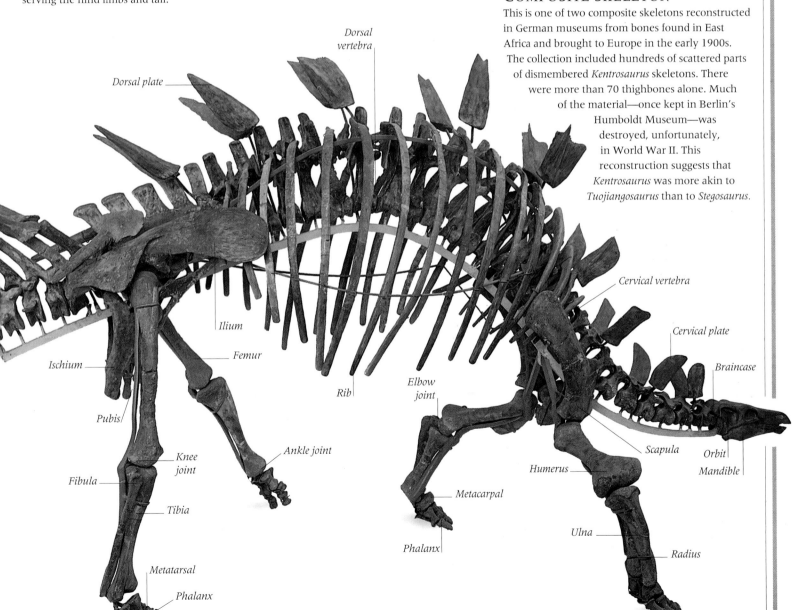

TUOJIANGOSAURUS

T UOJIANGOSAURUS ("Tuo River lizard") is the best-known plated dinosaur from southern China, where stegosaurs may have evolved before spreading to other continents. It was longer but lighter than today's heaviest rhinoceros and at the hips stood taller than a human. It had a typical stegosaur's small, low head with toothless beak and small teeth, an arched back, bulky body, heavy tail, and pillarlike limbs. Neck, back, and tail supported up to 15 pairs of pointed, vertical plates; rounded plates on the neck gave way to tall ones along the back. Two pairs of spikes stuck out from the tail-tip, and each shoulder may have borne a platelike spine.

LIFE RESTORATION
This lifelike restoration of the Chinese stegosaur Tuojiangosaurus *was based on the remains of two specimens.*

■ LIFE AND BEHAVIOR ■

Tuojiangosaurus plodded along river banks, browsing on the ferns and cycads that sprouted thickly in the rich river valley soil. Head slung low, the dinosaur cropped mouthfuls of leaves with its horny beak, stuffed them in its cheeks, chewed them between its small, ridged cheek teeth, and swallowed the pulp for digestion in its roomy gut. *Tuojiangosaurus* would have spent most of its waking life just eating, swallowing, and digesting leaves.

■ COMMUNITIES ■

Life was usually placid for this and other herbivores whose fossils now lie in the Shangshaximiao Formation of southern China: *Mamenchisaurus* and *Omeisaurus* (these were vast, long-necked sauropods), the small, primitive ornithischian *Gongbusaurus,* and two more plated dinosaurs—*Chialingosaurus* and *Chungkingosaurus.* When several species of stegosaurs lived closely together, distinctive plates or spines probably served as recognition signals. Occasionally, a *Tuojiangosaurus* male squared off against a rival or met a large, aggressive theropod. Only its spikes, plates, and hide could save this slow-moving quadruped from the fangs and claws of predators.

CAUDAL SPIKES

Four tall, slim, cone-shaped caudal (tail) spikes stuck up and outward from the end of the creature's tail. Paired tail defenses are also found in other well-preserved stegosaurs, including *Huayangosaurus, Kentrosaurus,* and *Stegosaurus.* Tail spikes evidently formed key defensive weapons for all members of the stegosaur group.

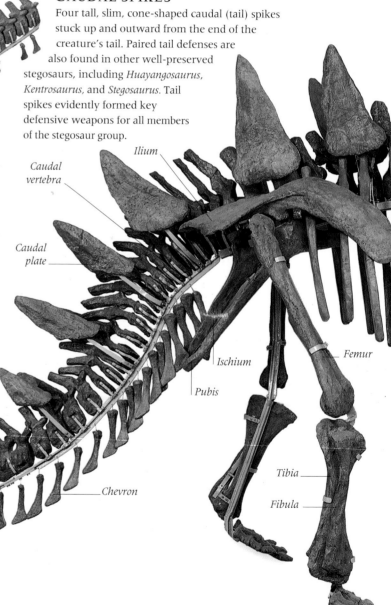

Ilium

Caudal vertebra

Caudal plate

Ischium

Pubis

Femur

Caudal spike

Chevron

Tibia

Fibula

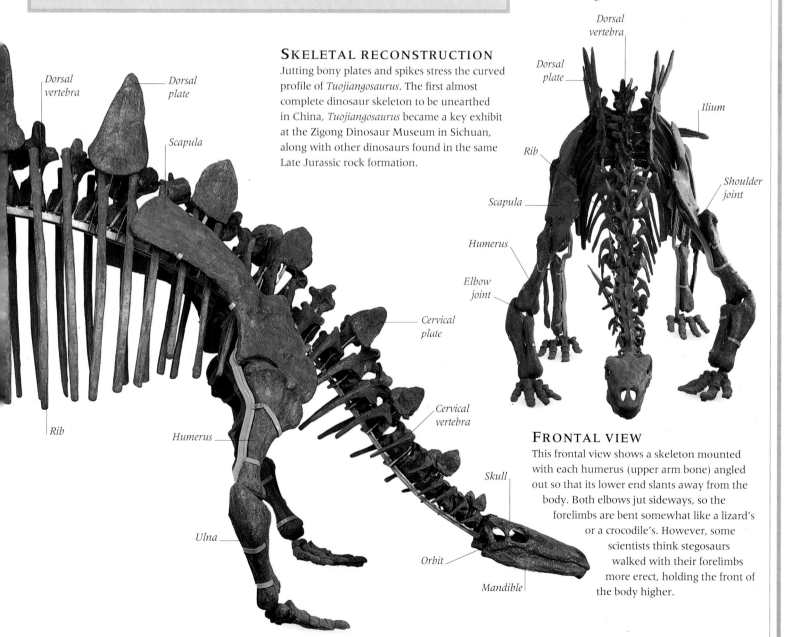

FACT FILE

TUOJIANGOSAURUS

Tuojiangosaurus was a quadrupedal plant-eater with a low head, two rows of protective plates from neck to tail, and spikes at the tip of the tail.

THE MESOZOIC ERA

MYA
248   208   144   65

TRIASSIC   JURASSIC   CRETACEOUS

SIZE
Length 23ft (7m)
Weight 1 ton

TIME
156MYA

LOCATION
China Sichuan

DIET
Low-growing plants

CLASSIFICATION
Family Stegosauridae
Infraorder Stegosauria
Suborder Thyreophora
Order Ornithischia

COMPARING TEETH

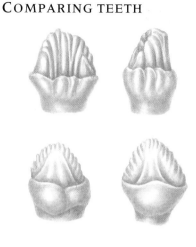

Tuojiangosaurus's cheek teeth (above) resembled those of *Stegosaurus* (top) in being small and ridged, well suited to a diet of leaves.

SKELETAL RECONSTRUCTION

Jutting bony plates and spikes stress the curved profile of *Tuojiangosaurus*. The first almost complete dinosaur skeleton to be unearthed in China, *Tuojiangosaurus* became a key exhibit at the Zigong Dinosaur Museum in Sichuan, along with other dinosaurs found in the same Late Jurassic rock formation.

Dorsal vertebra

Dorsal plate

Scapula

Rib

Humerus

Ulna

Cervical plate

Cervical vertebra

Skull

Orbit

Mandible

Dorsal vertebra

Dorsal plate

Ilium

Rib

Shoulder joint

Scapula

Humerus

Elbow joint

FRONTAL VIEW

This frontal view shows a skeleton mounted with each humerus (upper arm bone) angled out so that its lower end slants away from the body. Both elbows jut sideways, so the forelimbs are bent somewhat like a lizard's or a crocodile's. However, some scientists think stegosaurs walked with their forelimbs more erect, holding the front of the body higher.

EDMONTONIA

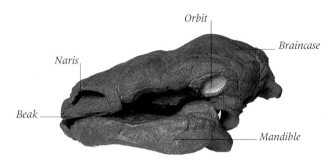

Orbit

Naris

Braincase

Beak

Mandible

EDMONTONIA ("OF EDMONTON") was one of the largest and latest of the nodosaurids—armored dinosaurs without the broad "horns," contorted nasal passages, and bony tail club of their relatives the ankylosaurids. *Edmontonia* was a barrel-bodied quadruped that had evolved tyrannosaur-resistant armor. A jigsaw puzzle of interlocking bony plates reinforced the pear-shaped skull. Three rows of large bony plates protected the neck and shoulders, and a pavement of small, ridged plates covered the back, hips, and tail. Long, bony, forward-angled spikes stuck out from the sides as defense for the flanks and shoulders.

SHEEPLIKE SKULL

Seen from one side, the long, narrow skull of *Edmontonia* resembled that of a sheep. Its bones were thick and the rows of teeth were deeply incurved, leaving room for large cheek pouches in which to store food.

Dorsal scute

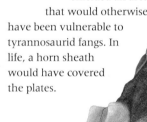

COLLAR PLATES

These two bony plates (left) are from the largest and hindmost of the three rows of armor that protected the top of *Edmontonia*'s neck and the area between its shoulders. The plates shielded an area that would otherwise have been vulnerable to tyrannosaurid fangs. In life, a horn sheath would have covered the plates.

■ LIFE AND BEHAVIOR ■

This heavy-bodied browser ambled slowly on pillarlike limbs through western North America's lowland glades and across meadows of herbaceous plants. Like today's Black Rhinoceros, *Edmontonia* was a relatively narrow-mouthed herbivore, which suggests that it was a selective feeder capable of cropping the juiciest low-growing plants. Sometimes, *Edmontonia* might have had to make do with tough-leaved shrubs: growth rings found in fossil trees suggest that although there were periods with good rainy seasons, these alternated with drier times in which tender-leaved, short-rooted plants would have withered.

■ SELF-DEFENSE ■

It used to be thought that when an *Edmontonia* was threatened, it would simply lie down with its legs beneath its body, turning itself into a living bomb shelter until the predator got tired and walked away. It is more likely that this formidably armed nodosaurid wheeled around to face its enemy, suddenly lunging forward so that its long shoulder spines inflicted crippling wounds to the carnosaur's vulnerable feet or shins. Flank and shoulder spines helped protect *Edmontonia* from an attack from the side, and wide hips gave the armored dinosaur a broad base that would have made it difficult to overturn. When two male *Edmontonia* met, they may have fought to win females or territory. Alternatively, the winner may simply have been the dinosaur with larger shoulder spines, scaring off the loser by a frontal threat display.

Crosswise row of armor

Shoulder spike capable of inflicting fearsome wounds

Armored head

Large cheek

Relatively narrow mouth

Large, heavy foot

VIEWS OF A TOOTH

The cheek teeth of *Edmontonia* had a ridged, leaf-shaped crown, flattened from side to side and enameled on both sides to resist wear. More primitive than most ornithischian teeth, they interlocked with no others and, although 1.6in (4cm) long including elongated root, were relatively small. Even so, nodosaurids had relatively larger teeth than ankylosaurids.

Ridged, leaf-shaped crown

Enameled, wear-resistant surface

Elongated root

EXTERNAL FEATURES

This restoration shows *Edmontonia*'s rock-like head, plated neck, and avenues of ridged plates covering the back and tail. Double-pointed shoulder spines posed a more serious wounding hazard to any predator. Even a tyrannosaurid would hesitate before it chanced its teeth on this heavy, armored herbivore.

Tough, scaly skin

Small, ridged plates covering the tail

Flank spike providing protection against attack from behind

Powerful hind limb

Sturdy forelimb

Splayed toes on large foot

Narrow snout

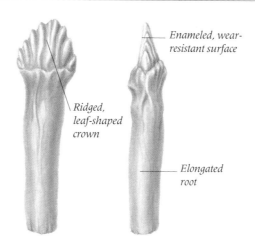
DISCOVERY

Several skulls and skeletons of *Edmontonia* are known. Two, complete with their armor, may have dried out after the animals died and before they were covered in silt by floodwaters.

THE SKULL ROOF

Viewed from above, the narrow snout gave the skull a pear-shaped appearance (left). Bony plates fused to the underlying skull thickened and reinforced its roof. The largest plate protected the braincase. Around the edges of this plate, smaller plates interlocked like pieces in a rigid jigsaw puzzle.

Interlocking small plates

Braincase plate

SAUROPELTA

S AUROPELTA ("SHIELDED LIZARD") was the earliest and most primitive member of the nodosaurid family known to have lived in what is now North America. Advanced nodosaurids like *Edmontonia* had big, bony shoulder plates, but *Sauropelta's* shoulders, back, and tail were covered with horn-sheathed, bony cones interspersed with rows of smaller bony studs. Other primitive features were premaxillary teeth (teeth in the top half of the beak); lack of a secondary palate (a device aiding simultaneous breathing and eating); and unfused neck bones nearest the skull. Like all nodosaurids, *Sauropelta* had a tapering tail with no tail club.

UNDER ATTACK
A Sauropelta *faces a pack of hungry* Deinonychus. *Its tough hide, protective cones and studs, and long shoulder spikes frustrated such small theropods. The armor-backed beast could defy even bigger enemies by crouching.*

■ LIFE AND BEHAVIOR ■

Like other ankylosaurs, as well as their relatives the stegosaurs, *Sauropelta* was an inoffensive, bulky-bodied herbivore that cropped low-growing plants with its beak and chewed them between its small, weak-looking cheek teeth. It lived in the late Early Cretaceous period in western North America, about 100 million years ago. Other herbivores of this period varied greatly in size and included relatively small bipedal hypsilophodontids and huge sauropods. Predators known to have lived then ranged from the turkey-size *Microvenator* to *Deinonychus* and ostrich dinosaurs related to *Struthiomimus*. Big theropods, still undiscovered today, might have been the main enemies of *Sauropelta*. This cumbersome quadruped usually moved no faster than a walking pace, although it probably had the ability to trot. Even so, its pillarlike legs could hardly raise a gallop in order to escape from a pack of long-legged, hungry dromaeosaurids. Confronted by their lethal, hooked talons, the nodosaurid would have been forced to stand its ground and rely on its armor for protection.

■ PRIMITIVE ARMOR ■

Sauropelta's armor, primitive compared to that of its advanced relative *Edmontonia*, consisted of chain-mail body covering, with spines on both sides of the neck. Spines probably also guarded the flanks, protecting the nodosaurid from an attack from the side. If ringed by enemies, *Sauropelta* may have lain down to protect the least well-guarded part of its body: its underbelly. The structure of the forelimb bones hints at this possibility, suggesting that the animal had strong shoulder muscles. These might have enabled *Sauropelta* to bend its arms with greater flexibility than other ankylosaurs.

EXTERNAL FEATURES

Based on partial finds of several specimens, this recreated *Sauropelta* has spikes along the sides of the neck, bony plates on the upper neck, triangular plates along the flanks, and crosswise, bony cones on the back in a sea of smaller bony studs.

Armored tail

BODY ARMOR

Bony cones and triangular plates ran across the upper body from neck to tail. Like the modern giant armadillo's banded armor, *Sauropelta's* body covering evolved to combine protection with flexibility.

Bony cone

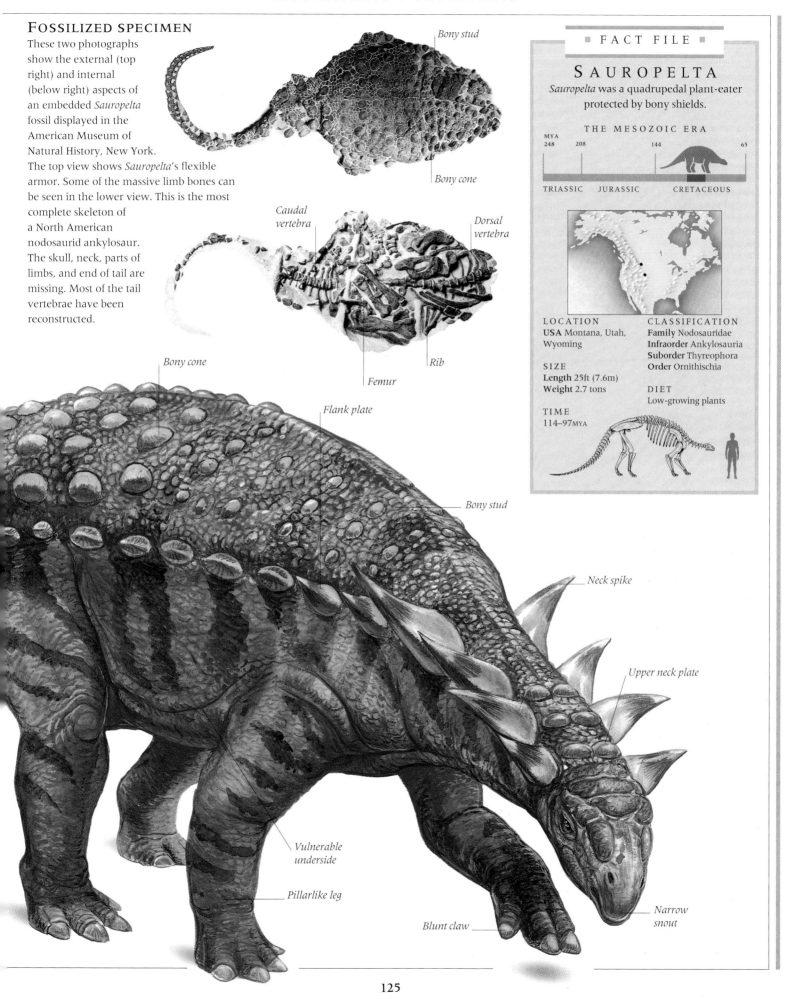

FOSSILIZED SPECIMEN

These two photographs show the external (top right) and internal (below right) aspects of an embedded *Sauropelta* fossil displayed in the American Museum of Natural History, New York. The top view shows *Sauropelta*'s flexible armor. Some of the massive limb bones can be seen in the lower view. This is the most complete skeleton of a North American nodosaurid ankylosaur. The skull, neck, parts of limbs, and end of tail are missing. Most of the tail vertebrae have been reconstructed.

Bony stud

Bony cone

Caudal vertebra

Dorsal vertebra

Femur

Rib

Bony cone

Flank plate

Bony stud

Neck spike

Upper neck plate

Vulnerable underside

Pillarlike leg

Blunt claw

Narrow snout

■ FACT FILE ■

SAUROPELTA

Sauropelta was a quadrupedal plant-eater protected by bony shields.

THE MESOZOIC ERA

MYA 248	208	144	65
TRIASSIC	JURASSIC	CRETACEOUS	

LOCATION
USA Montana, Utah, Wyoming

SIZE
Length 25ft (7.6m)
Weight 2.7 tons

TIME
114–97MYA

CLASSIFICATION
Family Nodosauridae
Infraorder Ankylosauria
Suborder Thyreophora
Order Ornithischia

DIET
Low-growing plants

125

MINMI

M INMI WAS THE first armored ornithischian to be found in the Southern Hemisphere. It is named after Minmi Crossing, a place near the site in Queensland, Australia where the first skeleton was found. This herbivore has two unusual features: bony rods grew backward from unique, flat bony plates beside the neural spines of the dorsal vertebrae; and a mosaic of small scutes (bony plates) protected the belly. *Minmi*'s classification is still uncertain. First placed in the nodosaurid family, it might prove to be a primitive ankylosaurid, or even part of a "new," third family of armored dinosaurs.

MINMI UNDER ATTACK
A theropod assaults a young Minmi *as older animals move in to drive it off. Predators like* Kakuru *preyed on the young, but small scutes helped protect their tender bellies.*

■ LIFE AND BEHAVIOR ■

Minmi was a four-legged, armored herbivore that stomped around on four sturdy limbs, cutting off leafy fronds with its beak and chewing them between its small, leaf-shaped cheek teeth. Its body was thickly covered with armor that would have discouraged attack. Even a theropod that succeeded in overturning a *Minmi* risked snapping off its teeth against the belly armor. The whole underside appears to have been covered with small, rounded scutes (bony plates) slightly over ¼in (about 5mm) in diameter. It is possible that *Minmi* may have preferred running to passive resistance. Its running may have been facilitated by *Minmi*'s most remarkable feature, not found in any other known ankylosaur. Beside each dorsal (back) vertebra there was a bony plate, known as a paravertebra, some 3¼in (2cm) long by 1½in (4cm) wide. Attached to this was a rod of bone, similar to the bony tendons found in ornithopods. The rods might have reinforced the spine and eased the strain on it when the lumbering animal pounded the ground as it ran.

NEW INFORMATION

The discovery of a second skeleton in 1990 shed new light on *Minmi*'s armor. Low, flat, sharp plates jutted from the hips. Triangular plates like giant thorns protected the tail, and bony scutes protected the shins. The front of the thigh shown in this restoration was probably incorporated within the body wall.

Triangular plates protect the tail

NEAR MINMI CROSSING
The first Minmi *was found on level grassland in Australia. In such landscapes, erosion is so slow that rocks yield fossils at a miserly rate, and good discoveries are rare.*

■ FOSSILIZATION ■

Two fossil skeletons have been discovered, both in Australia. The animals seem to have lived in open woodland, and both specimens seem to have been washed out to sea by rivers when they died, where they settled upside down on the seabed. Clay filled the body cavities, and then hard marine sediments encased the carcasses. Later still, the sea retreated, exposing the rocks in which the fossils lay entombed.

FOSSIL AND FINDER
Ian Ievers kneels beside the first Minmi, *which he discovered in 1964. Acetic acid was later used to free its bones from the blocks of hard calcareous concretions in which they were embedded.*

FOSSIL SKELETON

This partial skeleton shows an armored skull tapering to a narrow beak as well as neck plates and shoulder scutes (bony plates). Rows of scutes, each lying between two ribs, run down the wide body. Traces of the shelflike ilia remain, as do fragments of the limbs and tail.

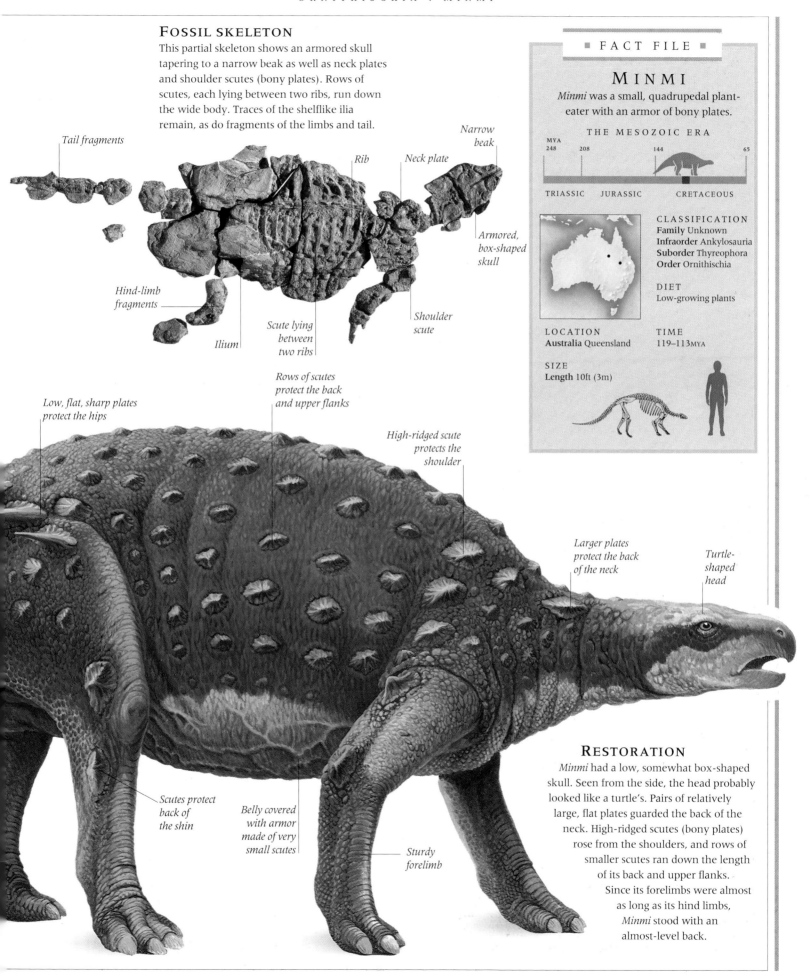

Tail fragments

Rib

Neck plate

Narrow beak

Armored, box-shaped skull

Hind-limb fragments

Ilium

Scute lying between two ribs

Shoulder scute

■ FACT FILE ■

MINMI

Minmi was a small, quadrupedal plant-eater with an armor of bony plates.

THE MESOZOIC ERA

| MYA 248 | 208 | 144 | 65 |

TRIASSIC   JURASSIC   CRETACEOUS

CLASSIFICATION
Family Unknown
Infraorder Ankylosauria
Suborder Thyreophora
Order Ornithischia

DIET
Low-growing plants

LOCATION
Australia Queensland

TIME
119–113MYA

SIZE
Length 10ft (3m)

Low, flat, sharp plates protect the hips

Rows of scutes protect the back and upper flanks

High-ridged scute protects the shoulder

Larger plates protect the back of the neck

Turtle-shaped head

Scutes protect back of the shin

Belly covered with armor made of very small scutes

Sturdy forelimb

RESTORATION

Minmi had a low, somewhat box-shaped skull. Seen from the side, the head probably looked like a turtle's. Pairs of relatively large, flat plates guarded the back of the neck. High-ridged scutes (bony plates) rose from the shoulders, and rows of smaller scutes ran down the length of its back and upper flanks. Since its forelimbs were almost as long as its hind limbs, *Minmi* stood with an almost-level back.

127

EUOPLOCEPHALUS

W ITH ITS TAIL CLUB, short, broad skull, and complex nasal passages, *Euoplocephalus* was a typical ankylosaurid dinosaur. Slabs of bony armor, like glued-on cobblestone paving, protected almost all of its skull. Bony eyelids drooped like steel shutters to protect the vulnerable eyes, and four short horns protected the back of the head. The neck, body, and base of the tail were strengthened by bands of bony studs, spikes, and large, ridged, horny plates, while the stiffened tail ended in a heavy, bony club. For all the armor, in time of danger (perhaps alerted through a keen sense of smell) *Euoplocephalus* was fairly agile, and could lumber along at some speed.

COUNTERATTACK
Agile for its size, Euoplocephalus *could have sidestepped a big theropod's flank attack and felled its formidable enemy with a bone-snapping tail blow to shin or ankle.*

LOCOMOTION
Euoplocephalus *could run faster than a sauropod, slower than a ceratopsian.*

■ LIFE AND BEHAVIOR ■

Isolated finds of more than 40 fossil specimens suggest that *Euoplocephalus* led a solitary life. Around 70 million years ago, however, it was the most abundant kind of armored dinosaur in western North America. This broad-beaked dinosaur ambled through forests, browsing on the undergrowth. It ate almost any low herbaceous plants, chewing the plant material between its small, ridged teeth. The crushed vegetation was then ground to a pulp inside a muscular enlargement of the intestine. The greatest danger for *Euoplocephalus* was that a carnosaur would turn it over to attack its relatively soft underbelly, which was less heavily armored than the rest of its body.

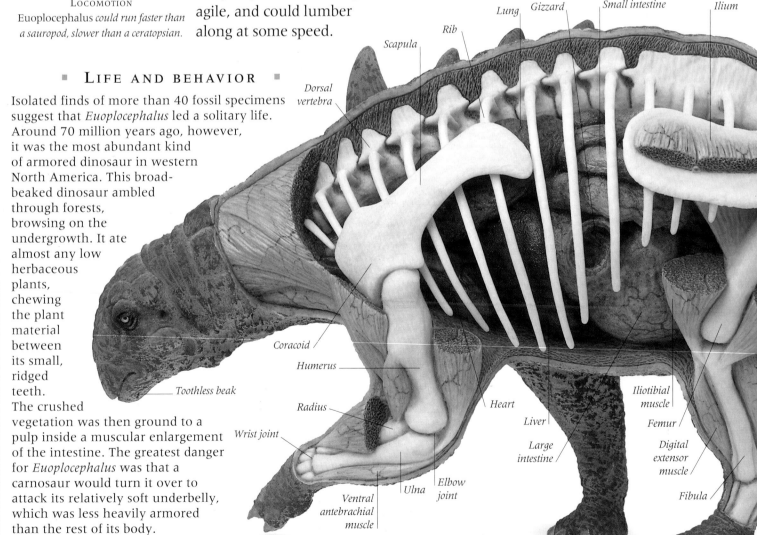

Scapula
Dorsal vertebra
Rib
Lung
Gizzard
Small intestine
Ilium
Coracoid
Humerus
Toothless beak
Radius
Heart
Wrist joint
Liver
Large intestine
Iliotibial muscle
Femur
Digital extensor muscle
Ventral antebrachial muscle
Ulna
Elbow joint
Fibula

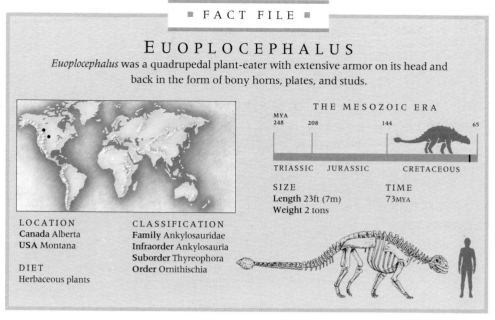

■ FACT FILE ■

EUOPLOCEPHALUS

Euoplocephalus was a quadrupedal plant-eater with extensive armor on its head and back in the form of bony horns, plates, and studs.

THE MESOZOIC ERA

MYA 248	208	144	65
TRIASSIC	JURASSIC	CRETACEOUS	

SIZE
Length 23ft (7m)
Weight 2 tons

TIME
73 MYA

LOCATION
Canada Alberta
USA Montana

DIET
Herbaceous plants

CLASSIFICATION
Family Ankylosauridae
Infraorder Ankylosauria
Suborder Thyreophora
Order Ornithischia

FOSSILIZED SKIN
A close-up view of part of *Euoplocephalus*'s hide shows the bony mosaic that formed a flexible armor combining protection with mobility.

INTERNAL ANATOMY

Deep, curved ribs enclosed this animal's heart and other internal organs, including the long, convoluted gut where plant food was broken down. Each massive scapula (shoulder blade) and strongly ridged humerus (upper arm bone) anchored forelimb muscles. In the hip region, fused spines rising from the vertebrae and broad shelf-shaped ilia braced the powerful muscles that moved the hind limbs and swung the tail club.

FOSSIL: TOP VIEW

Plates of tough skin set with small, bony studs along *Euoplocephalus*'s broad back show clearly in this fossil, along with lengthwise rows of taller, spikier defenses. The head end faces right but lacks a skull.

FOSSIL: BOTTOM VIEW

The same fossil appears here, from the underside and facing left. Clearly visible are the spinal column and strong hip "basket" where ribs grew out from the spine and fused with a shelflike ilium on either side.

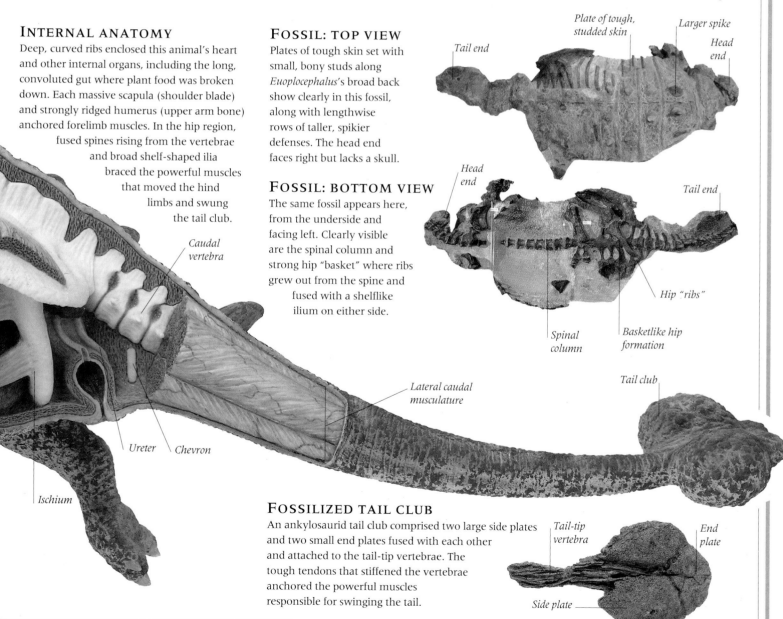

Plate of tough, studded skin

Larger spike

Head end

Tail end

Head end

Tail end

Hip "ribs"

Spinal column

Basketlike hip formation

Caudal vertebra

Ureter *Chevron*

Ischium

Lateral caudal musculature

Tail club

FOSSILIZED TAIL CLUB

An ankylosaurid tail club comprised two large side plates and two small end plates fused with each other and attached to the tail-tip vertebrae. The tough tendons that stiffened the vertebrae anchored the powerful muscles responsible for swinging the tail.

Tail-tip vertebra

End plate

Side plate

ORNITHOPODS

O RNITHOPODS, OR "BIRD FEET," comprised a suborder of bipedal and bipedal/quadrupedal plant-eating ornithischian dinosaurs with feet similar to a bird's, a horny beak, leaf-shaped cheek teeth, a backward-angled pubic bone, a ridged ischium, and bony tendons that stiffened the tail. From dog-sized early ornithischians like *Lesothosaurus* (commonly believed too primitive to be counted as a true ornithopod), the group evolved uniquely effective teeth and jaws for chewing vegetation, and gave rise to Late Cretaceous giants like *Edmontosaurus*. The eight known ornithopod families belonged to one of the longest-lived and largest of all the groups of ornithischians.

✳ PRIMITIVE ✳
ORNITHISCHIANS

LESOTHOSAURUS was a bipedal, Early Jurassic, ornithischian plant-eater, 3ft 3in (1m) long, from southern Africa. It lacked the roomy cheeks of more developed ornithischians, yet it was once placed in the fabrosaurids, a supposed ornithopod family thought to be ancestral to all ornithischians. Fabrosaurids later proved to be a rag-bag of unrelated genera, and scientists found that *Lesothosaurus* lacked some key features that identified true ornithopods. However, it did exhibit some ornithopod features.

✳ "SMALL" ✳
ORNITHOPODS

HETERODONTOSAURIDAE were agile, dog-sized, Early Jurassic ornithopods. Unlike other ornithopods, they had three types of teeth, including tusk-like canines and cheek teeth with high, chisel-shaped crowns with serrated edges. Five named genera are known from southern Africa, and a sixth genus comes from China. Scientists think that heterodontosaurids were more primitive than the other ornithopods. Like pachycephalosaurs, they had a gap between the front upper teeth and those behind. Other shared traits led the paleontologist Paul Sereno to the conclusion that ornithopods and marginocephalians sprang from a common ancestor and formed an ornithischian "supergroup," which he named the Cerapoda.

HYPSILOPHODONTIDAE had tiny, five-fingered hands, elongated shins, and four-toed feet. At least some had teeth in their upper beaks, a primitive ornithischian feature. There were perhaps 18 genera, from 3ft to 11ft (90cm to 3.4m) long, or more. The longest-lived ornithopod family, the hypsilophodontids, lived from Middle

ORNITHOPODS IN AUSTRALIA
A group of Leaellynasaura *roams the edge of a flood plain in Early Cretaceous southeast Australia. These and other hypsilophodontid ornithopods became the most successful small, plant-eating dinosaurs.*

Jurassic to Late Cretaceous times and occurred as far apart as North America, Europe, Asia, Australia, and Antarctica. DRYOSAURIDAE had the appearance of smaller versions of the iguanodonts (see below). Unlike *Hypsilophodon*, *Dryosaurus* had three-toed feet and a toothless beak. The fewer than six genera known were 9ft to 21ft (2.7m to 6.5m) long, and lived in North America, Europe, Africa, and New Zealand.

✳ IGUANODONTS ✳

CAMPTOSAURIDAE were named after *Camptosaurus*, with its long, low head, close-packed cheek teeth, and four-toed feet with hooflike claws. There are at least four genera of these bulky ornithopods, 11ft 6in to 23ft (3.5m to 7m) long, which lived from the Middle Jurassic to the Late Jurassic. Their fossils have been found in North America, Europe, and Australia (if *Muttaburrasaurus* was indeed a camptosaurid and not, as some would say, an iguanodontid). IGUANODONTIDAE were big, bulky, bipedal/quadrupedal ornithopods with long heads, powerful legs with three-toed feet, hooflike toe- and fingernails, and spiky thumbs. There may have been about ten genera, ranging from about 13ft to 29ft 6in (4m to 9m) long. Despite

ORNITHOPODS LARGE
AND SMALL
Iguanodon, *29ft 6in (9m) long, is shown towering over* Hypsilophodon. *Ornithopods ranged from dog-sized hypsilophodontids to 49ft (15m) long duck-billed hadrosaurs.*

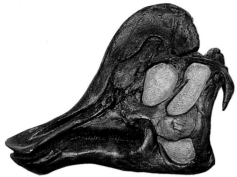

CORYTHOSAURUS SKULL

EDMONTOSAURUS SKULL

HETERODONTOSAURUS SKULL

THREE ORNITHOPOD SKULLS
Corythosaurus and Edmontosaurus *had toothless beaks, mobile upper jaws, and batteries of up to 1,000 cheek teeth for cropping and chewing leaves. The more primitive* Heterodontosaurus *had three kinds of teeth but a simpler jaw design.*

ORNITHOPOD FAMILY TREE

This diagram shows relationships among ornithopod families (the names ending in -idae), each of which is known to have contained several genera. All the members of the Ornithopoda had a premaxillary (upper front) tooth row below the level of the maxillary tooth row situated behind it, and a depressed jaw joint. *Lesothosaurus* was once called an ornithopod but lacked these typical features and was probably closely related to the ancestral ornithischian that gave rise to both ornithopods and marginocephalians. Heterodontosaurids had more kinds of teeth than other ornithopods. The Euornithopoda ("true ornithopods") were a subgroup with a long prepubic process and other distinctive features. Small kinds like *Hypsilophodon* gave rise to huge hadrosaurid and lambeosaurid hadrosaurs (duckbills) with toothless beaks and self-sharpening cheek teeth. These huge hadrosaurs were among the most common of the large, plant-eating dinosaurs of Late Cretaceous North America.

ORNITHOPOD

Euornithopoda

similarities between these genera, some scientists believe that not all belonged to one family. In fact, they consider *Iguanodon* and *Ouranosaurus* to be the only undoubted genera of Iguanodontidae. Iguanodontids in the broader sense lived from the Early to the Late Cretaceous in North (and perhaps also South) America, Africa, Europe, and Asia.

※ HADROSAURS ※

HADROSAURIDAE evolved from such ancestors as *Iguanodon*. Also known as "duckbills," these dinosaurs were ornithischians with wide, toothless beaks, pavements of self-sharpening cheek teeth, and flat skulls or skulls with bony bumps. Their hands had

four fingers, and the palms may have formed a fleshy pad. There are more than two dozen known genera, ranging from 12ft to 49ft (3.7m to 15m) long. They have been found in Late Cretaceous North and South America, Europe, and Asia. **LAMBEOSAURIDAE** had characteristic tall, hollow, bony head crests, but in other respects closely resembled hadrosaurids. Lambeosaurids are, as a result, often considered to be a subfamily of the Hadrosauridae. Both groups of these advanced ornithopods had keen senses, lived in herds, bred in colonies, and evidently tended their young. The fewer than a dozen lambeosaurid genera lived in Late Cretaceous North America and Asia.

HYPSILOPHODON HIP BONES
The long prepubis anchored a muscle that pulled the leg up and forward. The backward-angled pubis left room below the hips for a bulky gut. This placed the bipedal ornithopod's center of gravity conveniently below the hips.

Prepubis
Ilium
Ischium
Pubis

Lesothosaurus

Heterodontosauridae

Hypsilophodontidae

Dryosauridae

Camptosauridae

Iguanodontidae

Hadrosauridae

Lambeosauridae

KEY

⬤ Suborder

◯ Infraorder

Relationship uncertain

LESOTHOSAURUS

N O LONGER THAN a large dog, *Lesothosaurus* had a small head, perhaps with small fleshy cheeks, ridged cheek teeth, and a horny lower beak. Apart from a probably roomy belly, the little herbivore was lightly built, with a slim neck, hollow limb bones, long legs with elongated shins and upper toe bones, and short arms with five-fingered grasping hands (the fifth finger was smaller than the rest). Bony tendons stiffened its tail, counterbalancing the body at the hips. Such small ornithischians evolved the body plan for later two-legged, plant-eating dinosaurs.

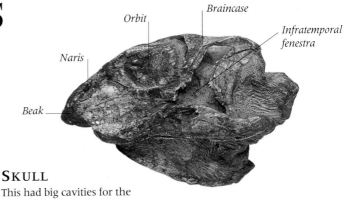

SKULL

This had big cavities for the eye and jaw muscles, an opening in front of the eye, a short, pointed snout, and a lower jaw that may have ended in a horny beak. Teeth slightly set in from the outside of the skull and mandible suggest there were small cheeks.

Orbit
Braincase
Naris
Infratemporal fenestra
Beak

■ LIFE AND BEHAVIOR ■

Lesothosaurus lived in the same kind of sandy semidesert as the small, early ornithopod *Heterodontosaurus*. Like that dinosaur, "Lesotho lizard" could have foraged on all fours, cropping leaves and tender shoots from low, shrublike plants. But its jaws seem to have been less efficient than those of *Heterodontosaurus,* using a vertical motion up and down rather than rotating to grind. As it ate, *Lesothosaurus* would have raised its head from time to time, gazing nervously around for enemies, always poised to race away if a large flesh-eater suddenly appeared. Long toe and shinbones show that *Lesothosaurus* was capable of running extremely fast. In many ways, the creature resembled a modern gazelle—a defenseless plant-eater on the alert at all times for danger because the only means of escaping an attacker is instant flight at high speed. The toe and shinbones are particularly like those of a gazelle.

■ IDENTITY OF FABROSAURUS ■

It is possible that the fossil bones named *Lesothosaurus* in 1978 are actually the same as those of *Fabrosaurus* ("Fabre's lizard"), named in 1964 from a worn piece of lower jaw. Although there is very little fossil evidence to allow an accurate comparison between the *Fabrosaurus* find and the later one, there are many authorities who are reasonably satisfied that the two creatures are the same animal. If the two sets of fossil bones named *Lesothosaurus* and *Fabrosaurus* do indeed turn out to be from one and the same dinosaur, then the creature will be called *Fabrosaurus*—the first name attributed to it. (In the event of duplicate identification, the name first given to an animal or plant always takes priority over any names it acquires later.)

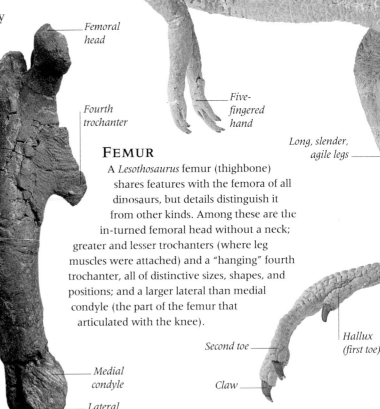

Slim neck

Shoulder

Short, strong forelimb

Femoral head

Fourth trochanter

Five-fingered hand

Long, slender, agile legs

FEMUR

A *Lesothosaurus* femur (thighbone) shares features with the femora of all dinosaurs, but details distinguish it from other kinds. Among these are the in-turned femoral head without a neck; greater and lesser trochanters (where leg muscles were attached) and a "hanging" fourth trochanter, all of distinctive sizes, shapes, and positions; and a larger lateral than medial condyle (the part of the femur that articulated with the knee).

Medial condyle

Lateral condyle

Second toe

Claw

Hallux (first toe)

FRONT VIEW

Seen from the front, *Lesothosaurus* might have resembled a very large lizard walking on its hind limbs. While a few lizards can briefly lift their bodies off the ground and run on hind limbs only, none can stand or pace along with upright limbs, as shown here. Holding its head high enabled *Lesothosaurus* to scan the surroundings for low-growing plants and spot hungry theropods before they crept close enough to launch a dangerous attack.

LESOTHOSAURUS HERD

This diminutive plant-eating dinosaur might have roamed southern Africa in herds, like the small, swift gazelles of today.

Hip

Stiffened tail acts as a counterbalance

TAIL The length was gauged from an incomplete set of caudal bones.

SIDE VIEW

Lesothosaurus was a small, primitive, lightly built plant-eater with some—but not all—of the features found in ornithopods rather than other ornithischians. Like a small ornithopod, it had short arms and hands but long legs and feet. As in most sprinting creatures, the lower parts of the hind limb were the longest. *Lesothosaurus's* shins were 25 percent longer than its thighs, and its three-toed feet were as long as its shins.

Short thigh

Elongated shin

Long "sprinter's" foot

■ FACT FILE ■

LESOTHOSAURUS

Lesothosaurus was a bipedal herbivore. Diminutive and agile, it had a small head, strong legs, and a lengthy tail.

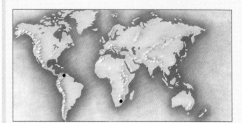

THE MESOZOIC ERA

MYA			
248	208	144	65

TRIASSIC JURASSIC CRETACEOUS

LOCATION
Lesotho Mafeteng
Venezuela

DIET
Low-growing plants

CLASSIFICATION
Family Unknown
Suborder Unknown
Order Ornithischia

SIZE
Length 3ft 3in (1m)

TIME
206MYA

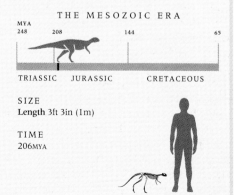

HETERODONTOSAURUS

MANY REPTILES POSSESS only one type of tooth. *Heterodontosaurus* ("different-teeth lizard") had three kinds: sharp upper front teeth that bit against a toothless, horny beak; long canine tusks that fitted into grooves in the top and bottom jaws; and high-crowned cheek teeth. This turkey-size plant-eater was one of the earliest and smallest ornithopods ("bird feet")—dinosaurs with three long, forward-facing toes on each foot. Other birdlike features included its fused lower-leg, ankle, and upper-foot bones. The arms were muscular and each grasping hand bore three long, blunt-clawed digits and a small fourth and fifth finger.

■ LIFE AND BEHAVIOR ■

Heterodontosaurus seems to have rambled over southern African semideserts, searching for tasty plants to eat. Standing and browsing on all fours, *Heterodontosaurus* probably nipped off leaves and stems one by one with its narrow beak, before stuffing them into its roomy cheek pouches, and then chewing them with a rotating action of its jaws. Each time its high-crowned top and bottom teeth met, the downstroke of the upper jaw would have forced the two sides of the lower jaw slightly inward. Unusual features of its shoulder, wrist, and hand joints could mean that *Heterodontosaurus* scrabbled in the sand for juicy roots and succulent tubers or tore open termites' nests to feast upon the insects hidden within. Competing adult males undoubtedly threatened and even bit each other with their pointed, caninelike fangs. Females and young males probably did not have these long, sharp teeth. *Heterodontosaurus*'s enemies included theropods, flesh-eating, mammal-like reptiles, and quick-footed crocodilians living on dry land. The agile small ornithopod would have run from these enemies at speed. Some experts claim that it galloped on all fours, but most scientists believe that it rose up and sprinted on its hind limbs only, lengthening its stride to increase speed. As it ran, its tail would have wagged furiously rather than sticking out rigidly like the stiffened tails of such later ornithopods as *Hypsilophodon*.

DISCOVERY

Heterodontosaurus was named in 1962 by Alfred Crompton and Alan Charig. This small ornithopod was discovered by a team of fossil hunters led by experts from the University of London and from South Africa.

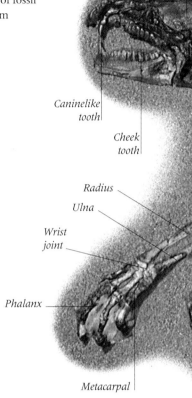

Palpebral bone

Orbit

Caninelike tooth

Cheek tooth

Radius

Ulna

Wrist joint

Phalanx

Metacarpal

Humerus

RESTORATION

A *Heterodontosaurus* pauses to lick a hand perhaps dirtied by digging up tubers or opening a termite mound.

ESCAPING AT SPEED

Surprised at a watering hole, seven small Heterodontosaurus *sprint off, pursued by two crested ceratosaurs. The ornithopods' tusks were no match for the theropods' teeth and claws.*

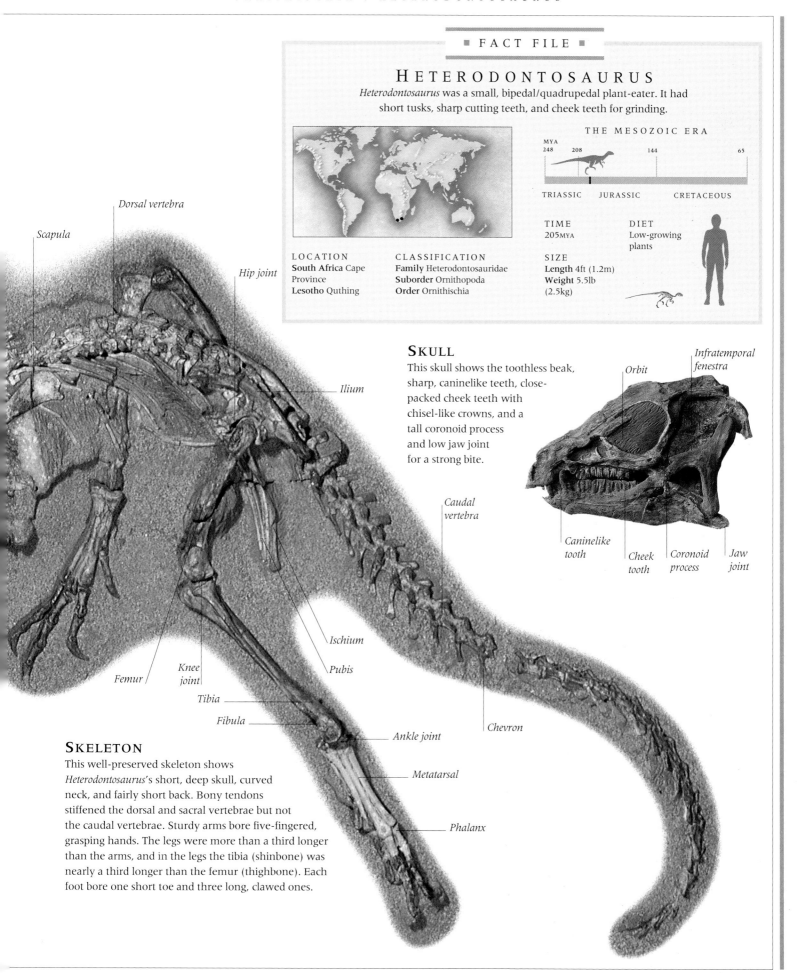

■ FACT FILE ■

HETERODONTOSAURUS

Heterodontosaurus was a small, bipedal/quadrupedal plant-eater. It had short tusks, sharp cutting teeth, and cheek teeth for grinding.

THE MESOZOIC ERA

MYA
248   208   144   65

TRIASSIC   JURASSIC   CRETACEOUS

TIME
205MYA

DIET
Low-growing plants

LOCATION
South Africa Cape Province
Lesotho Quthing

CLASSIFICATION
Family Heterodontosauridae
Suborder Ornithopoda
Order Ornithischia

SIZE
Length 4ft (1.2m)
Weight 5.5lb (2.5kg)

Scapula

Dorsal vertebra

Hip joint

Ilium

SKULL

This skull shows the toothless beak, sharp, caninelike teeth, close-packed cheek teeth with chisel-like crowns, and a tall coronoid process and low jaw joint for a strong bite.

Orbit

Infratemporal fenestra

Caninelike tooth

Cheek tooth

Coronoid process

Jaw joint

Caudal vertebra

Ischium

Pubis

Femur

Knee joint

Tibia

Fibula

Ankle joint

Chevron

SKELETON

This well-preserved skeleton shows *Heterodontosaurus*'s short, deep skull, curved neck, and fairly short back. Bony tendons stiffened the dorsal and sacral vertebrae but not the caudal vertebrae. Sturdy arms bore five-fingered, grasping hands. The legs were more than a third longer than the arms, and in the legs the tibia (shinbone) was nearly a third longer than the femur (thighbone). Each foot bore one short toe and three long, clawed ones.

Metatarsal

Phalanx

HYPSILOPHODON

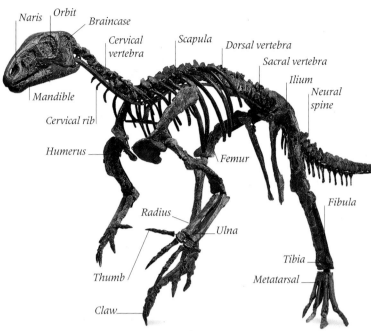

A N ORNITHOPOD little longer than a human, *Hypsilophodon* ("high ridge tooth") was a gazelle-like dinosaur, superbly engineered for both browsing and escaping danger. In its small head were large, keen eyes and a complex feeding mechanism: a horny beak with upper teeth; self-sharpening top and bottom cheek teeth that formed a cutting edge; strong, mobile jaws; and cheek pouches for storing food. *Hypsilophodon*'s short arms ended in five stubby digits tipped with strong claws. Its sprinter's hind limbs featured elongated shins and tall upper foot bones supported by three forward-facing, sharp-clawed toes.

Labels on skeleton: Naris, Orbit, Braincase, Cervical vertebra, Scapula, Dorsal vertebra, Sacral vertebra, Ilium, Neural spine, Mandible, Cervical rib, Humerus, Femur, Radius, Ulna, Fibula, Thumb, Tibia, Metatarsal, Claw

▪ LIFE AND BEHAVIOR ▪

Hypsilophodon nibbled low-growing plants among the lush fern and horsetail meadows that lay between the rivers, lakes, and swamps of the coastal floodplain that covered much of southern England 120 million years ago. This best-known member of the hypsilophodontid family nipped off fronds with its beak, stuffed them in roomy cheek pouches, and then pulped them with a powerful chewing action. Each time it closed its jaws, the upper jaws splayed out, but the lower jaws moved in, so that, as the jaws met, the top and bottom teeth obliquely sheared past one another. Chewing leaves eventually wore down even *Hypsilophodon*'s high-crowned cheek teeth, but new teeth grew to take their place. Timid *Hypsilophodon*'s survival probably depended on group living. Since 1849, the remains of about 24 *Hypsilophodon* have been discovered in the Isle of Wight. Some specimens lay close together, perhaps part of a herd trapped in prehistoric coastal quicksand. While most members of the herd were apparently eating with their heads down, a few could have been scanning the countryside for danger, just as in a herd of modern antelopes. Running away was the defenseless creatures' only option when attacked by hungry carnosaurs. *Hypsilophodon* was one of the fastest dinosaurs of all. At top speed it could also dodge from side to side to evade a pursuer. Its long, tendon-stiffened tail helped it keep its balance when running and maneuvering at speed. Without a few seconds' warning, however, even *Hypsilophodon* could not have escaped the big, swift theropods whose bones are also found on the Isle of Wight.

THOMAS HENRY
HUXLEY
In 1869 he named
Hypsilophodon.

SKELETON

Detailed study of its skeleton discloses that *Hypsilophodon* was a browsing sprinter, with an advanced jaw mechanism and longer shins than thighs. Unlike those more advanced ornithopods—the four-fingered, three-toed hadrosaurs—this ornithopod had five-fingered hands and four forward-facing toes. But the fifth finger was tiny, and the fourth toe was normally too short to reach the ground, much like the vestigial digits of many animals today.

A HYPSILOPHODON HERD

Eight timid *Hypsilophodon* keep close together as they hurry along, turning their heads watchfully from side to side. Each individual is safer from big theropods than if it roamed about independently.

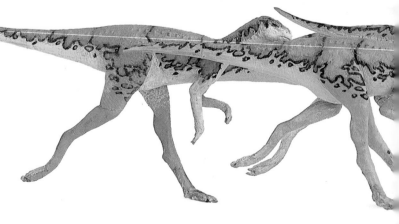

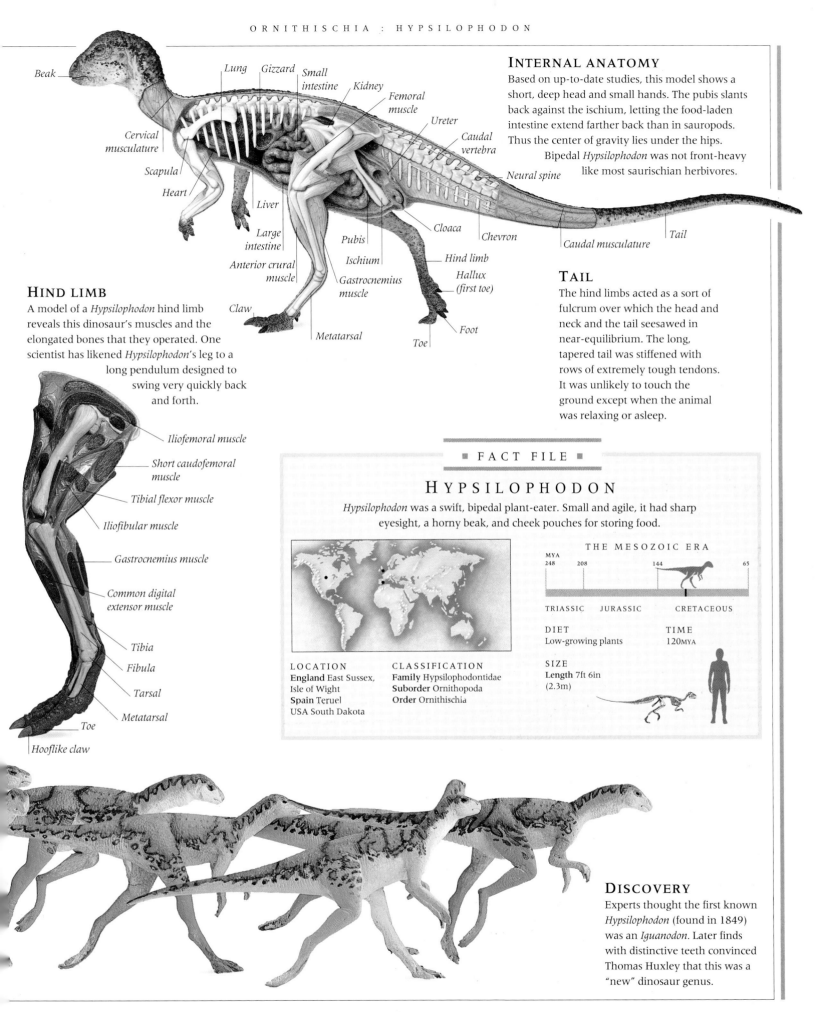

Beak

Cervical
musculature

Scapula

Heart

Lung

Gizzard

Small
intestine

Kidney

Femoral
muscle

Ureter

Caudal
vertebra

Neural spine

Liver

Large
intestine

Anterior crural
muscle

Claw

Metatarsal

Pubis

Ischium

Gastrocnemius
muscle

Cloaca

Chevron

Hind limb

Hallux
(first toe)

Foot

Toe

Caudal musculature

Tail

INTERNAL ANATOMY

Based on up-to-date studies, this model shows a short, deep head and small hands. The pubis slants back against the ischium, letting the food-laden intestine extend farther back than in sauropods. Thus the center of gravity lies under the hips.

Bipedal *Hypsilophodon* was not front-heavy like most saurischian herbivores.

HIND LIMB

A model of a *Hypsilophodon* hind limb reveals this dinosaur's muscles and the elongated bones that they operated. One scientist has likened *Hypsilophodon*'s leg to a long pendulum designed to swing very quickly back and forth.

Iliofemoral muscle

Short caudofemoral
muscle

Tibial flexor muscle

Iliofibular muscle

Gastrocnemius muscle

Common digital
extensor muscle

Tibia

Fibula

Tarsal

Metatarsal

Toe

Hooflike claw

TAIL

The hind limbs acted as a sort of fulcrum over which the head and neck and the tail seesawed in near-equilibrium. The long, tapered tail was stiffened with rows of extremely tough tendons. It was unlikely to touch the ground except when the animal was relaxing or asleep.

■ FACT FILE ■

HYPSILOPHODON

Hypsilophodon was a swift, bipedal plant-eater. Small and agile, it had sharp eyesight, a horny beak, and cheek pouches for storing food.

THE MESOZOIC ERA

MYA			
248	208	144	65

TRIASSIC   JURASSIC   CRETACEOUS

DIET
Low-growing plants

TIME
120MYA

SIZE
Length 7ft 6in
(2.3m)

LOCATION
England East Sussex,
Isle of Wight
Spain Teruel
USA South Dakota

CLASSIFICATION
Family Hypsilophodontidae
Suborder Ornithopoda
Order Ornithischia

DISCOVERY

Experts thought the first known *Hypsilophodon* (found in 1849) was an *Iguanodon*. Later finds with distinctive teeth convinced Thomas Huxley that this was a "new" dinosaur genus.

IGUANODON

I GUANODON ("IGUANA TOOTH") was a large, heavy ornithopod that existed in large numbers. This dinosaur owes its name to high-ridged cheek teeth, similar to those of a modern iguana lizard, but much larger. *Iguanodon* cropped vegetation with its horny beak and chewed with its cheek teeth, with an unusual sliding action of the jaws. It had five-fingered hands that were unique and highly specialized. Each had a spiked thumb, three middle fingers with hooflike claws, and a grasping fifth finger.

IGUANODON'S DISCOVERER
Iguanodon *was discovered by Dr Gideon Mantell, who named the dinosaur in 1825.*

Tall, unworn tooth

Short tooth worn down by chewing vegetation

LOWER CHEEK TEETH

Two lower cheek teeth of *Iguanodon* (above) reveal the effects of wear. The tall tooth has an unworn edge. The short tooth was worn down by chewing tough vegetation but was kept sharp by sliding against the upper teeth.

Dorsal vertebrae

Sacral vertebrae

Cervical vertebrae

■ LIFE AND BEHAVIOR ■

Iguanodon was probably a peaceful herbivore capable of standing and walking either on its hind limbs or on all fours. Young animals, with their relatively short arms, were probably usually two-legged. However, adults had longer, stronger arms and could have lowered the forward part of the body to rest on the three weight-bearing middle fingers of each hand, possibly to drink or to browse on low-growing horsetails. A few trackways suggest that adults sometimes walked on all fours too. Yet most fossil tracks attributed to *Iguanodon* show only prints left by its big, three-toed feet. *Iguanodon* could stand on its long, muscular hind legs to reach tree leaves. When walking on its hind limbs, it would have thrust its head forward, holding its back and tail stiff and nearly horizontal. *Iguanodon* could have escaped from large predators such as *Baryonyx* by running on two legs. If cornered, however, the ornithischian could have defended itself by jabbing out with its spiked thumbs. It is unlikely that any carnosaur would have dared tackle a whole group of *Iguanodon*, and quite likely this dinosaur did roam the land in herds. One clue is a group of fossil carcasses found close together at a site in Germany. Scientists suspect that a large herd was engulfed and drowned in a flash flood before it had a chance to escape.

Prepubic process

Ilium

Rib

Humerus

Ulna

Pubis

Femur

Tibia

Fibula

VERSATILE HANDS

The hoofed fingers formed a "foot" for walking. When the hand was raised, the wrist could rotate and bring the fifth finger in toward the palm. The spiked thumb was unable to bend.

Metatarsal

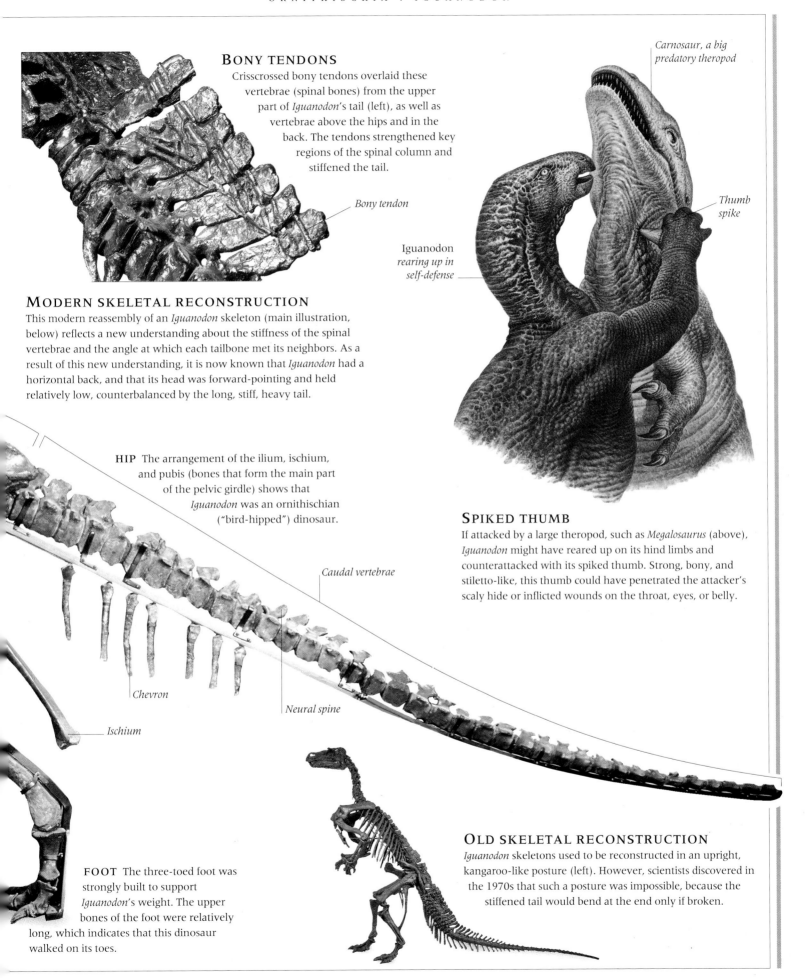

BONY TENDONS

Crisscrossed bony tendons overlaid these vertebrae (spinal bones) from the upper part of *Iguanodon*'s tail (left), as well as vertebrae above the hips and in the back. The tendons strengthened key regions of the spinal column and stiffened the tail.

Bony tendon

Carnosaur, a big predatory theropod

Thumb spike

Iguanodon *rearing up in self-defense*

MODERN SKELETAL RECONSTRUCTION

This modern reassembly of an *Iguanodon* skeleton (main illustration, below) reflects a new understanding about the stiffness of the spinal vertebrae and the angle at which each tailbone met its neighbors. As a result of this new understanding, it is now known that *Iguanodon* had a horizontal back, and that its head was forward-pointing and held relatively low, counterbalanced by the long, stiff, heavy tail.

HIP The arrangement of the ilium, ischium, and pubis (bones that form the main part of the pelvic girdle) shows that *Iguanodon* was an ornithischian ("bird-hipped") dinosaur.

Caudal vertebrae

SPIKED THUMB

If attacked by a large theropod, such as *Megalosaurus* (above), *Iguanodon* might have reared up on its hind limbs and counterattacked with its spiked thumb. Strong, bony, and stiletto-like, this thumb could have penetrated the attacker's scaly hide or inflicted wounds on the throat, eyes, or belly.

Chevron

Neural spine

Ischium

FOOT The three-toed foot was strongly built to support *Iguanodon*'s weight. The upper bones of the foot were relatively long, which indicates that this dinosaur walked on its toes.

OLD SKELETAL RECONSTRUCTION

Iguanodon skeletons used to be reconstructed in an upright, kangaroo-like posture (left). However, scientists discovered in the 1970s that such a posture was impossible, because the stiffened tail would bend at the end only if broken.

BREEDING BEHAVIOR

A model depicts a mother *Iguanodon* tending her nest and eggs. No known *Iguanodon* nests and eggs have ever been discovered, but most paleontologists are confident in assuming that this dinosaur constructed an earthen nest and cared for eggs and young in the same way as alligators do.

Tail balancing the body

Earth nest shaped with the hands

DISCOVERY

In 1825 *Iguanodon* became only the second dinosaur to gain a scientific name. An *Iguanodon* shinbone had been found in 1809, but not recognized; it was subsequently forgotten, until it was identified in the 1970s.

Naris

Large head

Toothless beak

MUTTABURRASAURUS

Orbit
Naris
Skull
Mandible
Cervical vertebra
Scapula
Rib
Humerus
Dorsal vertebra
Sternal bone
Ulna
Ilium
Femur
Radius
Pubis
Fibula
Tibia
Ischium
Chevron
Metatarsal
Neural spine

This 23ft (7m) Australian relative of *Iguanodon* had a hollow arch above its snout, much as in some hadrosaurs. Its toothless beak was similar to *Iguanodon*'s, but its cheek teeth were designed for shearing, unlike the grinding cheek teeth of *Iguanodon*.

OPEN-AIR DISPLAY
This model stands outside the Museum of Tropical Queensland in Australia.

MOUNTED SKELETON

This displays a large head, strong arms, and hands with five digits, including spiky thumbs.

DIET

Iguanodon probably browsed low down, feeding on the ferns and horsetails that formed great savannas on the low, marshy delta lands of northwest Europe. *Iguanodon* nipped off mouthfuls of foliage and then chewed it with an effective, sideways swinging action of the jaws.

Elbow

Spikelike thumb

Hand with five digits

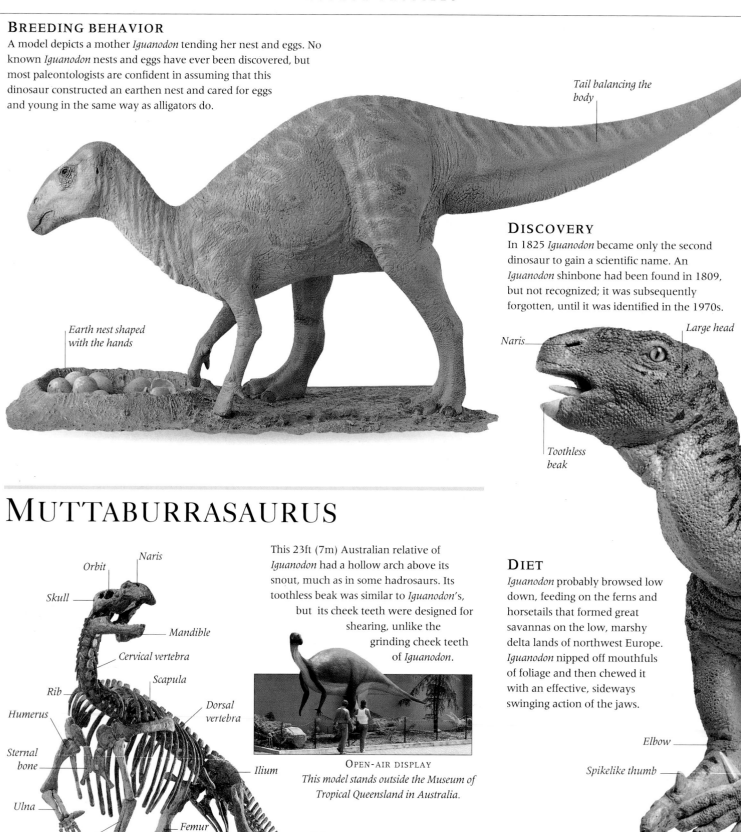

■ FACT FILE ■

IGUANODON

Iguanodon was a large bipedal/quadrupedal plant-eater with cheek teeth for grinding, hooflike claws, and spiky thumbs used for defense.

MYA 248	208	144	65
TRIASSIC	JURASSIC	CRETACEOUS	

SIZE
Length 29ft 6in (9m)
Weight 4.4 tons

TIME
140–110MYA

LOCATION
Belgium Hainaut
England Southeast
Germany Nordrhein-Westfalen
Spain Castellón, Cuenca, Teruel
USA South Dakota

CLASSIFICATION
Family Iguanodontidae
Suborder Ornithopoda
Order Ornithischia

DIET
Horsetails, ferns, possibly flowering plants

HIND LIMB ANATOMY

A restoration of the internal anatomy of an *Iguanodon* hind limb reveals its supporting structure of femur, tibia, fibula, and tarsal and metatarsal bones. Muscles joined to limb and pelvic bones worked in pairs to pull the whole leg back and forth. Other pairs of muscles contracted alternately to bend or straighten the lower leg at the knee.

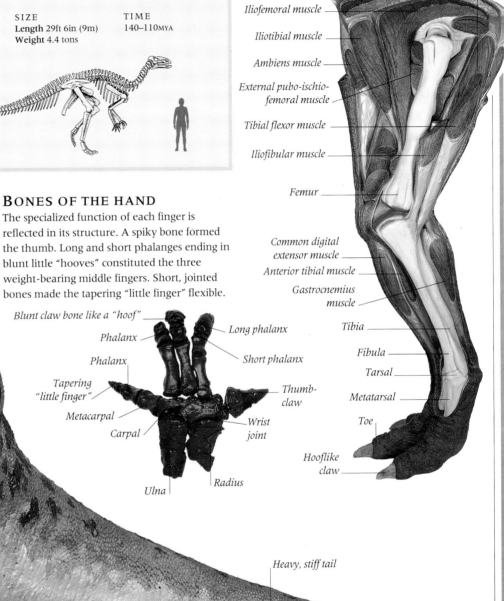

- Short caudo-femoral muscle
- Iliofemoral muscle
- Iliotibial muscle
- Ambiens muscle
- External pubo-ischio-femoral muscle
- Tibial flexor muscle
- Iliofibular muscle
- Femur
- Common digital extensor muscle
- Anterior tibial muscle
- Gastrocnemius muscle
- Tibia
- Fibula
- Tarsal
- Metatarsal
- Toe
- Hooflike claw

BONES OF THE HAND

The specialized function of each finger is reflected in its structure. A spiky bone formed the thumb. Long and short phalanges ending in blunt little "hooves" constituted the three weight-bearing middle fingers. Short, jointed bones made the tapering "little finger" flexible.

- Blunt claw bone like a "hoof"
- Phalanx
- Phalanx
- Tapering "little finger"
- Metacarpal
- Carpal
- Long phalanx
- Short phalanx
- Thumb-claw
- Wrist joint
- Radius
- Ulna

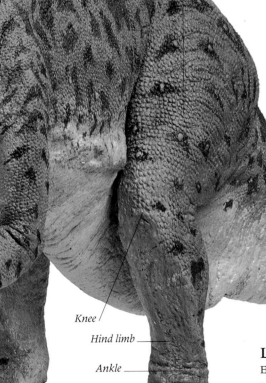

- Thigh
- Knee
- Hind limb
- Ankle
- Foot
- Hooflike nail
- Heavy, stiff tail

LOCOMOTION

Evidence for giving this model *Iguanodon* a bipedal pose includes fossil tracks left by big, three-toed feet in the same rock layers as *Iguanodon* skeletons. Only a few of the tracks include small imprints produced by the hands, so the creature's weight was for the most part only on the hind limbs.

OURANOSAURUS

A BLEND OF the familiar and the unusual, *Ouranosaurus* ("brave monitor lizard") had certain characteristics in common with its well-known relative *Iguanodon*. These included hind limbs that were longer and stronger than the forelimbs, hooflike claws on the toes and fingers, spiked thumbs, and teeth with high-ridged crowns. It also had distinctive features: low bumps over the eyes, a hadrosaur-like beak, and bony, sail-bearing blades jutting from the backbone.

SAHARA EXPEDITION
Paleontologists at a find of Ouranosaurus *bones in 1971.*

MARSH DWELLERS
The sail-backed ornithopod Ouranosaurus *shared lush African riversides with reptiles including* Sarcosuchus, *a crocodile up to 49ft (15m) long.*

■ LIFE AND BEHAVIOR ■

In behavior, *Ouranosaurus* was probably much like *Iguanodon*. The structure of its hands suggests that it rested and ambled on all fours. Its hands were smaller than *Iguanodon*'s but its wrist bones were very strong. Although each hand's three, hoofed middle fingers could not grasp, they could stretch out and bend back to form a weight-bearing "foot" when *Ouranosaurus* went down on all fours. To run, however, adults must have reared on their pillarlike hind limbs. The young would have walked on only their two back legs because their forelimbs were somewhat shorter. *Ouranosaurus* had a ducklike beak and powerful jaws with which it cropped and chewed such vegetation as low-growing cycadeoids and early flowering plants of the river floodplain. The purpose of the skin sail stretched across the high spines rising from its backbone is still not known. If males had taller sails than females, they might have served as visual signals to attract a mate or to scare a rival. The sail might also have served as a heat regulator. Like several other sail-backed dinosaurs and large prehistoric reptiles, *Ouranosaurus* lived in a hot, dry climate where there was a constant danger of overheating. During the hot afternoons, *Ouranosaurus* might have kept cool by standing with its sail edge-on to the sun and letting heat escape from the sail's skin. On chilly mornings it might have warmed up by standing broadside to the sun to let its rays warm the blood inside the sail.

SKELETON EXPOSED
A Tuareg tribesman gazes at the articulated skeleton of an Ouranosaurus. *The sand that covered it had simply blown away.*

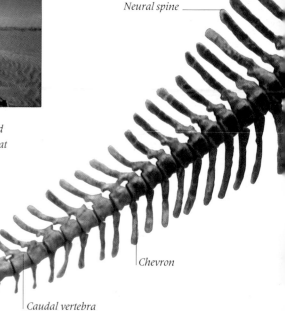

Neural spine

Chevron

Caudal vertebra

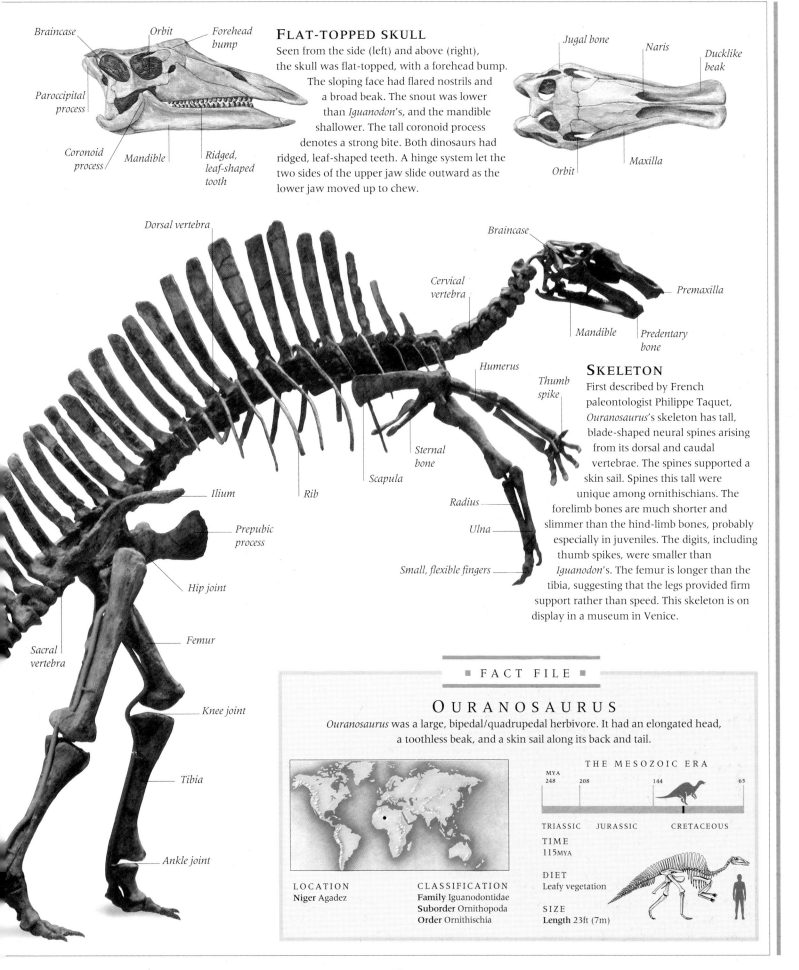

FLAT-TOPPED SKULL

Braincase — **Orbit** — **Forehead bump**

Paroccipital process

Coronoid process — **Mandible** — **Ridged, leaf-shaped tooth**

Seen from the side (left) and above (right), the skull was flat-topped, with a forehead bump. The sloping face had flared nostrils and a broad beak. The snout was lower than *Iguanodon*'s, and the mandible shallower. The tall coronoid process denotes a strong bite. Both dinosaurs had ridged, leaf-shaped teeth. A hinge system let the two sides of the upper jaw slide outward as the lower jaw moved up to chew.

Jugal bone — **Naris** — **Ducklike beak**

Orbit — **Maxilla**

Dorsal vertebra

Braincase

Cervical vertebra

Premaxilla

Mandible — **Predentary bone**

Humerus

Thumb spike

SKELETON

First described by French paleontologist Philippe Taquet, *Ouranosaurus*'s skeleton has tall, blade-shaped neural spines arising from its dorsal and caudal vertebrae. The spines supported a skin sail. Spines this tall were unique among ornithischians. The forelimb bones are much shorter and slimmer than the hind-limb bones, probably especially in juveniles. The digits, including thumb spikes, were smaller than *Iguanodon*'s. The femur is longer than the tibia, suggesting that the legs provided firm support rather than speed. This skeleton is on display in a museum in Venice.

Sternal bone

Scapula

Radius

Ulna

Small, flexible fingers

Ilium — **Rib**

Prepubic process

Hip joint

Femur

Sacral vertebra

Knee joint

Tibia

Ankle joint

■ FACT FILE ■

OURANOSAURUS

Ouranosaurus was a large, bipedal/quadrupedal herbivore. It had an elongated head, a toothless beak, and a skin sail along its back and tail.

THE MESOZOIC ERA

MYA			
248	208	144	65

TRIASSIC   JURASSIC   CRETACEOUS

TIME
115MYA

DIET
Leafy vegetation

SIZE
Length 23ft (7m)

LOCATION
Niger Agadez

CLASSIFICATION
Family Iguanodontidae
Suborder Ornithopoda
Order Ornithischia

EDMONTOSAURUS

L ONGER THAN the baseline of a tennis court and as heavy as an elephant, "Edmonton lizard" (of Edmonton, Canada) was one of the biggest duck-billed dinosaurs. With its powerful jaws, bulky body, small forelimbs, long, strong hind limbs, and deep tail, it resembled an unusually large *Iguanodon*. But it had a flatter, more ducklike beak, hundreds of close-packed cheek teeth, and inflatable skin flaps over large nasal cavities. Also, the backbone curved down sharply at the shoulders, and each hand bore only four digits embedded in a fleshy pad.

Teeth arranged in small groups

Dentary bone (jawbone)

DENTAL PAVEMENT

Tall, self-sharpening teeth formed a battery of up to 60 close-packed "families," each of three to five teeth sprouting in succession. When chewing, the maxillary (upper) teeth slid sideways over the dentary (lower) teeth.

■ LIFE AND BEHAVIOR ■

Duckbills were once thought to have been aquatic animals, gobbling soft water plants and swimming by thrusting water back with their webbed hands and by wagging their rudderlike tails. In fact, their fingers were not webbed (fossil evidence suggests a fleshy pad), their tails seem too inflexible for sculling, and their teeth appear designed for chewing tough-leaved land plants. Scientists now think *Edmontosaurus* lived on land. It could have stood or ambled on all fours but would have reared to hurry, striding on its great hind limbs with back held level and the ramrod-straight tail balancing the head, neck, arms, and chest. Sprinting at up to 30 mph (50 km/hr) seems possible, and the big duckbill could have loped along for miles at almost half that speed. Without sharp teeth or claws to protect it, *Edmontosaurus* would have had to flee from *Tyrannosaurus* or other carnosaurs that haunted western North America in the last days of the dinosaurs. Usually, *Edmontosaurus* wandered in slow-moving herds, perhaps made noisy by bellowing calls. Such calls, which caused the nasal skin flaps to inflate, might have been made to entice mates, to threaten rivals, or to summon straying young. The herds cropped herbaceous undergrowth and tree leaves in forests near the western shores of the great inland sea. Remains of undigested seeds, fruits, twigs, and pine-tree needles lay inside the carcass of one mummified *Edmontosaurus*; perhaps they formed the last meal that this animal ate before it died.

INFLATABLE NASAL SAC

Two illustrations depict the head of an *Edmontosaurus*. Normally, the facial skin lay flat and wrinkly, but *Edmontosaurus* could inflate it like a balloon, to emit a call of considerable resonance.

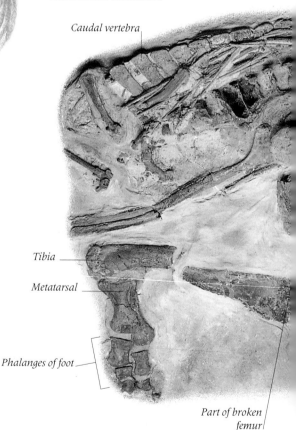

Caudal vertebra

Tibia

Metatarsal

Phalanges of foot

Part of broken femur

FOSSILIZED SKIN

Clustered bumps feature among the mass of smaller scales on Edmontosaurus's skin. These bumps may have formed brightly colored patches.

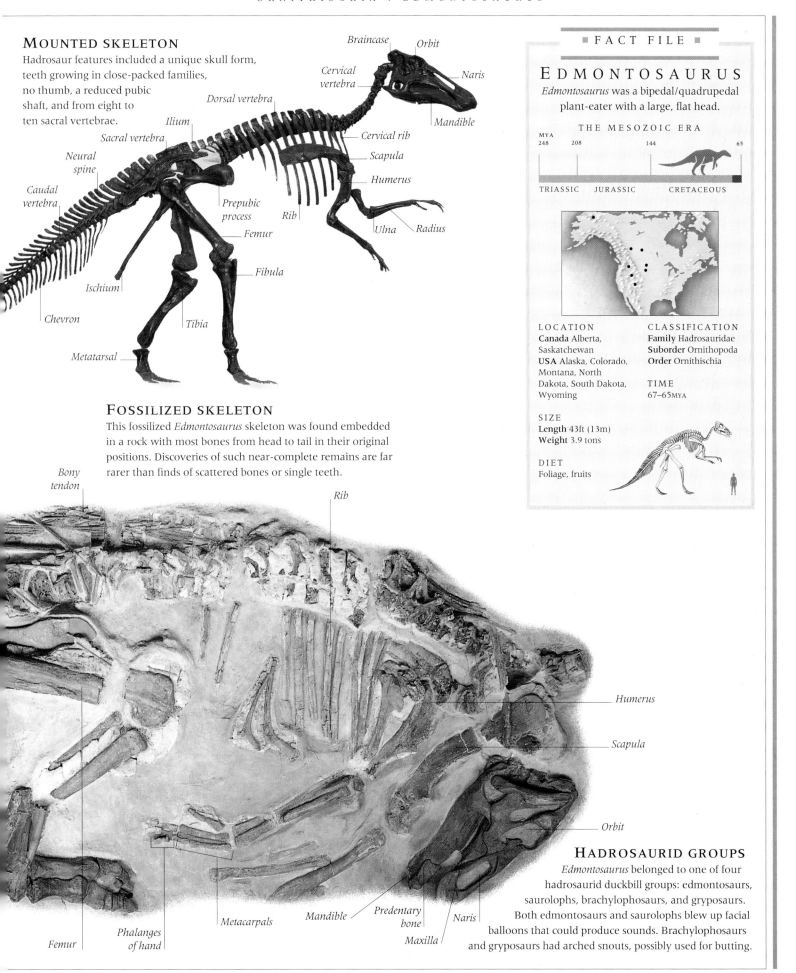

MOUNTED SKELETON

Hadrosaur features included a unique skull form, teeth growing in close-packed families, no thumb, a reduced pubic shaft, and from eight to ten sacral vertebrae.

Braincase
Orbit
Cervical vertebra
Naris
Dorsal vertebra
Mandible
Ilium
Cervical rib
Sacral vertebra
Scapula
Neural spine
Humerus
Caudal vertebra
Prepubic process
Rib
Ulna
Radius
Femur
Chevron
Fibula
Ischium
Tibia
Metatarsal

FOSSILIZED SKELETON

This fossilized *Edmontosaurus* skeleton was found embedded in a rock with most bones from head to tail in their original positions. Discoveries of such near-complete remains are far rarer than finds of scattered bones or single teeth.

Bony tendon
Rib
Humerus
Scapula
Orbit
Femur
Phalanges of hand
Metacarpals
Mandible
Predentary bone
Naris
Maxilla

■ FACT FILE ■

EDMONTOSAURUS

Edmontosaurus was a bipedal/quadrupedal plant-eater with a large, flat head.

THE MESOZOIC ERA

| MYA 248 | 208 | 144 | 65 |
| TRIASSIC | JURASSIC | CRETACEOUS |

LOCATION
Canada Alberta, Saskatchewan
USA Alaska, Colorado, Montana, North Dakota, South Dakota, Wyoming

CLASSIFICATION
Family Hadrosauridae
Suborder Ornithopoda
Order Ornithischia

TIME
67–65MYA

SIZE
Length 43ft (13m)
Weight 3.9 tons

DIET
Foliage, fruits

HADROSAURID GROUPS

Edmontosaurus belonged to one of four hadrosaurid duckbill groups: edmontosaurs, saurolophs, brachylophosaurs, and gryposaurs. Both edmontosaurs and saurolophs blew up facial balloons that could produce sounds. Brachylophosaurs and gryposaurs had arched snouts, possibly used for butting.

MAIASAURA

WITH ITS BROAD, ducklike beak, powerful jaws, and batteries of self-sharpening cheek teeth, *Maiasaura* ("Maia's lizard") is a typical example of the "duck-billed" dinosaurs. It is placed in the family Hadrosauridae on account of its lack of a hollow head crest, and in the subdivision known as the brachylophosaurs because of the solid, hornlike crest above its eyes and the triangular projections on its cheek bones. Maiasaura was first discovered in 1978; since then thousands of specimens have been found.

VULNERABLE YOUNG

Museum skeletons depict a young ornithopod falling prey to a hungry *Troodon*. Agile, lightweight theropods might have invaded a *Maiasaura* colony to seize defenseless infants.

MAIASAURA HATCHLING
This baby Maiasaura *has broken its eggshell and is about to emerge.*

■ LIFE AND BEHAVIOR ■

Immense herds of *Maiasaura* ranged along the upper level of the coastal plain between North America's Rocky Mountains and the prehistoric interior sea. Fossil finds suggest some were tens of thousands strong. Scientists believe these herds migrated north and south with the seasons in search of food, stamping broad trackways along the upper coastal plain. While they stayed close together in their herd, sheer size and numbers would have kept these bulky creatures fairly safe from attack by tyrannosaurids. Prowling tyrannosaurids would also explain why *Maiasaura* bred in colonies. Each year many females trekked back to the same nesting site, scooping out mud nests 6ft (about 2m) across and laying up to 20 sausage-shaped eggs. Heat from a covering layer of rotting vegetation then helped the eggs hatch.

Meanwhile, the mother stayed nearby to protect them. Like most birds, the mothers also brought their babies food. The worn teeth and unformed limb bones of some fossil *Maiasaura* babies show that they had been eating solid food before they had grown strong enough to forage on their own.

Sacral vertebrae

Caudal vertebrae

Ilium

Pubis

Ischium

Femur

Chevron

Neural spine

Tibia

JUVENILE SKELETON

Apart from its diminutive size, the skeleton of this juvenile *Maiasaura* differed from an adult's skeleton in several ways. The short snout and big eyes probably evoked a maternal response, as such features do in living mammals. In hatchlings, cartilage, not bone, formed the limb bones' undeveloped ends.

Fibula

Ankle joint

Phalang

Metatarsals

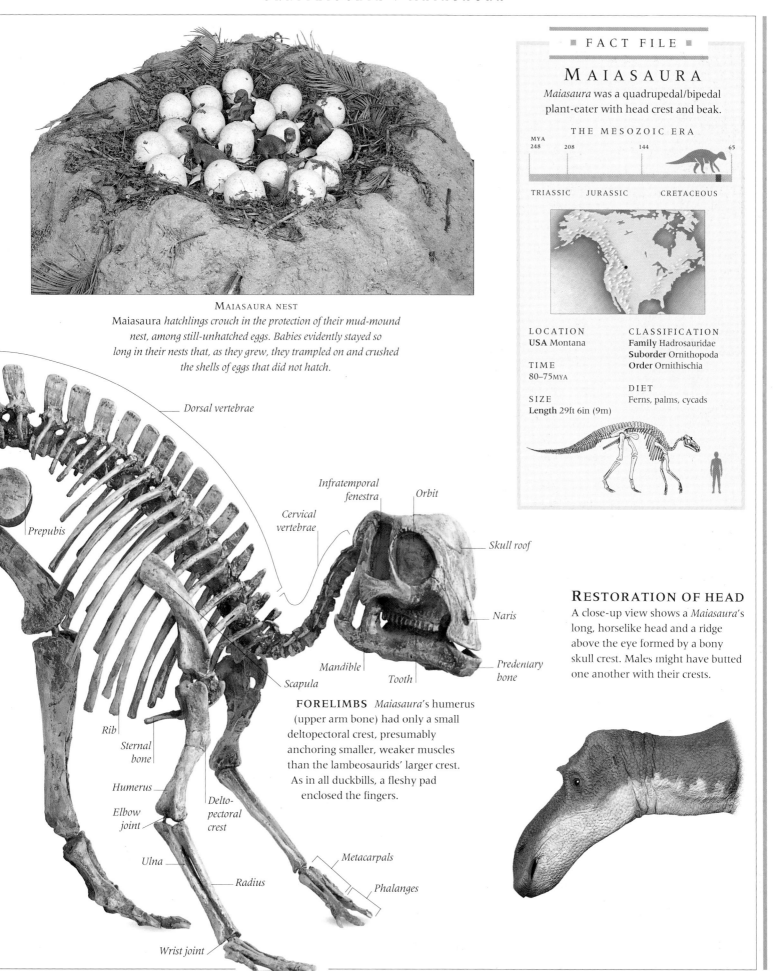

MAIASAURA NEST

Maiasaura *hatchlings crouch in the protection of their mud-mound nest, among still-unhatched eggs. Babies evidently stayed so long in their nests that, as they grew, they trampled on and crushed the shells of eggs that did not hatch.*

■ FACT FILE ■

MAIASAURA

Maiasaura was a quadrupedal/bipedal plant-eater with head crest and beak.

THE MESOZOIC ERA

| MYA 248 | 208 | 144 | 65 |

TRIASSIC | JURASSIC | CRETACEOUS

LOCATION
USA Montana

CLASSIFICATION
Family Hadrosauridae
Suborder Ornithopoda
Order Ornithischia

TIME
80–75MYA

SIZE
Length 29ft 6in (9m)

DIET
Ferns, palms, cycads

Dorsal vertebrae

Prepubis

Infratemporal fenestra

Cervical vertebrae

Orbit

Skull roof

Naris

Mandible

Tooth

Predentary bone

Scapula

Rib

Sternal bone

Humerus

Elbow joint

Delto-pectoral crest

Ulna

Radius

Metacarpals

Phalanges

Wrist joint

FORELIMBS *Maiasaura's* humerus (upper arm bone) had only a small deltopectoral crest, presumably anchoring smaller, weaker muscles than the lambeosaurids' larger crest. As in all duckbills, a fleshy pad enclosed the fingers.

RESTORATION OF HEAD

A close-up view shows a *Maiasaura's* long, horselike head and a ridge above the eye formed by a bony skull crest. Males might have butted one another with their crests.

147

CORYTHOSAURUS

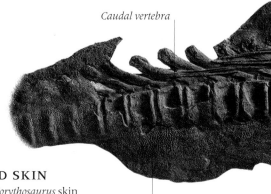

Caudal vertebra

Fossilized skin

TWO DOZEN OR SO identified skulls make *Corythosaurus* ("helmet lizard") one of the best-known of North America's duck-billed dinosaurs. High, hollow, bony head crests that enclosed convoluted nasal passages are characteristic of the lambeosaurid hadrosaurs, to which this large ornithopod belonged. Confusingly, not every *Corythosaurus* had an identical head crest—size and shape depended on sex and age. Before this was clarified, it was thought that there were seven species. Now just one is recognized.

COLLECTING CORYTHOSAURUS
In the early 1900s, flatboat-based fossil hunters found Corythosaurus *by the Red Deer River in Alberta.*

FOSSILIZED SKIN

Impressions of *Corythosaurus* skin have survived with this length of fossilized caudal vertebrae. The skin's scales are pebbly, not overlapping as in many reptiles.

Hip

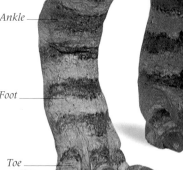

✳ LIFE AND BEHAVIOR ✳

Corythosaurus lived on the coastal plain between North America's western mountains and a prehistoric inland sea. Herds would have trampled paths through the rich forest of cycadophytes, magnolias, ferns, palms, and cypress trees, browsing upon low-growing tree leaves and fruits, and cropping low-growing flowering plants. Sometimes a *Corythosaurus* herd would have crossed paths with herds of other hadrosaurids; *Corythosaurus* fossils occur in a rock formation that holds those of *Gryposaurus*, *Prosaurolophus*, *Lambeosaurus*, and *Parasaurolophus*. If herds of different duckbills intermingled, distinctive head crests and a keen sense of smell would have helped herd members keep in touch with one another. Males' head crests must have been especially important in the breeding season, when the crest might have changed color to attract a mate. During courtship or to dominate rivals, the males probably produced a loud, low trumpeting sound by forcing air from the windpipe up into a cavity in the crest, then through two side pockets, and out through the nostrils. This amplified the male's voice, making it resonate.

Tail

Thigh

Knee

Hind limb

HADROSAUR UNGUAL

This fossil bone is from the tip of one of the three large fingers of a hadrosaur hand. It supported a large, blunt nail.

Ankle

Foot

Toe

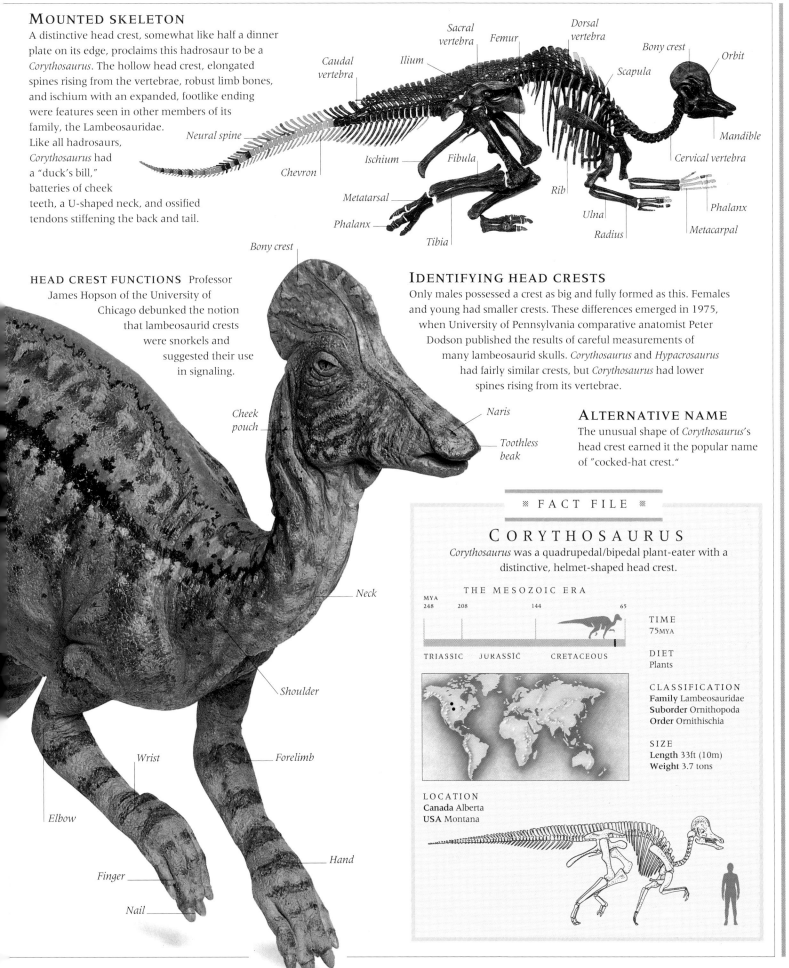

MOUNTED SKELETON

A distinctive head crest, somewhat like half a dinner plate on its edge, proclaims this hadrosaur to be a *Corythosaurus*. The hollow head crest, elongated spines rising from the vertebrae, robust limb bones, and ischium with an expanded, footlike ending were features seen in other members of its family, the Lambeosauridae. Like all hadrosaurs, *Corythosaurus* had a "duck's bill," batteries of cheek teeth, a U-shaped neck, and ossified tendons stiffening the back and tail.

Neural spine

Caudal vertebra

Chevron

Ilium

Sacral vertebra

Femur

Dorsal vertebra

Bony crest

Orbit

Scapula

Mandible

Cervical vertebra

Ischium

Fibula

Rib

Phalanx

Metatarsal

Phalanx

Tibia

Ulna

Radius

Metacarpal

HEAD CREST FUNCTIONS
Professor James Hopson of the University of Chicago debunked the notion that lambeosaurid crests were snorkels and suggested their use in signaling.

Bony crest

Cheek pouch

Neck

Shoulder

Wrist

Forelimb

Elbow

Finger

Hand

Nail

IDENTIFYING HEAD CRESTS

Only males possessed a crest as big and fully formed as this. Females and young had smaller crests. These differences emerged in 1975, when University of Pennsylvania comparative anatomist Peter Dodson published the results of careful measurements of many lambeosaurid skulls. *Corythosaurus* and *Hypacrosaurus* had fairly similar crests, but *Corythosaurus* had lower spines rising from its vertebrae.

Naris

Toothless beak

ALTERNATIVE NAME

The unusual shape of *Corythosaurus*'s head crest earned it the popular name of "cocked-hat crest."

※ FACT FILE ※

CORYTHOSAURUS

Corythosaurus was a quadrupedal/bipedal plant-eater with a distinctive, helmet-shaped head crest.

THE MESOZOIC ERA

MYA 248	208	144	65
TRIASSIC	JURASSIC	CRETACEOUS	

TIME
75MYA

DIET
Plants

CLASSIFICATION
Family Lambeosauridae
Suborder Ornithopoda
Order Ornithischia

SIZE
Length 33ft (10m)
Weight 3.7 tons

LOCATION
Canada Alberta
USA Montana

LAMBEOSAURUS

L AMBEOSAURUS ("LAMBE'S LIZARD") was a large, robust, duck-billed dinosaur with a head crest that has often been compared in shape to a hatchet. The crest was hollow: the cavity inside was an extension of the nasal passage, and very likely amplified the sound of the animal's calls. The crest may have supported a frill of skin that ran down the neck, back, and tail. Three species of *Lambeosaurus* are known, each with a differently shaped crest. The hadrosaurs or "duckbills" were a group comprising two families: lambeosaurids such as *Lambeosaurus* and *Corythosaurus*, with hollow crests and short lower jaws, and hadrosaurids such as *Edmontosaurus*.

■ LIFE AND BEHAVIOR ■

Finds of skeletons as far apart as Canada and Mexico suggest that *Lambeosaurus* ranged a long way to the north and the southwest of North America's Cretaceous inland sea. Herds probably migrated after a food supply that fluctuated with the seasons. As each *Lambeosaurus* slowly browsed its way across the countryside, its narrow beak could have snipped off the twigs and fronds of favorite species of plants. Hadrosaurid duckbills, with broader beaks, were probably less choosy eaters. Horned dinosaurs, with their parrotlike beaks, perhaps munched plants that neither group of duckbills was equipped to tackle. The varied feeding habits of the different duckbills and all the other ornithischians that shared the same habitat helped to prevent overcropping of the vegetation. The same sharing of food resources happens today among herbivores of the African savannas.

■ SIGNALS ■

Members of a *Lambeosaurus* herd could recognize each other visually by variations in their crests. If an animal lost sight of its herd, however, it would have been able to regain contact by sound. The tubes inside a *Lambeosaurus*'s crest acted as a sound box, amplifying the voice and producing low, resonant cries. It is plausible that the various lambeosaurid dinosaurs could all be recognized by their voices: *Lambeosaurus*'s crest would have made a different sound from that created by *Corythosaurus*'s helmet-shaped crest. *Prosaurolophus* lacked a crest but was equipped with nasal "balloons." These would have inflated when the animal was about to call, perhaps to produce a loud bellow like that of an elephant seal today.

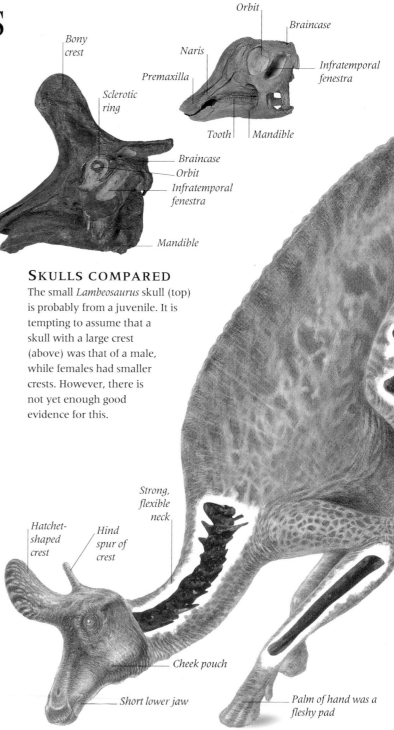

Orbit
Braincase
Bony crest
Naris
Premaxilla
Infratemporal fenestra
Sclerotic ring
Tooth
Mandible
Braincase
Orbit
Infratemporal fenestra
Mandible

SKULLS COMPARED

The small *Lambeosaurus* skull (top) is probably from a juvenile. It is tempting to assume that a skull with a large crest (above) was that of a male, while females had smaller crests. However, there is not yet enough good evidence for this.

Strong, flexible neck
Hatchet-shaped crest
Hind spur of crest
Cheek pouch
Short lower jaw
Palm of hand was a fleshy pad

Forward-bulging crest

Long crest with a tubular hollow

HEAD SHAPES

Lambeosaurus magnicristatus (left) had a forward-bulging crest. *Parasaurolophus* (right), another lambeosaurid, had a longer, backward-sweeping, bony crest. *Kritosaurus* (far right), a hadrosaurid duckbill, had a hump before the eyes, probably covered in thick skin, but no crest.

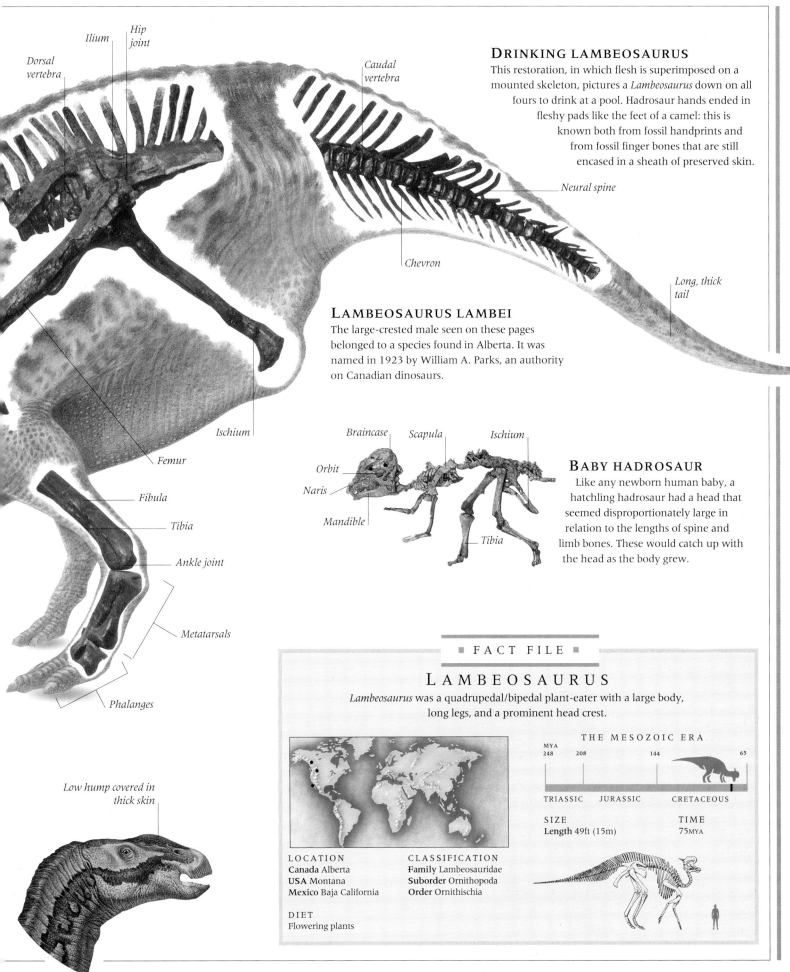

Dorsal
vertebra

Ilium

Hip
joint

Caudal
vertebra

Neural spine

DRINKING LAMBEOSAURUS

This restoration, in which flesh is superimposed on a
mounted skeleton, pictures a *Lambeosaurus* down on all
fours to drink at a pool. Hadrosaur hands ended in
fleshy pads like the feet of a camel: this is
known both from fossil handprints and
from fossil finger bones that are still
encased in a sheath of preserved skin.

Chevron

Long, thick
tail

LAMBEOSAURUS LAMBEI

The large-crested male seen on these pages
belonged to a species found in Alberta. It was
named in 1923 by William A. Parks, an authority
on Canadian dinosaurs.

Ischium

Femur

Braincase

Scapula

Ischium

Orbit

Naris

Mandible

Tibia

BABY HADROSAUR

Like any newborn human baby, a
hatchling hadrosaur had a head that
seemed disproportionately large in
relation to the lengths of spine and
limb bones. These would catch up with
the head as the body grew.

Fibula

Tibia

Ankle joint

Metatarsals

Phalanges

Low hump covered in
thick skin

■ FACT FILE ■

LAMBEOSAURUS

Lambeosaurus was a quadrupedal/bipedal plant-eater with a large body,
long legs, and a prominent head crest.

THE MESOZOIC ERA

MYA
248   208   144   65

TRIASSIC   JURASSIC   CRETACEOUS

SIZE
Length 49ft (15m)

TIME
75MYA

LOCATION
Canada Alberta
USA Montana
Mexico Baja California

CLASSIFICATION
Family Lambeosauridae
Suborder Ornithopoda
Order Ornithischia

DIET
Flowering plants

MARGINOCEPHALIANS

M ARGINOCEPHALIA ("margined heads") were a suborder of bipedal/quadrupedal plant-eating ornithischians with a narrow shelf or deep bony frill at the back of the skull; broad hips; no obturator process (a projection on the ischium); and no symphysis (cartilaginous union of bones) between the pubic bones. These dinosaurs probably shared an ancestor with the ornithopods. The first known marginocephalians were small, Late Jurassic bipeds with a tiny skull ridge. Late Cretaceous forms included huge, horned quadrupeds with bony skull frills, cutting beaks, self-sharpening cheek teeth, and powerful jaws. They were among the most abundant large, plant-eating dinosaurs of Late Cretaceous western North America. They are divided into two infraorders: Pachycephalosauria and Ceratopsia. Two closely related Ceratopsian families form the subgroup Neoceratopsia.

BREEDING HAZARDS
Two adults of the protoceratopsid Protoceratops *guard young from an oviraptorid dinosaur.*

❋ PACHYCEPHALOSAURIA ❋

"Thick-headed lizards" were very small to moderately large, bipedal herbivores that evolved broad, stocky bodies and immensely thick skulls decorated with knobs and sometimes spikes (most are only known from skullcap fragments). Rows of bony tendons stiffened most of the length of the tail. Primitive ornithischian features included teeth in the front of the jaw, and small, leaf-shaped cheek teeth. The group seemingly evolved in East Asia by Late Jurassic times, but most known genera lived during the Late Cretaceous, when one of the three families evidently spread to North America and another family apparently reached Europe.
CHAOYANGOSAURIDAE formed the earliest family known, with cheek projections a bit like those of *Psittacosaurus*, lobed upper front teeth, and sharp caninelike teeth. The two Late Jurassic genera in this family came from China.
PACHYCEPHALOSAURIDAE were the dome-headed pachycephalosaurs with a thick, high-domed cranium that evidently shielded the brain when rival males banged heads forcibly together. Pachycephalosaurids ranged from 3ft to 15ft (90cm to 4.6m) long. All the known types lived in Late Cretaceous times. Of the eight known genera, one was discovered in Madagascar, five in North America, and two in East Asia.
HOMALOCEPHALIDAE were flat-headed pachycephalosaurs. These resembed the pachycephalosaurids but their thick cranium was flat, not domed, and rival males probably engaged in head-to-head pushing contests. Homalocephalids ranged from 20in to 10ft (50cm to 3m). Three genera lived in Late Cretaceous East Asia, and one apparently in Europe.

❋ CERATOPSIA ❋

"Horned faces" were bipedal and quadrupedal ornithischians whose special features included flared cheekbones and a rostral bone that formed the top tip of a deep, narrow, parrotlike beak. The Psittacosauridae were apparently more primitive than either the Protoceratopsidae or the Ceratopsidae. In 1986, paleontologist Paul Sereno put these last two under the collective heading of Neoceratopsia ("new horned faces").
PSITTACOSAURIDAE or "parrot lizards" were basically bipedal herbivores around 6ft 6in (2m) long. Key features included an "old-fashioned" ornithischian body and a highly evolved skull. The snout was relatively shorter than any other ornithischian's and formed a deep,

TWO MARGINOCEPHALIANS
These models of a huge, horned, quadrupedal ceratopsid, Styracosaurus, *and a small bipedal pachycephalosaurid,* Stegoceras, *stress the contrasts in size and form found among marginocephalians.*

PSITTACOSAURUS SKULL

STEGOCERAS SKULL

TRICERATOPS SKULL

MARGINOCEPHALIAN SKULLS

Three photographs (not to scale) contrast the skull of the thick-skulled pachycephalosaurid Stegoceras (middle) with the skulls of two ceratopsians: the small, parrotlike psittacosaurid Psittacosaurus (top) and the immense ceratopsid Triceratops with long brow horns and neck frill (bottom).

MARGINOCEPHALIAN FAMILY TREE

This diagram shows relationships among the marginocephalian families (the names ending in -idae). Scientists long disagreed about where pachycephalosaurs belonged within the Ornithischia, and variously grouped them with stegosaurs, ankylosaurs, and ornithopods. The idea that the Pachycephalosauria were a sister group to the Ceratopsia was confirmed in the mid-1980s, when it was recognized that both groups shared features derived from a common ancestor. In the Late Cretaceous, pachycephalosaurids and protoceratopsids seemingly migrated, by a land bridge, to North America, where protoceratopsids probably gave rise to ceratopsids.

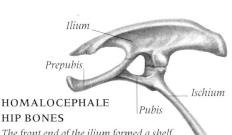

HOMALOCEPHALE HIP BONES

Ilium
Prepubis
Ischium
Pubis

The front end of the ilium formed a shelf above a prepubis far longer than the pubis. In ceratopsids the whole top of the ilium formed a shelf and the prepubis was a long, flared blade.

narrow beak with high nostril holes. The half dozen or so known species belonged to the genus *Psittacosaurus*, which lived in late Early Cretaceous Central, East, and Southeast Asia. (A species found in Thailand suggests that Indochina had joined with Asia before the Late Cretaceous). PROTOCERATOPSIDAE or "first horned faces" included about eight genera of quadrupedal and bipedal/quadrupedal herbivores 3ft 3in to 10ft (1m to 3m) long or more. All had a bony frill at the back of the skull, and some also had bumps above the brow and nose. Self-sharpening cheek teeth, only enameled on one side, were designed to shear and crush, and may have evolved to cope with the flowering plants arising in Late Cretaceous times. Protoceratopsids occurred in Central and East Asia, and spread to western North America.

CERATOPSIDAE or "horned faces" included some 18 named genera of quadrupedal, rhinoceros-like herbivores up to 29ft 6in (9m) long. Deep, shelflike, bony skull frills and brow and nose horns adorned their huge heads. There were two subfamilies: Centrosaurinae had short, deep faces, relatively short frills, and longer nose horns than brow horns; Chasmosaurinae had long, shallow faces, and relatively long frills and brow horns. Both of these Late Cretaceous groups lived in western North America.

MARGINOCEPHALIA

Pachycephalosauria

Ceratopsia

Neoceratopsia

Pachycephalosauridae

Homalocephalidae

Chaoyangosauridae

Psittacosauridae

Protoceratopsidae

Ceratopsidae

KEY

◯ Suborder

◯ Infraorder

◯ Subordinate group

PACHYCEPHALOSAURUS

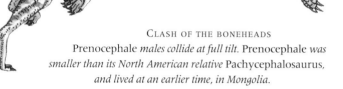

T HE LARGEST OF THE bone-headed dinosaurs, *Pachycephalosaurus* is known from only one skull and a few immensely thick skull roofs. "Thick-headed lizard" cushioned its brain inside a domed braincase up to 10in (25cm) thick. Bony knobs edged the dome's rear rim, and short spikes projected upward from the snout. The teeth were tiny. From what is known of other dinosaurs in the same family, it is surmised that *Pachycephalosaurus* was the length of a large car, with a fairly short, thick neck, short arms, a bulky body, long legs, and a heavy tail held rigid by a basketwork of hard, bony tendons.

CLASH OF THE BONEHEADS
Prenocephale *males collide at full tilt.* Prenocephale *was smaller than its North American relative* Pachycephalosaurus, *and lived at an earlier time, in Mongolia.*

※ LIFE AND BEHAVIOR ※

Scientists suspect that *Pachycephalosaurus* and its dome-headed relatives had been the bipedal dinosaurian equivalents of today's bighorn sheep. In the mating season, big males evidently ran at one another, clashing heads together to decide which would dominate and mate with a whole herd of females. Scientists have conjectured that the thickness and height of the dome on *Pachycephalosaurus*'s head varied with age. Besides crash-helmet skulls, evidence that they used their heads as battering rams lies in ridge-and-groove extensions of the spinal vertebrae. These enabled the vertebrae to interlock, so that they could hold the back and tail rigid. When two males banged heads, the shock of the impact would have traveled through the skull and along the backbone to the legs without damaging the brain. When faced with predators, however, even head-banging may not have been a sufficient defense. Self-preservation probably depended on an effective early-warning system and a quick getaway. Large olfactory lobes in the brain imply a keen sense of smell. Big eye sockets facing somewhat forward suggest that the animal had sharp eyes capable of binocular vision. While feeding, a *Pachycephalosaurus* herd would have been keenly aware of how close they could safely allow a tyrannosaur to approach before they ran away.

※ DIET ※

What the bone-headed dinosaurs ate is uncertain. Their small, ridged teeth could not have chewed up tough, fibrous plants as effectively as the teeth of the duckbills and horned dinosaurs, both of which lived at the same time as the thick-heads. Perhaps *Pachycephalosaurus* lived on a mixed diet of leaves, seeds, fruits, and insects.

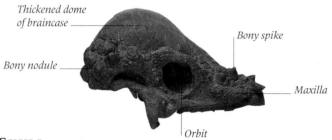

Thickened dome of braincase

Bony spike

Bony nodule

Maxilla

Orbit

SKULL
A thick, knobby, high-domed skull guarded the tiny brain, which was set deep in a mass of solid bone.

Heavy tail held rigid for most of its length

EXTERNAL FEATURES
This model's head is based on a superb skull found in Montana in 1940. Because remains other than those of skulls have not been found, the body proportions and size had to be estimated from the known skeletons of other pachycephalosaurs, especially *Stegoceras*. Comparisons between their skulls suggest that *Pachycephalosaurus* grew to 15ft (4.6m), in other words, to about twice the length of *Stegoceras*.

OTHER BONEHEADS

Prenocephale (far left) and *Stygimoloch* (left), like *Pachycephalosaurus*, were in the Pachycephalosauridae, a family of high-domed, bone-headed dinosaurs that clashed heads together. *Homalocephale* (below left) was in the Homalocephalidae, a family of flat-headed boneheads in which the males probably tussled head to head in nonviolent shoving contests.

PRENOCEPHALE

STYGIMOLOCH

HOMALOCEPHALE

Bony nodule

Skull shelf

Domed head

Scaly skin

Stout neck

Bony spikes projecting up from the snout

SKULL SHELF

The small rim of bony nodules jutting from the back of the head is evidence that, despite their bipedal stance, *Pachycephalosaurus* and its kin were not ornithopods, but relatives of the psittacosaurids and ceratopsians.

Short arm

Finger

Long leg— strong but perhaps not capable of running fast

STEGOCERAS

Stegoceras ("horny roof") was a goat-size pachycephalosaurid, known from one partial skeleton and dozens of mostly partial skulls. The skulls evidently became thicker and higher with age, especially in males. A male's dome overgrew the bony shelf around the back and sides of his skull. *Stegoceras* was about 8ft (2.5m) long, and lived in Alberta and Montana in the Late Cretaceous. This dinosaur was named in 1902, by Lawrence Lambe.

STANCE

Stegoceras typically held its back level, balancing the weight of its head and body with a heavy, stiffened tail.

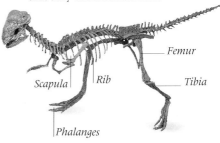

SKELETON

In *Stegoceras* and other pachycephalosaurs, the femur (thighbone) is longer than the tibia (shinbone). This pattern might suggest that they could not run fast.

Femur

Scapula

Rib

Tibia

Phalanges

※ FACT FILE ※

PACHYCEPHALOSAURUS

Pachycephalosaurus was a bipedal plant-eater. The largest of the bone-headed dinosaurs, it had a distinctive, thick, dome-shaped skull.

THE MESOZOIC ERA

MYA 248	208	144	65
TRIASSIC	JURASSIC	CRETACEOUS	

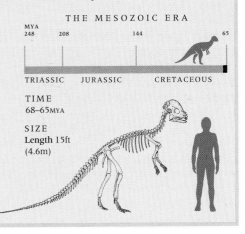

LOCATION
USA Montana, South Dakota, Wyoming

DIET
Plants

CLASSIFICATION
Family Pachycephalosauridae
Infraorder Pachycephalosauria
Suborder Marginocephalia
Order Ornithischia

TIME
68–65MYA

SIZE
Length 15ft
(4.6m)

PSITTACOSAURUS

P SITTACOSAURUS ("parrot lizard") was a two-legged herbivore about 6ft 7in (2m) long. It resembled the ornithopod *Hypsilophodon*, but had a deeper, longer body, shorter tail, longer arms, and four-fingered, grasping hands. The fourth finger and the first of the four toes were very short. But *Psittacosaurus*'s oddest feature was its short, deep head with a parrotlike beak formed partly by the rostral bone unique to ceratopsians. Other ceratopsian features included pointed cheek bones, cutting cheek teeth, and a tiny ridge foreshadowing the horned dinosaurs' huge neck frills. There were at least four species of *Psittacosaurus*, the sole known genus in the family Psittacosauridae.

❋ LIFE AND BEHAVIOR ❋

Psittacosaurus's cutting beak and self-sharpening cheek teeth suggest that it ate vegetation too tough for most other herbivores to tackle. Perhaps this ceratopsian dinosaur had evolved a way of getting nourishment from long-established kinds of plants. Yet it seems more than just coincidence that ceratopsians appeared about the same time as the flowering plants came on the scene. Maybe *Psittacosaurus* gnawed the juicy but fibrous trunks of young palm trees. Whatever it ate evidently demanded more than being simply ground up into short lengths in the mouth. *Psittacosaurus* used additional digestive measures: polished pebbles found with one skeleton had served as gastroliths or stomach millstones, grinding food inside a birdlike crop. Scientists believe that farther back inside the gut, bacteria and enzymes had probably completed the digestion process in special fermentation chambers. *Psittacosaurus* usually walked and ran on its hind limbs. While standing upright, it could have used its hands, which had stubby, short claws, to pull down branches to its mouth. Sometimes, however, it might have gone down on all fours, supported by its long, strong arms, while its jaws scissored through tough, low-growing leaves. Like the hands, the toes of *Psittacosaurus* also bore short, stubby claws. Without the sharp horns and bony neck frills of the later ceratopsians to deter carnosaurs, a threatened *Psittacosaurus* would have had to either flee or try to hide from its predators. The babies of *Psittacosaurus* are known from two fossils, which show them to have been only about the size of modern songbirds.

MOUNTED SKELETON

This reveals a rather ornithopod-like, bipedal dinosaur with a fairly long body balanced by the tail; robust arms; four-fingered, broad-clawed hands; hind limbs with slightly longer shins than thighs; and four-toed, broad-clawed feet. Unlike any ornithopod, it had a short, deep snout with a "parrot's beak."

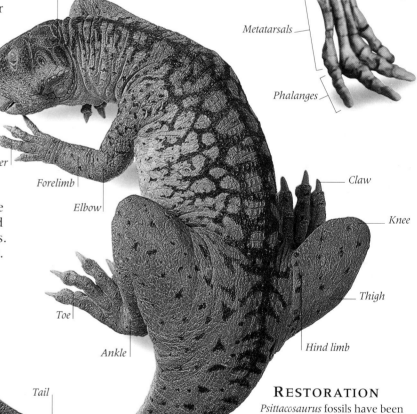

Sacral vertebrae
Caudal vertebrae
Chevron
Ilium
Ischium
Neural spine
Femur
Fibula
Tibia
Ankle joint
Metatarsals
Phalanges
Short, deep head
Finger
Forelimb
Elbow
Claw
Knee
Toe
Thigh
Ankle
Hind limb
Tail

RESTORATION

Psittacosaurus fossils have been found lying in this death pose. But quite healthy individuals probably also lay down on all fours to go to sleep, and an active *Psittacosaurus* might have used its sturdy arms as props when it lowered its head to drink or feed at ground level.

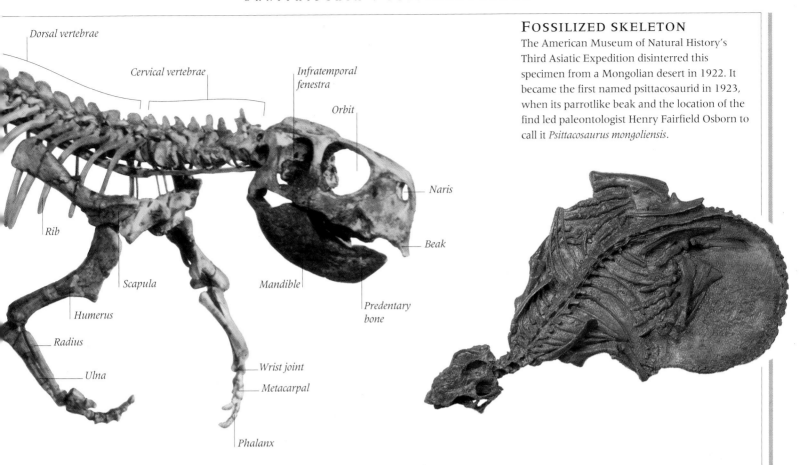

Dorsal vertebrae

Cervical vertebrae

Infratemporal fenestra

Orbit

Naris

Rib

Beak

Scapula

Mandible

Humerus

Predentary bone

Radius

Ulna

Wrist joint

Metacarpal

Phalanx

FOSSILIZED SKELETON

The American Museum of Natural History's Third Asiatic Expedition disinterred this specimen from a Mongolian desert in 1922. It became the first named psittacosaurid in 1923, when its parrotlike beak and the location of the find led paleontologist Henry Fairfield Osborn to call it *Psittacosaurus mongoliensis*.

SIMILARITIES WITH PARROTS

The dinosaur family Psittacosauridae takes its name from similarities between the skull of a *Psittacosaurus* (right) and the head of a macaw (far right), cockatoo, or other member of the Psittacidae (the parrot family). Parrots evolved deep, sharp beaks to slice through tough-skinned fruits and to crack open nuts. *Psittacosaurus*, with a deep, sharp beak and cheek teeth, was probably capable of cutting up hard plant material and chewing it as well.

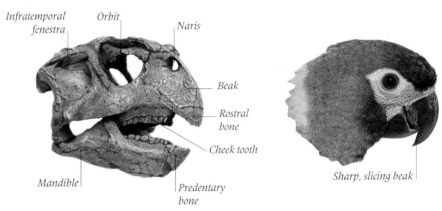

Infratemporal fenestra

Orbit

Naris

Beak

Rostral bone

Cheek tooth

Mandible

Predentary bone

Sharp, slicing beak

✻ FACT FILE ✻

PSITTACOSAURUS

Psittacosaurus was a small, bipedal plant-eater with a parrotlike beak and cheek horns.

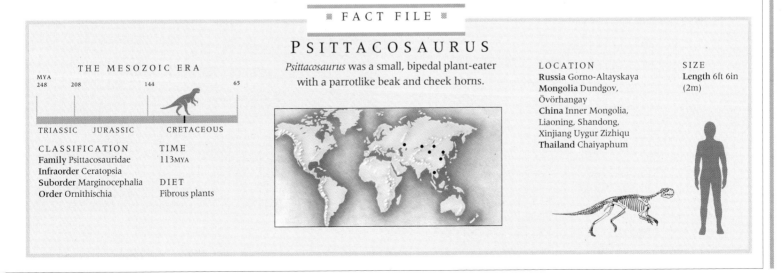

THE MESOZOIC ERA

MYA
248   208   144   65

TRIASSIC   JURASSIC   CRETACEOUS

CLASSIFICATION
Family Psittacosauridae
Infraorder Ceratopsia
Suborder Marginocephalia
Order Ornithischia

TIME
113MYA

DIET
Fibrous plants

LOCATION
Russia Gorno-Altayskaya
Mongolia Dundgov,
Övörhangay
China Inner Mongolia,
Liaoning, Shandong,
Xinjiang Uygur Zizhiqu
Thailand Chaiyaphum

SIZE
Length 6ft 6in
(2m)

PROTOCERATOPS

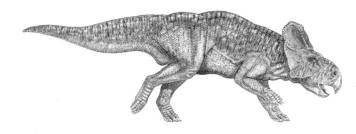

P ROTOCERATOPS ("first horned face") was discovered by an American expedition to Mongolia in the early 1920s. The numerous skeletons belonged to four-legged plant-eaters with oversized heads, bony neck frills, sharp, shearing cheek teeth, and parrotlike beaks. Some of these features identified *Protoceratops* as an early Asian model for the huge, horned dinosaurs of North America, the ceratopsids. *Protoceratops* gave its name to the protoceratopsids, a whole "new" family of dinosaurs. Finds of nests, eggs, and young gave the first clear indications of family life in a dinosaur community.

EGG DISCOVERER
Roy Chapman Andrews inspecting his great find of Protoceratops *eggs.*

EXTERNAL APPEARANCE

Protoceratops could run with reasonable speed but was a solidly built quadruped that was heavier, but not longer, than a tall human.

SKULL

The skull and jaws of *Protoceratops* appear almost absurdly overgrown. Like its later, larger relatives, *Protoceratops* had a deep beak, a ridge above the nose, and a large, bony frill that stuck out over the neck. As individuals matured, the bony frill grew bigger, for display, and the nose ridge taller, either for show or for use in butting contests.

Bony frill

Infratemporal fenestra

Jugal bone

Mandible

Dentary bone

Naris

Beak

Rostral bone

Predentary bone

※ LIFE AND BEHAVIOR ※

Protoceratops inhabited a hostile region of hot, dry, windswept sand dunes. The climate comprised a rainy season, during which water filled lakes and streams, and a dry season, during which the rains stopped and most of the surface water evaporated. Drought-resistant plants were able to thrive in this harsh environment, and it seems likely that *Protoceratops*'s massive jaws, sharp beak, and shearing teeth evolved to slice up the tough-leaved vegetation. This solidly built protoceratopsid probably lived in herds that wandered over a fairly small home range and came back to the same breeding grounds year after year.

※ BREEDING COLONIES ※

Evidence for such breeding grounds includes concentrated fossil finds of individuals of all ages near groups of nests, some of which were made on top of older ones. At mating time, males probably courted females by displaying their own relatively larger neck frills and nasal bumps. After mating, each female dug a shallow hole in the sand and filled it with a clutch of elongated, hard-shelled eggs laid in a spiral pattern. She then covered her eggs with sand and let the sun's heat hatch them. In the meantime, the mother had to guard her nest against plundering theropods. *Oviraptor* and *Velociraptor* bones have been unearthed in *Protoceratops* nesting colonies. *Oviraptor*'s strong, toothless beak could have crushed eggshells, while the more formidably armed *Velociraptor* could have preyed upon young and even adult protoceratopsids. One *Velociraptor* evidently died in combat with a *Protoceratops*, which also perished in the struggle.

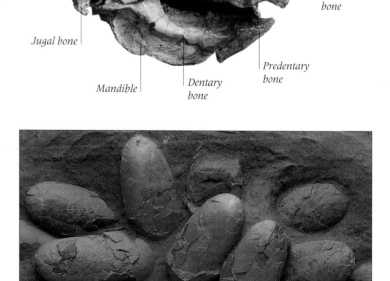

NEST AND EGGS
This fossil clutch of Protoceratops *eggs was found just as it had been laid more than 80 million years ago.*

MOUNTED SKELETON

Forelimb bones almost as long as those of the hind limbs helped support the heavy head. Like ceratopsids, *Protoceratops* had an arched sacrum (fused sacral vertebrae) that made its tail curve down. Unlike them, it had premaxillary (front upper) teeth, and the tibia and fibula (shinbones) were longer than the femur (thighbone).

Braincase

Orbit

Rostral bone

Parietal fenestra

Dorsal vertebra

Ilium

Femur

Hip joint

Sacrum

Caudal vertebra

Mandible

Predentary bone

Fibula

Shoulder joint

Ischium

Tibia

Chevron

Long foot

Wrist joint

Radius

Ulna

DIGITS Each forelimb had three long, spreading digits, tipped with blunt claws. The fourth and fifth digits were much reduced. Each hind limb ended in a long foot, with four toes tipped by bluntly tapered claws, and a trace of a fifth toe.

FOSSIL SKELETON

Seen from below, this articulated fossil skeleton reveals flared jugal (cheek) bones, which are a hallmark of the ceratopsian dinosaurs. Also visible is the rostral (beak) bone, another feature that differentiates the ceratopsians from other members of the marginocephalian group.

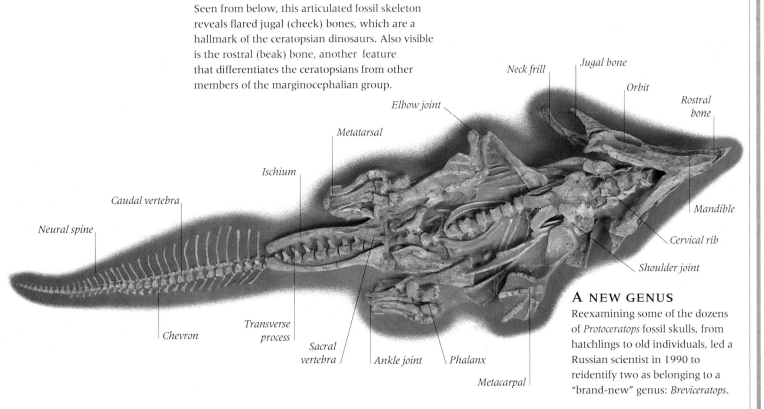

Neck frill

Jugal bone

Orbit

Rostral bone

Elbow joint

Metatarsal

Ischium

Caudal vertebra

Mandible

Neural spine

Cervical rib

Shoulder joint

Chevron

Transverse process

Sacral vertebra

Ankle joint

Phalanx

Metacarpal

A NEW GENUS

Reexamining some of the dozens of *Protoceratops* fossil skulls, from hatchlings to old individuals, led a Russian scientist in 1990 to reidentify two as belonging to a "brand-new" genus: *Breviceratops*.

CENTROSAURUS

T HE HORNED DINOSAUR *Centrosaurus* ("well-horned lizard") resembled a large rhinoceros. Like the rhinoceros, it had a heavy head, strong shoulders, pillarlike legs, broad-hoofed toes, a small tail, and a long, pointed nasal horn. In *Centrosaurus*, the massive head also had two small brow horns above the eyes. From the back of its rounded neck frill two long, bony hooks curved forward and down, and two shorter hooks curled back and inward. *Centrosaurus* grew to two-thirds the length of the largest horned dinosaur. It belonged to the centrosaurines: a ceratopsid subfamily whose members had short, deep faces, and a nose horn longer than the horns on its brows.

■ LIFE AND BEHAVIOR ■

As in *Triceratops* and other ceratopsids, the jaws of *Centrosaurus* were designed for munching tough, fibrous vegetation. Large muscles, some anchored to the neck frill, slammed shut these huge jaws to deliver an immensely powerful bite. Cheek teeth with long cutting blades scissored each mouthful of tough stems into small pieces. These pieces might then have been mashed by swallowed stomach stones, ready for digestion. *Centrosaurus* shared its habitat among the meandering rivers and swampy forests of what is now Alberta with other big plant-eaters: horned, duck-billed, bone-headed, and armored ornithischians, and with predatory dinosaurs of all sizes, from small elmisaurids and ferocious dromaeosaurids to the terrible tyrannosaurid *Albertosaurus*. Here, too, lived smaller animals: small mammals, birds, crocodiles, turtles, salamanders, frogs, and freshwater fish. Some of their relatives are still alive today.

■ MIGRATION ■

From Alberta's forests, *Centrosaurus* herds, thousands strong, probably migrated far north where plants grew quickly in the Arctic's mild, daylit summer months. These creatures could have rambled distances as great as 70 miles (about 110km) a day. Even if a flooded river blocked their path, instinct would have urged the densely crowded herd to plunge in and try to swim across. Sometimes, if the current proved too strong, hundreds would have drowned, their bodies eventually drifting to shore or foundering on a sandbar. The mountain of rotting meat would have then provided a feast for carnosaurs living in the surrounding area.

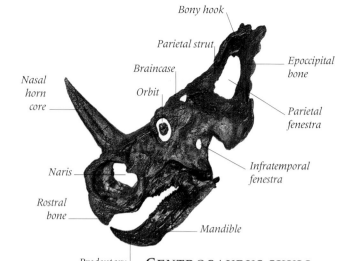

Bony hook
Parietal strut
Braincase
Epoccipital bone
Nasal horn core
Orbit
Parietal fenestra
Naris
Infratemporal fenestra
Rostral bone
Mandible
Predentary bone

CENTROSAURUS SKULL

A profile view of the skull (above) shows the long nasal horn and short, rounded neck frill pierced by windows. Two bony hooks overhung the frill from the back. Although they are shown in the profiled head (left), they might have been concealed by skin and muscle.

Bony hook
Rudimentary brow horn
Nose horn
Predentary bone

Ambiens muscle
Iliotibial muscle
Neural spine
Ischium
Lateral caudal musculature
Chevron
Knee joint
Gastrocnemius muscle
Ankle joint

HIPS, LEGS, AND TAIL

As in all ceratopsids, hipbones featured a broad, shelflike ilium, a long prepubis, and a downcurved ischium. In the legs, the femur was longer than the tibia. *Centrosaurus* had splayed, hoofed, four-toed feet. An arched sacrum made the base of the short, unstiffened tail slope down.

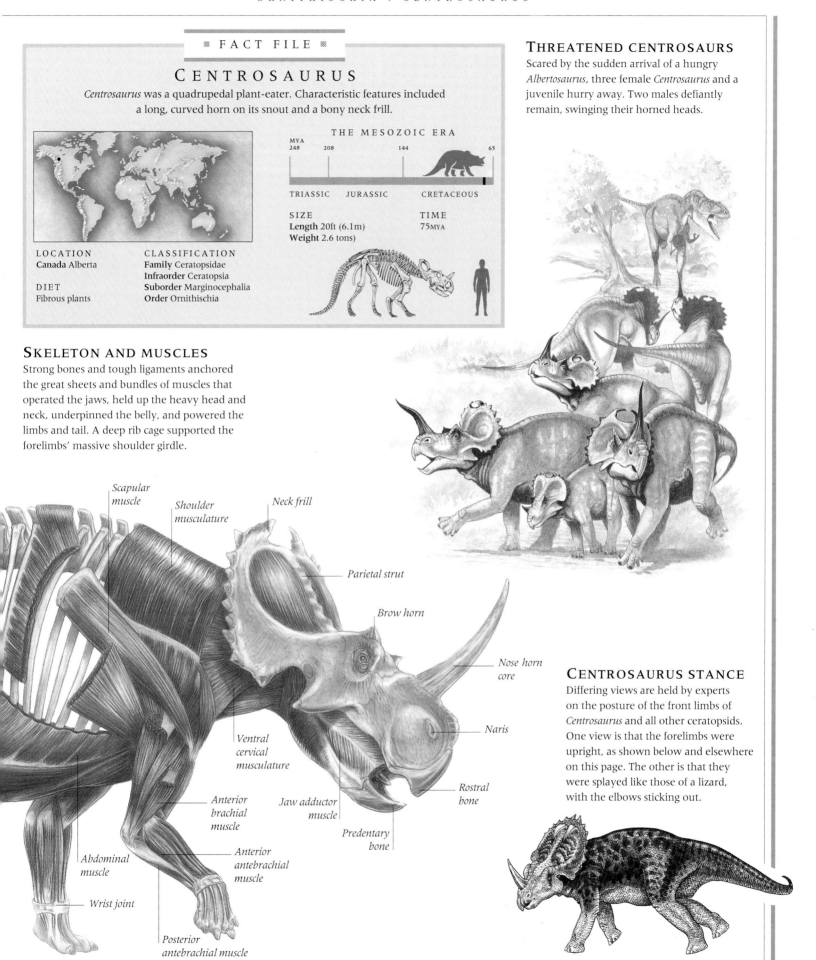

CENTROSAURUS

Centrosaurus was a quadrupedal plant-eater. Characteristic features included a long, curved horn on its snout and a bony neck frill.

THE MESOZOIC ERA

MYA 248	208	144	65
TRIASSIC	JURASSIC	CRETACEOUS	

SIZE
Length 20ft (6.1m)
Weight 2.6 tons)

TIME
75MYA

LOCATION
Canada Alberta

DIET
Fibrous plants

CLASSIFICATION
Family Ceratopsidae
Infraorder Ceratopsia
Suborder Marginocephalia
Order Ornithischia

THREATENED CENTROSAURS

Scared by the sudden arrival of a hungry *Albertosaurus*, three female *Centrosaurus* and a juvenile hurry away. Two males defiantly remain, swinging their horned heads.

SKELETON AND MUSCLES

Strong bones and tough ligaments anchored the great sheets and bundles of muscles that operated the jaws, held up the heavy head and neck, underpinned the belly, and powered the limbs and tail. A deep rib cage supported the forelimbs' massive shoulder girdle.

Scapular muscle

Shoulder musculature

Neck frill

Parietal strut

Brow horn

Nose horn core

Naris

Ventral cervical musculature

Anterior brachial muscle

Jaw adductor muscle

Rostral bone

Predentary bone

Abdominal muscle

Anterior antebrachial muscle

Wrist joint

Posterior antebrachial muscle

CENTROSAURUS STANCE

Differing views are held by experts on the posture of the front limbs of *Centrosaurus* and all other ceratopsids. One view is that the forelimbs were upright, as shown below and elsewhere on this page. The other is that they were splayed like those of a lizard, with the elbows sticking out.

STYRACOSAURUS

T HE HORNED dinosaur *Styracosaurus* ("spiked lizard") was so named because of the six long, bony spikes that stuck out fanwise from the back of its neck frill. These spikes were outgrowths of the small knobs known as epoccipital bones that gave a scalloped effect to the rim of the neck frill. The neck frill was a feature common to most ceratopsid dinosaurs, but the spikes were not. When *Styracosaurus* was alive, each of the four longest spikes of its neck frill, as well as its imposing nose horn, were probably about as long as a man's arm.

Frill spike

Supraorbital ridge

Naris

Parietal fenestra

Parietosquamosal frill

Nose horn core

Orbit

Mandible

SKULL AND HEAD

Features of *Styracosaurus*'s skull (above) included a neck frill with six long spikes and large, open "windows." In living animals, tough skin and muscle covered the frill windows (left).

■ LIFE AND BEHAVIOR ■

Styracosaurus's spiky head and neck frill would have shielded its neck and shoulders from attack by large predators akin to *Tyrannosaurus*. Rival males probably also brandished their nasal horns and frill spikes at each other in competition for mates. Two males might have edged sideways until their frill spikes interlocked, and then begun a shoving contest similar to the head-to-toe thrusting of two antlered Red Deer stags competing for a herd of doe. *Styracosaurus*'s powerful shoulders would have been extremely useful in this sort of fight. Pushing contests may not always have injured the contestants badly, but several ceratopsian skeletons do show that injuries did occur. Fights may have happened often.

■ CLASSIFICATION ■

Although the frill spikes and other skull features of *Styracosaurus* might seem to be very distinctive, some scientists think *Styracosaurus*, *Centrosaurus*, and some supposed specimens of *Monoclonius* all formed a single genus. It is possible that such features as the size and number of horns or spikes varied with age, sex, and perhaps species. To complicate this notion, a drawing published in 1990 suggested there may have been a species of *Styracosaurus* with only two frill spikes and a remarkable nasal horn that overhung the beak. Then in 1992 came news of a "missing link" between *Styracosaurus* and *Pachyrhinosaurus*. Such finds will shed new light on ceratopsid identities and evolution.

Relatively short tail

SKELETON

Styracosaurus's skeleton (below), featured a ceratopsid's typically deep beak, massive skull, sturdy shoulder and hip girdles, robust limb bones, roomy rib cage, and short tail. The short neck frill characterizes the subfamily Centrosaurinae. *Styracosaurus*'s long neck-frill spikes are usually thought to be unique to this genus.

Epoccipital bone

Braincase

Orbit

Nose horn core

Naris

Mandible

Predentary bone

Rostral bone

Metacarpal

Phalanx

Ulna

Radius

RESTORATION

As can be seen from this model, *Styracosaurus*'s most distinctive features were a long nose horn and a large neck frill with long spikes. *Styracosaurus* looked a little like *Centrosaurus* and *Monoclonius*, two ceratopsids that had long nose horns but no spikes on the neck frill.

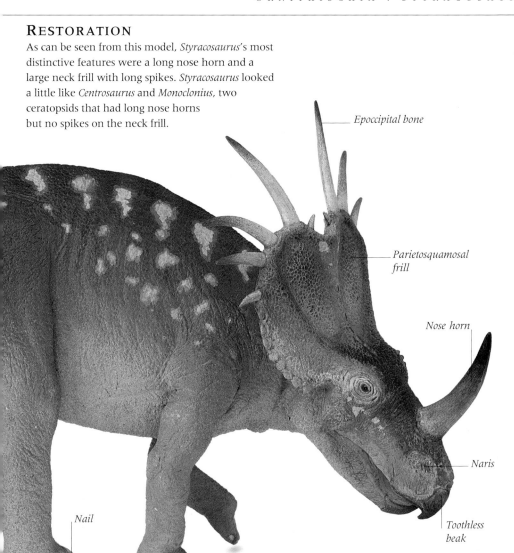

Epoccipital bone

Parietosquamosal frill

Nose horn

Naris

Toothless beak

Nail

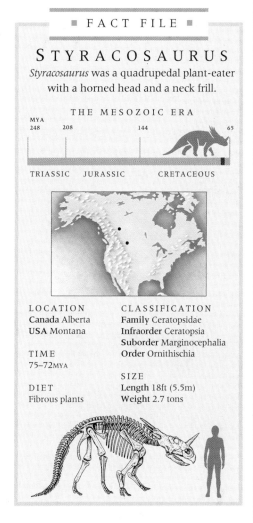

FACT FILE

STYRACOSAURUS

Styracosaurus was a quadrupedal plant-eater with a horned head and a neck frill.

THE MESOZOIC ERA

MYA				
248	208		144	65

TRIASSIC	JURASSIC	CRETACEOUS

LOCATION
Canada Alberta
USA Montana

TIME
75–72MYA

DIET
Fibrous plants

CLASSIFICATION
Family Ceratopsidae
Infraorder Ceratopsia
Suborder Marginocephalia
Order Ornithischia

SIZE
Length 18ft (5.5m)
Weight 2.7 tons

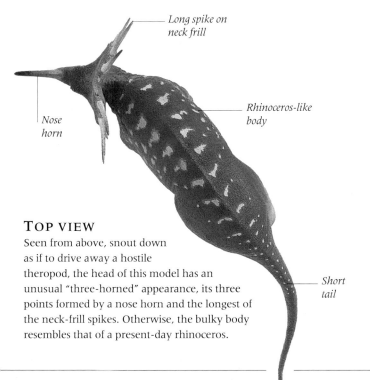

Long spike on neck frill

Nose horn

Rhinoceros-like body

Short tail

TOP VIEW

Seen from above, snout down as if to drive away a hostile theropod, the head of this model has an unusual "three-horned" appearance, its three points formed by a nose horn and the longest of the neck-frill spikes. Otherwise, the bulky body resembles that of a present-day rhinoceros.

PACHYRHINOSAURUS

"Thick-nosed reptile" was a horned dinosaur up to 19ft 6in (6m) long, with a short beak, and a low face crowned by a massive, bony boss. Males probably used their bosses in pushing contests. Up to 1,000 individuals were found in one bonebed in Alberta, Canada, and finds in Arctic Alaska suggest that *Pachyrhinosaurus* herds made long, seasonal migrations.

Bony boss

Neck frill

SKULL

Features included a bony boss, small hornlets on the neck frill, and, in some skulls, a unicorn-like horn in the middle of the frill.

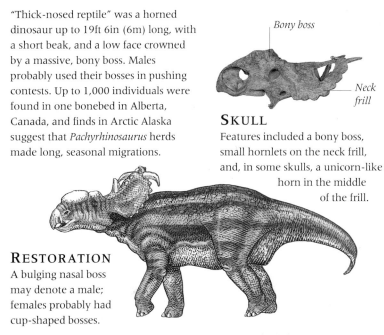

RESTORATION

A bulging nasal boss may denote a male; females probably had cup-shaped bosses.

TRICERATOPS

I N THE 1880s, HIGH PLAINS east of the Rocky Mountains yielded a strange pair of fossil brow horn cores. These were found to be from a huge, horned, plant-eating ornithischian. "Three-horned face" proved to be the largest-known ceratopsid—heavy as an elephant, with a massive body, and a head as long as an adult human's height. A broad, bony frill stuck out from the back of its deep-beaked skull, and two long, hollow-based brow horns jutted above its eyes. The nose horn was short. Despite its small frill, *Triceratops* was one of the chasmosaurines: a subfamily that was mainly long-frilled.

ADULT AND YOUNG
An old engraving shows a mother Triceratops *standing protectively over her baby. If a* Tyrannosaurus *menaced a* Triceratops *herd, the adults might have formed an outward-facing ring around their young.*

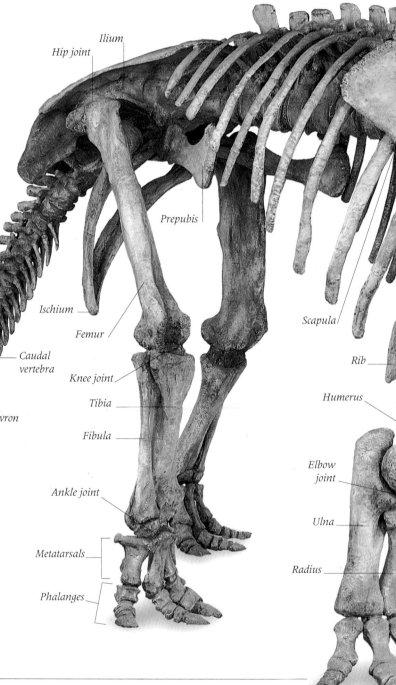

HATCHER'S SPRING
This discovery site is named after pioneer collector John Bell Hatcher.

LIFE AND BEHAVIOR

One of the last and most numerous of all the horned dinosaurs, *Triceratops* herds roamed through forests similar to today's, which thrived in the cool, dry climate to the west of North America's shrinking interior sea. Their heavy heads held low, the great creatures munched herbaceous plants. Perhaps they also used their long brow horns to press down low, leafy branches in order to chop off mouthfuls of twigs and leaves with the sharp sides of their beaks and to slice them up between batteries of shearing cheek teeth. The neck frill's rich blood supply probably served as a heat exchanger, shedding surplus heat when the body was in shade, and warming it when in sun. Sometimes a trial of strength decided which animal would dominate the herd: two males would meet head-to-head, lock horns, and twist until the weaker animal gave way. A hollow high in the skull functioned as a shock absorber, cushioning the brain. Evidence of old, healed wounds in the cheek and frill bones of some *Triceratops* skulls suggests injuries caused by horns when rival males fiercely fought each other. It is likely, however, that a male more commonly asserted his authority by a harmless display of threatening behavior: lowering his head to show off his frill, and then brandishing the frill from side to side to deter his rival and cause him to withdraw.

Ilium

Hip joint

Prepubis

Ischium

Femur

Caudal vertebra

Knee joint

Scapula

Rib

Tibia

Humerus

Fibula

Chevron

Neural spine

Elbow joint

Ankle joint

Ulna

Metatarsals

Radius

Phalanges

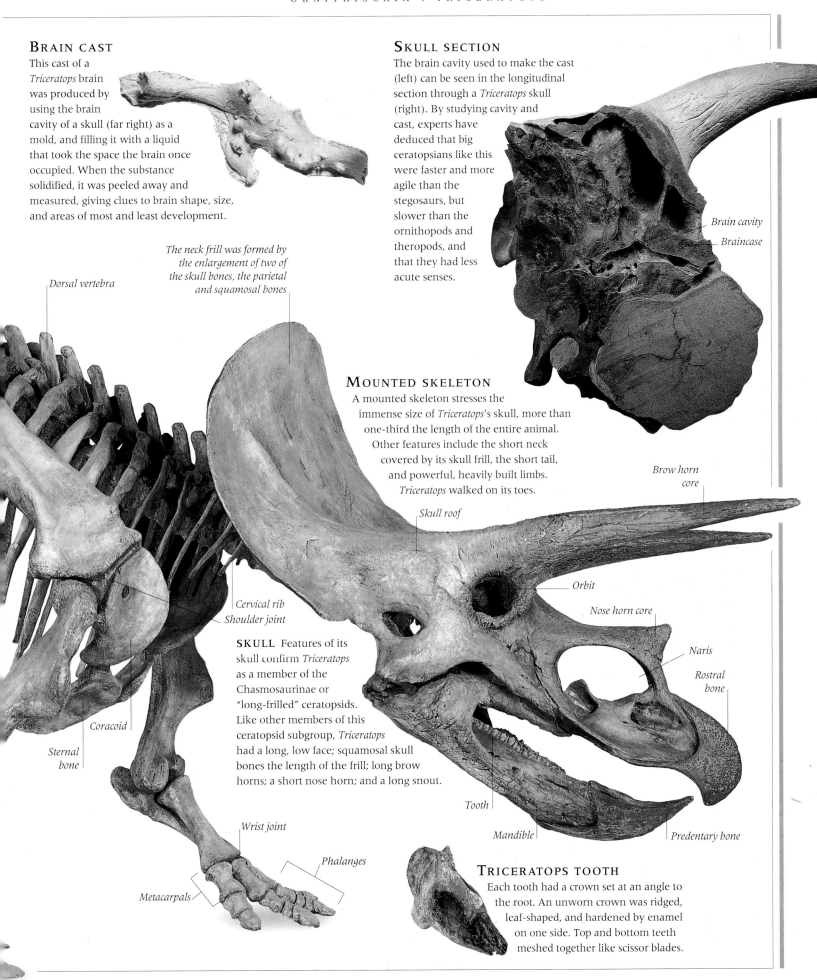

BRAIN CAST

This cast of a *Triceratops* brain was produced by using the brain cavity of a skull (far right) as a mold, and filling it with a liquid that took the space the brain once occupied. When the substance solidified, it was peeled away and measured, giving clues to brain shape, size, and areas of most and least development.

The neck frill was formed by the enlargement of two of the skull bones, the parietal and squamosal bones

Dorsal vertebra

SKULL SECTION

The brain cavity used to make the cast (left) can be seen in the longitudinal section through a *Triceratops* skull (right). By studying cavity and cast, experts have deduced that big ceratopsians like this were faster and more agile than the stegosaurs, but slower than the ornithopods and theropods, and that they had less acute senses.

Brain cavity

Braincase

MOUNTED SKELETON

A mounted skeleton stresses the immense size of *Triceratops*'s skull, more than one-third the length of the entire animal. Other features include the short neck covered by its skull frill, the short tail, and powerful, heavily built limbs. *Triceratops* walked on its toes.

Brow horn core

Skull roof

Cervical rib

Shoulder joint

Orbit

Nose horn core

Naris

SKULL

Features of its skull confirm *Triceratops* as a member of the Chasmosaurinae or "long-frilled" ceratopsids. Like other members of this ceratopsid subgroup, *Triceratops* had a long, low face; squamosal skull bones the length of the frill; long brow horns; a short nose horn; and a long snout.

Rostral bone

Coracoid

Sternal bone

Tooth

Mandible

Predentary bone

Wrist joint

Phalanges

Metacarpals

TRICERATOPS TOOTH

Each tooth had a crown set at an angle to the root. An unworn crown was ridged, leaf-shaped, and hardened by enamel on one side. Top and bottom teeth meshed together like scissor blades.

CHANGES IN CLASSIFICATION

Variations in the skulls of different *Triceratops* specimens once persuaded scientists that there had been 16 different species. A subsequent re-examination of the evidence led to the conclusion that there was only one. Since then there has been a fresh examination, which has caused some scientists to accept that there were probably two or three species.

LANDSCAPE
Triceratops inhabited a countryside of open woodland with flowering plants and conifers, many of which resembled species growing today.

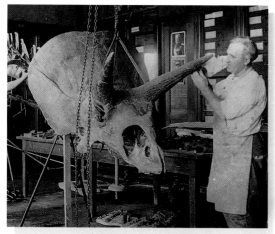

WORK IN PROGRESS
A museum craftsman examines a brow horn on a Triceratops *skull suspended from a hoist during reconstruction work.*

Thick, scaly skin

CHASMOSAURUS

This medium-size chasmosaurine ceratopsid grew up to 16ft (4.9m) long and weighed about 2.2 tons. Skulls of many specimens have been discovered in western North America, where *Chasmosaurus* predated its close relative *Triceratops* by several million years. One scientist has claimed to be able to tell males from females. He has also identified at least three *Chasmosaurus* species from what is now Alberta, and a fourth from Texas.

NECK FRILL AND SKULL
A front view of *Chasmosaurus*'s skull reveals narrow, bony struts—scaffolding to support the frill and reduce its weight. In life, skin covered the fenestrae (openings). From the back of the skull, the neck frill projected quite a way over the neck and shoulders.

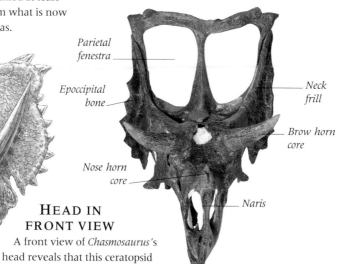

Parietal fenestra

Epoccipital bone

Nose horn core

Neck frill

Brow horn core

Naris

HEAD IN FRONT VIEW
A front view of *Chasmosaurus*'s head reveals that this ceratopsid had a small nose horn and two long brow horns similar to those of a cow.

Thigh

Ankle

Hind limb

Forelimb

Hooflike claw

EXTERNAL APPEARANCE

Triceratops resembled an immense rhinoceros. Like a rhinoceros, its heavy body depended for support on sturdy limbs, and short, broad feet with weight-supporting pads beneath the toes. But unlike any rhinoceros, this dinosaur had a bony neck frill, two long brow horns, and only one short nose horn. Largest of all horned dinosaurs, the monster is known from 50 complete or partial skulls. No complete *Triceratops* skeleton has yet been found.

Horn ended in a sharp point

TRICERATOPS HORN

The bony horn cores that sprout from fossil skulls were sheathed with horn in life. This model depicts a *Triceratops* horn as it would have appeared before its owner died. The result is a longer, sharper, and even more formidable weapon than fossil horn cores lead us to think. Fossil-hunter Othniel Marsh initially mistook such cores for prehistoric bisons' horns.

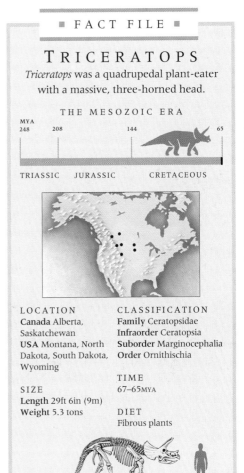

■ FACT FILE ■

TRICERATOPS

Triceratops was a quadrupedal plant-eater with a massive, three-horned head.

THE MESOZOIC ERA

MYA 248	208	144	65
TRIASSIC	JURASSIC	CRETACEOUS	

LOCATION
Canada Alberta, Saskatchewan
USA Montana, North Dakota, South Dakota, Wyoming

SIZE
Length 29ft 6in (9m)
Weight 5.3 tons

CLASSIFICATION
Family Ceratopsidae
Infraorder Ceratopsia
Suborder Marginocephalia
Order Ornithischia

TIME
67–65MYA

DIET
Fibrous plants

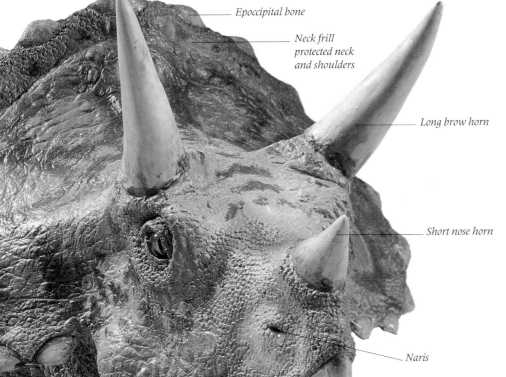

Epoccipital bone

Neck frill protected neck and shoulders

Long brow horn

Short nose horn

Naris

Toothless beak

Broad, blunt ending

Hooflike shape

TRICERATOPS UNGUAL

Three fingers on each "hand" and all four toes on each foot ended in a broad, blunt, rounded, hooflike ungual (terminal phalanx). A fossilized ungual is shown here. When *Triceratops* was alive, each ungual formed a tiny, horn-sheathed hoof. Most of the ceratopsids had hoofed toes; some protoceratopsids had sharp claws instead.

A TO Z OF DINOSAURS

T HIS SECTION is a dictionary including the names of all dinosaur genera that had appeared in print up to the time this book went to press. A total of 638 names are listed, 170 of which have proved (or appear to be) simply duplications of one kind or another. With each passing year, several new dinosaur genera are identified, and there may be thousands more still awaiting discovery.

A TO Z OF DINOSAURS

This section comprises a comprehensive list of currently known dinosaur genera. Each scientifically valid genus name is followed by a pronunciation guide. If a genus is covered in the **Dinosaur Profiles** (pp. 36–167), only a page reference is given. If a genus is not profiled, the **A to Z of Dinosaurs** also gives a derivation of the name, some notes about the animal, and a page reference that allows you to look up a dinosaur in the same family. Where no relative is profiled, details of the dinosaur's classification are listed. The letters *n.d.* (*nomen dubium* – "doubtful name") indicate that the genus is little known, or that it is invalid. Where a genus is listed with an equals sign (=), the second name is the scientifically valid name; if the second name has a question mark, this indicates that it is possibly the valid name. Informal or unofficial names appear in quotation marks.

A **Abelisaurus** (ah-BEEL-i-SORE-rus: "Abel's lizard") A bipedal carnivore 29ft 6in (9m) long: a ceratosaur related to *Carnotaurus* (p. 48). Lived in the Late Cretaceous. Found in Argentina.

Abrictosaurus (a-BRIK-toh-SORE-us: "awake lizard") A bipedal herbivore similar to *Heterodontosaurus* (p. 134). Found in South Africa.

Acanthopholis (ae-KAN-tho-FOLE-is: "spine bearer") A quadrupedal, armored herbivore 18ft (5.5m) long: an ankylosaur related to *Edmontonia* (p. 122). Lived in the Early and Late Cretaceous. Found in England. (*n.d.*)

Acrocanthosaurus (a-kroh-kan-thoh-SORE-us: "top-spined lizard") A sail-backed, bipedal carnivore up to 39ft (12m) long: a theropod related to *Allosaurus* (p. 52). Lived in the Early Cretaceous. Found in Oklahoma and Texas.

Adasaurus (ah-DAH-SORE-us: "Ada lizard") A bipedal carnivore 6ft 6in (2m) long: a theropod related to *Deinonychus* (p. 70). Lived in the Late Cretaceous. Found in Mongolia.

Aegyptosaurus (ee-jip-toh-SORE-us: "Egyptian lizard") A quadrupedal herbivore 53ft (16m) long: a sauropod related to *Saltasaurus* (p. 106). Lived in the Late Cretaceous. Found in Egypt and Niger.

Aeolosaurus (ee-OH-LOH-SORE-us: "wind lizard") A quadrupedal herbivore 53ft (16m) long: a sauropod related to *Saltasaurus* (p. 106). Lived in the Late Cretaceous. Found in Argentina.

Aepisaurus (ee-pi-SORE-us: "elephant lizard") A quadrupedal herbivore about 49ft (15m) long: a sauropod of unknown family. Lived in the Early Cretaceous. Found in France. (*n.d.*)

Aetonyx = *Massospondylus* (p. 88).

Agathaumas (aga-THOW-mas: "much wonder") A quadrupedal, horned herbivore; possibly *Triceratops* (p. 164). Lived in the Late Cretaceous. Found in Wyoming. (*n.d.*)

Agilisaurus (a-jil-i-SORE-us: "agile lizard") A small, bipedal herbivore: an ornithopod related to *Hypsilophodon* (p. 136). Lived in the Middle Jurassic. Found in China. Named in 1990.

Agrosaurus (ag-roh-SORE-us: "field lizard") A bipedal/quadrupedal herbivore: a prosauropod of unknown family and doubtful date (possibly Early Jurassic). Found in Australia. (*n.d.*)

Alamosaurus (AL-a-moh-SORE-us: "Alamo lizard") A quadrupedal herbivore up to 69ft (21m) long: a sauropod related to *Saltasaurus* (p. 106). Lived in the Late Cretaceous. Found in Utah and New Mexico.

Albertosaurus (al-BERT-oh-SORE-rus: "Alberta lizard") A bipedal carnivore up to 26ft (8m) long. Similar to *Tyrannosaurus* (p. 54). Lived in the Late Cretaceous. Found in western North America.

Albisaurus (al-bi-SORE-us: "white lizard") A dinosaur (or probable dinosaur) known only from sparse Late Cretaceous remains. Identity uncertain. Found in the Czech Republic. (*n.d.*)

Alectrosaurus (a-LEK-troh-sore-us: "eagle lizard") A bipedal carnivore 16ft 6in (5m) long. Related to *Tyrannosaurus* (p. 54). Lived in the Late Cretaceous. Found in China and Mongolia.

Algoasaurus (AL-goh-a-sore-us: "Algoa lizard") A quadrupedal herbivore 29ft 6in (9m) long: a sauropod known only from sparse remains. Lived in the Early Cretaceous. Found in South Africa. (*n.d.*)

Alioramus (ay-lee-oh-RAY-mus: "different branch") A bipedal carnivore 19ft 6in (6m) long with a low head. Related to *Tyrannosaurus* (p. 54). Lived in the Late Cretaceous. Found in Mongolia.

Aliwalia (ah-lee-WAL-ee-a: "Aliwal") An early, large, bipedal carnivore up to 36ft (11m) long. Related to *Herrerasaurus* (p. 40). Lived in the Late Triassic. Found in South Africa. (*n.d.*)

Allosaurus (al-oh-SORE-us) See p. 52.

Alocodon (ay-LOH-koh-don: "wing tooth") A small, bipedal herbivore: an ornithischian known only from teeth. Lived in the Late Jurassic. Found in Portugal. Classification uncertain.

Altispinax (al-ti-SPINE-ax: "high spines") A large, bipedal carnivore: a theropod known only from a tooth. Lived in the Early Cretaceous. Found in Germany. Classification uncertain. (*n.d.*)

Alvarezsaurus (AL-va-rez-SORE-us: "Alvarez lizard") A bipedal carnivore like *Struthiomimus* (p. 64) but unrelated. Lived in the Late Cretaceous. Found in Argentina. Named in 1991. Classification: Alvarezsauridae, Ceratosauria, Theropoda, Saurischia.

Amargasaurus (a-MAR-ga-SORE-us "Amarga lizard") A sail-backed, quadrupedal herbivore 29ft 6in (9m) long: a sauropod. Lived in the Early Cretaceous. Found in Argentina. Described in 1991. Classification: Dicraeosauridae, Sauropoda, Sauropodomorpha, Saurischia.

Ammosaurus (a-moh-SORE-us: "sand lizard") A bipedal/quadrupedal herbivore 8ft (2.4m) long: a prosauropod related to *Plateosaurus* (p. 86). Lived in the Early Jurassic. Found in Connecticut and Arizona.

Amphicoelias (am-fi-SEEL-yas: "with hollow-ended vertebrae") A large, quadrupedal herbivore: a sauropod related to *Diplodocus* (p. 100). Lived in the Late Jurassic. Found in Colorado.

Amphisaurus = *Anchisaurus* (p. 84).

Amtosaurus (am-toh-SORE-us: "Amtgay lizard") A large, bipedal/quadrupedal herbivore: a hadrosaur known only from a partial skull. Lived in the Late Cretaceous. Found in Mongolia. (*n.d.*)

Amygdalodon (ay-mig-DAL-oh-don: "almond tooth") A large, quadrupedal herbivore: a sauropod related to *Cetiosaurus* (p. 92). Lived in the Middle Jurassic. Found in Argentina.

Anatosaurus = *Edmontosaurus* (p. 144) and *Anatotitan*.

Anatotitan (an-at-oh-TIE-tan: "giant duck") A bipedal/quadrupedal herbivore 39ft (12m) long: a hadrosaur related to *Edmontosaurus* (p. 144). Lived in the Late Cretaceous. Found in western North America. Named in 1990.

Anchiceratops (AN-ki-SERRA-tops: "close-horned face") A quadrupedal, horned dinosaur up to 16ft 6in (5m) long: a ceratopsian related to *Triceratops* (p. 164). Lived in the Late Cretaceous. Found in western North America.

Anchisaurus (AN-ki-SORE-us) See p. 84.

Andesaurus (AN-dee-SORE-us: "Andes lizard") A large, quadrupedal herbivore: a sauropod related to *Saltasaurus* (p. 106). Lived in the Late Cretaceous. Found in Argentina. Named in 1991.

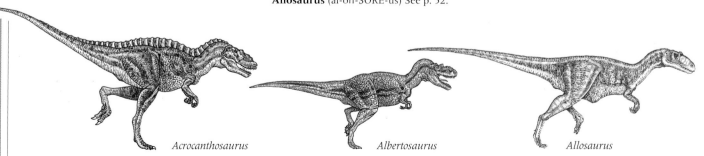

Acrocanthosaurus   *Albertosaurus*   *Allosaurus*

Ankylosaurus (an-KIE-loh-SORE-us: "stiff lizard") An armored dinosaur up to 33ft (10m) long, related to *Euoplocephalus* (p. 128). Lived in the Late Cretaceous. Found in western North America.

Anodontosaurus = *Dyoplosaurus*.

Anoplosaurus (an-oh-ploh-SORE-us: "unarmored lizard") A little known herbivore, probably *Acanthopholis*. Lived in the Early Cretaceous. Found in England. (*n.d.*)

Anserimimus (an-ser-ih-MEEM-us: "goose mimic") A bipedal, bird-like carnivore or omnivore: a theropod related to *Gallimimus* (p. 62). Lived in the Late Cretaceous. Found in Mongolia.

Antarctosaurus (an-tark-toe-SORE-us: "southern lizard") A quadrupedal herbivore about 59ft (18m) long: a sauropod related to *Saltasaurus* (p. 106). Lived in the Late Cretaceous. Found in Argentina.

Anthodon = *Paranthodon*.

Antrodemus = *Allosaurus* (p. 52).

Apatodon = *Allosaurus?* (p. 52).

Apatosaurus (ah-PAT-oh-SORE-us) See p. 102.

Aragosaurus (a-ra-goh-SORE-us: "Aragon lizard") A large, quadrupedal herbivore: a sauropod related to *Camarasaurus* (p. 96). Lived in the Early Cretaceous. Found in Spain.

Aralosaurus (ar-al-oh-SORE-us: "Aral lizard") A bipedal herbivore: a hadrosaur related to *Maiasaura* (p. 146). Lived in the Late Cretaceous. Found in Kazakhstan.

Archaeopteryx (ark-ee-OP-ter-iks) See p. 74.

Archaeornis = *Archaeopteryx* (p. 74).

Archaeornithoides (ark-ee-or-nee-THOY-deez: "like ancient bird") A small, bird-like carnivore. Skull features are reminiscent of *Troodon* (p. 68) and *Baryonyx* (p. 58). Lived in the Late Cretaceous. Found in Mongolia. Named in 1992. Classification: Archaeornithoididae, Tetanurae, Theropoda, Saurischia.

Archaeornithomimus (ark-ee-or-nee-thoh-MEEM-us: "ancient bird mimic") A bipedal, bird-like carnivore or omnivore: an ostrich dinosaur related to *Gallimimus* (p. 62). Lived in the Late Cretaceous. Found in China.

Arctosaurus (ark-toe-SORE-us: "Arctic lizard") A possible theropod known from a Late Triassic vertebra, from Arctic Canada. (*n.d.*)

Argyrosaurus (ahr-guy-roe-SORE-us: "silver lizard") A quadrupedal herbivore 69ft (21m) long, with thighbones more than 6ft 6in (2m) long: a sauropod related to *Saltasaurus* (p. 106). Lived in the Late Cretaceous. Found in Argentina and Uruguay.

Aristosaurus = *Massospondylus* (p. 88).

Aristosuchus = *Calamospondylus?*

"Arkansaurus" = *Archaeornithomimus?*

Arrhinoceratops (ay-rine-oh-SERRA-tops: "nose-horned face") A large, quadrupedal, horned herbivore: a ceratopsian related to *Triceratops* (p. 164). Lived in the Late Cretaceous. Found in Alberta, Canada.

Arstanosaurus (AHR-stan-oh-SORE-us: "Arstan lizard") Name for fossils of what proved to be a horned and a duck-billed dinosaur. Lived in the Late Cretaceous. Found in Kazakhstan. (*n.d.*)

Asiaceratops (AY-zya-SERRA-tops: "Asia horned face") A small, mainly bipedal, horned herbivore: a ceratopsian related to *Protoceratops* (p. 158). Lived in the Late Cretaceous. Found in Uzbekistan, Mongolia, and China. Named in 1989.

Asiatosaurus (AY-zya-toh-SORE-us: "Asian lizard") A large, quadrupedal herbivore: a sauropod perhaps related to *Camarasaurus* (p. 96) or *Mamenchisaurus* (p. 104). Lived in the Early Cretaceous. Found in Mongolia and China. (*n.d.*)

Astrodon (AS-troh-don: "star tooth") A quadrupedal herbivore perhaps more than 33ft (10m) long: a sauropod related to *Brachiosaurus* (p. 94). Lived in the Early Cretaceous. Found in eastern North America, England, and South Africa. (*n.d.*)

Astrodonius = *Astrodon*.

Atlantosaurus (at-lan-toh-SORE-us: "Atlas lizard") A quadrupedal herbivore 75ft (23m) long. (*n.d.*)

Atlascopcosaurus (AT-las-kop-koh-SORE-us: "Atlas Copco lizard") A bipedal herbivore about 9ft (2.7m) long: an ornithopod related to *Hypsilophodon* (p. 136). Lived in the Early Cretaceous. Found in Australia.

Aublysodon (oh-BLIS-oh-don: "blunt tooth") A bipedal carnivore similar to *Tyrannosaurus* (p. 54), but smaller. Lived in the Late Cretaceous. Found in western North America and China. Classification: Aublysodontidae, Tetanurae, Theropoda, Saurischia.

Austrosaurus (OS-troh-SORE-us: "southern lizard") A quadrupedal herbivore 49ft (15m) long: a sauropod perhaps related to *Cetiosaurus* (p. 92). Lived in the late Early and early Late Cretaceous. Found in Australia.

Avaceratops (AY-va-SERRA-tops: "Ava's horned face") A quadrupedal herbivore with a short nose horn: a ceratopsian related to *Centrosaurus* (p. 160). Lived in the Late Cretaceous. Found in Montana.

Avimimus (ay-vee-MEEM-us) See p. 76.

Avipes (AY-VEE-pace: "bird foot") A bipedal carnivore about 3ft 3in (1m) long: a theropod of doubtful identity. Lived in the Late Triassic. Found in Germany. (*n.d.*)

Azendohsaurus (ay-zen-doh-SORE-us: "Azendoh lizard") A bipedal herbivore 6ft (1.8m) long: perhaps related to *Thecodontosaurus*. Lived in the early Late Triassic. Found in Morocco.

B **Bactrosaurus** (bak-troh-SORE-us: "Bactrian lizard") A bipedal/quadrupedal herbivore up to 19ft 6in (6m) long: a primitive hadrosaur related to *Lambeosaurus* (p. 150). Lived in the Late Cretaceous. Found in China.

Bagaceratops (bag-a-SERRA-tops: "small horned face") A horned herbivore 3ft 3in (1m) long: a ceratopsian related to *Protoceratops* (p. 158). Lived in the Late Cretaceous. Found in Mongolia.

Bahariasaurus (ba-ha-ree-a-SORE-us: "Baharia lizard") A bipedal carnivore (or possibly omnivore): a theropod perhaps related to ostrich dinosaurs. Lived in the Late Cretaceous. Found in northern Africa.

Barapasaurus (bah-RAP-oh-SORE-us: "big leg lizard") A quadrupedal herbivore up to 59ft (18m) long: a primitive sauropod related to *Cetiosaurus* (p. 92) or in another family (Barapasauridae or Vulcanodontidae). Lived in the Early Jurassic. Found in India.

Barosaurus (bar-oh-SORE-us) See p. 98.

Barsboldia (barz-BOL-di-a: "Barsbold") A large, bipedal/quadrupedal herbivore: a hadrosaur related to *Lambeosaurus* (p. 150). Lived in the Late Cretaceous. Found in Mongolia.

Baryonyx (bar-ee-ON-iks: "heavy claw") See p. 58.

Becklespinax (bek-l-SPINE-ax: "Beckles' spines") A large, bipedal carnivore: a theropod with a skin and bone "sail" on its back. Named in 1991 from supposed *Altispinax* spinal bones. Lived in the Early Cretaceous. Found in England. Classification: Carnosauria, Tetanurae, Theropoda, Saurischia.

Anchisaurus   *Apatosaurus*   *Avimimus*

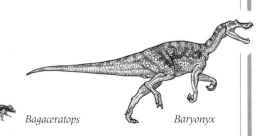

Bagaceratops   *Baryonyx*

Bellusaurus (bel-yoo-SORE-us) A quadrupedal herbivore at least 16ft 6in (5m) long: a sauropod related to *Cetiosaurus* (p. 92). Lived in the Middle Jurassic. Found in China.

Betasuchus (bee-ta-SYOO-kus: "B crocodile") A bipedal carnivore with slim thighbones: possibly related to *Carnotaurus* (p. 48). Lived in the Late Cretaceous. Found in the Netherlands.

Bihariosaurus (bi-HAR-i-oh-SORE-us: "Bihar lizard") A fairly large, bipedal/quadrupedal herbivore somewhat like *Iguanodon* (p. 138). Lived in the Late Cretaceous. Found in Romania. Named in 1989. Classification: Camptosauridae, Ornithopoda, Euornithopoda, Ornithischia.

Blikanasaurus (bli-KAHN-a-SORE-us: "Blikana lizard") A quadrupedal herbivore 16ft 6in (5m) long, with stocky hind limbs. Lived in the Late Triassic. Found in South Africa. Classification: Blikanasauridae, Prosauropoda, Sauropodomorpha, Saurischia.

Borogovia (bo-roh-GOH-vee-a: "Borogove") A small, bipedal carnivore with a large second toe-claw: a theropod related to *Troodon* (p. 68). Lived in the Late Cretaceous. Found in Mongolia.

Bothriospondylus (both-ree-oh-SPON-di-lus: "excavated vertebrae") A large, quadrupedal herbivore: a sauropod related to *Brachiosaurus* (p. 94). Lived in the Middle Jurassic–Early Cretaceous. Found in England, France, and Madagascar.

Brachiosaurus (brak-ee-oh-SORE-us) See p. 94.

Brachyceratops (brak-ee-SERRA-tops: "short horned face") A quadrupedal, horned herbivore up to 13ft (4m) long: a ceratopsian related to *Centrosaurus* (p. 160). Lived in the Late Cretaceous. Found in Alberta, Canada, and Montana.

Brachylophosaurus (brak-ee-lohf-oh-SORE-us: "short-crested lizard") A bipedal/quadrupedal herbivore: a hadrosaur related to *Maiasaura* (p. 146). Lived in the Late Cretaceous. Found in Alberta, Canada, and Montana.

Brachypodosaurus (brak-ee-pod-oh-SORE-us: "short-foot lizard") A quadrupedal, armored, or plated herbivore known only from an upper arm bone: a nodosaurid ankylosaur or perhaps a stegosaur. Lived in the Late Cretaceous. Found in India. (*n.d.*)

Brachyrophus = *Camptosaurus*.

Bradycneme = *Elopteryx?*

Breviceratops (brev-ee-SERRA-tops: "short horned face") A small, quadrupedal, horned, dinosaur, perhaps an ancestor of *Protoceratops* (p. 158). Lived in the Late Cretaceous. Found in Mongolia. Named in 1990.

Brontosaurus = *Apatosaurus* (p. 102).

Bruhathkayosaurus (broo-hath-kay-oh-SORE-us: "huge body lizard") A huge, bipedal carnivore: perhaps a ceratosaur related to *Carnotaurus* (p. 48). Lived in the Late Cretaceous. Found in India. Named in 1987. (*n.d.*)

C

Caenagnathus (seen-ag-NAYTH-us: "recent jaw") A small, bipedal carnivore, perhaps related to *Troodon* (p. 68). Lived in the Late Cretaceous. Found in western Canada. Classification: Caenagnathidae, Tetanurae, Theropoda, Saurischia.

Calamosaurus = *Calamospondylus*.

Calamospondylus (kal-a-moh-SPON-di-lus: "quill vertebrae") A small, bipedal carnivore: perhaps related to *Ornitholestes* (p. 78). Lived in the Early Cretaceous. Found in England.

Callovosaurus (kal-oh-voh-SORE-us: "Callovian lizard") A bipedal/quadrupedal herbivore 11ft 6in (3.5m) long: somewhat like *Iguanodon* (p. 138). Lived in the Middle Jurassic. Found in England. Classification: Camptosauridae, Euornithopoda, Ornithopoda, Cerapoda, Ornithischia.

Camarasaurus (kam-are-ah-SORE-us) See p. 96.

Camelotia (kam-el-OH-ti-a: "of Camelot") A quadrupedal herbivore 29ft 6in (9m) long: a prosauropod similar to *Riojasaurus* (p. 90). Lived in the Late Triassic. Found in England.

Camptonotus = *Camptosaurus*.

Camptosaurus (kamp-toh-SORE-us: "bent lizard") A bipedal/quadrupedal herbivore up to 23ft (7m) long: somewhat like *Iguanodon* (p. 138). Lived in the Late Jurassic to Early Cretaceous. Found in western USA, England, and Portugal. Classification: Camptosauridae, Euornithopoda, Ornithopoda, Ornithischia.

Campylodon = *Campylodoniscus*.

Campylodoniscus (kamp-i-LOH-don-isk-us: "bent toothed") A large, quadrupedal herbivore: a sauropod perhaps related to *Saltasaurus* (p. 106). Lived in the Late Cretaceous. Found in Argentina. (*n.d.*)

Carcharodontosaurus (kar-kar-o-don-toh-SORE-us: "Carcharodon lizard") A bipedal carnivore 26ft (8m) long with features seen in *Allosaurus* (p. 52) and *Tyrannosaurus* (p. 54). Lived in the late Early and early Late Cretaceous. Found in North Africa.

Cardiodon = *Cetiosaurus?* (p. 92).

Carnotaurus (kar-noh-TORE-us) See p. 48.

Cathetosaurus (kath-ee-toh-SORE-us: "upright lizard") A large, quadrupedal herbivore: a sauropod related to *Camarasaurus* (p. 96). Lived in the Late Jurassic. Found in Colorado. (*n.d.*)

Caudocoelus = *Teinurosaurus*.

Caulodon = *Camarasaurus* (p. 96).

Centrosaurus (SEN-troh-SORE-us) See p. 160.

Ceratops (SERRA-tops: "horned face") A quadrupedal, horned herbivore: a ceratopsian related to *Triceratops* (p. 164). Lived in the Late Cretaceous. Found in Colorado and Montana. (*n.d.*)

Ceratosaurus (seh-rat-oh-SORE-us) See p. 42.

Cetiosauriscus (see-tee-oh-SORE-is-kus: "like whale lizard") A quadrupedal herbivore 49ft (15m) long: a sauropod related to *Diplodocus* (p. 100). Lived in the Late Jurassic. Found in England and perhaps in Switzerland.

Cetiosaurus (see-tee-oh-SORE-us) See p. 92.

Changdusaurus (jang-doo-SORE-us: "Changdu lizard") A large, quadrupedal, plated herbivore: a stegosaur related to *Tuojiangosaurus* (p. 120). Lived in the Jurassic. Found in Tibet. (*n.d.*)

Chaoyangosaurus (kow-yung-oh-SORE-US: "Chaoyang lizard") A small, bipedal herbivore with jutting cheeks: perhaps an ancestor of marginocephalians, such as *Pachycephalosaurus* (p. 154) and *Psittacosaurus* (p. 156). Lived in the Late Jurassic. Found in China. Classification: Chaoyangosauridae, Pachycephalosauria, Marginocephalia, Ornithischia.

Chasmosaurus (kaz-moh-SORE-us) See p. 166.

Chassternbergia (chas-STERN-BERG-i-a: "Charles Sternberg") A large, quadrupedal, armored herbivore: an ankylosaur resembling *Edmontonia* (p. 122). Lived in the Late Cretaceous. Found in Alberta, Canada, and Montana. (*n.d.*)

Cheneosaurus = *Hypacrosaurus*.

Chialingosaurus (jya-ling-oh-SORE-us: "Chia-ling lizard") A quadrupedal, plated herbivore 13ft (4m) long: a stegosaur related to *Tuojiangosaurus* (p. 120). Lived in the Middle Jurassic. Found in China.

Chiayusaurus (jya-yoo-SORE-us: "Chia-yü lizard") A large, quadrupedal herbivore: a sauropod known only from teeth. Lived in the Late Cretaceous. Found in China. (*n.d.*)

Chilantaisaurus (ji-lan-tie-SORE-us: "Ch'i-lan-t'ai lizard") A large, bipedal carnivore related to *Allosaurus* (p. 52). Lived in the Late Cretaceous. Found in China.

Chindesaurus (chin-de-SORE-us: "ghost lizard") A bipedal carnivore up to 13ft (4m) long, similar to *Herrerasaurus* (p. 40). Lived in the early Late Triassic. Found in Arizona. Classification: Staurikosauridae, Theropoda, Saurischia.

Brachylophosaurus   *Camptosaurus*   *Carnotaurus*

Chingkankousaurus (jing-kan-koo-SORE-us: "Ch'ing-kang-kou lizard") A large, bipedal carnivore: perhaps like *Tyrannosaurus* (p. 54). Lived in the Late Cretaceous. Found in China.

Chinshakiangosaurus (KIN-sha-KYANG-oh-SORE-us: "Kinsha-kiang lizard") A large, quadrupedal herbivore: a prosauropod related to *Riojasaurus* (p. 90). Lived in the Early Jurassic. Found in China.

Chirostenotes (kie-ros-ten-OH-teez: "slender hands") A bipedal carnivore 6ft 6in (2m) long, with long, narrow fingers and claws. Lived in the Late Cretaceous. Found in Alberta, Canada. Classification: Elmisauridae, Tetanurae, Theropoda, Saurischia.

Chondrosteosaurus (kon-dros-ti-oh-SORE-us: "bony cartilage lizard") A large, quadrupedal herbivore: a sauropod perhaps like *Camarasaurus* (p. 96). Lived in the Early Cretaceous. Found in England.

Chondrosteus = *Chondrosteosaurus*.

Chuandongocoelurus (jwan-dong-oh-sel-YEW-rus: "Chuandong hollow tail") A small, bipedal carnivore related to *Ornitholestes* (p. 78). Lived in the Middle Jurassic. Found in China.

Chubutisaurus (choo-boo-ti-SORE-us: "Chubut lizard") A quadrupedal herbivore up to 75ft (23m) long: a sauropod possibly similar to *Brachiosaurus* (p. 94). Lived in the Late Cretaceous. Found in Argentina.

Chungkingosaurus (JOONG-KING-oh-SORE-us: "Chungking lizard") A quadrupedal, plated herbivore: a small stegosaur related to *Tuojiangosaurus* (p. 120). Lived in the Late Jurassic. Found in China.

Cionodon (sigh-OH-NOH-don: "columnar tooth") A large, bipedal/quadrupedal herbivore: a little known hadrosaur. Lived in the Late Cretaceous. Found in Colorado. Possibly *Edmontosaurus* (p. 144). (*n.d.*)

Claorhynchus = *Triceratops* (p. 164).

Claosaurus (klay-oh-SORE-us: "broken lizard") A bipedal/quadrupedal herbivore 12ft (3.7m) long: a primitive hadrosaur. Lived in the Late Cretaceous. Found in Kansas.

Clasmodosaurus (klaz-mod-oh-SORE-us: "fragment tooth lizard") A large, quadrupedal herbivore: a sauropod perhaps related to *Saltasaurus* (p. 106). Lived in the Late Cretaceous. Found in Argentina. (*n.d.*)

Clevelanotyrannus = *Nanotyrannus*.

Coelophysis (SEEL-oh-FIE-sis) See p. 46.

Coelosaurus = *Ornithomimus*?

Coeluroides (SEEL-yew-ROY-deez: "Coelurid form") A bipedal carnivore 6ft 6in (2m) long; perhaps related to *Ornitholestes* (p. 78). Lived in the Late Cretaceous. Found in India. (*n.d.*)

Coelurus (seel-YEW-rus: "hollow tail") A bipedal carnivore 6ft (1.8m) long: perhaps related to *Ornitholestes* (p. 78). Lived in the Late Jurassic. Found in Wyoming.

Coloradia = *Coloradisaurus*.

Coloradisaurus (kol-oh-rah-di-SORE-us: "Colorados lizard") A bipedal/quadrupedal herbivore: a prosauropod related to *Plateosaurus* (p. 86). Lived in the Late Triassic. Found in Argentina.

Compsognathus (komp-soh-NAY-thus) See p. 80.

Compsosuchus (komp-soh-SYOO-kus: "elegant crocodile") A large, bipedal carnivore: perhaps like *Allosaurus* (p. 52). Lived in the Late Cretaceous. Found in India.

Conchoraptor (KON-KOH-rap-tor: "conch thief") A small, bird-like, toothless carnivore related to *Oviraptor* (p. 66). Lived in the Late Cretaceous. Found in Mongolia.

Corythosaurus (koh-rith-oh-SORE-us) See p. 148.

Craspedodon (kras-PED-oh-don: "edge tooth") A large bipedal/quadrupedal herbivore: an ornithopod related to *Iguanodon* (p. 138). Lived in the Late Cretaceous. Found in Belgium.

Crataeomus (krat-ay-OH-mus: "great shoulder") A quadrupedal, armored herbivore about 6ft (1.8m) long: named from bones perhaps of the ankylosaurs *Danubiosaurus* and *Struthiosaurus*. Lived in the Late Cretaceous. Found in Austria and Romania. (*n.d.*)

Craterosaurus (krate-er-oh-SORE-us: "bowl lizard") A quadrupedal, plated herbivore 13ft (4m) long: related to *Stegosaurus* (p. 114). Lived in the Early Cretaceous. Found in England.

Creosaurus = *Allosaurus* (p. 52).

Cryptodraco (krip-toh-DRAK-oh: "hidden dragon") A quadrupedal, armored herbivore: an ankylosaur related to *Sauropelta* (p. 124). Lived in the Late Jurassic. Found in England.

Cryptosaurus = *Cryptodraco*.

Cumnoria = *Camptosaurus*.

D **Dacentrurus** (DAY-sen-TROO-rus: "pointed tail") A quadrupedal, plated herbivore 15ft (4.6m) long: a stegosaur similar to *Kentrosaurus* (p. 118). Lived in the Late Jurassic. Found in England, France, and Portugal.

Dachongosaurus (DA-JUNG-oh-SORE-us: "Dachong lizard") A large, quadrupedal herbivore: perhaps like *Cetiosaurus* (p. 92). Lived in the Jurassic. Found in China.

Dachungosaurus = *Dachongosaurus*.

Damalasaurus (DA-MAL-a-SORE-us: "Damala lizard") A huge, quadrupedal herbivore: a sauropod related to *Brachiosaurus* (p. 94). Lived in the Jurassic. Found in Tibet. (*n.d.*)

Dandakosaurus (dan-dak-oh-SORE-us: "Dandako lizard") A bipedal carnivore. Lived in the Early Jurassic. Found in India. Named in 1990. Classification uncertain. (*n.d.*)

Danubiosaurus (DAN-yoo-bee-oh-SORE-us: "Danube lizard") A small, quadrupedal, armored herbivore: an ankylosaur related to *Sauropelta* (p. 124). Lived in the Late Cretaceous. Found in Austria.

Daptosaurus = *Deinonychus* (p. 70).

Daspletosaurus (das-PLEE-toh-SORE-us: "frightful lizard") A large, bipedal carnivore resembling *Tyrannosaurus* (p. 54). Lived in the Late Cretaceous. Found in Alberta, Canada.

Datousaurus (dah-too-SORE-us: "Datou lizard") A quadrupedal herbivore 49ft (15m) long: a sauropod related to *Cetiosaurus* (p. 92). Lived in the Middle Jurassic. Found in China.

Deinocheirus (DINE-oh-KEE-rus: "terrible hand") A large, bipedal carnivore or herbivore with forelegs 8ft (2.4m) long: perhaps resembling a giant *Gallimimus* (p. 62). Lived in the Late Cretaceous. Found in Mongolia. Classification: Deinocheiridae, Tetanurae, Theropoda, Saurischia.

Deinodon = *Albertosaurus*?

Deinonychus (die-NON-i-kus) See p. 70.

Denversaurus (DEN-ver-SORE-us: "Denver lizard") A quadrupedal, armored herbivore: an ankylosaur similar to *Edmontonia* (p. 122). Lived in the Late Cretaceous. Found in South Dakota. (*n.d.*)

Dianchungosaurus (dyan-jong-oh-SORE-us: "Dianchung lizard") A small, bipedal herbivore, perhaps related to *Heterodontosaurus* (p. 134). Lived in the Early Jurassic. Found in China. (*n.d.*)

Diceratops (die-SERRA-tops: "two-horned face") A large, quadrupedal, horned dinosaur: a ceratopsian once believed to be *Triceratops* (p. 164). Lived in the Late Cretaceous. Found in Wyoming, USA.

Diclonius (die-KLONE-ee-us: "two stems") A large, bipedal/quadrupedal herbivore: a little known hadrosaur. Lived in the Late Cretaceous. Found in Montana. (*n.d.*)

Dicraeosaurus (die-KRAY-oh-SORE-us: "forked lizard") A quadrupedal herbivore 66ft (20m) long: a sauropod with forked spines rising from its vertebrae. Lived in the Late Jurassic. Found in Tanzania. Classification: Dicraeosauridae, Sauropoda, Sauropodomorpha, Saurischia.

Didanodon = *Lambeosaurus* (p. 150).

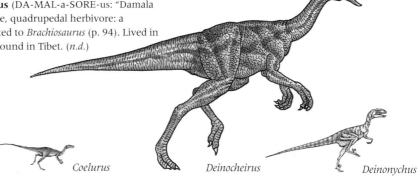

Chirostenotes   *Coelophysis*   *Coelurus*   *Deinocheirus*   *Deinonychus*

Dilophosaurus (die-LOAF-oh-SORE-us) See p. 44.

Dimodosaurus = *Plateosaurus* (p. 86).

Dinodocus = *Pelorosaurus*?

Dinosaurus = *Plateosaurus* (p. 86).

Diplodocus (di-PLOH-de-kus) See p. 100.

Diplotomodon (di-ploh-TOM-oh-don: "double cutting tooth") A large, bipedal carnivore known from a tooth, perhaps from *Dryptosaurus*. Lived in the Late Cretaceous. Found in New Jersey. (*n.d.*)

Diracodon (die-RAK-oh-don: "double tooth") A large, quadrupedal, plated dinosaur: a stegosaur probably descended from *Stegosaurus* (p. 114). Lived in the Late Jurassic. Found in Wyoming. (*n.d.*)

Dolichosuchus (DOL-i-koh-SYOO-kus: "long crocodile") A large, bipedal carnivore known from a limb bone, perhaps *Halticosaurus*. Lived in the Late Triassic. Found in Germany. (*n.d.*)

Doryphorosaurus = *Kentrosaurus* (p. 118).

Dracopelta (drak-oh-PEL-ta: "armored dragon") A quadrupedal, armored herbivore about 6ft 6in (2m) long: an ankylosaur related to *Sauropelta* (p. 124) Lived in the Late Jurassic. Found in Portugal.

Dravidosaurus (drav-id-oh-SORE-us: "Dravidanadu lizard") A quadrupedal, plated herbivore 10ft (3m) long: a stegosaur related to *Kentrosaurus* (p. 118). Lived in the Late Cretaceous. Found in India. (*n.d.*)

Drinker (DRIN-ker: "Drinker") A bipedal herbivore up to 6ft 6in (2m) long: an ornithopod perhaps related to *Hypsilophodon* (p. 136). Lived in the Late Jurassic. Found in Wyoming. Named in 1990.

Dromaeosaurus (DROH-may-oh-SORE-us: "running lizard") A bipedal carnivore 6ft (1.8m) long: like *Deinonychus* (p. 70). Lived in the Late Cretaceous. Found in Alberta, Canada; and Montana.

Dromiceiomimus (droh-MEE-see-oh-MEEM-us: "emu mimic") A bipedal, bird-like carnivore or omnivore: an ostrich dinosaur 11ft 6in (3.5m) long, related to *Struthiomimus* (p. 64). Lived in the Late Cretaceous. Found in Alberta, Canada.

Dromicosaurus = *Massospondylus* (p. 88).

Dryosaurus (dry-oh-SORE-us: "oak lizard") A bipedal herbivore 13ft (4m) long: an ornithopod similar to *Hypsilophodon* (p. 136), but may be more closely related to *Iguanodon* (p. 138). Lived in the Middle–Late Jurassic. Found in western USA and Tanzania. Classification: Dryosauridae, Ornithopoda, Euornithopoda, Ornithischia.

Dryptosauroides (drip-toh-SORE-OY-deez: "Dryptosaurus form") A large, bipedal carnivore: perhaps related to *Dryptosaurus*. Lived in the Late Cretaceous. Found in India. (*n.d.*)

Dryptosaurus (drip-toh-SORE-us: "wounding lizard") A bipedal carnivore 19ft 6in (6m) long with slender legs. Lived in the Late Cretaceous. Found in New Jersey. Classification: Dryptosauridae, Tetanurae, Theropoda, Saurischia.

Dynamosaurus = *Tyrannosaurus* (p. 54).

Dyoplosaurus (die-oh-ploh-SORE-us: "double-armed lizard") A large, quadrupedal herbivore: an ankylosaur like *Euoplocephalus* (p. 128). Lived in the Late Cretaceous. Found in Alberta, Canada.

Dysalotosaurus = *Dryosaurus*.

Dysganus (DISS-gah-nus: "rough luster") A large, quadrupedal, horned herbivore known from teeth: a ceratopsian of doubtful identity. Lived in the Late Cretaceous. Found in Montana. (*n.d.*)

Dyslocosaurus (diz-loh-koh-SORE-us: "bad place lizard") A large, quadrupedal herbivore: a sauropod like *Diplodocus* (p. 100) but with more (four or five) toe-claws per hind foot. Lived in the Late Jurassic or possibly Late Cretaceous. Found in Wyoming. Named in 1992.

Dystrophaeus (dis-troh-FAY-us: "coarsely jointed") A large, quadrupedal herbivore: a little-known sauropod: perhaps related to *Diplodocus* (p. 100). Lived in the Late Jurassic. Found in Utah. (*n.d.*)

Dystylosaurus (DIS-TIL-oh-SORE-us: "two beam lizard") A huge, quadrupedal dinosaur: a sauropod related to *Brachiosaurus* (p. 94). Lived in the Late Jurassic. Found in Colorado.

E **Echinodon** (EE-KIE-noh-don: "spiny tooth") A bipedal/quadrupedal herbivore 2ft (60cm) long: a primitive, possibly armored, ornithischian: perhaps related to *Scelidosaurus* (p. 112) or *Heterodontosaurus* (p. 134). Lived in the Late Jurassic. Found in England.

Edmontonia (ed-mon-TONE-ee-ah) See p. 122.

Edmontosaurus (ed-MON-toh-SORE-us) See p. 144.

Efraasia = *Sellosaurus*.

Elaphrosaurus (ee-LAF-roh-sore-us: "running lizard") A bipedal, bird-like carnivore or omnivore 11ft 6in (3.5m) long: an ostrich dinosaur more primitive than *Struthiomimus*. Lived in the Late Jurassic. Found in Tanzania and maybe Wyoming.

Elmisaurus (EL-mi-SORE-us: "foot lizard") A bipedal carnivore 10ft (3m) long with bird-like feet. Lived in the Late Cretaceous. Found in Mongolia and Alberta, Canada. Classification: Elmisauridae, Tetanurae, Theropoda, Saurischia.

Elopteryx (EE-LOP-ter-ix: "small wing") A small, bipedal carnivore: perhaps related to *Deinonychus* (p. 70). Lived in the Late Cretaceous. Found in Romania. (*n.d.*)

Elosaurus = *Apatosaurus* (p. 102).

Emausaurus (EE-mao-SORE-us ("EMAU lizard") Named in 1990 from the initial letters of a German university. An armored, quadrupedal herbivore 6ft 6in (2m) long, somewhat like *Scelidosaurus* (p. 112). Lived in the Early Jurassic. Found in Germany.

Embasaurus (EM-BA-sore-us: "Emba lizard") A large, primitive, little-known, bipedal carnivore named from two spinal bones. Lived in the Early Cretaceous. Found in Kazakhstan. (*n.d.*)

Enigmosaurus (en-ig-moh-SORE-us: "enigmatic lizard") A bipedal or quadrupedal carnivore or herbivore 23ft (7m) long: related to *Segnosaurus* (p. 108). Lived in the Late Cretaceous. Found in Mongolia.

Eoceratops (EE-oh-SERRA-tops: "early horned face") A large, quadrupedal, horned herbivore: perhaps *Chasmosaurus* (p. 166). (*n.d.*)

Eolosaurus = *Aeolosaurus*.

Eoraptor (EE-oh-RAP-tor: "early plunderer") A bipedal carnivore no bigger than a large dog: an early theropod more primitive than *Herrerasaurus* (p. 40). Thought to be close to the common ancestor of all dinosaurs. Lived in the Late Triassic. Found in Argentina. Described in 1993.

Epachthosaurus (e-PAK-thoh-SORE-us) A large, quadrupedal herbivore: a sauropod related to *Saltasaurus* (p. 106). Lived in the Late Cretaceous. Found in Argentina.

Epanterias = *Allosaurus*? (p. 52).

Erectopus (ee-REK-toh-pus: "upright foot") A bipedal carnivore related to *Carnotaurus* (p. 48). Lived in the Early Cretaceous. Found in France.

Erlikosaurus (AIR-lik-oh-SORE-us: "Erlik's lizard") A bipedal or quadrupedal carnivore or herbivore 16ft 6in (5m) long: related to *Segnosaurus* (p. 108). Lived in the Late Cretaceous. Found in Mongolia.

Euacanthus = *Polacanthus*.

Eucamerotus = *Chondrosteosaurus*.

Eucentrosaurus = *Centrosaurus* (p. 160).

Eucercosaurus (yoo-ser-koh-SORE-us: "well-tailed lizard") A little-known large herbivore: perhaps an ornithopod, related to *Iguanodon* (p. 138). Lived in the Early Cretaceous. Found in England.

Eucnemesaurus = *Euskelosaurus*.

Euhelopus (yoo-HEL-oh-pus: "good marsh foot") A quadrupedal herbivore 49ft (15m) long: a sauropod related to *Mamenchisaurus* (p. 104). Lived in the Late Jurassic. Found in China.

Euoplocephalus (you-op-loh-SEF-ah-lus) See p. 128.

Eureodon = *Tenontosaurus*.

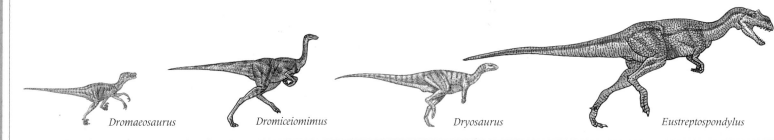

Dromaeosaurus   *Dromiceiomimus*   *Dryosaurus*   *Eustreptospondylus*

Euronychodon (YOO-roh-NIKE-oh-don: "European nail tooth") A bipedal carnivore known from teeth: perhaps like *Deinonychus* (p. 70). Lived in the Late Cretaceous. Found in Portugal. Named in 1991. (*n.d.*)

Euskelosaurus (yoo-SKEL-oh-SORE-us: "primitive leg lizard") A quadrupedal herbivore 33ft (10m) long: a prosauropod related to *Plateosaurus* (p. 86). Lived in the Late Triassic. Found in South Africa.

Eustreptospondylus (yoo-STREP-toh-SPON-die-lus) See p. 50.

F **Fabrosaurus** (FAB-roh-sore-us: "Fabre's lizard") A small, bipedal herbivore. Might be *Lesothosaurus* (p. 132).

Fenestrosaurus = *Oviraptor* (p. 66).

Frenguellisaurus = *Herrerasaurus* (p. 40).

"Fukuisaurus" (foo-KOO-i-SORE-us: "Fukui lizard") Informal name of a large, bipedal/quadrupedal herbivore: perhaps like *Iguanodon* (p. 138). Lived in the Early Cretaceous. Found in Japan.

Fulengia (foo-LENG-ee-a: "Lufeng beast" – in anagram form) A bipedal/quadrupedal herbivore perhaps related to *Plateosaurus* (p. 86): a "lizard" redescribed as a baby prosauropod. Lived in the Early Jurassic. Found in Lufeng, China.

Fulgurotherium (FOOL-GOO-roh-THEE-ree-um: "lightning beast") A bipedal herbivore 6ft 6in (2m) long: like *Hypsilophodon* (p. 136). Lived in the Early Cretaceous. Found in Australia.

"Futabasaurus" (foo-tah-bah-SORE-us: "Futaba lizard") Informal name of a large, bipedal carnivore: perhaps like *Tyrannosaurus* (p. 54). Lived in the Late Cretaceous. Found in Japan.

G **"Gadolosaurus"** (gad-oh-loh-SORE-us: mistranslation of hadrosaur) A large, bipedal/quadrupedal herbivore: an ornithopod related to *Iguanodon* (p. 138). Lived in the Early Cretaceous. Found in Central Asia.

Gallimimus (gal-lee-MEEM-us) See p. 62.

Garudimimus (ga-roo-dee-MEEM-us: "Garuda mimic") A bird-like, bipedal carnivore or omnivore: an ostrich dinosaur related to *Gallimimus* (p. 62), but with short toes. Lived in the Late Cretaceous. Found in Mongolia.

Gasosaurus (gas-oh-SORE-us: "gas lizard") A bipedal carnivore 13ft (4m) long: perhaps *Kaijiangosaurus*. Lived in the Middle Jurassic. Found in China.

Genyodectes (GEN-yoh-DEK-teez: "biting jaw") A large, bipedal carnivore with long, curved fangs. Lived in the Late Cretaceous. Found in Argentina. Classification uncertain.

Geranosaurus (GER-AN-oh-SORE-us: "crane lizard") A small, bipedal plant-eater: an ornithopod like *Heterodontosaurus* (p. 134). Lived in the Early Jurassic. Found in South Africa. (*n.d.*)

Gigantosaurus = *Pelorosaurus* and *Barosaurus* (p. 98).

Gigantoscelus = *Euskelosaurus*.

Gilmoreosaurus (GIL-more-oh-SORE-us: "Gilmore's lizard") A bipedal herbivore: a small, primitive hadrosaur. Lived in the Late Cretaceous. Found in China.

Giraffatitan = *Brachiosaurus* (p. 94).

Gongbusaurus (GONG-boo-SORE-us: "Gongbu lizard") A bipedal herbivore about 5ft (1.5m) long: perhaps like *Hypsilophodon* (p. 136). Lived in the Late Jurassic. Found in China.

Gorgosaurus = *Albertosaurus*?

Goyocephale (GOY-oh-SEF-ah-lee: "decorated head") A bipedal herbivore 6ft 6in (2m) long: a bone-headed dinosaur with a flatter skull than *Pachycephalosaurus* (p. 154). Lived in the Late Cretaceous. Found in Mongolia. Classification: Homalocephalidae, Pachycephalosauria, Marginocephalia, Ornithischia.

Gravisaurus (GRAV-i-SORE-us: "heavy lizard") A large, quadrupedal herbivore: an ornithopod related to *Iguanodon* (p. 138). Lived in the Early Cretaceous. Found in Niger. Named in 1988.

Gravitholus (GRAV-i-THOH-lus: "heavy dome") A bipedal herbivore 10ft (3m) long: a bone-headed dinosaur related to *Pachycephalosaurus* (p. 154). Lived in the Late Cretaceous. Found in Alberta, Canada.

Gresslyosaurus = *Plateosaurus* (p. 86).

Griphornis = *Archaeopteryx* (p. 74).

Griphosaurus = *Archaeopteryx* (p. 74).

Gryponyx = *Massospondylus* (p. 88).

Gryposaurus (GRIPE-oh-SORE-us: "griffin lizard") A large, bipedal/quadrupedal herbivore: a hump-nosed hadrosaur related to *Maiasaura* (p. 146). Lived in the Late Cretaceous. Found in Alberta, Canada.

Gyposaurus = *Anchisaurus* (p. 84).

H **"Hadrosauravus"** = *Gryposaurus*.

Hadrosaurus (HAD-roh-SORE-us: "big lizard") A bipedal/quadrupedal herbivore up to 33ft (10m) long: a hook-nosed hadrosaur related to *Edmontosaurus* (p. 144). Lived in the Late Cretaceous. Found in New Jersey.

Halticosaurus (HAL-ti-coh-SORE-us: "nimble lizard") A bipedal carnivore 18ft (5.5m) long: a primitive, predatory dinosaur. Lived in the Late Triassic. Found in Germany and perhaps France. Classification: Halticosauridae, Ceratosauria or Tetanurae, Theropoda, Saurischia.

Haplocanthosaurus (hap-loh-KANTH-oh-SORE-us: "single-spine lizard") A quadrupedal herbivore up to 72ft (22m) long: a sauropod related to *Cetiosaurus* (p. 92). Lived in the Late Jurassic. Found in Colorado and Wyoming.

Haplocanthus = *Haplocanthosaurus*.

Harpymimus (HAR-pee-MEEM-us: "harpy mimic") A bipedal, bird-like carnivore or omnivore: an ostrich dinosaur related to *Gallimimus* (p. 62). Lived in the late Early Cretaceous. Found in Mongolia.

Hecatasaurus = *Telmatosaurus*.

Heishansaurus (hay-shan-SORE-us: "Mount Hei lizard") A little-known quadrupedal or bipedal herbivore: perhaps an ankylosaur or pachycephalosaur. Lived in the Late Cretaceous. Found in China.

Helopus = *Euhelopus*.

Heptasteornis (HEP-tas-tee-OR-nis: "seven mountains bird") A small, bipedal carnivore: a troodontid or dromaeosaurid theropod. Perhaps *Elopteryx*. Lived in the Late Cretaceous. Found in Romania. (*n.d.*)

Herrerasaurus (eh-ray-rah-SORE-us) See p. 40.

Heterodontosaurus (HET-er-oh-DONT-oh-SORE-us) See p. 134.

Heterosaurus = *Iguanodon* (p. 138).

Hierosaurus = *Nodosaurus*?

Hikanodon = *Iguanodon* (p. 138).

"Hironosaurus" (hi-ron-oh-SORE-us: "Hirono-machi lizard") Informal name for a large, bipedal/quadrupedal herbivore: a hadrosaur. Lived in the Late Cretaceous. Found in Japan.

"Hisanohamasaurus" (his-an-oh-ham-ah-SORE-us: "Hisano-hama lizard") Informal name for a large, quadrupedal herbivore: a sauropod perhaps like *Diplodocus* (p. 100). Lived in the Late Cretaceous. Found in Japan.

Homalocephale (home-ah-loh-SEFF-ah-lee: "even head") A bipedal herbivore 10ft (3m) long: a bone-headed dinosaur with a flatter head than *Pachycephalosaurus* (p. 154). Lived in the Late Cretaceous. Found in Mongolia. Classification: Homalocephalidae, Pachycephalosauria, Marginocephalia, Ornithischia.

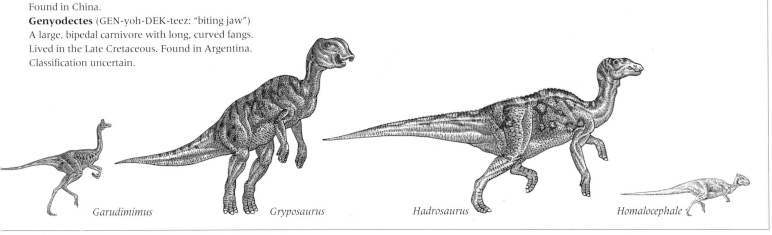

Garudimimus　　　*Gryposaurus*　　　*Hadrosaurus*　　　*Homalocephale*

Hoplitosaurus = *Polacanthus*.

Hoplosaurus = *Struthiosaurus*.

Hortalotarsus = *Massospondylus* (p. 88).

Huayangosaurus (hoy-YANG-oh-SORE-us: "Huayang lizard") A quadrupedal, plated herbivore 15ft (4.6m) long: a primitive stegosaur with front teeth. Lived in the Middle Jurassic. Found in China. Classification: Huayangosauridae, Stegosauria, Thyreophora, Ornithischia.

Hulsanpes (HUL-SAN-pes: "Khulsan foot") A small, bipedal carnivore related to *Deinonychus* (p. 70). Lived in the Late Cretaceous. Found in Mongolia.

Hylaeosaurus (HIGH-lee-oh-SORE-us: "woodland lizard") A quadrupedal, armored herbivore 13ft (4m) long: an ankylosaur related to *Sauropelta* (p. 124). Lived in the Early Cretaceous. Found in England.

Hypacrosaurus (high-PAK-roh-SORE-us: "high-spined reptile") A bipedal/quadrupedal herbivore 29ft 6in (9m) long: a hadrosaur very similar to *Corythosaurus* (p. 148). Lived in the Late Cretaceous. Found in western North America.

Hypselosaurus (HIP-sel-oh-SORE-us: "high ridge lizard") A quadrupedal herbivore 39ft (12m) long: a sauropod related to *Saltasaurus* (p. 106). Lived in the Late Cretaceous. Found in France and Spain.

Hypsibema (HIP-si-BEE-ma: "high step") A name based on fossil hadrosaur scraps. Lived in the Late Cretaceous. Found in North Carolina. (*n.d.*)

Hypsilophodon (hip-sih-LOH-foh-don) See p. 136.

Hypsirophus = *Stegosaurus* (p. 114).

I   **Iguanodon** (ig-WHA-noh-don) See p. 138.

    Iguanosaurus = *Iguanodon*.

Iliosuchus (eye-li-oh-SYOO-kus: "crocodile-hipped") A moderately sized, bipedal carnivore: perhaps related to *Megalosaurus*. Lived in the Middle Jurassic. Found in England.

Indosaurus (in-doh-SORE-us: "Indian lizard") A moderately sized, bipedal carnivore: perhaps with a horned head, related to *Carnotaurus* (p. 48). Lived in the Late Cretaceous. Found in India.

Indosuchus (in-doh-SYOO-kus: "Indian crocodile") A large, bipedal carnivore, perhaps related to *Abelisaurus*. Lived in the Late Cretaceous. Found in India.

Ingenia (in-GAY-nee-a: "Ingenia") A small, bird-like, bipedal, toothless carnivore or omnivore related to *Oviraptor* (p. 66). Lived in the Late Cretaceous. Found in Mongolia.

Inosaurus (ee-noh-SORE-us: "In lizard") A bipedal predator about 6ft 6in (2m) long: perhaps related to *Ornitholestes* (p. 78). Lived in the Early Cretaceous. Found in Niger. (*n.d.*)

Ischisaurus = *Herrerasaurus* (p. 40).

Ischyrosaurus = *Pelorosaurus*.

Itemirus (EE-tem-EE-rus: "Itemir lizard") A small, bipedal carnivore: perhaps related to the much larger *Tyrannosaurus* (p. 54). Lived in the Late Cretaceous. Found in Uzbekistan.

J   **Janenschia** (YAN-ENSH-ee-a: "Janensch") A large, quadrupedal herbivore: a sauropod related to *Saltasaurus* (p. 106). Lived in the Late Jurassic. Found in Tanzania and Zimbabwe. Named in 1991.

Jaxartosaurus (jak-SART-oh-SORE-us: "Jaxartes lizard") A bipedal/quadrupedal herbivore 29ft 6in (9m) long: a hadrosaur related to *Corythosaurus* (p. 148). Lived in the Late Cretaceous. Found in Kazakhstan and China.

"Jiangjunmiaosaurus" (jyang-joon-mee-ow-SORE-us: "Jiang Jun-miao lizard") Informal name for a large carnivore not yet formally described: perhaps a primitive relative of *Allosaurus* (p. 52). Lived in the Late Jurassic. Found in China.

Jubbulpuria (jab-al-POOR-yah: "from Jabalpur") A bipedal carnivore 4ft (1.2m) long. Lived in the Late Cretaceous. Found in India. (*n.d.*)

Jurapteryx = *Archaeopteryx* (p. 74).

Jurassosaurus (joo-RAS-oh-SORE-us: "Jurassic lizard") A quadrupedal, armored herbivore 10ft (3m) long: a primitive ankylosaur with protective plates. Lived in the Middle Jurassic. Found in China. Named in 1992.

K   **"Kagasaurus"** (ka-ga-SORE-us: "Kaga lizard") Informal name for a large, bipedal carnivore: perhaps related to *Megalosaurus*. Lived in the Late Cretaceous. Found in Japan. Classification uncertain.

Kaijiangosaurus (kie-jang-oh-SORE-us: "Kaijang lizard") A large, bipedal carnivore. Lived in the Middle Jurassic. Found in China.

Kakuru (KA-ka-roo: "rainbow serpent") A bipedal carnivore about 8ft (2.4m) long, with slim shinbones. Lived in the late Early Cretaceous. Found in Australia. Classification uncertain.

Kangnasaurus (kang-na-SORE-us: "Kangna Ranch lizard") A small, bipedal plant-eater somewhat like *Hypsilophodon* (p. 136). Lived in the Early Cretaceous. Found in South Africa. Classification: Dryosauridae, Euornithopoda, Ornithopoda, Ornithischia. (*n.d.*)

"Katsuyamasaurus" (kat-soo-yah-mah-SORE-us: "Katsuyama lizard") Informal name for a large, bipedal carnivore: perhaps related to *Allosaurus* (p. 52). Lived in the Early Cretaceous. Found in Japan.

Kelmayisaurus (kel-a-MAY-ee-SORE-us: "Kelmayi lizard") A little-known, large, bipedal carnivore. Lived in the Early Cretaceous. Found in China. Classification uncertain. (*n.d.*)

Kentrosaurus (KEN-troh-SORE-us) See p. 118.

Kentrurosaurus = *Kentrosaurus* (p. 118).

"Kitadanisaurus" (kit-ah-dan-ee-SORE-us: "Kitadani lizard") Informal name for a small, bipedal carnivore known from a tooth: perhaps related to *Deinonychus* (p. 70). Lived in the Early Cretaceous. Found in Japan.

"Klamelisaurus" (kla-mel-ee-SORE-us: "Klameli lizard") Informal name for a large, quadrupedal herbivore: a sauropod perhaps related to *Mamenchisaurus* (p. 104). Lived in the Late Jurassic. Found in China.

Koreasaurus (koh-ree-oh-SORE-us: "Korean lizard") A small, bipedal carnivore: perhaps *Deinonychus* (p. 70). Lived in the Cretaceous. Found in South Korea. (*n.d.*)

Kotasaurus (KOH-ta-SORE-us: "Kota lizard") A large, quadrupedal herbivore: a sauropod perhaps related to *Cetiosaurus* (p. 92). Lived in the Early Jurassic. Found in India.

Kritosaurus (KRITE-oh-SORE-us: "noble lizard") A large, bipedal/quadrupedal herbivore: a hump-nosed hadrosaur related to *Maiasaura* (p. 146). Lived in the Late Cretaceous. Found in western North America, and remains attributed to it have been found in Argentina.

Kunmingosaurus (KOON-MING-oh-SORE-us: "Kunming lizard") A large, quadrupedal herbivore: a primitive sauropod. Lived in the Early Jurassic . Found in China. Classification: Vulcanodontidae, Sauropoda, Sauropodomorpha, Saurischia.

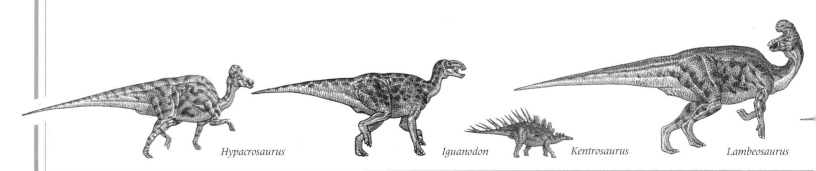

Hypacrosaurus   *Iguanodon*   *Kentrosaurus*   *Lambeosaurus*

L **Labocania** (la-boh-KAY-nee-ah: "La Bocana") A large, bipedal carnivore: perhaps related to *Tyrannosaurus* (p. 48). Lived in the Late Cretaceous. Found in Mexico.

Labrosaurus = *Allosaurus* (p. 52).

Laelaps = *Dryptosaurus*.

Laevisuchus (LEE-VEE-syoo-kus: "slender crocodile") A bipedal carnivore 6ft 6in (2m) long, perhaps like *Calamospondylus*. Lived in the Late Cretaceous. Found in India. (*n.d.*)

Lambeosaurus (LAM-bee-oh-SORE-us) See p. 150.

Lametasaurus (la-met-a-SORE-us: "Lameta lizard") Named from mixed fossils, some from a big, quadrupedal herbivore: a sauropod related to *Saltasaurus* (others from a carnivorous dinosaur and a crocodile). Lived in the Late Cretaceous. Found in India. (*n.d.*)

Lanasaurus (lahn-ah-SORE-us: "wool lizard") A small, bipedal/quadrupedal herbivore: an ornithopod related to *Heterodontosaurus* (p. 134). Lived in the Early Jurassic. Found in South Africa.

Lancangjiangosaurus (lan-kang-jyang-oh-SORE-us: "Lancangjian lizard") A large, quadrupedal herbivore: a sauropod perhaps related to *Cetiosaurus* (p. 92). Lived in the Middle Jurassic. Found in Tibet. (*n.d.*)

Lancangosaurus = *Datousaurus*.

Laosaurus (LAY-oh-SORE-us: "fossil lizard") A small, bipedal herbivore: an ornithopod perhaps related to *Hypsilophodon* (p. 136). Lived in the Late Jurassic. Found in Wyoming. (*n.d.*)

Laplatasaurus = *Titanosaurus*.

Lapparentosaurus (la-pa-rent-oh-SORE-us: "Lapparent's lizard") A huge, quadrupedal herbivore: a sauropod related to *Brachiosaurus* (p. 94). Lived in the Middle Jurassic. Found in Madagascar.

Leaellynasaura (LEE-EL-IN-a-SORE-a: "Leaellyn's lizard") A small, bipedal herbivore: an ornithopod related to *Hypsilophodon* (p. 136). Lived in the Early Cretaceous. Found in Australia. Named in 1989.

Leipsanosaurus = *Struthiosaurus*.

Leptoceratops (lep-toh-SERRA-tops: "slim horned face") A mainly quadrupedal herbivore 8ft (2.4m) long: a ceratopsian related to *Protoceratops* (p. 158). Lived in the Late Cretaceous. Found in Alberta, Canada and Wyoming.

Leptospondylus = *Massospondylus* (p. 88).

Lesothosaurus (le-SOO-too-SORE-us) See p. 132.

Lexovisaurus (lex-OH-vi-SORE-us: "Lexovii lizard") A quadrupedal, plated herbivore 19ft 6in (6m) long: a stegosaur akin to *Kentrosaurus* (p. 118). Lived in the Middle Jurassic. Found in England and France.

Liliensternus (LIL-ee-en-SHTERN-us: "Lilienstern") A bipedal carnivore 16ft 6in (5m) long: a ceratosaur. Lived in the Late Triassic. Found in Germany.

Limnosaurus = *Telmatosaurus*.

Lisboasaurus (leesh-voh-a-SORE-us: "Lisbon lizard") A crow-sized, bipedal carnivore: a "lizard" redescribed in 1991 as a theropod perhaps related to *Troodon* (p. 68) or *Archaeopteryx* (p. 74). Lived in the Late Jurassic. Found in Portugal.

Loncosaurus (LON-koh-SORE-us: "lance head lizard") A bipedal carnivore: a theropod based on a tooth. Lived in the Late Cretaceous. Found in Argentina. (*n.d.*)

Longosaurus (lon-goh-SORE-us: "Long's lizard") A bipedal carnivore 10ft (3m) long: perhaps *Coelophysis* (p. 46). Lived in the Late Triassic. Found in New Mexico. (*n.d.*)

Lophorhothon = *Prosaurolophus*?

Loricosaurus = *Neuquensaurus*?

Lufengocephalus = *Lufengosaurus*.

Lufengosaurus (loo-FUNG-oh-SORE-us) See p. 89.

Lukousaurus (loo-kow-SORE-us: "Lukou lizard") A small, bipedal carnivore: probably a theropod, but of unknown family. Lived in the Late Triassic/Early Jurassic. Found in China.

Lusitanosaurus (LOOZ-i-TANE-oh-SORE-us: "Lusitania lizard") A quadrupedal, armored herbivore related to *Scelidosaurus* (p. 112). Lived in the Early Jurassic. Found in Portugal.

Lycorhinus (LIE-koh-RINE-us: "wolf snout") A small, bipedal, tusked herbivore: an ornithopod like *Heterodontosaurus* (p. 134). Lived in the Early Jurassic. Found in South Africa.

M **Macrophalangia** = *Chirostenotes*.

Macrurosaurus (mak-ROO-roh-sore-us: "long-tailed lizard") A large, quadrupedal herbivore: a sauropod possibly related to *Saltasaurus* (p. 106). Lived in the Early Cretaceous. Found in England. (*n.d.*)

"Madsenius" (mad-SEN-ee-us: "Madsen") A large, bipedal carnivore still to be described: a relative of *Allosaurus* (p. 52).

Magnosaurus = *Megalosaurus*?

Magyarosaurus = *Titanosaurus*?

Maiasaura (MY-ah-SORE-ah) See p. 146.

Majungasaurus (mah-JOON-gah-SORE-us: "Majunga lizard") A large, bipedal carnivore: perhaps related to *Carnotaurus* (p. 48). Lived in the Late Cretaceous. Found in Madagascar and perhaps Egypt and India.

Majungatholus (mah-JOON-ga-THOH-lus: "Majunga dome") A bipedal herbivore about 4ft 6in (1.4m) long: a bone-headed ornithischian related to *Pachycephalosaurus* (p. 154). Lived in the Late Cretaceous. Found in Madagascar.

Maleevosaurus (mah-LAY-ev-oh-SORE-us: "Maleev's lizard") A large, bipedal carnivore related to *Tyrannosaurus* (p. 54). Lived in the Late Cretaceous. Found in Mongolia. Named in 1992.

Maleevus (mah-LAY-ev-us: "Maleev") A large, quadrupedal, armored dinosaur: an ankylosaur related to *Euoplocephalus* (p. 128). Lived in the Late Cretaceous. Found in Mongolia.

Mamenchisaurus (mah-MEN-chee-SORE-us) See p. 104.

Mandschurosaurus (mand-CHOO-roh-SORE-us: "Manchurian lizard") A large, bipedal/quadrupedal herbivore: a hadrosaur resembling *Gilmoreosaurus*. Lived in the Late Cretaceous. Found in China.

Manospondylus = *Tyrannosaurus* (p. 54).

Marmarospondylus = *Bothriospondylus*.

Marshosaurus (MARSH-oh-SORE-us: "Marsh's lizard") A bipedal carnivore resembling various kinds of theropods including *Coelurus*. Lived in the Late Jurassic. Found in Utah.

Massospondylus (MAS-oh-SPON-die-lus) See p. 88.

Megacervixosaurus (MEG-a-SER-vix-oh-SORE-us: "big neck lizard") A large, quadrupedal herbivore: a sauropod related to *Diplodocus* (p. 100). Lived in the Late Cretaceous. Found in Tibet. (*n.d.*)

Megadactylus = *Anchisaurus* (p. 84).

Megadontosaurus = *Microvenator*.

Megalosaurus (MEG-ah-loh-SORE-us) See p. 51.

Melanorosaurus (MEL-an-or-oh-SORE-us: "black mountain lizard") A quadrupedal herbivore 24ft (7.5m) long: a prosauropod related to *Riojasaurus* (p. 90). Lived in the Late Triassic. Found in South Africa.

Metriacanthosaurus (MET-REE-a-kan-thoh-SORE-us: "moderately spined lizard") A bipedal carnivore 26ft (8m) long. Lived in the Early Jurassic. Found in England. Classification uncertain.

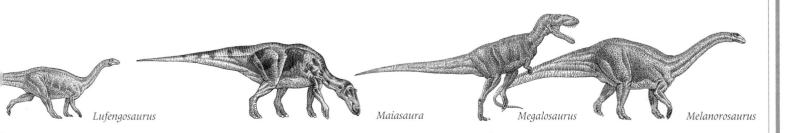

Lufengosaurus   *Maiasaura*   *Megalosaurus*   *Melanorosaurus*

Microceratops (mik-roh-SERRA-tops: "tiny horned faced") A mainly bipedal, horned dinosaur under 2ft 8in (80cm) long: a ceratopsian related to *Protoceratops* (p. 158). Lived in the Late Cretaceous. Found in China and Mongolia.

Microcoelus (mik-roh-SEEL-us: "tiny hollow") A large, quadrupedal herbivore: perhaps the sauropod *Saltasaurus* (p. 106). Lived in the Late Cretaceous. Found in Argentina.

Microdontosaurus (mik-roh-DONT-oh-SORE-us: "tiny tooth lizard") A large, quadrupedal herbivore: a prosauropod or sauropod. Lived in the Middle Jurassic. Found in Tibet. Classification uncertain. (*n.d.*)

Microhadrosaurus (mik-roh-HAD-roh-SORE-us: "tiny *Hadrosaurus*") A bipedal herbivore 8ft (2.4m) long: a hadrosaur. Lived in the Late Cretaceous. Found in China. (*n.d.*)

Micropachycephalosaurus (mik-roh-pak-ee-SEF-a-loh-SORE-us: "tiny thick-headed lizard") A tiny, bipedal herbivore 20in (50cm) long: a pachycephalosaur of unknown family. Lived in the Late Cretaceous. Found in China.

Microsaurops = *Microcoelus*.

Microvenator (mik-roh-ven-AH-tor: "tiny hunter") A small, bipedal carnivore: perhaps related to *Chirostenotes*. Lived in the Early Cretaceous. Found in Montana.

"Mifunesaurus" (mih-FOON-e-SORE-us: "Mifune lizard") Informal name of a large, bipedal carnivore based on a tooth. Lived in the Late Cretaceous. Found in Japan. Identity uncertain.

Minmi (min-MY) See p. 126.

Mochlodon = *Rhabdodon*.

Mongolosaurus (mon-gol-oh-SORE-us: "Mongolian lizard") A large herbivore: perhaps a sauropod or a segnosaur. Lived in the Early Cretaceous. Found in China. (*n.d.*)

Monkonosaurus (mon-kon-oh-SORE-us: "Monko lizard") A large, quadrupedal, plated herbivore: perhaps related to *Tuojiangosaurus* (p. 120). Lived in the Early Cretaceous. Found in Tibet.

Monoclonius (mon-oh-KLOH-ni-us: "single stem") A quadrupedal, horned herbivore: a ceratopsian related to *Centrosaurus* (p. 160). Lived in the Late Cretaceous. Found in Alberta, Canada and Montana.

Monolophosaurus (mon-oh-loaf-oh-SORE-us: "single ridge lizard") A large, bipedal carnivore: a theropod perhaps related to *Allosaurus* (p. 52) or *Eustreptospondylus* (p. 50). Lived in the Middle Jurassic. Found in China.

Montanoceratops (mon-tan-oh-SERRA-tops: "Montana horned face") A quadrupedal, horned dinosaur: a ceratopsian akin to *Protoceratops* (p. 158). Lived in the Late Cretaceous. Found in Montana.

Morinosaurus = *Pelorosaurus*.

Morosaurus = *Camarasaurus* (p. 96).

Moshisaurus = *Mamenchisaurus* (p. 104).

Mussaurus (mus-OR-us: "mouse lizard") A bipedal/quadrupedal herbivore possibly up to 10ft (3m) long: a prosauropod related to *Plateosaurus* (p. 86). Lived in the Late Triassic. Found in Argentina.

Muttaburrasaurus (MUT-a-BUR-a-SORE-us) See p. 140.

N **Nanosaurus** (nan-oh-SORE-us: "dwarf lizard") A bipedal herbivore 3ft (90cm) long: an ornithopod perhaps like *Hypsilophodon* (p. 136). Lived in the Late Jurassic. Found in Colorado and Utah.

Nanotyrannus (NAN-oh-tie-RAN-us: "tiny tyrant") A bipedal carnivore 16ft 6in (5m) long, related to *Tyrannosaurus* (p. 54). Lived in the Late Cretaceous. Found in Montana.

Nanshiungosaurus (nan-SHOONG-oh-SORE-us: "Nanshiung lizard") A heavy-bodied carnivore or herbivore, probably related to *Segnosaurus* (p. 108) and *Therizinosaurus*. Lived in the Late Cretaceous. Found in China.

Nemegtosaurus (nem-EG-toh-SORE-us: "Nemegt lizard") A large, quadrupedal herbivore: a sauropod with a low head. Lived in the Late Cretaceous. Found in Mongolia and China. Classification: Dicraeosauridae, Sauropoda, Sauropodomorpha, Saurischia.

Neosaurus = *Parrosaurus*.

Neosodon = *Pelorosaurus*.

Neuquensaurus (NYOO-kyen-SORE-us: "Neuquén lizard") A large, quadrupedal herbivore: a sauropod related to *Saltasaurus* (p. 106). Lived in the Late Cretaceous. Found in Argentina.

Ngexisaurus (n-gay-shee-SORE-us: "Ngexi lizard") A small, bipedal carnivore related to *Ornitholestes* (p. 78). Lived in the Middle Jurassic. Found in Tibet. (*n.d.*)

Nipponosaurus (nip-ON-oh-SORE-us: "Japanese lizard") A bipedal/quadrupedal herbivore: a small hadrosaur related to *Corythosaurus* (p. 148). Lived in the Late Cretaceous. Found on Sakhalin Island (now in Russia).

Noasaurus (noh-ah-SORE-us: "north-west Argentina lizard") A bipedal carnivore 8ft (2.4m) long, with a switchblade toe-claw. Lived in the Late Cretaceous. Found in Argentina. Classification: Noasauridae, Ceratosauria, Theropoda, Saurischia.

Nodosaurus (no-doh-SORE-us: "node lizard") A large, quadrupedal, armored herbivore: an ankylosaur related to *Edmontonia* (p. 122). Lived in the Late Cretaceous. Found in Kansas and Wyoming.

Notoceratops (NOH-TOH-SERRA-tops: "southern horned face") A little-known, quadrupedal herbivore: perhaps related to the ceratopsians. Lived in the Late Cretaceous. Found in Argentina. (*n.d.*)

Nouerosaurus = *Nurosaurus*.

Nurosaurus (NYOO-roh-SORE-us: "Nur lizard") A huge, quadrupedal herbivore 85ft (26m) long: a sauropod related to *Mamenchisaurus* (p. 104). Lived in the Early Cretaceous. Found in China. Named in 1991.

Nuthetes (nyoo-THEE-teez: "monitor") A small, bipedal carnivore: perhaps a juvenile related to *Megalosaurus*. Lived in the Early Cretaceous. Found in England. (*n.d.*)

Nyasasaurus (nie-as-a-SORE-us: "Nyasa lizard") A bipedal/quadrupedal herbivore 6ft 6in (2m) long: possibly like *Anchisaurus* (p. 84). Lived in the Middle Triassic. Found in Tanzania.

O **Ohmdenosaurus** (OHM-den-oh-SORE-us: "Ohmden lizard") A quadrupedal herbivore 13ft (4m) long: a primitive sauropod. Lived in the Early Jurassic. Found in Germany. Classification: Vulcanodontidae, Sauropoda, Sauropodomorpha, Saurischia.

Oligosaurus = *Rhabdodon*.

Omeisaurus (oh-my-EE-SORE-us: "Omei lizard") A quadrupedal herbivore 66ft (20m) long: a sauropod probably related to *Mamenchisaurus* (p. 104). Lived in the Late Jurassic. Found in China.

Omosaurus = *Dacentrurus*.

Onychosaurus = *Rhabdodon*.

Opisthocoelicaudia (oh-PIS-thoh-SEEL-i-KOW-dee-a: "tail vertebrae cupped behind") A quadrupedal herbivore 39ft (12m) long: a sauropod related to *Camarasaurus* (p. 96). Lived in the Late Cretaceous. Found in Mongolia.

Microceratops   *Minmi*   *Ornithomimus*   *Orodromeus*   *Ouranosaurus*

Oplosaurus = *Pelorosaurus*.

Orinosaurus = *Euskelosaurus*.

Ornatotholus (OR-nat-oh-THOH-lus: "ornate dome") A bipedal herbivore 8ft (2.4m) long: a bone-headed relative of *Pachycephalosaurus* (p. 154). Lived in the Late Cretaceous. Found in Alberta, Canada.

Ornithodesmus (OR-nith-oh-DEZ-mus: "bird ligament") Probably a small, bipedal carnivore: perhaps like *Troodon* (p. 68). Once thought to have been a "pterosaur", but redefined in 1993. Lived in the Early Cretaceous. Found in England.

Ornithoides = *Saurornithoides*.

Ornitholestes (OR-nith-oh-LES-teez) See p. 78.

Ornithomerus = *Rhabdodon*.

Ornithomimoides (OR-nith-oh-MEE-moy-deez: "bird-form mimic") A little-known, large, bipedal carnivore. Lived in the Late Cretaceous. Found in India. (*n.d.*)

Ornithomimus (OR-ni-thoh-MEE-mus: "bird mimic") A bipedal omnivore up to 11ft 6in (3.5m) long: an ostrich dinosaur similar to *Struthiomimus* (p. 64). Lived in the Late Cretaceous. Found in western North America.

Ornithopsis = *Pelorosaurus*.

Ornithotarsus = *Hadrosaurus*.

Orodromeus (OR-oh-DROH-mee-us: "mountain runner") A bipedal herbivore 6ft 6in (2m) long: an ornithopod like *Hypsilophodon* (p. 136). Lived in the Late Cretaceous. Found in Montana.

Orosaurus = *Euskelosaurus*.

Orthogoniosaurus (OR-thoh-GON-ee-oh-SORE-us: "straight angle lizard") A large, bipedal carnivore known from an unusual tooth. Lived in the Late Cretaceous. Found in India. (*n.d.*)

Orthomerus (OR-thoh-MER-us: "with straight parts") A large, little-known, bipedal/quadrupedal herbivore: a hadrosaur perhaps like *Maiasaura* (p. 146). Lived in the Late Cretaceous. Found in the Netherlands, and maybe Spain and the Ukraine. (*n.d.*)

Oshanosaurus (oh-SHAN-oh-SORE-us: "Oshan lizard") A large, quadrupedal herbivore: a sauropod perhaps like *Cetiosaurus* (p. 92). Lived in the Early Jurassic. Found in China. (*n.d.*)

Othnielia (oth-ni-EL-ee-a: "Othniel") A bipedal herbivore up to 13ft (4m) long: an ornithopod related to *Hypsilophodon* (p. 136). Lived in the Late Jurassic. Found in Colorado, Utah, and Wyoming.

Ouranosaurus (OO-ran-oh-SORE-us) See p. 142.

Oviraptor (OHV-ih-RAP-tor) See p. 66.

Ovoraptor = *Velociraptor*.

P **Pachycephalosaurus** (PAK-ee-SEF-a-loh-SORE-US) See p. 154.

Pachyrhinosaurus (PAK-ee-RINE-oh-SORE-us) See p. 163.

Pachysauriscus = *Plateosaurus* (p. 86).

Pachysaurops = *Plateosaurus* (p. 86).

Pachysaurus = *Plateosaurus* (p. 86).

Pachyspondylus = *Massospondylus* (p. 88).

Palaeopteryx (PAL-ee-OP-ter-ix: "ancient wing") A little-known, small bipedal carnivore: perhaps related to *Archaeopteryx* (p. 74) or *Troodon* (p. 68). Lived in the Late Jurassic. Found in Colorado. (*n.d.*)

Palaeoscincus (PAL-ee-oh-SKINK-us: "ancient skink") A large, quadrupedal, armored herbivore: a nodosaur based on teeth. Lived in the Late Cretaceous. Found in Montana. (*n.d.*)

Panoplosaurus (pan-OP-loh-SORE-us: "armored lizard") A quadrupedal, armored herbivore 23ft (7m) long: an ankylosaur related to *Edmontonia* (p. 122). Lived in the Late Cretaceous. Found in western North America.

Paraiguanodon = *Bactrosaurus*.

Paranthodon (PAR-AN-thoh-don: "beside *Anthodon*") A quadrupedal, plated herbivore: a stegosaur 16ft 6in (5m) long, related to *Kentrosaurus* (p. 118). Lived in the Early Cretaceous. Found in South Africa.

Parasaurolophus (par-a-SORE-oh-LOAF-us: "beside *Saurolophus*") A bipedal/quadrupedal herbivore 33ft (10m) long: a hadrosaur related to *Corythosaurus* (p. 148). Lived in the Late Cretaceous. Found in western North America, including perhaps Alaska.

"Parhabdodon" = *Rhabdodon*.

Parksosaurus (PARX-oh-SORE-us: "Parks's lizard") A bipedal herbivore 8ft (2.4m) long: an ornithopod related to *Hypsilophodon* (p. 136). Lived in the Late Cretaceous. Found in Alberta, Canada.

Paronychodon (par-on-EYE-koh-don: "beside the nail (or claw) tooth") A bipedal carnivore 6ft 6in (2m) long: perhaps like *Deinonychus* (p. 70). Lived in the Late Cretaceous. Found in Montana. (*n.d.*)

Parrosaurus (PAHR-oh-SORE-us: "Parr's lizard") A little-known, large quadrupedal herbivore: a sauropod. Lived in the Late Cretaceous. Found in Missouri.

Patagosaurus (PAT-a-goh-SORE-us: "Patagonian lizard") A large, quadrupedal herbivore: a sauropod related to *Cetiosaurus* (p. 92). Lived in the Late Jurassic. Found in Argentina.

Pectinodon = *Troodon* (p. 68).

Peishansaurus (PAY-shan-SORE-us: "Mount Pei lizard") Perhaps a quadrupedal, armored herbivore, but little-known. Lived in the Late Cretaceous. Found in China. (*n.d.*)

Pelorosaurus (PEL-oh-roh-SORE-us: "monstrous lizard") A huge, quadrupedal herbivore: a sauropod related to *Brachiosaurus* (p. 94). Lived in the Early Cretaceous. Found in England and France.

Peltosaurus = *Sauropelta* (p. 124).

Pentaceratops (PEN-ta-SERRA-tops: "five-horned face") A quadrupedal, horned herbivore: a ceratopsian related to *Triceratops* (p. 164). Lived in the Late Cretaceous. Found in New Mexico.

Phaedrolosaurus (FEED-rol-oh-SORE-us: "gleaming lizard") A bipedal carnivore: perhaps similar to *Deinonychus* (p. 70). Lived in the Early Cretaceous. Found in China. (*n.d.*)

Phyllodon (FIL-oh-don: "leaf tooth") A bipedal herbivore, perhaps only 3ft (90cm) long: perhaps like *Hypsilophodon* (p. 136). Lived in the Late Jurassic. Found in Portugal.

Piatnitzkysaurus (pee-at-NITS-kee-SORE-us: "Piatnitzky's lizard") A bipedal carnivore 14ft (4.3m) long: perhaps related to *Allosaurus* (p. 52). Lived in the Middle Jurassic. Found in Argentina.

Pinacosaurus (pin-AK-oh-SORE-us: "plank lizard") A quadrupedal, armored herbivore: an ankylosaur 16ft 6in (5m) long related to *Euoplocephalus* (p. 128). Lived in the Late Cretaceous. Found in China and Mongolia.

Pisanosaurus (pee-SAN-oh-SORE-us: "Pisano's lizard") A bipedal herbivore 3ft (90cm) long: a primitive ornithischian. Lived in the early Late Triassic. Found in Argentina. Classification uncertain.

Piveteausaurus (PEEV-eh-toh-SORE-us: "Piveteau's lizard") A bipedal carnivore perhaps 36ft (11m) long: possibly related to *Megalosaurus*. Lived in the Middle Jurassic. Found in France.

Plateosauravus = *Euskelosaurus*.

Plateosaurus (PLAT-ee-oh-SORE-us) See p. 86.

Pleurocoelus (PLEW-roh-SEEL-us: "hollow side") A large, quadrupedal herbivore: a sauropod related to *Brachiosaurus* (p. 94). Lived in the Early Cretaceous. Found in Maryland, Texas, and England.

Parasaurolophus   *Pinacosaurus*   *Plateosaurus*

Pleuropeltus = *Struthiosaurus*.

Podokesaurus (po-DOH-kee-SORE-us: "swift-footed lizard") A bipedal carnivore 3ft (90cm) long: perhaps related to *Coelophysis* (p. 46). Lived in the Early Jurassic. Found in Connecticut.

Poekilopleuron (peek-il-oh-PLEW-ron: "varying side") A bipedal carnivore 29ft 6in (9m) long, with short, strong arms: perhaps related to *Megalosaurus*. Lived in the Middle Jurassic. Found in France. Classification uncertain.

Polacanthoides = *Hylaeosaurus*.

Polacanthus (pol-a-KAN-thus: "many spines") A quadrupedal, armored herbivore related to *Sauropelta* (p. 124). Lived in the Early Cretaceous. Found in the Isle of Wight, England, and South Dakota.

Polyodontosaurus = *Troodon* (p. 68).

Polyonax = *Triceratops* (p. 164).

Prenocephale (pren-oh-SEF-a-lee: "sloping head") A bipedal herbivore 8ft (2.4m) long: a bone-headed relative of *Pachycephalosaurus* (p. 154). Lived in the Late Cretaceous. Found in Mongolia.

Priconodon (PRY-kon-oh-don: "serrated conical tooth") A large, quadrupedal, armored herbivore: perhaps like *Sauropelta* (p. 124). Lived in the Early Cretaceous. Found in Maryland. (*n.d.*)

Priodontognathus (PRY-oh-dont-oh-NAY-thus: "saw-toothed jaw") A quadrupedal, armored herbivore, perhaps like *Sauropelta* (p. 124). Lived in the Late Jurassic. Found in England.

Probactrosaurus (PROH-BAK-troh-SORE-us: "before *Bactrosaurus*") A bipedal/quadrupedal herbivore: an ornithopod related to *Iguanodon* (p. 138) and the hadrosaurs. Lived in the Late Cretaceous. Found in China and Mongolia.

Proceratops = *Ceratops*.

Proceratosaurus (PROH-ser-AT-oh-SORE-us: "before *Ceratosaurus*") A medium-size, bipedal carnivore with a single nose horn. Lived in the Middle Jurassic. Found in England. Classification uncertain.

Procerosaurus (PROH-SER-oh-SORE-us: "first horned lizard") A bipedal or quadrupedal herbivore: perhaps *Iguanodon* (p. 138), known only from a single, incomplete bone. Lived in the Late Cretaceous. Found in Czech Republic. (*n.d.*)

Procheneosaurus = *Corythosaurus* (p. 148) and *Lambeosaurus* (p. 150).

Procompsognathus (PROH-KOMP-soh-NAY-thus: "before *Compsognathus*") A bipedal carnivore 4ft (1.2m) long: an early theropod related to *Coelophysis* (p. 46). Lived in the Late Triassic. Found in Germany.

Prodeinodon (PROH-DINE-oh-don: "before *Deinodon*") A large, bipedal carnivore: perhaps *Alectrosaurus*. (*n.d.*)

Prosaurolophus (PROH-sore-oh-LOAF-fus: "before *Saurolophus*") A bipedal/quadrupedal herbivore: a hadrosaur related to *Edmontosaurus* (p. 144). Lived in the Late Cretaceous. Found in Alberta, Canada, and Montana.

Protiguanodon = *Psittacosaurus* (p. 156).

Protoavis (PROH-TOH-AY-vis: "first bird") A small, bird-like carnivore of uncertain relationships. Lived in the Late Triassic. Found in Texas. Described in 1991.

Protoceratops (PROH-toh-SERRA-tops) See p. 158.

Protognathosaurus (PROH-toh-NAY-thoh-SORE-us: "early jaw lizard") A large, quadrupedal herbivore: a sauropod related to *Cetiosaurus* (p. 92). Lived in the Middle Jurassic. Found in China. Named in 1991. (*n.d.*)

Protognathus = *Protognathosaurus*.

Protorosaurus = *Chasmosaurus*.

Psittacosaurus (Si-TAK-oh-SORE-us) See p. 156.

Pteropelyx (ter-oh-PEL-ix: "wing pelvis") A large, bipedal/quadrupedal herbivore: a hadrosaur, possibly *Corythosaurus* (p. 148) or *Hypacrosaurus*. Lived in the Late Cretaceous. Found in Montana. (*n.d.*)

Pterospondylus (ter-oh-SPON-di-lus: "winged vertebrae") A small, bipedal carnivore: perhaps a ceratosaur. Lived in the Late Triassic. Found in Germany. (*n.d.*)

Q **Quaesitosaurus** (ky-sit-oh-SORE-us: "unusual lizard") A large, quadrupedal herbivore: a sauropod that might be *Nemegtosaurus*. Lived in the Late Cretaceous. Found in Mongolia.

R **Rapator** (RAP-ah-tor: "plunderer") A bipedal carnivore 33ft (10m) long: perhaps a relative of *Carnotaurus* (p. 48). Lived in the Early Cretaceous. Found in Australia.

Rebbachisaurus (reb-BATCH-i-SORE-us: "Rebbachi lizard") A large, quadrupedal herbivore: a sauropod related to *Dicraeosaurus*. Lived in the Early Cretaceous. Found in Morocco, Tunisia, Niger, Mali, and Algeria.

Regnosaurus (REG-noh-SORE-us: "Sussex lizard") A quadrupedal herbivore (sauropod or, more likely, stegosaur), known from a piece of jaw. Lived in the Early Cretaceous. Found in England. (*n.d.*)

Revueltosaurus (rev-WEL-toh-SORE-us: "Revuelto lizard") A small, bipedal herbivore, perhaps like *Lesothosaurus* (p. 132). Lived in the Late Triassic. Found in New Mexico. Named in 1989. (*n.d.*)

Rhabdodon (RAB-doh-don: "rod tooth") A bipedal herbivore 13ft (4m) long: an ornithopod with features seen in *Hypsilophodon* (p. 136) and *Iguanodon* (p. 138). Lived in the Late Cretaceous. Found in Spain, France, Austria, and Romania.

Rhodanosaurus = *Struthiosaurus*.

Rhoetosaurus (reet-oh-SORE-us: "Rhoetos lizard") A quadrupedal herbivore over 49ft (15m) long: a sauropod related to *Cetiosaurus* (p. 92). Lived in the Middle Jurassic. Found in Australia.

Ricardoestesia (ri-KARD-oh-es-TEEZ-i-a: "Richard Estes") A small, bipedal carnivore known only from teeth and bits of lower jaw. Lived in the Late Cretaceous. Found in Alberta, Canada; and Montana and Wyoming. Named in 1990. Classification uncertain.

Richardoestesia = *Ricardoestesia*.

Rioarribasaurus = *Coelophysis* (p. 46).

Riojasaurus (ree-O-ha-SORE-us) See p. 90.

Roccosaurus = *Melanorosaurus*.

S **Saichania** (sigh-CHAN-ee-a: "beautiful") A quadrupedal, armored herbivore 6.6m (22ft) long: an ankylosaur like *Euoplocephalus* (p. 128). Lived in the Late Cretaceous. Found in Mongolia.

Saltasaurus (Sal-te-SORE-us) See p. 106.

Saltopus (SALT-oh-pus: "leaping foot") A tiny, bipedal carnivore 2ft (60cm) long: a ceratosaur. Lived in the Late Triassic. Found in Scotland. (*n.d.*)

"Sanchusaurus" (san-choo-SORE-us: "Sanchu lizard") Informal name for a bird-like, bipedal carnivore (or omnivore): an ostrich dinosaur like *Gallimimus* (p. 62). Lived in the Late Cretaceous. Found in Japan.

"Sangonghesaurus" (san-gong-eh-SORE-us: "Sangonghe lizard") A quadrupedal, armored herbivore: an ankylosaur like *Euoplocephalus* (p. 128). Lived in the Late Cretaceous. Found in China. (*n.d.*)

Sanpasaurus (san-pa-SORE-us: "Sanpa lizard") Named from mixed-up fossils of a sauropod and an ornithopod. Lived in the Middle Jurassic. Found in China. (*n.d.*)

Prosaurolophus   *Riojasaurus*   *Saltasaurus*   *Saurolophus*

Sarcolestes (sar-koh-LES-teez: "flesh robber") A quadrupedal, armored herbivore: an early ankylosaur related to *Sauropelta* (p. 124). Lived in the Middle Jurassic. Found in England.

Sarcosaurus (SAR-koh-sore-us: "flesh lizard") A bipedal carnivore 11ft 6in (3.5m) long: a ceratosaur of unknown family. Lived in the Early Jurassic. Found in England.

Sauraechinodon = *Echinodon.*

Saurolophus (SORE-oh-LOAF-us: "ridged lizard") A bipedal/quadrupedal herbivore 29ft 6in (9m) long: a hadrosaur related to *Edmontosaurus* (p. 144). Lived in the Late Cretaceous. Found in Alberta, Canada, California, and Mongolia.

Sauropelta (SORE-oh-PEL-ta) See p. 124.

Saurophagus = *Allosaurus* (p. 52).

Sauroplites (SORE-op-LITE-eez: "lizard hoplite") A quadrupedal, armored herbivore: an ankylosaur perhaps like *Euoplocephalus* (p. 128). Lived in the Early Cretaceous. Found in China.

Saurornithoides (sore-OR-nith-OID-eez: "bird-like lizard") A bipedal carnivore 6ft 6in (2m) long: like *Troodon* (p. 68). Lived in the Late Cretaceous. Found in Mongolia.

Saurornitholestes (sore-OR-nith-oh-LES-teez: "bird-robbing lizard") A bipedal carnivore 6ft (1.8m) long: like *Deinonychus* (p. 70). Lived in the Late Cretaceous. Found in Alberta, Canada.

Scelidosaurus (skel-IDE-oh-SORE-us) See p. 112.

Scolosaurus = *Euoplocephalus* (p. 128).

Scutellosaurus (skoo-TEL-oh-SORE-us) See p. 113.

Secernosaurus (si-KER-noh-SORE-us: "severed lizard") A bipedal/quadrupedal herbivore 10ft (3m) long: probably a primitive hadrosaur. Lived in the Late Cretaceous. Found in Argentina.

Segisaurus (SAY-hee-SORE-us: "Segi [Canyon] lizard") A bipedal carnivore 3ft 3in (1m) long: a ceratosaur perhaps like *Coelophysis* (p. 46). Lived in the Early Jurassic. Found in Arizona.

Segnosaurus (SEG-noh-SORE-us) See p. 108.

Seismosaurus (SIZE-moh-SORE-us: "earth-shaking lizard") A huge, quadrupedal herbivore reportedly 130ft (40m) long (the longest known dinosaur): a sauropod related to *Diplodocus* (p. 100). Lived in the Late Jurassic. Found in New Mexico. Described in 1991.

Sellosaurus (SEL-oh-SORE-us: "saddle lizard") A bipedal/quadrupedal herbivore 21ft (6.5m) long: a prosauropod related to *Plateosaurus* (p. 86). Lived in the Late Triassic. Found in Germany.

Shamosaurus (SHAM-oh-SORE-us: "Gobi [Desert] lizard") A large, quadrupedal, armored herbivore: an ankylosaur like *Euoplocephalus* (p. 128). Lived in the Early Cretaceous. Found in Mongolia.

Shanshanosaurus (shan-SHAN-oh-SORE-us: "Shanshan lizard") A bipedal carnivore 8ft (2.4m) long: perhaps related to *Aublysodon.* Lived in the Late Cretaceous. Found in China.

Shantungosaurus (shan-TUNG-oh-SORE-us: "Shantung lizard") A bipedal/quadrupedal herbivore 49ft (15m) long: a hadrosaur like *Edmontosaurus* (p. 144). Lived in the Late Cretaceous. Found in China.

Shunosaurus (SHOO-noh-SORE-us) See p. 93.

Shuosaurus = *Shunosaurus* (p. 93).

Siamosaurus (sigh-AM-oh-SORE-us: "Siam lizard") A large, bipedal carnivore, perhaps like *Spinosaurus* (p. 60). Lived in the Late Jurassic. Found in Thailand.

Silvisaurus (SIL-vih-SORE-us: "forest lizard") A quadrupedal, armored herbivore 13ft (4m) long: an ankylosaur related to *Sauropelta* (p. 124). Lived in the Early Cretaceous. Found in Kansas.

Sinocoelurus (SINE-oh-seel-YEW-rus: "Chinese *Coelurus*") A small, bipedal carnivore known only from teeth. Lived in the Late Jurassic. Found in China. (*n.d.*)

"Sinornithoides" (sine-ORN-ith-OID-eez: "Chinese bird-like") A small, bipedal carnivore like *Troodon* (p. 60), not yet formally described. Lived in the Early Cretaceous. Found in China.

Sinosaurus (SINE-oh-SORE-us: "Chinese lizard") A bipedal carnivore 8ft (2.4m) long, perhaps like *Herrerasaurus* (p. 40). Lived in the Early Jurassic. Found in China. (*n.d.*)

Sphenospondylus = *Iguanodon* (p. 138).

Spinosaurus (SPINE-oh-SORE-us) See p. 60.

Spondylosoma (SPON-di-loh-SOH-ma: "vertebra body") A little-known, bipedal carnivore: perhaps a primitive theropod related to *Staurikosaurus.* Lived in the early Late Triassic. Found in Brazil.

Staurikosaurus (stor-IK-oh-SORE-us: "[Southern] Cross lizard") A bipedal carnivore 6ft 6in (2m) long: a primitive theropod somewhat like *Herrerasaurus* (p. 40). Lived in the early Late Triassic. Found in Brazil. Classification: Staurikosauridae, Theropoda, Saurischia.

Stegoceras (ste-GOS-er-as) See p. 155.

Stegopelta = *Nodosaurus.*

Stegosauroides (STEG-oh-sore-OIDE-eez: "stegosaur form") A quadrupedal, armored herbivore: an ankylosaur perhaps like *Euoplocephalus* (p. 128). Lived in the Late Cretaceous. Found in China. Classification uncertain. (*n.d.*)

Stegosaurus (STEG-oh-SORE-us) See p. 114.

Stenonychosaurus = *Troodon* (p. 68).

Stenopelix (STEN-oh-PEL-ix: "narrow pelvis") A bipedal herbivore 5ft (1.5m) long: perhaps a primitive pachycephalosaur. Lived in the Early Cretaceous. Found in Germany.

Stenotholus = *Stygimoloch.*

Stephanosaurus = *Lambeosaurus* (p. 150).

Stereocephalus = *Euoplocephalus* (p. 128).

Sterrholophus = *Triceratops* (p. 164).

Stokesosaurus (STOKES-oh-SORE-us: "Stokes's lizard") A bipedal carnivore 13ft (4m) long: perhaps related to *Allosaurus* (p. 52). Lived in the Late Jurassic. Found in Utah. Classification uncertain.

Strenusaurus = *Riojasaurus* (p. 90).

Struthiomimus (STRUTH-ee-oh-MEEM-us) See p. 64.

Struthiosaurus (STRUTH-ee-oh-SORE-us: "ostrich lizard") A quadrupedal, armored dinosaur 6ft (1.8m) long: an ankylosaur related to *Sauropelta* (p. 124). Lived in the Late Cretaceous. Found in Austria and Romania. Formal redescription pending. (*n.d.*)

Stygimoloch (STIJ-i-MOH-lok: "[River] Styx demon") A bipedal herbivore: a bone-headed relative of *Pachycephalosaurus* (p. 154). Lived in the Late Cretaceous. Found in Montana and Wyoming.

Styracosaurus (sty-RAK-oh-SORE-us) See p. 162.

"Sugiyamasaurus" (SOO-gee-YAH-mah-SORE-us: "Sugiyama lizard") Informal name for a large, quadrupedal herbivore: a sauropod known only from teeth. Lived in the Late Cretaceous. Found in Japan. Not yet formally described.

Supersaurus (SUE-per-SORE-us: "super lizard") A huge, quadrupedal herbivore 98ft (30m) long: a sauropod related to *Diplodocus* (p. 100). Lived in the Late Jurassic. Found in Colorado.

Symphyrophus = *Camptosaurus.*

Syngonosaurus = *Acanthopholis*?

Syntarsus (sin-TAR-sus: "fused ankle") A bipedal carnivore 10ft (3m) long: related to *Coelophysis* (p. 46). Lived in the Early Jurassic. Found in South Africa, Zimbabwe, and Arizona.

Syrmosaurus = *Pinacosaurus.*

Scelidosaurus   *Shantungosaurus*   *Shunosaurus*   *Spinosaurus*

Szechuanosaurus (sich-WAN-oh-SORE-us: "Sichuan lizard") A bipedal carnivore 26ft (8m) long: related to *Allosaurus* (p. 52). Lived in the Late Jurassic. Found in China.

T **Talarurus** (tal-a-ROO-rus: "basket tail") A quadrupedal, armored herbivore 19ft 6in (6m) long: an ankylosaur like *Euoplocephalus* (p. 128). Lived in the Late Cretaceous. Found in Mongolia.

Tanius (TAN-i-us: "of the Tan") A bipedal/quadrupedal herbivore: probably a primitive hadrosaur. Lived in the Late Cretaceous. Found in China.

Tanystrosuchus = *Halticosaurus.*

Tarascosaurus (TA-RAS-koh-SORE-us: "Tarasque lizard") A bipedal carnivore: a relative of *Carnotaurus* (p. 48). Lived in the Late Cretaceous. Found in France. Named in 1991.

Tarbosaurus (TAR-boh-SORE-us: "alarming lizard") A bipedal carnivore 33ft (10m) long: like *Tyrannosaurus* (p. 54). Lived in the Late Cretaceous. Found in China and Mongolia.

Tarchia (TAR-kee-a: "brain") A quadrupedal, armored herbivore 28ft (8.5m) long: an ankylosaur related to *Euoplocephalus* (p. 128). Lived in the Late Cretaceous. Found in Mongolia.

Tatisaurus (DAH-DEE-SORE-us: "Ta-Ti lizard") A quadrupedal, armored or plated dinosaur: perhaps related to *Scelidosaurus* (p. 112) or *Huayangosaurus*. Lived in the Early Jurassic. Found in China.

Taveirosaurus (ta-VEE-roh-SORE-us: "Taveiro lizard") A bipedal herbivore known only from teeth: thought to be a bone-headed ornithischian dinosaur, perhaps related to *Homalocephale*. Lived in the Late Cretaceous. Found in Portugal. Named in 1991.

Tawasaurus = *Lufengosaurus.*

Technosaurus (TEK-noh-SORE-us: "Texas lizard") A small, bipedal herbivore: a primitive ornithischian perhaps much like *Lesothosaurus* (p. 132). Lived in the Late Triassic. Found in Texas. (*n.d.*)

Teinurosaurus (TEYN-you-roh-SORE-us: "extended lizard") A small, bipedal carnivore, known only from one tailbone. Lived in the Late Jurassic. Found in France. Classification uncertain. (*n.d.*)

Telmatosaurus (tel-mat-oh-SORE-us: "marsh lizard") A large, bipedal/quadrupedal herbivore: a primitive hadrosaur. Lived in the Late Cretaceous. Found in Romania.

Tenantosaurus = *Tenontosaurus.*

Tenchisaurus = *Tianchisaurus.*

Tenontosaurus (TEH-NON-toh-SORE-us: "sinew lizard") A bipedal/quadrupedal herbivore up to 24ft (7.5m) long: an ornithopod with features seen in *Dryosaurus* and *Iguanodon* (p. 138). Lived in the Early Cretaceous. Found in Montana, Oklahoma, Texas, and Utah.

Tetragonosaurus = *Lambeosaurus* (p. 154).

Thecocoelurus = *Calamospondylus.*

Thecodontosaurus (THEEK-oh-DON-toh-SORE-us: "socket-toothed lizard") A bipedal herbivore 8ft (2.4m) long: the most primitive of the prosauropods. Lived in the Late Triassic. Found in England. Classification: Thecodontosauridae, Prosauropoda, Sauropodomorpha, Saurischia.

Thecospondylus (THEEK-oh-SPON-di-LUS: "socket vertebrae") A dinosaur known only from a fragmentary fossil. Lived in the Early Cretaceous. Found in England. Classification uncertain. (*n.d.*)

Therizinosaurus (THER-ih-ZINE-oh-SORE-us: "scythe lizard") A bipedal or bipedal/quadrupedal carnivore, insectivore, or herbivore up to 39ft (12m) long, named from scythe-like claws. Perhaps related to *Segnosaurus* (p. 108). Lived in the Late Cretaceous. Found in Mongolia.

Therosaurus = *Iguanodon* (p. 138).

Thescelosaurus (thes-kel-oh-SORE-us: "wonderful lizard") A bipedal/quadrupedal herbivore 11ft (3.4m) long: an ornithopod somewhat like *Hypsilophodon* (p. 136). Lived in the Late Cretaceous. Found in western USA and Alberta, Canada.

Thespesius = *Edmontosaurus*? (p. 144).

Thotobolosaurus (thoh-toh-boh-loh-SORE-us: "Thotobolo lizard") A large, quadrupedal herbivore: probably a prosauropod related to *Riojasaurus* (p. 90). Lived in the Late Triassic. Found in Lesotho.

Tianchisaurus (ti-an-chih-SORE-us: "Tianchi lizard") A quadrupedal, armored herbivore: an ankylosaur perhaps like *Euoplocephalus* (p. 128). Lived in the Middle Jurassic. Found in China. (= *Jurassosaurus*?)

Tianchungosaurus = *Dianchungosaurus*?

Tichosteus (tik-os-TEE-US: "walled bone") A little-known, large, bipedal/quadrupedal herbivore: perhaps like *Hypsilophodon* (p. 136). Lived in the Late Jurassic. Found in Colorado. (*n.d.*)

Tienshanosaurus (tyen-shan-oh-SORE-us: "Tienshan lizard") A quadrupedal herbivore up to 39ft (12m) long: a sauropod related to *Camarasaurus* (p. 96) or *Mamenchisaurus* (p. 104). Lived in the Late Jurassic. Found in China.

Titanosaurus (tie-TAN-oh-SORE-us: "titanic lizard") A quadrupedal herbivore 39ft (12m) long: a sauropod related to *Saltasaurus* (p. 106). Lived in the Late Cretaceous. Found in India. (Name also used in the past for *Atlantosaurus*.)

Tochisaurus (toe-chee-SORE-us: "Tochi lizard") A small, bipedal carnivore related to *Troodon* (p. 68). Lived in the Late Cretaceous. Found in Mongolia. Named in 1991.

Tomodon = *Diplotomodon.*

Tornieria (tor-NEAR-ee-a: "Tornier") A large, quadrupedal herbivore: a sauropod related to *Diplodocus* (p. 100). Lived in the Late Jurassic. Found in Tanzania. (=*Barosaurus*?)

Torosaurus (tor-oh-SORE-us: "bull lizard") A quadrupedal, horned dinosaur 24ft (7.5m) long with the largest head of any known land animal: a ceratopsian related to *Triceratops* (p. 164). Lived in the Late Cretaceous. Found in western North America.

Torvosaurus (tor-voh-SORE-us: "savage lizard") A bipedal carnivore up to 33ft (10m) long, with short, strong arms: related to *Megalosaurus*. Lived in the Late Jurassic. Found in Colorado. Classification uncertain.

Trachodon (TRAK-oh-don: "rough tooth") A large, bipedal/quadrupedal herbivore: a hadrosaur known only from fragments including teeth. Lived in the Late Cretaceous. Found in Montana and England. Classification uncertain. (*n.d.*)

Triceratops (try-SERRA-tops) See p. 164.

Trimucrodon (try-MEW-kroh-don: "three-grooved tooth") A small, bipedal herbivore, perhaps related to *Lesothosaurus* (p. 132). Lived in the Late Jurassic. Found in Portugal. (*n.d.*)

Troodon (TROH-oh-don) See p. 68.

Tsintaosaurus (chin-TAY-oh-sore-us: "Tsintao lizard") = *Tanius* mixed up with other fossils.

Tugulusaurus (TOO-goo-loo-SORE-us: "Tugulo lizard") A bipedal carnivore about 10ft (3m) long: perhaps like *Ornitholestes* (p. 78). Lived in the Early Cretaceous. Found in China.

Tuojiangosaurus (toh-HWANG-oh-SORE-us) See p. 120.

Turanoceratops (too-RAHN-oh-SERRA-tops: "Turan horned face") A quadrupedal, horned dinosaur: a ceratopsid. Lived in the Late Cretaceous. Found in Uzbekistan. Named in 1989.

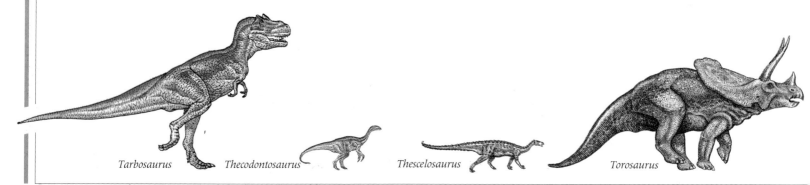

Tarbosaurus   *Thecodontosaurus*   *Thescelosaurus*   *Torosaurus*

Tylocephale (tie-loh-SEF-ah-lee: "swollen head") A bipedal herbivore 6ft 6in (2m) long: a pachycephalosaur related to *Pachycephalosaurus* (p. 154). Lived in the Late Cretaceous. Found in Mongolia.

Tylosteus = *Pachycephalosaurus* (p. 154).

Tyrannosaurus (tie-RAN-oh-SORE-us) See p. 54.

U **Udanoceratops** (oo-dan-oh-SERRA-tops: "Udan horned face") A large, quadrupedal herbivore: a ceratopsian related to *Protoceratops* (p. 158). Lived in the Late Cretaceous. Found in Mongolia. Named in 1992.

Ugrosaurus = *Triceratops*? (p. 164).

Uintasaurus = *Camarasaurus* (p. 96).

Ultrasauros (ult-ra-SORE-os: "ultra lizard") A huge, quadrupedal herbivore up to 89ft (27m) long: a sauropod like *Brachiosaurus* (p. 94) but even larger. Lived in the Late Jurassic. Found in Colorado. Name respelled in 1991 to avoid duplication of previously published *Ultrasaurus*.

Ultrasaurus (ult-ra-SORE-us: "ultra lizard") A quadrupedal herbivore like *Brachiosaurus* (p. 94), but smaller. Lived in the Early Cretaceous. Found in South Korea. Named in 1983. (*n.d.*)

Umarsaurus = *Barsboldia*.

Unquillosaurus (un-keel-yo-SORE-us: "Unquillo lizard") A bipedal carnivore 36ft (11m) long, known only from a hipbone. Lived in the Late Cretaceous. Found in Argentina. Classification uncertain.

"Utahraptor" (YOO-tah-RAP-tor: "Utah plunderer") A bipedal carnivore 19ft 6in (6m) long: akin to *Deinonychus* (p. 70). Lived in the Late Jurassic. Found in Utah. Not yet formally described.

V **Valdoraptor** (VAL-doh-RAP-tor: "Wealden plunderer") A large, bipedal carnivore, perhaps like *Allosaurus* (p. 52). Lived in the Early Cretaceous. Found in England. Named in 1991.

Valdosaurus (VAL-doh-SORE-us: "Wealden lizard") A bipedal herbivore 10ft (3m) long: an ornithopod like *Hypsilophodon* (p. 136). Lived in the Early Cretaceous. Found in England, Romania, and Niger. Classification: Dryosauridae, Ornithopoda, Euornithopoda, Ornithischia.

Vectensia = *Hylaeosaurus*?

Vectisaurus (VEK-ti-SORE-us: "Isle of Wight lizard") A large, bipedal/quadrupedal herbivore: like *Iguanodon* (p. 138). Lived in the Early Cretaceous. Found in England.

Velocipes (vel-O-si-peez: "quick foot") A small, bipedal carnivore known from part of one bone: perhaps a ceratosaur. Lived in the Late Triassic. Found in Germany. (*n.d.*)

Velociraptor (vel-O-si-RAP-tor: "quick plunderer") A bipedal carnivore 6ft (1.8m) long: similar to *Deinonychus* (p. 70). Lived in the Late Cretaceous. Found in China and Mongolia.

Velocisaurus (vel-O-si-SORE-us: "quick lizard") A small, bipedal carnivore with unusual upper foot bones. Lived in the Late Cretaceous. Found in Argentina. Named in 1991. Classification: Velocisauridae, Ceratosauria, Theropoda, Saurischia.

Volkheimeria (VOLK-hie-mer-i-a: "Volkheimer's") A large, quadrupedal herbivore: a sauropod related to *Brachiosaurus* (p. 94). Lived in the Middle Jurassic. Found in Argentina.

Vulcanodon (vul-KAN-oh-don: "volcano tooth") A quadrupedal herbivore 21ft (6.5m) long: a small, primitive sauropod. Lived in the Early Jurassic. Found in Zimbabwe. Classification: Vulcanodontidae, Sauropoda, Sauropodomorpha, Saurischia.

W **Wakinosaurus** (wah-keen-oh-SORE-us: "Wakin lizard") A large, little-known, bipedal carnivore, perhaps like *Allosaurus* (p. 52). Lived in the Early Cretaceous. Found in Japan. Named in 1992. (*n.d.*)

Walgettosuchus = *Rapator*?

Walkeria (wauk-EAR-i-a: "Walker's") A bipedal carnivore about 4ft (1.2m) long: possibly related to *Herrerasaurus* (p. 40). Lived in the Late Triassic. Found in India. Classification uncertain.

Wannanosaurus (wan-an-oh-SORE-us: "Wannan lizard") A tiny, bipedal herbivore (one of the smallest dinosaurs) about 2ft (60cm) long: a flat-headed pachycephalosaur related to *Goyocephale*. Lived in the Late Cretaceous. Found in China.

Wuerhosaurus (WER-oh-SORE-us: "Wuerho lizard") A quadrupedal, plated herbivore 19ft 6in (6m) long: related to *Stegosaurus* (p. 114). Lived in the Early Cretaceous. Found in China.

X **Xenotarsosaurus** (zen-oh-tar-soh-SORE-us: "strange-ankle lizard") A large, bipedal carnivore: related to *Carnotaurus* (p. 48). Lived in the Late Cretaceous. Found in Argentina.

Xiaosaurus (SHEE-ah-o-SORE-us: "Xiao lizard") A bipedal herbivore 5ft (1.5m) long: perhaps an ornithopod related to *Hypsilophodon* (p. 136). Lived in the Middle Jurassic. Found in China. (*n.d.*)

Xuanhanosaurus (shwan-HAN-oh-SORE-us: "Xuanhan lizard") A bipedal/quadrupedal carnivore 19ft 6in (6m) long, with sturdy arms. Lived in the Middle Jurassic. Found in China. Classification uncertain.

Xuanhuasaurus (SHWAN-hwah-SORE-us: "Xuanhua lizard") A small, bipedal herbivore: a pachycephalosaur related to *Chaoyangosaurus*. Lived in the Late Jurassic. Found in China. (*n.d.*)

Y **Yaleosaurus** = *Anchisaurus* (p. 84).

Yandusaurus (YAN-doo-SORE-us: "Yandu lizard") A bipedal herbivore 6ft 6in (2m) long: an ornithopod related to *Hypsilophodon* (p. 136). Lived in the Middle Jurassic. Found in China. (See *Yubasaurus*.)

Yangchuanosaurus (yang-choo-AHN-oh-SORE-us: "Yangchuan lizard") A bipedal carnivore 29ft 6in (9m) long: perhaps related to *Eustreptospondylus* (p. 50). Lived in the Late Jurassic. Found in China. Classification uncertain.

Yaverlandia (YAV-er-land-ee-ah: "of Yaverland") A bipedal herbivore or a quadrupedal, armored herbivore: possibly a pachycephalosaur, but may be an ankylosaur, perhaps related to *Hylaeosaurus*. Lived in the Early Cretaceous. Found in England. (*n.d.*)

Yaxartosaurus = *Jaxartosaurus*.

Yingshanosaurus (ying-SHAN-oh-SORE-us: "Mt. Ying lizard") A quadrupedal, plated herbivore: a stegosaur probably related to *Tuojiangosaurus* (p. 120). Lived in the Jurassic. Found in China.

Yubasaurus = *Yandusaurus* (or vice versa, if *Yubasaurus* was named first).

Yunnanosaurus (yoo-NAN-oh-SORE-us: "Yunnan lizard") A bipedal/quadrupedal herbivore 23ft (7m) long: a prosauropod with self-sharpening, spoon-shaped teeth. Lived in the Early Jurassic. Found in China. Classification: Yunnanosauridae, Prosauropoda, Sauropodomorpha, Saurischia.

Z **Zapsalis** = *Paronychodon*.

Zephyrosaurus (ZEF-ear-o-SORE-us: "west wind lizard") A bipedal herbivore 6ft (1.8m) long: an ornithopod like *Hypsilophodon* (p. 136). Lived in the Early Cretaceous. Found in Montana.

Zigongosaurus = *Omeisaurus*.

Zizhongosaurus (zeez-HONG-oh-SORE-us: "Zizhong lizard") A quadrupedal herbivore 29ft 6in (9m) long: a primitive sauropod perhaps like *Vulcanodon*. Lived in the Early Jurassic. Found in China.

Velociraptor   *Wuerhosaurus*   *Yandusaurus*   *Yangchuanosaurus*

GLOSSARY

Acetabulum The hip socket.
Ankylosaurs Quadrupedal, armored thyreophoran ornithischians.
Antorbital fenestra A hole in the skull in front of each eye: a hallmark of the archosaurs.
Archosaurs A group of reptiles that includes dinosaurs, crocodiles, pterosaurs, and "thecodonts."
Armored dinosaurs Dinosaurs with bodies protected by bony plates or studs. They included ankylosaurs. Some sauropods were also armored in a similar fashion.
Bipedal Walking on hind legs only.
Bone-headed dinosaurs The pachycephalosaurs.
Braincase Bones of the skull containing and guarding the brain.
Carnivore A meat-eating animal.
Carnosaurs Big bipedal theropods: a group of tetanurans formally named the Carnosauria.
Carpals The bones of the wrist.
Caudal vertebrae Tailbones.
Cenozoic era The geological time span covering the last 65 million years: "Age of Mammals." It comprised the Tertiary and Quaternary periods.
Cerapoda A great group of related ornithischian dinosaurs comprising the ornithopods and the marginocephalians.
Ceratopsians Bipedal and quadrupedal marginocephalians comprising psittacosaurids (parrot lizards) and neoceratopsians.
Ceratosaurs One of two major groups of theropods.
Cervical vertebrae Neck bones.
Chevron bones Bones projecting down from the caudal vertebrae (tailbones).
Clade A group of organisms (such as dinosaurs) that share uniquely evolved anatomical features.
Class A group of organisms consisting of one or more related orders (sometimes grouped in subclasses). Classes traditionally include Aves (birds), Reptilia (reptiles), and Mammalia (mammals).
Cloaca A combined outlet for body wastes and sperm or eggs.
Coelurosaurs Mainly small, bipedal saurischian theropods forming a group called the Coelurosauria.
Cold-blooded Depending for body warmth upon heat from the sun.
Coracoid A short bone joined to a dinosaur's scapula that helps to form its shoulder girdle.
Coronoid process An upward projection of the mandible's dentary bone, anchoring the jaw muscles.
Cranium See **Braincase**.
Cretaceous period The third and last part of the Mesozoic era or "Age of Dinosaurs."
Dentary The main, tooth-bearing bone of the lower jaw.
Denticles Tiny, pointed projections such as those on the cutting edges of some dinosaurs' teeth.

Dinosaurs A great group of advanced, small to immense archosaurs, probably including the ancestors of birds.
Dorsal vertebrae Spinal bones supporting the back, between the cervical vertebrae and the sacrum.
Duck-billed dinosaurs A popular name for the large, flat-beaked ornithopods known as hadrosaurs.
Euornithopods Advanced ornithopods.
Family Related organisms comprising a genus or several genera. Formal family names end in -idae, as in Tyrannosauridae; informal family names end in -ids, as in tyrannosaurids.
Femur The thighbone.
Fenestra An opening in the skull.
Fibula The calf bone in the leg.
Gastralia Belly ribs.
Genetic change Change to the minute hereditary units called genes found in living cells. Genes program an individual's development. Generations of accumulating genetic changes cause new species to evolve.
Genus (plural: genera) A group of closely related organisms within a family. A genus consists of one or more species. In print, the name of a genus appears in italics with a capital first letter.
Gizzard A thick-walled, muscular bulge in the gut, with a tough, horny lining that helps grind up food. Occurs in birds and in some dinosaurs.
Gizzard stones (gastroliths) Stones that are swallowed that help grind up food in a gizzard.
Hadrosaurs Big ornithopods with ducklike beaks. They comprised two families, known as the Hadrosauridae and Lambeosauridae.
Herbivore A plant-eating animal. Ornithischians and sauropodomorphs were herbivorous dinosaurs.
Horned dinosaurs Big, quadrupedal ceratopsians forming the family Ceratopsidae. They had huge skull frills and a nose horn and/or brow horns.
Humerus The upper arm bone.
Ilium (plural: ilia) One of a pair of bones forming the top of the pelvis, bladelike or shelflike in dinosaurs. Ilia anchored hind-limb muscles, also the spinal column's sacral vertebrae, thus transferring body weight to the hind limbs.
Infraorder A major subdivision of an order.
Ischium (plural: ischia) One of a pair of rear, lower hipbones (ischia), rodlike in dinosaurs. The ischium anchored hind-limb muscles that pulled the leg in and back.
Jugal bone A bone below the eye. In ceratopsians it formed a flaring cheekbone.
Jurassic period The second part of the Mesozoic era or "Age of Dinosaurs."
Mandible The lower jaw.
Maniraptorans Small coelurosaurian theropods with a distinctive wrist design. Many scientists think maniraptorans gave rise to birds.

Marginocephalians Ornithischians with a skull ridge or shelf: the pachycephalosaurs and ceratopsians.
Maxilla (plural: maxillae) The upper jaw, and, in particular, one of its pair of main tooth-bearing bones.
Mesozoic era The geological time span of 248–65 million years ago, also called "Age of Dinosaurs." It comprised three geological periods: Triassic, Jurassic, and Cretaceous.
Metacarpals The "palm" bones, situated between the wrist (carpus) and the fingers.
Metatarsals Bones of the upper foot, between the ankle bones and the toe bones.
Naris (plural: nares) Opening of the nasal passage(s).
Neoceratopsians Small to large, chiefly quadrupedal ceratopsians, many with huge, horned heads: the Protoceratopsidae and Ceratopsidae.
Neural spines Bones that project up from vertebrae.
Order A group of organisms below subclass level.
Ornithischians "Bird-hipped" dinosaurs: herbivores comprising one of the two major dinosaur groups.
Ornithodires The group of archosaurs including dinosaurs and pterosaurs (and arguably birds).
Ornithopods "Bird feet": small to very large, mainly bipedal, plant-eating ornithischians.
Pachycephalosaurs Bipedal marginocephalians with an immensely thick skull.
Palaeozoic Era The geological time span of 570–248 million years ago. Fish, amphibians, and reptiles appeared during this time.
Parrot lizards The psittacosaurids: a family of small ceratopsians with parrotlike beaks.
Pelvis The hip, comprising a left and a right ilium, pubis, and ischium.
Phalanges (singular: phalanx) Toe bones or finger bones (excluding metacarpals and metatarsals).
Plated dinosaurs See **Stegosaurs**.
Predentary bone A toothless bone located at the tip of the lower jaw of ornithischians.
Preparator A scientist specializing in the removal of fossils from rock.
Prosauropods Mainly bipedal/ quadrupedal and wholly quadrupedal, small to large, early sauropodomorphs.
Pterosaurs Warm-blooded flying reptiles related to dinosaurs.
Pubis (plural: pubes) One of a pair of front, lower hipbones, rodlike in dinosaurs. Some pubes had a long, forward extension, or prepubis. In many dinosaurs the pubis anchored a muscle that pulled a leg forward.
Quadrupedal Walking on all fours.
Radius One of two forearm bones.
Reptiles "Cold-blooded," scaly vertebrates breeding on land. Some dinosaurs and pterosaurs were atypical.

Rostral bone A bone forming the tip of the upper jaw of ceratopsians.
Sacral vertebrae The bones of that part of the backbone or spinal column attached to the pelvis.
Sacrum Fused vertebrae that are joined to the pelvis.
Saurischians "Lizard-hipped" dinosaurs: herbivores and carnivores comprising one of the two major dinosaur groups.
Sauropodomorphs Mainly large to immense, long-necked, long-tailed, quadrupedal, herbivorous saurischian dinosaurs. They comprised the prosauropods and sauropods.
Sauropods Large to immense sauropodomorphs.
Scapula The shoulder blade. (See also **Coracoid**.)
Sclerotic ring A "pineapple ring" of bony plates supporting the eye; found in birds, dinosaurs, and other vertebrates.
Scutes Bony plates set in the skin to protect it against the teeth and jaws of predators. The outer surfaces of scutes were often horn-covered.
Segnosaurs A puzzling group of saurischian dinosaurs: perhaps bizarre theropods.
Skull The head's bony framework that protects the brain, eyes, ears, and nasal passages.
Species In the classification of living things, the level below genus. *Tyrannosaurus rex* is a species in the genus *Tyrannosaurus*.
Stegosaurs Quadrupedal thyreophoran ornithischians with two tall rows of plates and/or spines running down the neck, back, and tail.
Subclass The major subdivision of a class.
Suborder The major subdivision of an order.
Tarsals Ankle bones. In dinosaurs they included a distinctively shaped astragalus bone.
Tetanurans One of two major groups of theropods.
"Thecodonts" A mixed group of archosaurs that includes ancestors of dinosaurs, crocodilians, and pterosaurs.
Theropods Bipedal, carnivorous saurischian dinosaurs.
Thyreophorans The armored ankylosaurs, plated stegosaurs, and their close relatives.
Tibia The shinbone.
Triassic period The first part of the Mesozoic era or "Age of Dinosaurs."
Ulna One of the two bones of the forearm.
Ungual phalanges Terminal toe or finger bones bearing claws, hooves, or nails.
Vertebrae Bones of the spinal column.
Vertebrates Backboned animals: fish, amphibians, reptiles, birds, and mammals.
Warm-blooded Maintaining body warmth by turning food into heat inside the body.

INDEX

Page numbers in **bold** refer to dinosaur profiles; page numbers in *italics* refer to entries in the glossary

ACKNOWLEDGMENTS

Dorling Kindersley would like to thank:
Museums and other organizations: Mary Dawson, Pam Pochapin, and Betty Hill, The Carnegie Museum of Natural History, Pittsburgh, Pennsylvania; Professor W.-D. Heinrich, Museum für Naturkunde, Humboldt-Universität, Berlin, Germany; Paul Howard and Stuart Ogilvy, Yorkshire Museum, York, UK; Margherita and Gilda Majani, Erizzo Editrice, Venice, Italy; John Martin, Leicestershire Museum, Leicester, UK; Dr. Teresa Maryanska and Dr. Wojciech Skarzynski, Polish Academy of Sciences, Warsaw, Poland; Mark Norell and Barbara Mathe, The American Museum of Natural History, New York, NY; Kevin Padian, Museum of Paleontology, University of California at Berkeley; Dr. Jaime E. Powell, Instituto Miguel Lillo, Universidad Nacional de Tucumán, Argentina; Dr. Philip Powell, Oxford University Museum, Oxford, UK; Dr. Monty Reid, Royal Tyrrell Museum of Paleontology, Alberta; Dr. G.W. Rougier, Museo Argentino de Ciencias Naturales, Buenos Aires, Argentina; Professor A. Rozanov and Dr. S.M. Kurzanov, Paleontological Institute, Moscow, Russia; Raymond Rye, Caroline Newman, Pamela Baker, and Chip Clark, National Museum of Natural History, Smithsonian Institution, Washington, DC; Dr. Charles R. Schaff, Museum of Comparative Zoology, Harvard University, Massachusetts; Bruce Selyem, Museum of the Rockies, Montana State University, Bozeman; Mary Ann Turner, Lynette Jordan, Eric Hoag, and Barbara Narendra, Peabody Museum, Yale University, New Haven, Connecticut; Hiromi Yamazaki, Fuji Television Network Inc., Tokyo, Japan; Professor Dong Zhiming, Institute of Vertebrate Paleontology and Paleoanthropology, Beijing, China.
Additional paleontology assistance: Tracy Ford, William Lindsay, Jack Macintosh, George Olshevsky
Additional design assistance: Paul Calver, Dirk Kaufman, Gwyn Lewis, Salim Qurashi, Chris Walker, Bryn Walls
Additional editorial assistance: Mike Darton, Paul Docherty, Ellen Dupont, Martyn Page, Mukul Patel, Cathy Rubinstein, Louise Tucker
Index: Sue Bosanko
Retouching: Roy Flooks, Selwyn Hutchinson, David Pugh
US research: Mary Ann Lynch
Special thanks to Susannah Massey for coordinating and interpreting in Russia
The Essential Dinosaur designed by Clare Shedden

ILLUSTRATORS
Simone Boni/L.R. Galante: 26–27, 152 tr, 160 cr, 162 tc, 166 bl
Roby Braun: 21 mr, 50–51, 60–61, 66–67, 77 c, 79 c, 104–105, 114–115, 150–151, 160–161
Simone End: 10 tr, 10 bl, 10 br, 24 tr, 39 bl, 64 bc, br, 78 cr, br, 83 tr, 84 bc, 86 tr, 88 br, 91 bc, 92 tr, 109 br, 111 tr, 116 c, 121 tr, 123 tc, 131 tr, 144 c, cra, 153 tl
John Holmes: 20 c, 59 br, 89 r, 93 crb, 105 br, 120 tr
Dave Hopkins/Ian Fleming Associates: 56 tl, 164 tr
Andrew Hutchinson: 108–109 c, 110 tr, 112–113
Steve Kirk: 43 tl, 46 c, 60 tr, 65 b, 67 tl, tc, tr, cra, 74 tr, cr, br, 113 tc, 124-125, 162 bc
Janos Marffy: cladograms, family trees, and skeletons and silhouettes for Fact File boxes, 44 tr, 79 br, 80 tr, 111 c, ca, bc, 143 tl, tr
Ikkyu Murakawa: 155 tl
Andrew Robinson: 40 bc, 77 tl, 106 br, 108 tr, 109 tl, tc

Colin Rose: 12 (main image), 53 tl, cla
Graham Rosewarne: 12 (small images), 13 (small images), 14 c, 17 tm, 19 tm, 46 tr, 60 c, 66 bl, 76 tr, 82 tr, 124 tr, 126 tr, 133 tl, 134 br, 158 tr, 161 tr, 161 br, 163 br
John Sibbick: 6 full page, 11 tr, 15 r, 17 r, 18 c, 19 r, 22 br, 23 tr, 38 tl, 40 tr, 42 bl, 47 r, 62 bl, 68 cr, 70 bc, 82 bl, 95 tr, 102 br, 110 bl, 130 tr, 138 br, 139 tr, 142 tr, 150 bc, br, 151 bl, 152 tr
John Temperton: 50 tr, 51 bc, 60 br, 72 cl, bc, 88 tr, 90 bc, 93 ca, 96 tr, 102 tr, 106 tr, 118 tr, 154 tr

MODEL MAKERS
Roby Braun: 38 bl (*Allosaurus, Compsognathus*), 40–41, 44 c, 45 br, 48–49, 48tc, 49 tl, 52 mr, br, 53 br, 56 cr, 63 tl, 80–81, 81 r, 84–85, 84 cr, 85 br, 106–107, 116 t, bm, 117 c, 130 bl (*Iguanodon*), 132–133, 133 tr, 136–137, 140 t, 152 bl (*Styracosaurus*), 154–155, 162–163, 163 bl
Centaur Studios: 54 tr, 54–55, 58–59, 94 cr, 94–95, 98–99, 140–141, 148–149, 166–167
David Donkin: 14 tr, 16 tr, 18 tr
John Holmes: 34–35 (*Gallimimus* sequence), 38 bl (*Gallimimus*), 63 bc, 128–129, 130 bl (*Hypsilophodon*), 137 tc

SKELETAL AND FOSSIL MATERIAL
American Museum of Natural History, New York, NY: 23 br, 32–33, 32 bl, cb, 33 cl, tr, 57 br, 98 tr, 149 tr, 157 tr, 158 br, 159 bc, 160 tr, 162 tr, 166 bc
Institute und Museum für Geologie und Paläontologie der Universität Tübingen, Germany: 86 bc, 86–87, 87 bc, 117 tc, tl, 118–119, 119 tl
Instituto Miguel Lillo, Universidad Nacional de Tucumán, Argentina: 40 cr, 41 tc, 90–91, 91 tc, 106 ca, 107 cra
Leicestershire Museum, Leicester, UK: 92–93
Museo Argentino de Ciencias Naturales, Buenos Aires, Argentina: 29bc, 48 bc, 49 tr
Museum für Naturkunde, Humboldt-Universität, Berlin, Germany: 75 tr, 95 tl
The Natural History Museum, London, UK: 24 br, 26 br, 42 tr, 52–53, 58 tr, br, 59 tl, 82 cra, 88–89, 92 b, 92 bc, 100–101 c, 112 cr, br, 113 c, 120–121, 124 br, 132 tr and bc, 136 t, 138–139, 144–145, 165 bc, 167 tc
Naturmuseum Senckenberg, Frankfurt, Germany: 55 br, 56–57, 100–101, 139 bc
Oxford University Museum, Oxford, UK: 50 c, cr, bc, 51 cl
Peabody Museum, Yale University, New Haven, Connecticut: 70–71, 72 tl, 84 tc, 85 r, 102 cr
Queensland Museum, South Brisbane, Australia: Bruce Cowell (photographer) 127 tc, 140 bl
Royal Tyrrell Museum of Paleontology, Alberta: 20 tr, 21 tl, 21 br, 23 mr, 38 tr, cr, crb, 44–45, 47 bc, 55 cr, 56 tc, 64 ca, 64–65, 87 cra, 129 br, 131 cl, 135 cr, 146–147, 150 cra, tr, 152 bl, 155 tr, cr, 163 crb, 164–165
Section of Vertebrate Fossils, Carnegie Museum of Natural History, Pittsburgh, Pennsylvania: 10 bm, 102–103, 103 cr, 115 cr
© 1992 Smithsonian Institution, Washington, DC: 24 tl, 27 ml, 30–31, 42–43, 83 cla, 96–97, 97 tr, 100 tr, 145 tc, 148 tr, 165 tr
Staatliches Museum für Naturkunde, Stuttgart, Germany: 52 tr
Yorkshire Museum, York, UK and The Institute of Vertebrate Paleontology and Paleoanthropology, Beijing, China: 89 cra, 93 br, 120 c, 121 cr

PICTURE CREDITS
Courtesy Department of Library Services, American Museum of Natural History, New York: 26 tl (Neg.no. 356084), 125 tc (Neg. no. 314802); 125 ca (Neg. no. 314803); 148 cl (Neg. no. 13547); 158 cla (Neg. no. 410764)
Stuart Baldwin, Witham, Essex, UK (from *Dinosaur Stamps of the World*): 9 tc, 37 tc, 169 tc
The Hulton Deutsch Collection: 166 cl
The Bridgeman Art Library: 100 br
Bristol City Museums and Art Gallery, Bristol: 112 ca, tr
Dr. Eric Buffetaut, Laboratoire de Paléontologie des Vertèbres, Paris, France: 61 br
Bruce Coleman Limited/Jane Burton: 73 tc, 80 bl
Canadian Museum of Nature, Ottawa: 69 tr (model of *Dinosauroid* by Ron Séguin in collaboration with Dr. Dale A. Russell)
Section of Vertebrate Fossils, Carnegie Museum of Natural History, Pittsburgh, Pennsylvania: 31 tr (Neg. no. 8P25), cra (Neg. no. 18P26), 33 br (Neg. no. B376), 46 ba (Neg. no. 10P26), 78 tr (Neg. no. 1086); 98 cl (Neg. no. 1095); 99 bc (Neg. no. 1012); 99br (Neg. no. 170); 100 cl (Neg. no. C1058); 164 cl (Neg. no. 61)
Fuji Television Network Inc., Tokyo, Japan and Paleontological Institute, Moscow, Russia: 76 cr, 156–157
Robert Harding Picture Library: 25 bl
Dr. Ian Ievers and Dr. Ralph E. Molnar, South Brisbane, Australia: 126 cb, bc
Dr. S.M. Kurzanov/Paleontological Institute, Moscow, Russia: 76 clb, bc
Ligabue Studies and Researches Centre Archive, Venice, Italy: 142 cla, cb, 142–143, 151 cr, 158 cr, 159 tc
Museo Argentino de Ciencias Naturales, Buenos Aires, Argentina: 29 bc
Museum für Naturkunde, Humboldt-Universität, Berlin, Germany: 75 cl, 94 cl, 118 c, cr
Museum of the Rockies, Montana: Bruce Selyem (photographer) 69b, 146 tr
National Museum of Natural Science, Taichung, Taiwan: 34 tr, 75 tl
The National Museum of Wales, Cardiff, UK and The Institute of Vertebrate Paleontology and Paleoanthropology, Beijing, China: 29 tc, ca, 104 bc
The Natural History Museum Picture Library, London, UK: 35 c, cra, crb, 54 bc, 58 c, 72–73, 74 bl, 89 tr (John Holmes), 93 crb (John Holmes), 94 tr, 96 cl, 105 br (John Holmes), 120 tr (John Holmes), 122 c, tr, 123 br, 129 cra, crb, 134 c, 136 c, 137 cl, 138 tc, 139 tl, 144 bc, 166 tr
John Ostrom/Peabody Museum, Yale University, New Haven, Connecticut: 28 tr, br, 73 cra, crb
Oxford Scientific Films: 25 br
Paleontological Museum, Uppsala University, Sweden: Christer Bäck (photographer) 105 c, cr
Dr. Jaime E. Powell, Instituto Miguel Lillo, Universidad Nacional de Tucumán, Argentina: 29 br, 48 bl
Queensland Museum, South Brisbane, Australia: 26mr, 140 bm
Wojciech Skarzynski, Institute of Paleobiology, Polish Academy of Sciences, Warsaw, Poland: 30 bl, 30 tr, 62 tr
Smithsonian Institution, Washington, DC: 31 br (Photo no. 28269)
South African Museum, Cape Town, South Africa and Museum of Comparative Zoology, Harvard University, Massachusetts: Al Coleman (photographer) 134–135